The Boys from Syracuse

The Boys from Syracuse

The Shuberts' Theatrical Empire

Foster Hirsch

Cooper Square Press

First Cooper Square Press edition 2000

This Cooper Square Press paperback edition of *The Boys from Syracuse* is an
unabridged republication of the edition first published in Carbondale, Illinois,
in 1998, with the addition of eighteen textual emendations. It is reprinted by
arrangement with Southern Illinois University Press.

Published by Cooper Square Press
An Imprint of the Rowman & Littlefield Publishing Group
150 Fifth Avenue, Suite 911
New York, New York 10011

Distributed by National Book Network

Library of Congress Cataloging-in-Publication Data

Hirsch, Foster.
    The boys from Syracuse : the Shuberts' theatrical empire / Foster
Hirsch.—1st Cooper Square Press ed.
        p. cm.
    Originally published: Carbondale, Ill. : Southern Illinois
University Press, 1998.
    Includes bibliographical references and index.
    ISBN 0-8154-1103-0 (pbk. : alk. paper)
        1. Shubert, Lee, 1873?-1953. 2. Shubert, Sam S., 1875-1905.
3. Shubert, Jacob J., 1878?-1963. 4. Theater—New York (State)—
New York—History—20th century. 5. Theater—United States—History—
20th century. 6. Theatrical producers and directors—United States—
Biography. 7. Shubert Organization—History. 8. Shubert family. I. Title.

PN2285 .H56 2000
792'.0232'09227471—dc21
[B]   00-043093

The Shuberts? They were hardly human.
　　　　　　　　　—Agnes de Mille, Choreographer

The Shuberts had their human side too, you know.
　　　　　　　　　—John Kenley, Producer

Contents

Illustrations

Acknowledgments

ᠺᢣ

I would like to thank the following people: the late George Abbott; Barbara Barondess; Kristofer Batho; the late Michael Bavar; the late Irving Caesar; Imogene Coca; Alexander Cohen; Don Costello; the late Agnes de Mille; Dorothy Derman; Alan Eisenberg; L. Marc Fields; Janet Cantor Gari; Max Gendel; Jeremy Gerard; Ruth Goetz; Viola Seff Goldberg; Ethel Lynne; Abraham Grossman; Jack Hagstrom; Charlotte Harmon; Lewis Harmon; Judy Haven; the late Helen Hayes; Murray Helwitz; Emily Hewlett; Lori Inman; the late Bernard B. Jacobs; Sol Jaccobson; Anne Jeffreys; Garson Kanin, Eileen Kelly; John Kenley; N. R. Kleinfield; Abner Klipstein; Joan Lavender; the late Lawrence Shubert Lawrence, Jr.; Lucille Lawrence; Kevin Lewis; Marjorie Light; Joe Masteroff; Valerie Mitchell; Hobe Morrison; Grafton Nunes; the late Bill O'Connell; Ellen Orbach; Richard Osk; Annette Packer; William Packer; Harold Prince; Miriam Krengel Pulvers; Dorothy Tewlow Reissman; Anthony W. Robins; Gerald Schoenfeld; Dorothy Seegar; Henry Senker; the late John Shubert; Syd Silverman; Sandra Epstein; Judith Teichmann Steckler; the late Ezra Stone; Evelyn Teichmann; the late Howard Teichmann; Ned Wayburn, Jr.; Esther Weiser; Gerson Werner; Max Wilk; Alan Williams; Iva Withers; the five who spoke on condition of anonymity; Ruth Nathan, who persevered; Walt Bode, who edited; and Kathryn Koldehoff, who copyedited.

I also thank The Billy Rose Theatre Collection, The New York Public Library for the Performing Arts at Lincoln Center; the libraries of Brooklyn College of the City University of New York, Columbia University, and New York University; The Onondaga Historical Society; and The Shubert Archive. I am deeply indebted to The State Historical Society of Wisconsin. They own the John Shubert/Howard Teichmann 1959–1960 tapes and the material within. Mr. Robert B. Thomasgard, Jr., acting director of the Society, and Mrs. Barbara Kaiser, former executive of the archives division, gave Mrs. Teichmann permission to use the twenty-five reels of tapes, and she allowed me to use the valuable interviews. At Southern Illinois University Press, I would like to thank Jim Simmons, Carol Burns, Kyle Lake, and Lisa Bayer.

The Boys from Syracuse

Prologue: The Last Shubert

John Shubert, the sole direct heir to the vast Shubert theatrical empire, began the last day of his life—Friday, November 16, 1962—exactly as he began every workday, arriving at his office on the sixth floor of the Sardi Building a few minutes before noon. After a smile for the receptionist, he went into his outer office, where two secretaries, Eileen Kelly and Sandra Epstein, had been sorting through his mail and taking calls from employees and producers who wanted appointments. Announcing that he was leaving town ("a business trip to Florida"), he asked Miss Epstein to cancel his appointments for Monday, Tuesday, and Wednesday and to have his car waiting for him in Shubert Alley within an hour. Before making their calls, the secretaries, who knew what "going to Florida" meant, winked at each other.

In his office, John took off his navy blue overcoat and black hat and hung them on a coat-tree in the corner of the fourteen- by fifteen-foot room that was his home away from home. Two walls were lined with glass-enclosed shelves that held leather-bound classics in expensive gold leaf, uncut and unread. A dust-encrusted window looked out onto the cement wall of the *New York Times* plant scarcely four feet away. From the large windows at the north end of the room, he could survey the north side of West Forty-fourth Street—Shubert Alley, and the three Shubert theatres, the Majestic, the Broadhurst, and the Shubert, which were the architectural center of the American commercial theatre.

He sat down behind the imposing desk that had once belonged to his father, J. J. Shubert, and that John felt was still rightfully his father's property. Though he was the de facto head of the business, John considered himself just an extension of the vast Shubert organization founded by his Uncle Sam at the turn of the century and ruled by Sam's brothers, Lee and J. J., for nearly half a century. In less than a month, on December 13, 1962, John would be fifty-three years old. Although he was no matinee idol, he had long outgrown the gooney look he had had as a kid; he was not only the best-liked Shubert since Sam—his father and his Uncle Lee were decidedly unpopular—he was also the handsomest. He looked dour and dissipated, but his thick, graying hair and his deep, rough-sounding voice gave him an unexpected outlaw sex appeal, which only seemed to increase with age. Women who liked him often claimed he reminded them of Humphrey Bogart. Beneath his chocolate brown eyes, which took on a kind of boyish, pleading quality when he was with women who attracted him, were dark circles that John always insisted were hereditary, though friends blamed fast living—too many pills, too much liquor, too many late nights, and too much sex—instead. He smoked about two packs of cigarettes a day and mixed large amounts of alcohol with a variety of pills, mostly Nembutals and Miltowns. "I'm a hypochondriac," John admitted. "When I travel I carry more drugs than clothes."[1] "He used to take pills to sleep, and pills to wake up, and he drank a lot," Sandra Epstein recalled. "I remember looking at his attaché case and saying, 'This is a regular drugstore in here, and I think you should shape up.' I felt he was going to wear himself thin, which I think he finally did."[2] John, at 167 pounds, weighed a bit too much for his five-foot nine-inch frame, but his addiction to alcohol and to desserts defeated his intentions to go on a diet.

This Friday John was planning to spend no more than an hour at the office, as opposed to his usual seven or eight. He stayed just long enough to go over some pressing paperwork and to make two calls that were part of his daily ritual. The first was to his mother, Catherine Mary, who, though it was only early afternoon, was already in her cups; Catherine Mary drank sherry from the time she got up until she fell back onto her bed late at night. Despite her drinking, her nagging, her greed, and the horrendous childhood her catastrophic marriage to his father had caused him, John had remained a dutiful son. He told his mother he would be in Florida until Wednesday; and like his secretaries, Catherine Mary knew what that meant. John then telephoned his wife, Kerttu, nicknamed "Eckie," who was also a heavy drinker, though like John she drank mostly at night. He'd be back by Wednesday, he reminded her; and like the others Eckie knew where John was going and why. He told her that, if she needed him, she could reach him through the company switchboard.

Both his mother and his wife, who despised each other, complained to John about the other. Trying to effect a truce between the two women, John was a hapless go-between, the man in the middle who could never make his mother and his wife stop hating each other, as he had never been able to banish the bitterness between his parents or to stem the rising animosity with which his father and his Uncle Lee regarded each other across West Forty-fourth Street, where the two Shubert offices had been located for decades.

After he had made his duty calls to Catherine Mary and to Eckie, John went up to the penthouse where his father lived to say good-bye. Surrounded by a cook, a nurse, his second wife, Muriel, and what was left of his memories, J. J. seemed not to understand the purpose of John's visit. Still stocky and with the pink complexion of his youth in his sagging face, the old man stared at a daytime television show. Though J. J.'s parenting had consisted of equal doses of intimidation and neglect, John had never really ceased wanting his father's approval.

After kissing his father and telling Muriel that he would be away until Wednesday, John walked across the street to stop by the offices of the longtime Shubert lawyers, Gerald Schoenfeld and Bernard B. Jacobs, located in the suite of offices above the Shubert Theatre. John's admonition to the lawyers, to keep an eye on the business while he was away, was unnecessary; both men were well trained and extremely conscientious and, as time would reveal, only too willing to mind the store.

John then walked down to his car, which was waiting for him in Shubert Alley. His second cousin, Lawrence Shubert Lawrence, Jr., was already in the car. "I drove with John down to Penn Station, where he was to take the 4:35 for Clearwater," Lawrence said. "I was John's assistant and next in line. I told him I'd talk to him every day. On the way to the station he seemed all right to me. He certainly didn't look like somebody who had only a few hours to live."[3]

At the station, after Lawrence had dropped him off, John had time for one quick call to Eileen Kelly. "He called to remind me that I had forgotten to give him a book—I think it was *Hotel Paradiso*—that was about to be done either as a musical or a play. He said, 'You know where to send it.' Then he said he had to go. That was the last time I spoke to him. That was the last time anybody in New York spoke to him."[4]

As scheduled, the West Coast Champion rolled away from the platform at 4:35. When the train emerged from the darkness of the tunnel that runs beneath the Hudson River and came out into the fading light descending on the New Jersey flatlands, John settled back in his drawing room to relax. In New York he had disciplined himself to drink only after the nightly count-up; now, with no phone calls to make, no producers to placate, no one to scold him or to ask for favors, no one at all to be responsible to, he opened the bottle of Dewar's he had packed and poured himself a double Scotch.

John made only one concession to the seductive southern climate he was headed toward: he changed from his signature blue serge suit into a navy suit of lighter weight. No vanilla Palm Beach suit or gaily colored Hawaiian shirt; when he entered the dining car for a six o'clock dinner, he looked the way he always looked on the sixth floor of the Sardi Building: like a banker prepared to turn down a loan. A somber-looking gentleman whose diffident manner did not betray the fact that he was heir to one of the greatest private fortunes in America, John Shubert spoke to none of the three other passengers who sat at the same table. After finishing his dinner, topped by a whiskey and coffee, he undertipped the waiter and returned to his drawing room. Placing a "Do Not Disturb" sign on the door had, for him, a special significance. He rooted around in the supply of assorted pills and capsules he had packed in plastic holders, and after looking over some scripts that were potential candidates for Shubert theatres in the upcoming spring season, he took a handful of pills and washed them down with the remaining contents in the bottle of Dewar's.

He didn't appear at breakfast. At one o'clock, the porter knocked to announce that lunch was being served but received no answer. Later, when the train was two stops away from the important passenger's destination, the conductor went to the door that still had the "Do Not Disturb" sign posted on it. When there was no response to his loud cries of "Mr. Shubert! Mr. Shubert!" the conductor used a skeleton key from a large brass ring to unlock the door.

His face contorted, his open eyes unseeing, John Shubert lay sprawled on the floor of the compartment, dead.

On the platform of the Clearwater station, an attractive, dark-haired young woman waited eagerly to greet her husband. As different from Eckie as Eckie was from Catherine Mary, Nancy was John Shubert's other wife. And at the couple's modest beachfront bungalow, tucked in cribs and taking their afternoon naps, were John's two then-illegitimate children, a boy named John Jason (another J. J., named in tribute to the boy's famous grandfather) and a girl, Sally. Only John's secretaries, his mother, his "first" wife, Lawrence, the lawyers, and a very few others knew of John's second family. Soon, in the kind of headlines the elder Shuberts had tried all their lives to avoid, everyone would learn that the Shubert heir was a bigamist.

John was truly the last Shubert to run the business according to the methods his father and uncles had established. Lawrence Shubert Lawrence, Jr., headed the firm for ten years following John's death, but Larry Lawrence, as he was known along Broadway, was a Shubert in name only.

The three founding brothers, Sam, Lee, and J. J., were empire builders second to none, and as they fought fearlessly and resourcefully with a procession of opponents, they compiled a record as theatrical czars likely to remain unmatched. Moving downstate to New York from Syracuse at the turn of the century—Sam first, then Lee, and finally J. J.—the Shubert brothers seemed unlikely casting for the most ruthless titans in the history of the American theatre. Their unprepossessing appearance and lack of cultivation inspired predictions of doom, which underestimated the Shubert will, the Shubert resilience, and the Shubert relish for a fight. Driven by a seemingly unquenchable acquisitiveness, they built, leased, or booked a record number of theatres both in New York and throughout the country and produced a record number of plays and musicals. Both on their way up and once they were the unchallenged rulers of Broadway, the brothers squared off against labor unions, actors, dramatists, composers, other producers and theatre owners, and the local, state, and federal governments. Over the course of their long careers, they were embroiled, often eagerly, in thousands of lawsuits. But, perhaps not surprisingly, no matter how much money or power or sex they seized, they never seemed to have enough. They were the conquerors of the American theatre, millionaires many times over who would save pennies in the hit production of *Hellzapoppin'* by reducing the size of the paper cups in a gag. They once charged Noël Coward seven dollars for paint for his dressing room.

As they amassed and then kept strict watch over their theatrical and other real estate holdings, their interlocking corporations, and their almost unimaginable wealth (the exact accounting of their worth continues to be a matter of speculation, though at the height of their power in the twenties they were rumored to be good for around four hundred million), they were feared, admired, despised, mocked, and even sometimes, though rarely, simply liked. No one who ever dealt with them was neutral. Despite their influence over every nook and cranny of this most public business, they were obsessively private men. Garson Kanin, an old pal, wondered if Lee ever had any "real" friends.[5] And Larry Lawrence recalled that "J. J. used to have different cronies but nobody could ever last with him because nobody could really understand him."[6] In private they had humor, temperament, and vigor, but in public they appeared clumsy and abrasive. Lacking a gift for oratory or showmanship, they avoided the limelight as often as possible.

As husbands, fathers, and siblings, they were singularly untalented, and so it is no accident that there is no living Shubert managing the still-thriving Shubert Organization, Inc. The Shuberts dedicated their prodigious energies to Mammon, and it is only fitting that the vast Shubert fortune has been channeled back into the business, which may well endure as long as there continues to be commercial theatre in America.

The Shubert family history, capped by John Shubert's bigamy, includes a series of bizarre secret marriages and divorces; paternity both denied and abused; and a fierce, lifelong rivalry between Lee and J. J. None of the brothers had any apparent interest in training a successor. Sam, first in the field and dead at twenty-nine, was probably homosexual. Although secretly married in 1936, Lee lived as if he were a bachelor and had no children, at least none he was willing to acknowledge. J. J., who also behaved like a bachelor for most of his life, produced the only direct heir but did not properly train his son to take over the business; John succeeded to the throne only by default, after J. J. had become senile. "It was terrible for John, working for his father," Larry Lawrence recalled. "J. J. was awful to him, truly mean. He seemed threatened, as if he thought John wanted to steal the business away from him."[7] John himself avoided becoming a father. He forced his first wife to have at least two abortions, and then he mysteriously permitted his "other" wife to bear two children whose rights to the family business he failed to secure before his early and unexpected death.

Famous for handing out money to panhandlers and to former employees down on their luck, the Shuberts were kinder to strangers than to their own. "They were an odd family," Larry Lawrence said. "They weren't what you would expect from a Jewish family: they weren't close, and over the years the bitterness between Lee and J. J. grew."[8] Nonetheless, however buried or disfigured, an atavistic bond linked the embattled brothers; distrustful of everyone, they shared an abiding belief, broken only near the end of their lives, that neither one would ever cheat the other in business. Both were equally reluctant to cede control of any aspect of the great business they had built.

Though their first real achievement was to destroy the Theatrical Syndicate, a pernicious monopoly, they became in time as tyrannical as their first and fiercest rivals. "The Shuberts were bad men whose only genius was a genius for greed," Agnes de Mille said. "They turned a potential art and a fine profession into an unseemly, vicious, and disgusting traffic. And while someone must have liked them or spoken well of them, I have never in a long life met anyone who did."[9] While de Mille's is certainly not a universally accepted judgment, it's fair to say that the Shuberts were no better than they had to be in order to maintain their sovereignty. During their long run, they controlled the kinds of shows theatregoers saw and where they saw them, and many of the policies they established about the business of theatre remain in force to this day. They left behind not only a collection of historic buildings and a flourishing business but also a way of doing business. The caution and the fear of retaliation they instilled in employees and adversaries, the distrust they both lived by and engendered, endure.

"I won't talk," Gerson Werner, a former Shubert employee (and relative) snapped in a gruff, coarse voice when I called to request an interview.[10] "Be careful—remember that you're not dealing with ladies and gentlemen," another former employee warned me.[11] "I have to watch what I say about those guys up there—they're very shrewd," Larry Lawrence said at his home in Boca Raton, Florida, eighteen years after Gerald Schoenfeld and Bernard Jacobs had become "the

Shuberts."[12] Speaking conspiratorially, Lawrence confirmed that, even without a Shubert in charge, the business continues to be run in a distinctly Shubertian mode.

Centered on Broadway, the Shubert saga covers the entire sweep of American theatre in the twentieth century, but the roots of the story reach back to Syracuse in the last two decades of the nineteenth century.

1

∾

The Boys in Syracuse

*S*yracuse, New York, was the place of our birth," begins an unfinished memoir by Lee Shubert.[1] In fact, however, Lee, his two brothers, and three of his
four sisters, were born in Europe, though exactly where and when remain
uncertain. "They came from a small town on the border between Germany and
Poland," John Shubert said.[2] An 1892 census taken in Syracuse is probably the
most reliable source of placing the family. "Polland" is given as the birthplace for
the entire family, whose name is spelled Shurburt, though elsewhere it was Shubard,
Schubart, or Szemanski.[3]

Though on the surface the story of their origins seems commonplace enough,
Lee's fictional reconstructions about where and when he and his brothers were
born make it clear that he felt he had something to hide. His father, Duvvid
Schubart (as he usually spelled it), married Katrina Helwitz in 1870. Katrina's
dowry included a pair of tall pewter candlesticks, a brass samovar, a quilt stuffed
with goose feathers, and a collection of relatives in the United States. Like every
Jew in Europe at the time, Duvvid looked to America to escape from pogroms and
poverty. There was a higher tax on tea in Germany than in Poland, so Duvvid
earned a marginal living smuggling tea across the border in the pockets of his
overcoat to support the six children Katrina gave birth to in Poland. Finally in
1881, the whole family—Duvvid and Katrina; their three sons, Levi, Sammy, and
Jacob; and their three daughters, Fanny, Sarah, and Lisa—boarded a ship in Ham-
burg and descended to steerage, where they huddled with other emigrants in dank,
foul conditions for a journey that took about seven weeks. They were part of a
vast exodus of eastern European Jews fleeing Lithuania, Romania, Poland, and

Russia in the hope that, whatever America offered, it would be better than the persecution and hunger that had stalked them at home. Between 1880 and 1914, close to two million Jews emigrated from eastern Europe to America, and most of them, like the Schubarts and their relatives, settled in the city of New York.

On their arrival, the Schubarts stayed in Jamaica, in what is now Queens, with the Helwitzes, Katrina's relatives. Although their names were anglicized—Duvvid Schubart became David Shubart, Katrina became Catherine—David refused to assimilate and refused to work. A religious fanatic, he spent his time praying and allowed his family to be dependent on the generosity of his wife's relatives. After a few months, the strain of two large families living in a single cramped apartment (there were eight Helwitzes to match the eight Shubarts) became unbearable. The Shubarts had to move. This time David turned to his own relatives: a married sister in Syracuse found the Shubarts a rickety wooden house with two small bedrooms.[4]

When the family moved into their new home in 1882, Levi was about seven, Sam was about five, and Jacob was only about three. The first two boys, at least, were old enough to be aware of the family's squalid circumstances and of the shame attached to the fact that their new house, at 110 Grape Street, stood behind another house. A privy was located in back of their house, and behind that were the railroad tracks. The family became accustomed to the chugging and pounding of the engines, the acrid smell of the smoke, and hot cinders. Since they could not afford coal for the stove in the kitchen, the three boys picked up lumps of coal that fell from the engines of the passing trains. David's sister and an Orthodox congregation helped the family through the first winter in Syracuse. David prayed while his frail, short wife, barely five feet, bore another daughter, Dora, cooked and washed and cleaned and became increasingly haggard. "My grandfather was a religious man who believed the Lord would provide if he kept the faith," John said scornfully, clearly repeating the family-accepted version of their origins. "No one in the family liked to talk about it, but one of the younger daughters, Lisa, died of malnutrition that first winter. The generation before mine rarely mentioned it, and when they did the women would get tears in their eyes and Father and Uncle Lee would always look away."[5]

In the early 1880s, when the Shubart family moved there, Syracuse had a population of one hundred twenty-one thousand people and was one of the largest manufacturing cities in the state. More than twenty-five hundred firms were in business, in either manufacturing or trade. Their home at 110 Grape Street was located in the city's Seventh Ward, a thriving, thickly settled ghetto with a scattering of Irish and Italians amid the Jews from Germany, Poland, and Lithuania.[6] In the 1880s, Grape Street was a major thoroughfare with three meat markets, a bakery, four Jewish restaurants, a fish store, a liquor store, and two dry-goods stores. At the corner of Grape and Harrison stood a three-story building that was the vital center of Jewish life in Syracuse, a place where the traditions of the Old World were reverently preserved. On the first floor were Rubin's kosher meat market, Abe Rothchild's barbershop, Yutke Manheim's fish market, Lazarus's bakery, Mayeroshke the cobbler, Sara Eddlestein's dressmaking shop, Etta Grossman's millinery shop, and Kahn's saloon. The second floor was a kosher boardinghouse, and the entire third floor was Rubin's Hall, for weddings and parties. Although there was some tension between the German and Polish Jews, the immigrants helped each other, as the Shubarts could certainly testify, and stood together against outsiders, who referred to them as "the Israelites of the Seventh Ward."

"Conscious of the prejudice against them they bring into the battle for their rights that dogged zeal and distinctive power of concentration which have demanded for them the admiration of honest men," the *Syracuse Standard* commented in an editorial on June 13, 1890. The *Standard's* benevolent racism may have been intended to counter the more brutal kind that Jews regularly experienced. "We believe the descendants of Abraham in Syracuse have not contributed very largely to swell the city's relief funds, and this fact is highly creditable to them as a people," the editorial continued.

While most of the Jewish immigrants worked hard and prospered, David, who was stocky and healthy looking with a fine pink complexion, did not. He placed his family under a double disgrace: not only did he fail to thrive, he was also an alcoholic. To be a Jew who drank in this cohesive community, where neighbors knew each other's business and looked out for each other, meant humiliation of the worst sort for both David and his family.

David finally went to work as a peddler, the standard occupation for Jewish immigrants. Peddlers, who were itinerant department stores carrying dry goods into rural areas, got their supplies in Syracuse from Jewish merchants like Shimberg, Silverman, and Thalheimer. On Sunday nights the Shubart boys, like Jewish sons throughout the Seventh Ward, helped their father arrange his packs, which might contain socks, suspenders, underwear, bedspreads, towels, pins, needles, napkins, aprons, bibs, ladies' stockings, and men's workshirts.[7] On Monday mornings David would strap the packs on his back, carry one in each hand, and march to the train station along with the other peddlers. They boarded trains for Oswego or Canandaigua or Binghamton and then walked for miles, often over rugged terrain, to the farmers who were their regular customers. Sometimes the farmers paid in cash for dry goods; sometimes they traded poultry and eggs. It was a hard living, but many enterprising peddlers flourished, expanding their routes and eventually saving up enough money to become shopkeepers. But not David, who suffered from rheumatism and complained loudly about it. "That's one of the reasons he was such a bad peddler," John said. "And when the family had very, very little money, just barely enough to send him, he used to go to a watering resort to 'cure' his condition."[8]

When Levi (later Lee), his oldest son, turned ten, David terminated the boy's schooling and brought him into the business. With a pack strapped on his back, Levi followed his father along the rutted country roads. After a few weeks, Levi traded a used baseball glove and a well-knicked bat for a child's wagon, which could carry three times the weight Levi could manage on his back. David slapped his son not because the wagon was a bad idea—in fact, it was good for business— but because it had not been his own idea. David was often surly and brutal, especially when he drank. "All the boys took the old man on for a fistfight at some point along the line," John said.[9]

Once he put Levi to work, David withdrew into alcoholic and religious isolation, leaving his wife and sons to take care of themselves, of their sisters, and of him. At this point, in effect, David writes himself out of the Shubert family history, becoming the father who never was. When the boys moved their mother and sisters down to New York a decade later, after they had established themselves as Broadway impresarios, David stayed behind. A year or so after that, he retraced his steps, retiring to Jamaica and the Helwitz household. He ended his life in America exactly where he began it, in a dark walk-up apartment overlooking the rattling elevated tracks. His sons supported him, though he had virtually no contact with them or with his estranged wife. "He and my grandmother never got back together again," John said. "I don't think that they ever actually spoke after they broke up in Syracuse. When they came on down to the Big Time, Old Man Shubert just wouldn't accept it. He found he was no longer the boss of the family. His position had been usurped by Lee, and his wife had become too much of a boss in the family. He went back to Jamaica because there an Orthodox family understood him."[10]

A last image of the Shubert paterfamilias: the managers of the Shubert-owned theatres in Brooklyn used to give David passes, which he would then peddle in front of his sons' theatres. For the rest of their lives, his three sons rejected David's example as fiercely as they denied that they had been immigrants. Unlike their father, Lee, Sam, and Jacob did not drink, remained almost defiantly inattentive to their Jewish heritage ("I have never seen them at any point favor anything that was Jewish," John recalled[11]), and were phenomenally hardworking. Where David was mystical, his sons were blatantly materialistic; where David had no interest or ability in accumulating money, his sons worshiped devoutly at the altar of the false god of riches and avarice. From David's worldly failure arose the demons that haunted and drove the Shubert brothers all their lives; and no matter how much capital or property they were to acquire, submerged but never forgotten were the image of their selfish, lazy, inebriated father, who loved his God far more than he ever cared for them, and the specter of hunger that shadowed their early childhoods. And in the pathological attitude toward fatherhood both Lee and Jacob were to exhibit, David was surely an unexorcized presence, a bit of antimatter in their souls. "No, we don't glorify old Grandfather David," John said. "He gave his wife and children a rough time."[12]

Attempting to counteract her husband's inadequacy, Catherine Shubart took in boarders and arranged for her daughters to get paid for sewing at home. Unlike David, she felt pride rather than rivalry as her sons went to work with a vengeance. In photographs taken after her sons had become rich and famous, Catherine looks severe; she pulls back from the camera's prying gaze the way her sons did. John recalled that "her hands were very small, her feet were very small, her body was very small; in fact it seemed almost impossible that she had given birth to all the children that she had."[13] Far from oozing the warmth and personality of the traditional Jewish matron, she seemed painfully constrained and self-conscious. The son of one of her boarders said that his father remembered Mrs. Shubart pushing her sons out the door when they came home for lunch. "You want corned beef?" she would ask. "Here's ten cents, go buy yourself a corned beef sandwich."[14]

While the girls were kept at home, the boys were enrolled in school. Levi and Sammy were restless, indifferent students who went to only one school, which was run by a Rabbi Levy, a short man with red hair and whiskers who held class in his living room. "Most of his students were sons of poor pack peddlers—Levy received a dollar a month for each pupil, and he averaged fifty at a time," writes Willie Provol, who attended Rabbi Levy's classes with the Shubart boys and Marcus Heiman, who would later become a Shubert business partner. Levy was a disciplinarian, who yanked the ears of misbehaving boys, and something of a moral philosopher. He devoted half of each day to "lectures on self-reliance, resourcefulness and ambition. Hundreds of his former pupils, scattered over the United States, testify lovingly to his beneficial influence."[15]

Levi, ten, and Sammy, eight, were relieved when David pulled them out of school so they could go to work to support him, but Jacob, only six, refused to quit school. He started working when he turned eight, as his father demanded, but he also continued his education. At fourteen, to David's mortification, Jacob graduated from a Catholic grammar school. David, of course, would not pay for his schooling, so Jacob paid for it himself from the money he earned selling newspapers. In later years, as John recalled, his father said he was "grateful for the discipline the nuns had instilled."[16]

After he became famous, there were persistent rumors that Lee could neither read nor write. John Kenley, a play reader for Lee Shubert in the thirties, scoffed, "Lee could read but with some difficulty. He never did read a play in his entire life, however. I told him to read; I encouraged him to read; but he wouldn't. He once asked me to make him a synopsis of the *Reader's Digest*. All his letters were written by attorneys, though he did memos, short dictation, only a few lines at a time. J. J. read a lot, on the other hand, but he didn't understand what he read."[17]

"Lee basically didn't get any education," John maintained.

I would say that toward the end of his life he was able to read a newspaper well, and he could probably read through a letter, but I don't think he could write at all. I think he would write his name, and a few elementary notes, but I never saw him write a full letter of any kind in longhand, or even a short memorandum to anyone. My father told me that Sam, who had just as little time in school as Lee had, maybe even less time, was able to read and write easily.[18]

With minimal education and a father who offered neither financial support nor moral guidance, the three Shubart boys were responsible for their own survival, and for that of their family, from a startlingly early age. As youngsters in Syracuse, they quickly demonstrated the native shrewdness that was to earn them more money from the theatre than anyone else in the history of American show business.

Thin and sallow, Levi inherited his father's sharp, Asian-looking eyes, and even as a youngster he regarded the world with suspicion. In childhood photographs he has the look of the most unpopular kid in class, a born loner. While he pulled the wagon for his father during the day, at night he ran bets on ball games and prizefights for a cigar operator who carried on an underground operation. The boy who had held the job before him had been caught, but Levi, like his father the former tea smuggler, never was. After about eighteen months, a drummer in the cigar store told Levi of a day job at a cigar factory. Reluctantly, David released him from peddling on the condition that Levi bring him two cigars every day.

The boy never succeeded as a cigar maker. He started with either too much filler or too little, and he consistently cut his fingers with the small, curved knife cigar makers constantly wield. On the bench next to him sat a young man whose skill was greater than Levi's but whose distaste for the work proved equal. Joe Rosenthal, who was impressed by the way Levi could master figures in his head, said he wanted to open a haberdashery shop and needed a partner. Rosenthal told Levi that he would have to put in one hundred dollars to become a partner. Levi had managed to save about fifty dollars, an enormous sum (especially so in light of the fact that David demanded his entire weekly salary) and an early indication of his financial ability; he may have accumulated the money on the sly when he worked for the bookie. Levi asked his father's rabbi to recommend someone who could lend him the fifty dollars he needed; the rabbi gave him a letter of introduction to Joseph W. Jacobs, a well-to-do merchant. Impressed by the boy's earnest manner, Jacobs advanced him the money. Rosenthal, it turned out, had no money of his own, but he had the connections Levi needed to move forward. Joe introduced him to the son of one of the wealthiest German Jewish families in Syracuse. The son agreed to enter into partnership with Levi, and once the firm of Shubart and Mirbach was founded, Levi hired Joe Rosenthal as a clerk.

Under Levi's watch, the store never prospered, though it probably wouldn't have mattered to Levi if it had. He found the work tedious and spent most of his time staring out at the horse-drawn carriages on the bustling main street of downtown Syracuse.[19] Despite his small, unrevealing eyes, Levi could be persuasive: he had convinced Joe Rosenthal, David's rabbi, Joseph Jacobs, and the Mirbach family that he was worth taking a chance on.

Where Levi was dour and hidden and had developed an expert poker face at an early age, Jacob was a live wire with a ripping temper. In contrast to his slender brothers, Jacob had the physique of a heavyweight: thick neck, broad, sloping shoulders, a pair of big fists. He was the only son who never cried after one of David's beatings. "Father was the handsomest of the bunch," John claimed. "He had curly hair, a good complexion, and he was very strong physically, tremendously strong."[20] But from the beginning, Jacob seemed branded as the "other" Shubart, an outsider, even within the family. He was the son who openly defied David, as when he continued attending Catholic school despite his father's enraged objections. David punished Jacob more frequently and more vigorously than he did his two other boys, and perhaps as a consequence Jacob in turn fought with his brothers. From very early on, Sammy and Levi formed a bond from which the youngest brother was at least partially excluded.

Jacob's first job was selling newspapers outside a hotel on the seamy side of town where gamblers, hoodlums, and politicians gathered to shoot dice, play cards, and bet on ponies. Cunningly, the boy figured that winners might feel expansive enough to give him a tip when they bought a paper. Jacob regularly fought off other kids who wanted the same spot. "He was the little bully who used to protect his corner from the other news kids," John said. "He found out that if you're really tough, people leave you alone."[21] Word of his success reached the circulation manager of the *Union News*, who offered the boy a job selling newspapers and magazines on the train that went from Syracuse to Rochester. In the Darwinian struggle for survival into which their father had tossed them, both boys were remarkably adept. Ambition, vitality, and love of money drove them, even then.

It was their middle brother, Sammy, who gave them the chance to move into a more exciting world than selling clothes and newspapers. Painfully thin, "pasty-faced and sallow," according to John, Sammy was Mrs. Shubart's favorite son, the boy she thought could do no wrong. "He was sort of a dreamy-eyed character," John said. "Lee had none of the dreamy eyes in him, neither did Father, and neither did the girls. Sammy was sort of off in left field, all by himself, and maybe that's how genius runs. He was the one who had the drive and the foresight to really start up this whole deal."[22]

With his small hands and feet—he walked with a slight limp—and his delicate features, Sammy looked vulnerable, and his mother and sisters felt he needed special looking after. Once he left home, he incited the maternal instinct of practically every woman he was to meet. Moreover, as Lee writes, "Even at [an] early age, and despite his diminutive size, Sam had an impressive personality and a winning way, going about whatever he had to do with a zeal and a self-assurance that inspired confidence and made friends."[23] The only Shubart boy who looked as if he might have a touch of the poet, Sammy may have seemed frail, but in fact he needed no one's protection: from the age of eight, when his father ordered him to go to work, Sammy, like his brothers, was a cunning businessman.

There are two versions of how Sammy got his start in show business. In the first, which J. J. passed on to John, he is a shoeshine boy working near the alley of the Grand Opera House in downtown Syracuse; when winter comes, the slender boy begins to shiver as the cold wind from the nearby Erie Canal whips through his worn, hand-me-down jacket. The house manager of the Grand, Charles Plummer, takes pity on him and invites him to sit in a back row during a performance. The boy, who has never been to a theatre, is enchanted by the color and spectacle of a touring production of *The Black Crook*, an extravaganza first produced in 1868 that is routinely cited as the aboriginal American musical.

In his autobiographical fragment, Lee Shubert supplies a second version of Sammy's debut. Lee claims that he and his brothers had been regular Saturday matinee theatregoers ever since they had seen one of the annual visits of a "Tom show"—*Uncle Tom's Cabin*, the biggest stage hit of the nineteenth century. As the boys wait with other theatregoers, the house manager chooses Sammy for the honor of handing out programs, in exchange for which he gets to see the show for free.[24]

The first narrative, with Sammy being invited into the theatre from out of the cold by a man who felt sorry for him, is the more plausible. It is unlikely that the Shubart boys, as Lee claims, had the money, the time, or even the inclination to be regular Saturday afternoon theatregoers; their father would never have allowed it. Besides, they would have been expected to observe the Sabbath.

However Sammy Shubart first gained entrance into the Grand Opera House, Mr. Plummer liked him enough to hire him as program boy for $1.50 a week, despite Lee's assertion that the only pay Sammy received was the right to see every show for free. Like his brothers, Sammy was not satisfied working at only one job.

With Willie Provol, an enterprising friend, he formed an interlocking partnership. "We became the boy candy kings of Syracuse," Provol writes in *The Pack Peddler*, his charming memoir about his early days in Syracuse. "Irish kids would try to steal Sammy's candy, and it was up to me to defend him. Sammy was a clean-cut little fellow, rather delicate in health but very shrewd and I was a strong stocky boy. Whenever Sammy got into a fight he would yell for Willie." Sammy and Willie also peddled fruit to immigrants; delivered newspapers, which required them to be up at 3:00 A.M. on Sundays; and sold handbills at the Grand. Without Willie, Sammy secured the opera-glass concession at the theatre. (Provol offers a rare instance of a Shubert without money on the brain: "On Sunday afternoons, in the basement of their humble home, Sammy constructed an opera house from old soap boxes and cast-off lumber and built his own shifting scenery as well as [a] drop curtain.")[25]

Precise dating is not possible, but Sammy probably had his first theatre job early in 1887. Within eighteen months, he was promoted to the box office, the sanctum sanctorum in the Shubert saga. Sammy was so small that customers could not see him in the ticket booth, and he had to stand on a wooden crate. Like Levi, he was a wizard with numbers, able to add sums in his head and to quote daily grosses to the penny. Sammy did everything—from speaking to advancing his career—quickly, and by the end of 1888, he was assistant treasurer at the Grand. The following year, the foremost theatre in town, the Wieting, offered him a position as treasurer and he left the Grand, with Plummer's approval. Mrs. John Wieting, who had inherited the theatre from her late husband, was impressed by her new employee; and in 1891 she asked Sam Shubart, scarcely five feet tall and weighing a feather or two over one hundred pounds, to become the house manager of her theatre. Sammy immediately hired Levi to take charge of the ushers in the balcony. His older brother, still confined during the day to the drudgery of waiting on customers at his haberdashery, leapt at the chance.

Within a year after Sammy became house manager, the family moved to a larger residence, at 922 Orange Street, which this time was not hidden in the back. By this point, delicate-looking Sammy, who had the gift of arousing the interest and confidence of people who were in a position to help him, had replaced both his father and his older brother as the family breadwinner. With the kind of speed that was to be typical of his whirlwind career, Sammy had risen from program boy to assistant treasurer to treasurer to house manager; his next step, to producer, marked a major transition for this young man in a hurry.

There are also two versions of Sammy's debut as a producer. In both, the play was *A Texas Steer*, a farce by Charles Hoyt, a long-forgotten playwright who in his day was the box office king of the American theatre. In version number one, re-counted by John Shubert, the company manager of a touring edition of *A Texas*

Steer skipped town with the receipts—a fairly common occurrence at the time. During the week's engagement at the Wieting, the actors had become friendly with the young and personable house manager and now turned to Sammy to help them: could he raise the money to continue the tour? Sammy first had to convince Mrs. Wieting to keep the show on for another week while he sought backing and secured the rights from Charles Hoyt. Since the house had no prior booking and Mrs. Wieting found Sammy to be an irresistible combination of charm and common sense, she readily agreed. Beginning a practice that would eventually change theatre history, Sammy got the funds to keep the production afloat from sources outside the theatre. Sunday night Sammy took a train down to New York; Monday morning, with a check for a thousand dollars in hand, he called at Hoyt's office. The playwright was reluctant to admit his young caller, but Sammy got his attention when he announced that he had come not to borrow money but to offer it. Explaining to Hoyt what had happened in Syracuse, he asked for the rights to *A Texas Steer*. Hoyt, taking the measure of the eager youngster and his check, shook Sammy's hand, congratulating him on becoming a producer.

Returning on the next train to Syracuse, Sammy brought his brothers in on the very first Shubart production. Jacob, around seventeen, had the job of overseeing a stagehand adjust the letters on the marquee. The billing was to have read "Samuel Shubart Presents," but the stagehand ran out of *A*s, so he used an extra *E*. Shubert with an *e* became the family name that Monday evening, and Shubert with an *e* it has remained ever since. "Father swears that's the way it happened," John said, "but whenever the story was told Uncle Lee would just shrug."[26]

In the second version of Sammy's first play (Lee's again), calculation rather than chance is the impelling force. As treasurer and as house manager, Sammy had studied the audiences as much as the productions. He noticed that Hoyt's farces were consistent crowd pleasers and that, of the many Hoyt shows he had seen, *A Texas Steer*—a farce set in Washington during the days of the robber barons—elicited the heartiest laughs. When Hoyt went to Syracuse with a new play called *A Contented Woman*, Sammy asked the playwright about his plans for *A Texas Steer*. Hoyt said he had put the play to rest. Sure that the play still had some kick to it, Sammy offered to buy it for a road tour. Hoyt was "a bit surprised that a sixteen-year-old boy should come forward with such a proposition," Lee writes, "and a trifle skeptical about his ability to carry it through." But as ever, Sammy's manner "commanded respect," and Hoyt became "seriously interested."[27] Typically playing fast and loose with his brother's age, as he would all his life alter his own, Lee states that Sammy became a producer at sixteen, which would place the date of Sammy's negotiations with Hoyt in 1892 or 1893: unlikely for a number of reasons. *A Texas Steer* opened in New York on January 8, 1894, and Hoyt would not have released the rights until after that date. Sammy must have seen the show for the first time in 1893 during the long pre-Broadway tour. Once he secured the rights, Sammy negotiated with the Syndicate for theatres in which to present the play—the Syndicate was organized in August 1896. It is likely, therefore, that Sammy presented his first play late in 1896 or early in 1897, when he would have been twenty or twenty-one, remarkably young but not quite the sixteen-year-old wunderkind Lee presents.

To launch his tour, Lee continues, Sammy needed five thousand dollars, which he raised from friends and local businessmen. Money in hand, Sammy went down to New York to buy the rights from Frank McKee, Hoyt's eagle-eyed partner and business manager. The first attraction to be presented under Shubert management was, as Lee writes, "from the start a money-maker for [Sammy] and his backers."[28]

This second scenario of how Sammy became a producer, in which he courts a famous playwright, is the one that rings true; he had a reputation as someone who impressed his elders, as someone worth taking a chance on. Sammy's performance as a novice producer was so successful that the hard-nosed firm of Hoyt and McKee appointed him the following season to take over the tours of two other Hoyt shows, *A Contented Woman* and *A Stranger in New York*.

The young man with the gentle manner and soft brown eyes, who seemed to listen to every word older people spoke, was adept not only in gaining the trust of the prominent, he also had a knack for catching the attention of people who would become important, as a meeting in February 1885 with future director and playwright David Belasco attests. At the time, Belasco was stage manager and casting director for a show called *May Blossoms*, produced by Daniel Frohman; the play needed four local boys to appear as extras, and Belasco hired three from a nearby elementary school and selected the fourth when he noticed Sammy outside the theatre jauntily giving out handbills for coming attractions. Belasco offered Sammy a dollar for the show's Syracuse run—the first and only time on the boards for any of the Shubert brothers.

Although he was not yet a celebrity, Belasco, a major figure whose emphasis on scenic realism helped modernize the American stage, had already cultivated a florid, grand manner. Sammy was impressed by Belasco's commanding personality; and when he embarked on his career as an impresario, he tried to emulate Belasco's speech and gestures. He even let his hair grow in the style Belasco affected. A notorious rake and a Jew who sought a clerical appearance by wearing a reverse collar, Belasco was "a great director and a total fraud," according to George Abbott.[29] Sam was to enlist Belasco's support in his battle with the Syndicate; and with Belasco's prestige on his side, Sam's career rounded an important corner. Later still, Lee and J. J. named two of their most successful operettas, *Maytime* and *Blossom Time*, in memory of the show that linked Shubert with Belasco.

Clearly, Sammy had a way with people. He won Belasco's attention and he convinced Charles Plummer, Mrs. Wieting, Charles Hoyt, Frank McKee, and a core of eminent Jewish merchants in Syracuse to give *him*, a pint-sized kid from nowhere, a chance. The omnivorous, often brutal Shubert theatrical empire was inaugurated by a boy with charm.

It is significant that the first Shubert presentation was one of the most financially successful plays in the history of the American theatre. In choosing *A Texas Steer* as his maiden offering and in pursuing Charles Hoyt, Sam demonstrated the Shuberts' atavistic desire to make money from the theatre. "In the early nineties there was not a more important man in New York's theatrical circles," writes theatre historian Douglas L. Hunt. "A millionaire before he was thirty, the lessee of the most successful theatre in the city, renowned as a wit and good fellow about town, Charles Hoyt was truly a Broadway big shot."[30]

Between 1883 and his death in 1900, Hoyt wrote and produced seventeen farces and one comic operetta; and fifteen of his shows were box office bonanzas. Hoyt, before he turned to playwriting, had been a drama critic for the *Boston Post* from 1878 to 1883. He presented himself as an avowed populist, claiming to speak only for the average theatregoer who wanted to have a good time on a night out. Once he began to write plays, Hoyt collaborated with his audiences, adding or deleting material according to the way the crowds responded on the long pre-Broadway tours his shows received. If Hoyt's work has no enduring literary merit, it is because it was never intended to. Nonetheless, with their vernacular subject matter and vigorous colloquial dialogue, his plays form part of an important movement to Americanize the American theatre in the late nineteenth century.

Like Charles Hoyt, Sam Shubert became adept at taking the public's pulse. Standing at the back of the orchestra night after night, the young man received a thorough education in the popular theatre of the era. Willie Provol records that he and Sammy handed out bills for and saw Joseph Jefferson in *Rip Van Winkle*; Henry Dixey in *Adonis*; Sir Henry Irving and Dame Ellen Terry in *The Merchant of Venice*; Edwin Booth in *Richard III*; Richard Mansfield in *Dr. Jekyll and Mr. Hyde*; James O'Neill in *The Count of Monte Cristo*; *Wang*, with DeWolf Hopper; *The Mikado*; a Joe Weber and Lew Fields show, with Lillian Russell; Lew Dockstader's minstrels; a vaudeville show with Eddie Foy.[31] Provol's list is impressive and revealing. First, it is clearly star oriented, a point fully absorbed by the vigilant young Shubert, who noted well that Syracuse audiences, like those across the country, paid more readily to see stars than plays. Second, Provol remembers primarily American stars.

By the time Willie and Sammy were handing out programs in the mid 1880s, American players had begun to compete with the great European stars. An American acting tradition had been building at least since the time of the Astor Place

Riot in 1849 in which supporters of Edwin Forrest (1806–1872), the first American-born star, had clashed violently with the fans of William Macready, an aristocratic British actor who openly mocked the American's interpretation of classical roles. In the 1880s, foreign stars still commanded special respect, and few American players could match the adulation that greeted a Sarah Bernhardt, an Eleanora Duse, a Tommaso Salvini, or an Adelaide Ristori; but the American stage could boast a group of native-born star performers, as well as homegrown versions of musical comedy, burlesque, melodrama, and vaudeville. While foreign actors had been appearing in America throughout the nineteenth century, it wasn't until July 19, 1884, when Augustin Daly's company appeared in London, that a foreign city received American players. In 1886, Daly's was the first American troupe to appear in France and Germany.

Moreover, the theatre business itself had recently undergone a seismic transformation. Until after the Civil War, the local stock company, in which a permanent group of actors performed a series of plays, had been the dominant form of theatrical presentation. Beginning in the 1870s, the combination system—in which actors were cast for a role in a single play, which was then sent out on tour—became increasingly popular. In the transition period between the heyday of the stock companies and the rise of the combination system, visiting stars were often supported by local stock players, often with slapdash results.

The combination system, which remains the reigning theatrical mode, radically altered the economics of theatre. Just at the time the Shuberts were entering it, theatre, for the first time, became a big business. In a financial sense, at least, the new combination method was good for practically everyone—stars, agents, theatre owners, and producers. Stock companies may have been healthy for actors, artistically speaking, but their rapid demise suggests that audiences clearly preferred the new system. The only one for whom the combination system was decidedly not good was the manager, who directed and sometimes acted with his own handpicked players in a season of rotating plays, some of which he may have written himself, performed at his own theatre. The stock company autocrat was not an empire builder, eager to acquire a string of theatres or to produce plays for other managements; he was an artist concerned only with his single theatre and his own troupe. As a businessman, he was strictly small-scale.

The combination system and its purely commercial basis inevitably ended the era of the stock company over which Augustin Daly, the leading manager of the pre-Shubert era, had presided magisterially.[32] The new arrangement not only forced theatres to compete for shows originating from New York but also spawned middlemen, the bookers who routed shows to provincial theatre owners clamoring for product. Beginning their careers during this combustible transition period, when control was shifting from resident artistic managers like Augustin

Daly to businessmen based in New York who were driven by visions of a national circuit of theatres, the Shuberts' timing could not have been better.

On December 14, 1897, Sam Shubert became the manager of the Bastable Theatre in Syracuse, and for the first time the budding impresario had a theatre of his own. Sam leased the theatre at an annual rental of about seven thousand dollars. "Mr. Shubert carries a very old head on very young shoulders," the *Syracuse Standard* reported, adding that Sam, "known for his tact" and for his "uniform courtesy to patrons," had been chosen from among a dozen bidders to run a theatre whose previous manager, "some would say, has not done all that was possible for the house."[33] Sam faced strong competition from the Wieting, a house booked by the newly hatched Theatrical Syndicate. As a Syndicate operation, the Wieting had first claim on hit shows direct from Broadway or on revivals of past hits featuring their original stars.

To get his feet on the ground, and simply to keep the Bastable open, Sam offered "an old-fashioned stock company in old-fashioned plays at old-fashioned prices." For his second season, however, Sam renovated the theatre and its programming, boldly announcing he would book touring combinations only. His plan placed him in open competition with the Syndicate, which by 1898 had already established virtually monopolistic control over the booking and routing of first-class productions from New York. In challenging the Syndicate and its tyrannical chieftain, Abraham Lincoln Erlanger, Sam launched what was to be the longest, bloodiest, and most decisive battle in Shubert history.

With his perpetual scowl, his mouth turned downward in disdain, his beady eyes, which looked with suspicion at colleague and opponent alike, his comically pudgy physique, and the harsh voice in which he barked commands, Abraham Lincoln Erlanger was brilliantly equipped to play his role as one of the most vivid villains in American theatrical history. Rather than emulate his namesake, Erlanger styled himself after Napoléon, stuffing his office with military and imperial artifacts. Like the Shuberts, he maintained a lifelong zest for high-stakes combat. Erlanger was almost universally disliked, and the description J. J. provides in a fragmentary memoir written in the 1940s may be only slightly exaggerated: "He was a short, bald, stubby, undersized, thickset man with a bulldog head. He was cold, callous, and calculating, and the milk of human kindness never permeated his curious ego. With no education of account, and profane to the last word, he would not brook any argument. His mind was usually made up before you got to him. He had no pity for the unfortunate, and he always boasted that his word was his bond. His God was money."[34]

Born in Buffalo in 1860 and raised in Cleveland, Erlanger had a background as humble as the Shuberts'. Like them, he was thrust into a struggle for survival at an age when later laws would have mandated attendance at school. At age eight, an errand boy in a dry-goods shop, he had to be up by 6:00 A.M., which is when he started his days for the rest of his life. Like Sam, he began his theatre career early—before he had even entered his teens. Handing out opera glasses at the Academy of Music in Cleveland, he impressed his employers at an astonishingly young age and was promoted to the post of assistant treasurer, then treasurer. Like Sam again, the young Erlanger knew how to gain the confidence of power brokers: when the Academy of Music passed into the hands of industrialist Mark Hanna, the national chairman of the Republican Party and the man most responsible for the election of President William McKinley, Erlanger made himself indispensable to Hanna's theatrical interests and became a fast friend.

In the early 1880s, when he became a road manager, he observed firsthand the operations of the theatre's primitive booking system. His first important assignment was for one of Joseph Jefferson's perennial tours in *Rip Van Winkle*. As an advance man—a crucial cog in the theatrical wheel of those days—Erlanger arrived in town before the show to look over the theatre that had been booked, to confer with the theatre owner or the manager, to make reservations at a hotel or boardinghouse for the company, to make sure that bills were posted around town, to spread "paper" (free tickets given to the newspapers and to local merchants who could help boost the show), and to oversee box office procedures to make sure that the producer he worked for was not being cheated. If his show was booked for a week, Erlanger would be in town for one or two days, but if he was representing a one-night-stand attraction, then he would race through his responsibilities in a morning or an afternoon and be off to the next town on the route. In those days, advance men could spell the difference between the success or failure of a tour.

Tireless, swift, and with an ability to be ingratiating when he had to be, Erlanger was a splendid advance man. Promoting a known attraction like Joseph Jefferson did not fully test Erlanger's mettle, however. The campaign that made him renowned in theatrical circles was the one he orchestrated in the South for an actress named Effie Ellsler, whose fame at the time did not extend beyond the major cities of the East. On each stop of the route, Erlanger appeared two weeks prior to the star's arrival and deluged the town with publicity, plastering photographs on billboards and planting enticing interviews in local papers. His P. T. Barnum–like tactics and their effectiveness became his calling card in New York.

Erlanger's partner on the Ellsler routing was another advance man, Marc Klaw, who was to be his close business associate for more than three decades. A Kentuckian born in 1858, Klaw was a lawyer who went to work as an advance man when he was unable to find clients. Klaw and Erlanger, as they were invariably called after they rose to power, were a potent team. Tall and lean and with a characteristically tight-lipped expression, which made him look as if he had just eaten a very sour pickle, Klaw played the diplomat to Erlanger's fiery imperator. "He was shrewd, calculating, a Uriah Heep, always ingratiating himself, making the balls for Erlanger to fire, helping Erlanger feed with venom against somebody. He was the go-between," J. J. writes, "always professing friendship, but the die was always cast. His office was not as pretentious as Erlanger's, and he would only be called in on the most important matters. He was very untrustworthy, but very tactful, which Erlanger was not."[35]

Before the Theatrical Syndicate arose, managers of provincial theatres journeyed to New York in the summer to sign up a slate of attractions for the coming season. Transactions were conducted alfresco, out on the sidewalks surrounding Union Square, then New York's theatrical hub. The casual system was often hazardous for both buyers and sellers. As insurance against the real possibility that a promised show might be canceled or booked elsewhere at the time it had been scheduled, local managers often double-booked their theatres, just as New York producers sometimes booked the same attraction into more than one theatre for the same play dates. Local theatre owners were often at the mercy of New York producers, who might cancel their shows if they had been unable to secure a full season's bookings; producers themselves were dependent on the railroads for transporting their shows; and too often their profits were eroded by a route in which there were great distances between one booking and the next and in which there was too much time between engagements.

Their experiences on the road made Klaw and Erlanger keenly aware of the need for a middleman who could bring order to booking and routing. In 1894 they decided to open a booking agency of their own. They were not the first middlemen (before they opened they bought out the Taylor Booking Agency on Union Square), but no one before them had such great ambition. At their new agency, out-of-town theatre owners could book an entire season from the roster of attractions that Klaw and Erlanger had rounded up from independent producers.

The agency offered both theatre owners and producers a service not previously available, and in the process Klaw and Erlanger helped regularize a business that had been notoriously catch-as-catch-can. Filling a need, they became successful so quickly they charged whatever they thought they could, from one-third of the net to 5 percent of the gross to the theatre owner and, in addition, up to 50 percent of the profits to the producer, and they refused to do business with anyone who would not meet their terms.

Early in 1896, a theatre owner and booker named Al Hayman approached Klaw and Erlanger with a plan for extending their agency onto a nationwide level by assuming control of a vast network of theatres that would agree to book attractions on terms the agency would set. With visions of John D. Rockefeller—a little shopkeeper from Erlanger's hometown of Cleveland who had gained control of the oil business by eliminating inefficiency and competition—already dancing in his head, Erlanger leapt at Hayman's proposal for establishing what in effect would be a nationwide theatrical trust.

Having worked in San Francisco for impresario M. B. Leavitt, who claimed to have pioneered the circuit scheme, Hayman learned firsthand how to build and control a network of theatres. Working for Leavitt, he had started out by managing a single theatre; then he quickly branched out on his own to gain exclusive control of the booking of several West Coast houses. By the time he spoke with Klaw and Erlanger, he was able to dictate bookings in important cities between the Missouri River and the Pacific Ocean. Born Raphael Hayman in what in 1852 was Wheeling, western Virginia, "he was very much the type of Erlanger," J. J. observes. "Machiavellian in makeup, brutal, forceful. He spent the early part of his life in Australia (there were rumors of a forced residence), and he spoke in a vaguely English accent. He was hard and cruel in his decisions, and abrogated his contract and his word when it suited him."[36]

On August 31, 1896, Erlanger, Klaw, and Hayman, together with three other men—producer Charles Frohman ("C. F."), theatre owners and sometime producers Samuel Nixon and Fred Zimmerman—met for lunch at the Holland House Hotel on Union Square to establish the American Theatrical Syndicate. Although the participants said that their coming together was merely by chance, like everything else that they did it was in fact calculated. Five of the six partners had financial control of theatres in different parts of the country, and when they pooled their resources their influence stretched from coast to coast. Klaw and Erlanger had strong affiliations in the East and the South; Hayman had a lock on the Far West; Nixon and Zimmerman were partners who had a monopoly in Philadelphia and Ohio. Frohman, the one genuine producer in the group (who would keep his distance from the others), brought to the table a much-needed touch of class.[37]

The historic Holland House meeting signaled both the advent and the triumph of the businessman in the theatre. For the first time on such a scale, a mere functionary, a go-between responsible neither for the show nor for the theatre, attained a position of virtually absolute power. Those who wrote plays and those who produced them were, in short order, at the mercy of the Syndicate, and the theatregoing public was placed in the passive position of taking what the Syndicate (which came increasingly to mean what Abraham Lincoln Erlanger) was pleased to send it. "One cannot but admire the magnificent audacity of their purpose," Alfred L. Bernheim writes in his landmark economic history of the American theatre.[38] With evident respect, Lee Shubert describes the Syndicate as "a concentration of authority never known before or since in the legitimate theatre."[39] Monopolies were the era's economic currency; a 1904 survey revealed that 319 industrial trusts had absorbed about fifty-three hundred formerly independent concerns.[40] And the Theatrical Syndicate operated with the megalomania that was rampant in the trust-building frenzy of the time.

Sam launched his career as a producer just months after the Syndicate had been formed; and from the beginning, even before he openly defied the Syndicate at the Bastable, he had felt the lash of Erlanger's tyrannical methods. After he had secured the rights for a tour of A Texas Steer, Sam needed a route and so went directly to the source, the fledgling Syndicate, which had already wrapped its tentacles around most of the best theatres in the Northeast. At the time Sam, a green kid from the provinces who limped, spoke in a soft voice, and had a disarming manner, posed no threat. Peering imperiously over his mammoth desk at the thin young man, Erlanger asked Sam why he thought he had the right to go into show business. Sam glanced downward in silence. He spent the rest of his life, however, providing Erlanger a vivid answer to his question.[41]

In that first meeting, all Erlanger had to go on was the fact that Sam had obtained the rights to a hit show from Hoyt and McKee, known in the business as sharp traders. Impressed, he booked Sam's show into first-class theatres. But as soon as "better" attractions became available, Erlanger began to reroute A Texas Steer into one-night stands and run-down theatres. The show was booked in New Orleans at Mardi Gras, but at the last minute Erlanger put another show in its place. ("Even today, once you get in the South and get in trouble, you're in real trouble," John said in 1959.[42]) Sam had no choice but to stop the tour. He made no attempt to retaliate—then.

When he acquired another Hoyt play, A Contented Woman, Sam once again had to apply to the Syndicate for theatres, but by this time, aware of Erlanger's tactics, he bribed a Syndicate booker. "Erlanger didn't pay too much attention to the show, which he thought was second-rate, and the booker never showed Erlanger the real books," John said, "and so in that way the booker helped the show to sneak through."[43] When he was on tour with the show in Philadelphia, Sam outfoxed Erlanger again, this time by enlisting Syndicate partner Samuel Nixon as a secret ally. "Nixon was the best of the whole lot of the Syndicate," J. J. writes. "He was not in any way vindictive, but he was very vacillating, you could not depend on his decision. (He and his partner Zimmerman, a very affable man dominated by Nixon, should not have been in show business.)"[44]

"Nixon and Sam made an arrangement that if the Shuberts got any theatre or show, Nixon would come in on it and put up the necessary financial part of his interest," John said. "But it would have to be kept very, very secret, as Erlanger would never permit Nixon to make any deal with Shubert."[45] (Only a few years later, however, Nixon and Zimmerman openly coproduced A Chinese Honeymoon with Sam.)

Throughout Sam's early career, then, the Theatrical Syndicate was an unavoidable obstacle that had to be alternately confronted and ducked, cajoled and outwitted. To survive, Sam began to employ Erlanger's own strategies. Bribery, double cross, evasion, and lying became part of the Shubert way of conducting business. As he built up a minicircuit in the Mohawk Valley behind Erlanger's back, Sam for the most part skillfully disguised his actions. Decades after his first encounter with Sam, Erlanger was asked why he hadn't crushed the frail-looking boy from Syracuse. He is supposed to have answered, according to John, "Why, I wouldn't have done that—he was Jewish."[46] Indeed, Sammy Shubert was one of his own, the kind of son Erlanger might himself have raised if he had ever raised a son. The bond between Erlanger and Sam was psychological as well: both relished money and power and a good fight; and in Sam and his brothers, the Syndicate warlord was to confront the wiliest and most tenacious opponents of his career.

In his second season at the "new" Bastable, when Sam booked competitively against the Syndicate-controlled Wieting, he featured spectacles, extravaganzas, sensation melodramas, variety bills, and farces. Since the big stars were likely to be booked at the Wieting, Sam had to feature the play itself or some aspect of the production as the enticement. The only stars on his programs at this time—the team of Bert Williams and George Walker, as well as Marie Dressler—were from vaudeville, which was not under Syndicate domination.

In the kinds of shows he presented and in the way he advertised them, Sam was simply following the fashions of the period. True to what was to become Shubert house policy, he was a canny copycat rather than an innovator. Because it had proven to be good for business, Sam used "New York" as a consistent selling point; for the road, "direct from New York" or "as seen in New York" were important pedigrees. Advertising was often evasive about whether audiences would be seeing the New York company; in most cases they would not, but a show guaranteed to be an authentic replication of a New York hit was often a strong enough lure.

For his opening attraction up against the Wieting, Sam presented Hoyt's *Stranger in New York*, a hit musical comedy. Other shows that crucial season were described as "a big scenic production" (*The Queen of Chinatown*); a romance "exactly as performed at the Eagle Theatre, New York"; "a kaleidoscopic mechanical trick dramatic spectacle in three acts"; a sensational melodrama (*King of the Opium Den*) "as performed for one hundred nights at the Academy of Music, New York"; a "world-famous" magician; a "big vaudeville farce"; and "the greatest naval drama ever seen in New York."[47]

In Syracuse at the end of the century, as in theatres everywhere else, bigger clearly was better. Long evenings of four-act plays filled with spectacle—battles, hurricanes, real horses—were major drawing cards, indicating how avid theatre-goers were for the kind of scenic realism and large-scale action set pieces the movies would begin to offer in the new century. With a program selling size and sensation, Sam was running a carnivalesque playground, a "people's theatre" with something for everyone.

In his first season against the Syndicate, Sam not only held his own, he quickly expanded by leasing the Grand Opera House. He appointed Lee as manager, and in the fall of 1899 opened the theatre as a venue for "high-class" vaudeville. "If it's at the Grand it must be good," the theatre boasted; and typical of vaudeville houses throughout the country, the Grand was promoted as the "home of clean, bright, honest entertainment." By the time the Shuberts were presenting it, vaudeville had been trying for two decades to overcome its origins in raffish concert saloons where male patrons, milling together in packed, smoky rooms, came to drink and to carouse with often scantily clad waitresses. "Variety" was the term used for the program of singers, dancers, and comedians the saloons offered, and it came to connote a low popular form, a kind of rude, profane entertainment that helped give show business its air of scandal.

In presenting "refined" vaudeville, the Shuberts were capitalizing on the efforts of the genre's pioneers. Tony Pastor, the father of upscale variety, opened a theatre in New York in 1879 that outlawed alcohol and prostitution and presented "clean" shows, promoting talent rather than vice. Where saloon variety played to working-class men, Pastor aimed to attract a middle-class clientele, women as well as men. Keeping a strict watch over his one theatre, Pastor, like the typical nineteenth-century manager, thought small—variety didn't become big business until B. F. Keith and his partner, E. F. Albee, invaded the field in the mid 1880s.

Like the Shuberts, Keith and Albee were born empire builders. They constructed a chain of regally appointed theatres for their "high-class" entertainment, in the process banishing the word "variety" for the French word *vaudeville*, which they felt gave the form a cultural patina. Both men were ardent moralists who permitted no suggestion of off-color material on their stages and tolerated no personal vulgarity from any of the performers whose careers they controlled. Where Sam had to buck the Syndicate, Lee had to compete with Keith and Albee, who by 1900 enjoyed a virtual monopoly in vaudeville.

In booking the Grand, Lee did not have access to the name performers in the field. They were under contract to Keith and Albee or to one of the handful of other czars of the vaudeville big time. Rather than building toward a headliner, programs at the Grand featured acrobats, animal acts, and oddities. For the week beginning Monday, December 4, 1899, with matinees daily at two and evening shows at eight, the Grand offered a ten-act program that included feet balancers,

Indian-club artists, a Hebrew impersonator, masters of the silver rings, a sketch by George M. Cohan, and with a glance at the future, the "Kinodrome," a moving picture process that offered "animated views of special current events."[48]

After Sam became the lessee of the Bastable and the Grand, he was two-for-one against the Syndicate in his hometown. But the Syndicate had a lock on the best theatre in town and a binding contract with most of the first-class attractions "direct from New York," and to survive Sam had to expand his reach beyond Syracuse. In rapid succession, he obtained leases on other upstate New York theatres that the Syndicate had not yet seized or did not want: the Majestic in Utica, the Rand Opera House in Troy, the Cook Opera House in Rochester, and Harmanus Hall in Albany. To conceal his movements from Erlanger, Sam often had one of his partners sign the lease. But even with this form of protection, Sam's expansionist moves demanded extraordinary nerve: a kid with a couple of theatres, Sam eagerly took on the octopus-like Syndicate.

The odds against a Shubert success in Rochester, for instance, were steep. The Cook, like most of the houses the Syndicate had bypassed, was a "Jonah," a jinx house that had seen about ten different managers in three or four years. Since J. J. (as Jacob was now known) was familiar with Rochester from his newspaper route, Sam appointed him his Rochester deputy. Abe Wolf, the owner-manager of the Lyceum, the opposition house, greeted J. J. by assuring him that, as J. J. later told John, he didn't have "a Chinaman's chance" and that the Shuberts wouldn't last longer than two weeks.[49]

Sam was optimistic about the first attraction he had signed for the theatre, the Henocksberg Cummings Stock Company (John Henocksberg was co-lessee of the theatre) with Jessie Bonstelle, the first lady of regional stock, as leading woman. However, when J. J. went to place an ad in the local paper, he was abruptly dismissed; the former managers had left unpaid bills, and the paper wanted $150 in advance, which J. J. didn't have. As the Shuberts often did in their early days, J. J. borrowed the money from a Syracuse crony, in this case Phil Lenen, a former manager at the Wieting. When J. J. went to place the order for the posters announcing the Cook's opening show, he was rebuffed by the owner of the bill-posting plant, a local big shot and bully. "This Mr. Stalbrodt, a most insulting man, wouldn't take my father seriously—I mean a kid that age," John recalled. Reluctantly, Stalbrodt agreed to print bills for the week but only if J. J. paid for the posting in advance, allowed Stalbrodt to decide where the bills were to be placed, and also paid in advance for covering up the postings with blank paper. Stalbrodt was more pessimistic than Wolf; he was certain the Shuberts "would not last out the week."[50]

The Shuberts made liars of both men. They lowered prices, charging half what other theatres were—ten cents for all seats at matinees, twenty-five cents for all seats at night—and Henocksberg Cummings did capacity business for six months. For good measure, as he was to do throughout his career, J. J. claimed an eye for an eye: he got even with the "insulting" Stalbrodt by opening a bill-posting business of his own. J. J.'s company charged one and two cents a sheet, where Stalbrodt's charged four or five cents, and succeeded in attracting national as well as local advertisers. J. J. himself, working at night with stagehands, would tear down Stalbrodt's posters, throw them into the Genessee River, and replace them with his own sheets. He got the best locations by offering landlords free tickets to all shows at the Cook. When Stalbrodt saw that his best locations were starting to go, he realized too late that, as J. J. gleefully recalled to John, "we Shuberts meant business."[51]

J. J.'s assault on Rochester was set back eight months later when their partner, Henocksberg, sold the lease of the Cook Opera House without the Shuberts' knowledge or consent. One morning J. J. arrived at work to find his office furniture out on the sidewalk. To avoid arousing Erlanger's suspicion, the lease had been in Henocksberg's name, and there was nothing J. J. could do. But he was far from defeated. There was a closed hotel around the corner from where he was living, and he thought it would make a fine location for a theatre. The hotel was owned by a Mrs. Baker, a member of one of the city's oldest and most prosperous families. She was now an elderly woman who, like many in her generation, disapproved of the theatre. But like Sam and Lee, J. J. could be persuasive; and after a number of meetings with Mrs. Baker and her attorney, he convinced them to build the Baker Theatre on the site of the deserted hotel.

To sign the ten-year lease with Mrs. Baker, the Shuberts had to come up with a deposit of seventy-five hundred dollars. They raised the money from the circle of Jewish businessmen in Syracuse who had been funding them from the beginning, although the final twenty-five hundred came only after the Shuberts made a pact with the enemy. Abe Wolf at the rival Lyceum in Rochester had refused to sign with the Syndicate rather than give it 33⅓ percent of his profits or 5 percent of his gross. Sam, realizing that a Syndicate contract for the Baker was his only chance to convince his Syracuse backers that the Shuberts could succeed in Rochester, went to see Erlanger hat in hand. Erlanger, like others at the time, may well have thought Sam and his brothers were naive young upstarts who would be out of business soon. Noting Sam's youth and seeming fragility, he may also have thought Sam could be easily dominated. It's also possible that he may have been genuinely impressed by Sam's eagerness and savvy. Perhaps for all these reasons, Erlanger signed an agreement stating that the Shuberts' Baker Theatre was to be the Syndicate house in Rochester. With that, Aaron Graff, owner of the largest furniture store in Syracuse, gave Sam the money he needed.

Then, in a move that would ultimately cost him his empire, Erlanger double-crossed the Shuberts. On hearing that Sam had secured the Syndicate bookings, Abe Wolf had a change of heart. Erlanger then assigned a season's supply of attractions to Wolf's Lyceum Theatre without informing the Shuberts. J. J. learned about the new deal for the first time when he read in the paper that the Lyceum was to become the Syndicate bastion in Rochester. Sam once again went down to see Erlanger in New York, but for the first time his charm did not register. Erlanger refused to consider any change in the Rochester bookings. "The Shuberts had staked their all, and had no attraction to open their theatre," John said.[52] After a delay, they booked Francis Wilson's company as the first offering—Wilson, a prominent comic-opera performer, was one of only a handful of stars who refused to work for the Syndicate. Following Wilson, the theatre struggled along without first-class attractions, playing stock and popular-priced shows.

The battle that was joined, first in Syracuse and then in Rochester, between the Shuberts and Abraham Lincoln Erlanger would last, with brief interregnums, for nearly three decades. In 1899, however, as Sam amassed his upstate circuit behind Erlanger's back, the contest was wildly unequal: Sam had only a handful of theatres while Erlanger was master of nearly two thousand theatres located in major cities and towns throughout the United States and Canada. Expanding his operations while sidestepping Erlanger gave Sam the kind of challenge he thrived on, but he quickly realized that, to become a major figure on a national level, he would have to establish a base in New York City, the heart of commercial theatre. By the end of 1899, after having been in full-time management for only two years, Sam felt secure enough to think of taking on the Syndicate on their own ground. Leaving Lee and J. J. to superintend his expanding interests on the home front, Sam went to New York accompanied by a few members of his Syracuse cabal, including Joe Jacobs, David Feinstone, and Aaron Graff.

On March 31, 1900, after three months in New York, Sam signed a three-year lease starting May 1 for his first theatre on the Great White Way, the Herald Square, at the corner of Thirty-fifth and Broadway, where Macy's now stands. Lee and a group of Syracuse investors were partners of the first part, while Sam was party of the second part. Sam's name alone was on the marquee, however, as lessee, and his name alone was on early program covers, as manager. Lee was resentful, and one Saturday night he went to New York from Syracuse to put up a new sign, which announced Sam Shubert and Lee Shubert as lessees. When Sam saw the new sign on Monday morning, he called his lawyer, William Klein, to protest that Lee had acted without authority.[53]

Tired of being Sam's lieutenant, Lee had rebelled. He was the oldest son, and here he was taking orders from his younger brother. Lee's shame can be seen in the fact that all his life he maintained that Sam was the firstborn. As time went by, Lee increased the distance between his own and his "older" brother's age.

"Sam wouldn't let Lee move to New York for at least a year," John said. Once he moved down to New York, Lee continued to compete with the imperial authority Sam had claimed. "Lee had a tendency to want to take over," John observed. "He'd try to take over anything."[54] Lee even managed to gain control of Sam's money and, according to William Klein, would often cause Sam considerable embarrassment. After Sam went to London in 1904 on a scouting expedition for theatres, he complained to Klein that Lee had not given him enough money. Once he arrived in Southampton, Sam had to borrow money.[55]

Feeling slighted by Sam, Lee was to displace his anger onto his younger brother; if Sam had made Lee feel like a second wheel, Lee bolstered his own sense of importance by keeping J. J. in a secondary position for as long as he could. "Lee wouldn't accept Father as an equal," John said.[56] As the youngest brother and the only one of the Shubert boys who was unable to mask his feelings, J. J. was particularly vulnerable. Often ostracized and humiliated by his older brothers, Jacob had beaten up Lee and Sammy more than once when they were children, just as he had more than once fought with their father. In later years, the growing enmity between Lee and J. J. was sometimes explained, as John Kenley said, by the fact that "as a boy, J. J. had dared to use his fists against Sam. Lee mentioned it to me often, and he just couldn't forgive J. J. for having done that to Sam."[57]

Pricked by resentment and competition, the Shubert boys from their earliest days made war on each other. Nonetheless, and despite bitter feelings, which were to become part of Broadway lore, from beginning to end the Shubert brothers closed ranks against outsiders; they were bound by blood ties of atavistic force. They were brothers, after all, and Jewish brothers at that. "There was jealousy and rivalry between them at a very early age," John said.

> Oh, not to the degree they didn't speak to each other, and heaven help you if you attacked one to the other, they'd rise up and defend each other. But among themselves there was a rivalry: Sam at first did not want Lee or J. J. in New York because he wanted the glory all for himself. But as young people getting started in a tough, cutthroat business they were deeply dependent on each other. They never made many friends because they basically didn't trust people. And so they stuck to themselves. At night, they would plot how to get ahead. Maybe this is a success formula—that you plan for the next day in secret so your competitors don't know.[58]

Despite the hostilities that divided them, the grievances that Lee and J. J. were to nurse for their entire lives, a deep loyalty bound them together, as did, as Larry Lawrence observed about John's relationship with J. J., "a peculiar kind of love."[59]

2

Sam Shubert Goes to Town

*A*s if with one eye on history, Sam Shubert moved to New York from Syracuse in the first week of the first month of a new century. He set up the Shubert Organization, Inc., which exists to this day, and in less than five years laid the foundations of Broadway's sturdiest empire. He moved speedily, and he spoke so quickly, in a rat-a-tat staccato, that he could find only one secretary fast enough to take dictation. At five feet, four inches—he had stopped growing at age thirteen—he had "the physique of a delicate child, the stoop of an old man, and the pallid skin of an invalid, but he was electric with energy and never walked but moved up and down Broadway at a dogtrot," according to the *New York Sun*. High-strung and twitchy—his fingers or his feet jiggled whenever his face was still—he was so full of energy that "even his hair looked as if it might crackle and emit sparks at a moment's notice."[1]

"He was the rawest boy who ever attempted to make good as a New York theatre manager," the *New York Herald-Tribune* commented. "Physically he was less presentable than any man who ever ran a Broadway playhouse. There never was a person who made as little impression upon a stranger as Sam Shubert."[2] When Channing Pollock, a future playwright, was job hunting in August 1900, he mistook Sam for an office boy. "A diminutive, dark-skinned youth took my card and told me Sam Shubert was too busy to see me. As I was about to protest, someone entered into conversation with the boy, who proved to *be* Sam Shubert." "Any one of the brothers might have been mistaken for an office boy," Pollock adds, noting that "they knew little more of literature and drama than a cow knows of the albuminous content of milk."[3] Sam's boyish appearance and his cultural ig-

norance were assets, a kind of protective coloring, and his early inroads against
the Syndicate were due, at least in part, to his seemingly harmless air: a thin, nervous, woefully uneducated boy couldn't possibly constitute a threat to the hefty,
prosperous burghers of the Syndicate.

Up to a point, it was to Sam's advantage to present himself as wide-eyed in
Babylon. Old-time managers by and large dismissed him as a yokel who had a
crackpot idea that he could break into the big time. Sam's "innocence" was part
of his knack—really, his genius—for inducing others, enemies as well as friends,
to speak well of him. "In amassing his fortune he always found time to show his
good will toward his fellow man," theatrical manager M. B. Leavitt writes.[4] Historian Robert Grau notes that "a generation provides three or four instances of
extraordinary tact in the conduct of theatrical management. First came Barnum,
then J. H. Haverly, then Sam Shubert."[5]

In photographs taken in his early days in New York, Sam posed in the style
of his idol, David Belasco. These formal portraits, in which Sam seems to com-
mune with otherworldly thoughts, belie the fact that his visions were more material than mystical. Though like Belasco he cultivated a monastic appearance, Sam
was in fact a wheeler-dealer in perpetual motion. Unlike Belasco, a Jewish satyr,
Sam was not a lady-killer. "He was one of the boys, a homosexual," opined producer John Kenley, who worked for Lee Shubert in the thirties.[6] In July 1901, a
rumor circulated that Sam was engaged to Lulu Glaser, a soubrette he had under
contract, but Glaser denied that there was any relationship between them, and
there was to be no marriage to Glaser or to anyone else. Given what Sam accomplished in so short a period, he could hardly have had time for much of a private
life of any kind.

A master of dissimulation who concealed his will to conquer under a mask of
diffidence, Sam had a layered, complex personality. Despite his humble background,
he assumed a genteel aura and was the one Shubert in any generation who could
claim even a hint of polish. An early, revealing article (in the *New York Herald-Tribune*,
December 13, 1903) tellingly entitled "The Shuberts—Jake, Lee and Sam and the
greatest of these is Sam," called him "the young Napoléon of the theatre." "Lee
attends to the financial part of the business, but it is Sam's judgment that accepts or
rejects the chances that may be involved in an undertaking—and from that judgment there is no appeal. What Sam says goes! And yet there is nothing in the least
aggressive or domineering about the little man who is scarcely past his boyhood."
Far from filling the role of an up-and-coming Broadway impresario in the usual
way, Sam was an original, a soft-spoken, dreamy-eyed young man out for the kill.

When Sam got to town in January 1900, Broadway was flourishing. More than
fifty shows were on the boards; and as he had in Syracuse, Sam went nightly to

the theatre, to gauge what was selling and why. He was an astute spectator whose tastes were in step with contemporary popular judgment, and from the beginning he was a frankly commercial producer who delivered far more hits than flops. If for him the theatre was in any way a temple, it was a temple filled with money changers he wished to join rather than expel.

In the vital, profane, popular theatre of 1900, ravishment for the eye and ear was clearly the dominant trend. Melodramas with spectacular action sequences, comic operas with exotic settings and costumes and lush melodies, alluring chorus lines, and stars, stars, and more stars were the chief attractions. The variety stage—vaudeville, revue, burlesque, and what was left of minstrelsy—was thriving. In 1900 the American theatre, by and large, still had a colonial relationship to England and the Continent. American musical theatre had yet to find a clear voice of its own; most shows were either direct imports or Americanized versions of British musical farces or Continental operettas. Producers and stars seeking prestige presented revivals of classics or iconoclastic, contemporary foreign pieces rather than original American plays. As soon as he was firmly established in New York, Sam began to make regular expeditions abroad to sign up plays and players. Neither then nor later did Sam or his brothers care about Americanizing the American stage—they simply wanted to produce the kinds of shows that made money; and when they were getting started, imports and adaptations of foreign works were often the big tickets.

Audiences, typically, were socially mixed, and at an ornate house like the Casino, society swells mingled with roughnecks from Hell's Kitchen who paid fifty cents for a seat upstairs. The theatre was now liberated from the Puritan prejudice that had trailed it for most of its history in the New World, and rituals that began to surround going to the theatre marked its elevated status. By the turn of the century, a visit to one of the large and lavish restaurants (called "lobster palaces" in the lingo of the era) that lined the Great White Way was a frequent prologue. Amid sumptuous Old World decor, Shanley's, Reisenweber's, and the Cafe Metropole offered gargantuan bird-and-bottle suppers and live musicians. The popular favorite was Rector's, which opened in 1899 on Broadway between Forty-third and Forty-fourth Streets. This "Cathedral of Froth" was the scene of nightly revelry, as leading figures from sports, journalism, society, and Wall Street hobnobbed with actors, dancers, opera singers, and theatrical impresarios, their images reflected in the ceiling-high mirrors that covered the soaring, two-tiered restaurant. The thick Irish linen was imported from Belfast; the green-and-gold decor was Louis XIV. The Sardi's of its day, Rector's was the place to see and be seen.[7]

The theatre district's center was in the thirties and edging up to Forty-second Street, but theatres were located all over town, from the Bowery up to Harlem, and in the boroughs as well. From the romantic escape provided by the typical

operetta to the thrills of cliff-hanging melodramas to the urban urgencies reflected in the comic sketches in vaudeville, the theatre before the era of mechanical reproduction offered respite and refreshment on a scale that will never be du-
plicated. The sheer abundance of theatres and shows quickened Sam's designs for
an empire of his own.

Sam's first goal in New York was to acquire a theatre, not an easy job because
by 1900 the Syndicate and their allies controlled almost all the first-class theatres
in town. The only theatre Sam could get, the Herald Square, was run down and
had an unsavory reputation. After he leased the unpromising house, paying at
least two or three times what the street said it was worth, a Syndicate spokesman
joined the growing list of those predicting an early death for the newcomers.
"Who are the Shuberts? Tell those kids to save their money. I feel sorry for them.
This is a man's game and they'll have to go back to Syracuse on foot."[8]

The Herald Square proved to be a success, however, for two reasons: Sam's
method of financing and the shows he presented. As he had been from the beginning, Sam was supported at the Herald Square by a group of investors who were
not themselves theatre people. "Beginning as early as 1894, with funding from
Syracuse clothier J. W. Jacobs and factory owner Jesse Oberdorfer, the Shuberts
relied on outside, sometimes shady, sources for investment capital," writes historian Peter Davis.[9] "Using little of their own money initially, the Shuberts allowed
silent partners to finance expansion. While this forced them to share ownership
with investors who were not directly involved with the management of the company, it also gave them plentiful and accessible funding necessary for rapid expansion." And as long as they made money, nontheatrical people would be less
likely than knowledgeable backers to interfere with Shubert strategy. No matter
how many corporations they were to establish (and eventually they were to have
fifty-one), the Shuberts themselves were in control; as Davis notes, their "internal
management structure always remained the same, with Sam as president [suc-
ceeded by Lee], with Lee or J. J. as vice-president, and a small collection of their
most trusted investors as the board of directors."

The Syndicate was organized as a pool, or combination, and as Davis points
out, "pools were typically viewed as informal or 'friendly' agreements to cooperate, relying entirely upon the trust of the individual members."[10] Despite their
differences, the Shuberts were a family who maintained vigilant and legally binding management of the outside capital that fueled their expansion; whereas the
Syndicate was a more loosely organized consortium whose members did not want
to restructure their independent firms and, as Nixon did when he signed an agreement on the sly with Sam, would sometimes break ranks to make separate deals.
The partners put in unequal amounts of capital and received unequal cuts of the
pie, a dangerous arrangement for a school of sharks.

"Monopolies are not all the same," Davis writes, and history was to prove that the Shuberts' kind, organized according to then-new corporate methods, with venture capitalists ceding control to an executive team responsible for returns on investors' money, was sturdier than the outmoded pooling system the Syndicate had adopted. Sam's pleasing personality was importantly backed up by his more efficient, up-to-date means of raising and watching over money.

Sam's financing got him the fast money he needed to lease the Herald Square, but he was able to stay in business because of the quick profits he returned to his investors. And in this crucial first outing in New York, Sam continued the winning streak he had established upstate. His far-from-desirable lease required him to honor the theatre's prior contracts, and a spate of failures might well have discouraged his backers and ended his metropolitan career. Two of the three shows Sam was forced to play were standard musical comedies built around stars: *The Cadet Girl* with Adele Ritchie and Dan Daly, and Charles Frohman's production of *The Girl from up There* with Edna May and the comedy team of David Montgomery and Fred Stone. Their short, predictable runs kept Sam afloat, but the ship was beginning to leak. The third booking, a Western by Augustus Thomas called *Arizona*, however, was a landmark in American theatre of the period. It featured not only the spectacle and action premovie theatre audiences craved but an aura of literary distinction as well—the dialogue had more vigor and the characters greater depth than the usual commercial fare. The play was a smash for the Shubert-run Herald Square. Sam concluded his first season with a production of his own, his first in New York, with a young, not-yet-famous Lionel Barrymore in a small role; *The Brixton Burglary*, which opened on May 20, 1901, was a routine English melodrama Sam had bought in London several months earlier.

Sam's successful first season was due in part to the Syndicate, who had supplied attractions (Frohman, after all, was a Syndicate partner) and who still more or less underrated the boys from Syracuse. But after the first season, as Lee writes in his memoirs, Klaw and Erlanger "openly revealed their resentment at Sam's entrance into competition with them in New York, refused to furnish him with attractions and warned their associates not to send plays to his theatre." As he had upstate, Sam considered stopgap measures to keep the house open. He rejected stock on the grounds that it was an outmoded form in New York by that point, and presenting stock at the Herald Square would have been a sign of defeat. Vaudeville was a more likely possibility, but here he was blocked by another monopoly, that of the Keith–Albee circuit who, according to Lee, "froze" them out and "declined to let us have acts [because] the Herald Square Theatre was in the territory which it recently had assigned to F. F. Proctor."[11]

Faced with the specter of an empty house, Sam realized that the only solution was to engage a star, and with typical nerve he pursued Richard Mansfield, perhaps the biggest star in the theatre at that time. The previous season, Mansfield had been booked by Klaw and Erlanger, but Sam knew that Mansfield, along with other leading players like Minnie Maddern Fiske, Joseph Jefferson, Francis Wilson, and Nat Goodwin, had openly protested the Syndicate's formation. Throughout the fall of 1896 and into 1897, Mansfield and the others delivered stirring anti-Syndicate curtain speeches, often in theatres booked by the Syndicate. The curtain was brought down on Mansfield during a particularly fiery declamation in the Chestnut Street Opera House in Philadelphia, a Syndicate stronghold operated by Nixon and Zimmerman. While the stars were intense in their opposition to the new theatrical trust, they did not have the leadership, the money, or the determination that were to carry the Shuberts to victory over the Syndicate. With the valiant exception of Mrs. Fiske, abetted by her husband, Harrison Grey Fiske, editor of the anti-Syndicate *New York Dramatic Mirror*, the actors, lured by generous Syndicate contracts, capitulated. By the end of 1897, as Mansfield's biographer Paul Wilstach writes, the actor "saw only futility in the fight and his ardor cooled perceptibly. But in the fullest sense of the word he was an Independent to the end of his career. He was fighting for an independence which opened the desirable Syndicate houses to him, yet left him free to play anywhere else he wished. This he achieved."[12]

Sam's decision to approach Mansfield, then, was well judged—there was a chance that, if he presented an attractive enough offer, he might be able to entice Mansfield to the Herald Square. "Can give you important Broadway theatre for your fall engagement on very advantageous terms. Would you be interested?" he asked Mansfield in a telegram sent to the actor's summer residence in New London, Connecticut.[13] Mansfield responded immediately and invited Sam to lunch on his yacht the following Monday. Surprisingly, as he preferred working alone, Sam asked Lee to join him in his make-or-break attempt to charm Mansfield into signing a Shubert contract. Lee's sullen demeanor could hardly have been an asset in a circumstance where striking the apt social tone was crucial.

The Shubert boys approached their fateful encounter with trepidation. They knew that if the moody, imperious actor could not be won over, their Broadway adventure might be ended. When the brothers appeared on his yacht, the near-sighted actor squinted at them through his monocle, demanding to know where Mr. Shubert was. When Sam said that he was Mr. Shubert, "the great one," "unable to conceal his astonishment at the frail figure before him, ejaculated, 'God bless my soul.' " Mansfield inquired what theatre young Mr. Shubert had in mind. Sam had omitted citing the Herald Square in his telegram, correctly fearing its malodorous reputation would repel the actor. "Why, that theatre is of no importance!" Mansfield exploded, and turned his back. Sam's response was a turning point in the fortunes of his fledgling empire. "No, Mr. Mansfield, but when *you* appear there it *will be* important. Any house you play becomes important."[14] Flattered, Mansfield agreed and in his very next breath inquired about terms. With his backers' consent, Sam was prepared to offer more generous terms than Mansfield was likely to have received from any Syndicate house. Satisfied, Mansfield gave Sam a letter to his manager, who was plainly "astonished." "How in the world did you do it?" he asked Sam.

There, of course, lay the secret of Sam Shubert's success. "We could not answer him definitely," Lee reports,

> but my opinion is that it was Sam's persuasive personality, and his direct convincing manner, which inspired confidence that he knew his business. . . . A dozen older, established managers in New York would have jumped at the opportunity to secure Richard Mansfield for their theatres and here was a boy of not yet twenty years of age [again, Lee is lowering Sam's age; Sam would have been about twenty-five in 1901] who had won the difficult, exacting, opinionated star over at the very first contact to playing in a house that was considered to be not of the very first class such as he always demanded. . . . The news was received with ill grace at the office of Klaw and Erlanger.[15]

Mindful of the reflected glory his presence bestowed on them, the Shuberts catered to their new star in a way that was quite different from their often notorious mistreatment of actors in the future. Mansfield demanded, and received, a new dressing room with rose pink drapes and a private bathroom boasting a tub made of onyx rather than porcelain, as well as a new coat of paint for the theatre's auditorium, a light white that would complement his complexion.

On December 2, 1901, presented by Samuel S. Shubert (the *S* was simply for sonority) Richard Mansfield appeared in Booth Tarkington's *Monsieur Beaucaire*, playing a coxcomb whose preening vanity and affectation were ideally suited to him. The show was a hit, and as Lee writes, "We had the satisfaction of seeing the finest class of theatre patrons in the city visit the house: prestige came with prosperity."[16] Mansfield was so pleased with his first season at the Herald Square that he returned for a second, opening on December 1, 1902, as Brutus in *Julius Caesar*.

To establish a solid presence in New York, Sam needed more than one theatre; his aim was a circuit of theatres in which to present his own productions. His success at the Herald Square convinced his backers to allow him to acquire the lease on another theatre, the Princess at Twenty-ninth and Broadway, which also had a dismal reputation. As a burlesque house, it had had several names, including Jack's and the Theatre Comique. After renovating the house over the spring and summer, Sam opened it on October 1, 1902, with another English import, a melodrama called *The Night of the Party*. (In the teens, the Princess would be the home

of a series of charming, intimate, historically important shows, with scores by
Jerome Kern and books and lyrics mostly by the team of Guy Bolton and P. G.
Wodehouse, which have come to be known as the Princess musicals.)

For his third New York theatre, Sam acquired a house with a lustrous reputation. From the time of its opening in 1882, the Casino had been the home of
exactly the kind of commercial entertainment Sam had always had his eye on:
comic opera containing generous portions of spectacle, lilting melodies, and romantic intrigue spiced with low comedy. Its original manager, Rudolph Aronson,
employed a permanent stock company, which he presented in a series of musical
spectacles with bejeweled fantasy settings. Six months after he opened, Aronson
installed a sumptuous roof-garden theatre, the first of its kind in New York, where
he presented concerts and variety programs. Aronson's exotic theatre matched his
offerings. Its Moorish design, featuring a prominent minaret, rounded arches, and
intricate stonework, provided a glittering setting for Aronson's musical extravaganzas. In its heyday in the eighties and nineties, the Casino was considered an
"uptown" house at Thirty-ninth and Broadway. Later, the rialto migrated in
stages from Union Square to Madison Square (at Twenty-third Street) to Herald
Square (at Thirty-fourth Street) and ultimately to Longacre Square (from Forty-
second to Forty-fifth Streets), and the theatre was usually either north or south
of the action. But when Sam sought tenancy, the Casino was ideally located.

Aronson presided until 1893, when he made the mistake of abandoning comic
opera for vaudeville. He went bankrupt, and George Lederer, often called "the
father of musical comedy," took over. Lederer's first production, *The Passing Show*,
which opened on May 12, 1894, is often cited as the first revue in America. From
his very first days in New York, Sam pursued Lederer. By the end of his first week
in New York, in fact, Sam purchased from Lederer the rights to a musical comedy,
The Belle of New York. The play had not been a success when Lederer had first
presented it at the Casino in 1897, but it later ran in London for 674 performances.
Sam was able to obtain the American touring rights for the hit show for the same
reason he would be able to take over the lease of the Casino two years later—
though Lederer was a brilliant showman, he was a befuddled accountant who always seemed to need cash and who had earned a reputation for not paying his
bills.

Sam, during one of his many visits to Lederer's office, met William Klein,
who was to become the principal Shubert lawyer for almost half a century. Then
a clerk in the office of Julius Lehmann, Klein had been assigned to see that Lederer
paid off his debt to the Eaves Costume Company in modest weekly installments,
which Klein personally collected each Saturday. In addition to his financial mismanagement, Lederer had refused to open the Casino to Syndicate attractions.

Erlanger blacklisted him, and—unlike Sam—Lederer had neither the savvy nor the backing to withstand the Syndicate.

In the early spring of 1902, Sam proposed taking over the Casino's lease, and Lederer was interested. He was exhausted from the theatrical wars and needed the money Sam was offering, but he shared his lease with the Sire brothers. Claiming that the Shuberts had paid Lederer but not them, the Sires, as William Klein reports, "put armed men into the Casino and barricaded [the theatre]."[17] The Bixby Estate, the owner of the property, went to court, together with the Shuberts, to try to dispossess the Sires. But a Judge Bolte ruled against them. "The defendants' case was entirely perjured," Klein maintains, adding that the Judge who decided against them was "thereafter disbarred and removed from the bench, the proceedings in our case being the basis of the action to remove him."

"The Shuberts Driven off at Gunpoint," a *Herald-Tribune* headline announced.[18] Although Klein filed an appeal, Sam had an expensive musical ready to go into the inaccessible theatre and didn't have the time to wait for the legal process to address his grievance. Klein claimed they would have been "ruined if nothing was done," and so, in late spring, like many Shubert cases in the future, this first legal skirmish in New York was settle out of court. Never admitting that the Shuberts had paid only one of the lessees, Klein gingerly said that they were "compelled to adjust the difficulties with the Sires and pay them $25,000 for them to step out of possession of the theatre and turn same over to the Shuberts."

The brouhaha, which might have provided a farcical subplot for one of the Casino's comic operas, stimulated interest in Sam as well as in his new show. Opening on June 2, 1902, *A Chinese Honeymoon* was Sam's first original New York hit, and the prototype for scores of later Shubert musicals. Sam shared producing credit with Nixon and Zimmerman, Syndicate partners still in business with Erlanger, whom they suspected of cheating them out of part of their share of the Syndicate take.

Yet another London import, *A Chinese Honeymoon* typified the trends in musical theatre. Though billed as a musical comedy, it was almost as fragmented as a vaudeville program. Continuity in plot and characterization was less important than the specialty numbers, which regularly interrupted the thin farce plot in which the hero, Simon Pineapple, takes his bride on a honeymoon in China, where he innocently kisses a young lady only to learn that local custom decrees that he must marry her. Treating the London original with an indifference customary at the time, Sam hired American composers William Jerome and Jean Schwartz to write some new songs to be interpolated into the free-form narrative.

"It is only another variation of a senseless species of stage entertainment which defies all intelligent criticism," the *Theatre* scoffed in its July review. But

Sam had produced a sight-and-sound spectacle: it didn't need critical approval. Exploiting the vogue for Oriental settings, the show enticed theatregoers to the Casino for a record full year's run. Even the disdainful critic for the *Theatre* admitted that "the stage settings and costumes are as beautiful as have ever been seen in this city. The Chinese gowns constitute a veritable orgy of splendid coloring."

At the Casino, Sam was the custodian of an already-established musical theatre tradition; what he needed now was a theatre he could put his own stamp on. His models were Charles Frohman, who had built a loyal carriage-trade clientele at his elegant Empire, and David Belasco, who the year before had leased the Republic Theatre and renamed it after himself. To build his first metropolitan theatre, the new Lyric Theatre, Sam entered into partnership with composer Reginald De Koven, whose money came from *Robin Hood*, his phenomenally successful comic opera (Sam and Lee were actually the theatre's first lessees). Sam wanted the Lyric to resemble the Casino, a house with a single policy. American "opera" was to be the specialty, the kind De Koven wrote, but Sam in fact opened the theatre with his ace in the hole, Richard Mansfield.

While he was still negotiating with De Koven for the Lyric, Sam pressed his luck with Mansfield. Each night Sam would visit the star backstage at the Herald Square, trying to persuade Mansfield to open the Lyric Theatre with *Heidelberg*, a play then concluding a disappointing run at Sam's Princess Theatre. Mansfield was reluctant, but Sam's account of the play's doomed romance between a prince and a commoner excited him enough to see one of the final performances at the Princess. Mansfield loved the play and saw a last chance, at age fifty, to perform a romantic leading role. But he hesitated, first, because it was clearly unwise for a star of his stature to appear next season in a play that had already failed and, second, because he was not sure if even *his* abilities at self-transformation and the most flattering lighting could make him a prince of college age.

Sam persisted, continuing to visit Mansfield backstage at the Herald Square several times a week, until he finally exacted the commitment he sensed was there all along. "I admire your courage and perseverance," Mansfield said. "I will take the play. You win." "No, Mr. Mansfield," Sam answered, again finding the *mot juste*, "it is you who win." "God bless my soul, you always have a ready answer, don't you? We will both win."[19]

As indeed they did. Mansfield opened the Lyric Theatre on October 12, 1903, in the play that was now called *Old Heidelberg*, and the show, the star, and the new playhouse elicited raves. It was a tribute to Mansfield's star presence that he was admired rather than mocked in a role he was at least thirty years too old for. (*Old Heidelberg* would be recycled through the Shubert factory for a third incarnation, as an operetta, *The Student Prince*, which was to become one of the Shuberts' most enduring offerings.)

Despite the dazzling premiere, Mansfield lasted only two seasons at the Lyric, and Sam's partnership with Reginald De Koven also foundered. The Lyric ceased being the "home of native American opera," although Sam continued to regard the theatre as an important part of his New York operation. Although the Lyric never became the prestigious flagship house Sam had envisioned, the theatre is important in Shubert history because of its location. In choosing Forty-second Street (a little north of the theatre district's 1903 boundaries) for his new theatre, Sam once again demonstrated superb timing.

Since the Shuberts built more theatres in the area than anyone else and thereby provided Broadway with the configuration it has maintained to this day, they are indeed the Fathers of Times Square (which, in 1903, was called Longacre Square). But once again they were following another's lead. It was Oscar Hammerstein I, grandfather of the celebrated lyricist and one of the great impresarios of the day, who first recognized that the hub formed by the intersection of Broadway, Seventh Avenue, and Forty-second through Forty-fourth Streets could become a teeming theatrical crossroads. In 1895 when Hammerstein decided to build his monumental Olympia Theatre on the east side of Broadway between Forty-fourth and Forty-fifth Streets, he was a lone pioneer daring audiences to travel uptown beyond the theatrical rialto, then centered around Thirty-fourth Street. "My theatre will make a place for itself, because I will give the public what they have never had before," Hammerstein declared in the ringing tones of a born showman.[20] And when his theatre opened on November 25, 1895, in the "wilderness" above Forty-second Street, he gave New York a playhouse of unprecedented magnificence.

On the ground floor, the Olympia contained not one but three elaborate theatres—the Music Hall, the Concert Hall, and the Lyric Theatre—which could seat six thousand spectators. The roof held a vast garden theatre, which could be glassed in for winter and opened for summer. Hammerstein called his roof theatre the Winter Garden, a name the Shuberts were to appropriate, as indeed they also appropriated the name of the Lyric Theatre. In addition, there was an Oriental café, a billiards room, and lounging rooms. It was a palatial entertainment complex, but like Hammerstein's epic battle to defy the Metropolitan Opera by creating a company of his own, the Olympia was a glorious failure, too grandiose ever to have succeeded. The Olympia closed on June 8, 1898, and less than a year later Hammerstein opened the Victoria, which was to become a raucous vaudeville venue. Modestly sized and appointed—even Hammerstein was incapable of erecting another Olympia—the new showcase at the corner of Forty-second Street and Seventh Avenue was the first house on what was to become the Forty-second Street of theatrical legend. In 1900 Hammerstein built the Republic Theatre on the adjacent lot.

Because Hammerstein was a musical maestro and the Republic was designed for plays, he remained for just one year, leasing the theatre in 1901 to David Belasco. Sam chose the site of his Lyric Theatre not only for its forward-looking uptown location but because placing his own theatre next to Belasco's was tangible evidence of his penetration of Broadway's inner circle. A third reason was that Klaw and Erlanger were building a theatre across the street. Sam's theatre was ready first; Klaw and Erlanger's New Amsterdam opened a month later.[21]

When he moved into his office above the Lyric Theatre in the spring of 1903, Sam had by no means achieved parity with Klaw and Erlanger. He was still the new kid in town. But as he acquired one theatre after another in New York and in strategic points on the road, and as he began to produce a string of popular shows, he was clearly a man on the move; and the fact that he chose to place his office directly opposite those of his adversaries was a symbolic gesture the Syndicate could not ignore. The Syndicate's response to Sam's new eminence was a renewed attempt to put him out of business.

"It was after the Shuberts had the lease on six New York houses that Erlanger and his henchman, Al Hayman, thought of a way to destroy us," J. J. writes in his memoirs. "At the time [1903] we were very vulnerable, and we knew that we could not get by unless we had help from other producers. We got to Mose Reis, a producer who was always ready to do what he could to help us." But Erlanger had gotten to Reis first, urging him to convince the Shuberts to book their theatres through Klaw and Erlanger. Encouraged by Reis, Sam signed up with the opposition despite Erlanger's having violated each of his previous contracts with the Shuberts. Sam needed attractions to fill his expanding circuit, and not enough independent productions were available. Charging the Shuberts 50 percent of the annual profits of each theatre he booked for them, Erlanger promised Sam "only the best attractions."[22]

The truce between Erlanger and the boys from Syracuse exploded when Sam refused to accept the Primrose and Dockstader minstrel show as the opening attraction in September 1903 at his newly acquired Garrick Theatre in Chicago. When Sam had taken over the lease of the theatre, it had been called the Dearborn and was a popularly priced house with a seedy reputation he was determined to overturn. Sam dismissed the minstrel show as a violation of his announced first-class policy, and Erlanger, who may well have been waiting for Sam to defy him, pounced. On August 31, 1903, Sam received a registered letter from Al Hayman, on behalf of Klaw and Erlanger, "declaring," as J. J. writes, "that the Shuberts had breached a contract and that they would not furnish us with any attractions. This was a desperate situation for us—as a rule the season opened on September first, and there we were without a single attraction with the exception of our own shows." When Sam tried to get an appointment to see Erlanger, he was refused and told to see Al Hayman instead. After a considerable wait, Sam and Lee were ushered into Hayman's office, where they discovered Klaw and Erlanger lurking conspiratorially. "Hayman was the most brutal scoundrel you have ever seen," Lee writes in his memoirs. "He raved for fifteen minutes, and said he was going to put us out of business. How dare we, a couple of kids from Syracuse, try to destroy the show business by boosting rents, taking theatres away from managers, and paying outrageous salaries." (Hayman's charges were not accurate.) Sam and Lee were informed that the Syndicate would not book Shubert plays or theatres; and as a parting shot, Erlanger, ominously quiet up to this point, "hurled these words at my brother: 'Go back to Syracuse—there is no place for you in the theatrical business—it belongs to us.' "[23]

After this meeting, the Shuberts were nearly ruined. Erlanger notified the managers of all Syndicate houses and the producers within the Syndicate fold that they would be blacklisted if they dared to conduct any business whatsoever with the Shuberts. Once again, and not for the last time, Erlanger misjudged his young opponents: the more he tried to evict them, the more determined they became to stand up to him. Recalls Lee, "Even at that early day Sam was under no awe of Erlanger or Hayman or Frohman, but felt that he could compete with them in all phases of the business despite their apparently impregnable position."

In the fall of 1903, as the Syndicate's opposition flared into open warfare, Sam laid out the strategy his brothers were to maintain over the next two decades. Continuing to do what he had already begun, but now at a heightened pace, Sam extended his circuit and aggressively sought stars, producers, and theatre owners who would join him in his challenge to the theatrical leviathan. His aim was to gain control of enough theatres in important cities so that he could assure producers of a full season's bookings. Only then could producers even consider defying the Syndicate. After seven seasons in the clutches of a tyrant, and with local managers unorganized and actors seemingly unfitted for the task, it was time for a "hero" to come forward to liberate the American theatre. To the contemporary managers, Sam's determination to resist the Syndicate seemed, and was, heroic; only later did it become apparent that his goal was not to liberate but to conquer the theatre.

As a further defense against the Syndicate, Sam began in 1903 to increase the number of his own productions—a Samuel S. Shubert hit in New York could be toured in Shubert theatres season after season. Building an arsenal of hits of his own reduced his dependence on outside producers, who could always defect to the Syndicate, and also boosted his own profits.

His early experience with Richard Mansfield had confirmed Sam's belief in star power. In April 1903, he added his good friend Fay Templeton, the queen bee at Weber and Fields's Music Hall famed for her imitations of celebrities, to the cast of his already-running show, *Runaways*. Sam's ploy to attract Templeton's Music Hall fans succeeded. The next season, on December 24 at the Lyric, Sam presented Lillian Russell, the first lady of comic opera, in a musical version of *The School for Scandal* called *Lady Teazle*. By 1904 Russell was past her prime; her many well-publicized nights on the town with Diamond Jim Brady, when two of the biggest eaters of the nineteenth century indulged in champagne and lobster suppers, had taken their toll. But Sam was determined to present Russell exactly as her fans expected her to be seen. Sam's three adapters performed a hatchet job on Richard Sheridan's sparkling eighteenth-century comedy of manners, and this Shubertized version of Sheridan required a cast of one hundred, including sixty chorus girls. The real point of the show, after all, was the sheer spectacle of Lillian Russell in huge feathered hats and strapped into formfitting blue, white, and green gowns as she snapped oversized fans and sang many songs in a voice reported by the *New York Times* to be "no worse than [the one] she has [had] for years and years."[24]

Sam continued to exploit the Oriental craze with his 1904 revival of *Wang*, a musical about the romantic misadventures of the regent of Siam, first produced in 1890 for the tall comic actor DeWolf Hopper, who had toured in the show ever since. "Sam S. Shubert, managing director of the DeWolf Hopper Company, presents DeWolf Hopper in a sumptuous production of *Wang*, a comedy operetta under the personal direction of Sam S. Shubert," the program announced. Made for the same audience who had supported *A Chinese Honeymoon* for its year's run, *Wang* was a massive production, which featured two elaborate settings, a village and harbor and the royal palace at Bangkok, and twenty-four musical numbers, including a Siamese wedding march, a coronation march, and a banjo interlude.

Typical of later Shubert practice, in which a hit bred numerous revivals and in-house imitations, Sam used *A Chinese Honeymoon* as the model for his first original show, *Fantana*, which opened at the Lyric on January 14, 1905. The show was Sam's idea, and he more or less cowrote the libretto. When his coauthor, Robert B. Smith, claimed to have done all the actual writing, Sam admitted that he had but would not change the credits. Sam's mechanical, unnecessarily complicated story of thwarted young lovers (played by Douglas Fairbanks and Julia Sanderson, both to become stars) was almost irrelevant—what Sam was selling was three and one-half hours of scenery and costumes, including exquisite black-and-gold dresses, a monumental gateway, and a huge ship, fancifully shaped and decorated. Produced at a cost of sixty thousand dollars, *Fantana* solidified Sam's growing reputation as a Broadway big spender.

A month after that show premiered, Sam went to London to secure the all-important first booking for his new Waldorf Theatre, which was to open in London in four months. As early as 1903, Sam had begun to plan for a London theatre of his own; in May 1904 he took a two-year lease on the Waldorf, then being built on the Strand. Although Syndicate partner Charles Frohman had established a strong presence in London, the other members of the Syndicate had not, and Sam felt that a theatre there would give him an edge over his rivals in the international market. And with a London base and a British staff working for him, he would be able to bid for the rights to the latest hits.

But from the beginning, his London venture was ill-starred. "The opening of the Waldorf means everything to us," Sam wrote to Lee from London on February 25, his frustration mounting as he failed to find a suitable attraction. "Naturally [Charles Frohman] will not deal with us as he disliked the idea of our coming to London," he fumed, after Frohman refused to discuss possibilities.[25] Desperate, Sam asked Lee to try to arrange with David Belasco to present David Warfield in *The Music Master*. When that failed to work out, he even considered putting on Julian Mitchell's production of *Babes in Toyland*, although he felt it was not elevated enough for the kind of London opening he envisioned.

Finally, though he felt gouged by the terms—75 percent was to go to the attraction, only 25 percent to the theatre—Sam signed a contract with British manager Henry Russell for what may well have been the most illustrious of all Shubert openings: a season of split weeks of grand opera featuring Emma Calvé, alternating with Eleanora Duse and her company in repertory. A man after Sam's own heart, Russell had challenged Covent Garden's monopoly in opera by securing the exclusive rights to a few operas and opera divas. Sam was concerned, however, that the powerful Covent Garden management would undermine Russell, and they may well have done so since neither grand opera nor Duse turned a profit for the Shuberts.

Back in New York in March, Sam put together his greatest achievement in star packaging, and his last. For what was announced as "a farewell American tour" (though in fact there would be three others), Sam enlisted Sarah Bernhardt, as he had Richard Mansfield, to help him in his fight against the Syndicate. Casting himself as a feisty independent, he appealed to Bernhardt's antiroyalist sympathies. But there were other reasons the great star found the young impresario compelling. Like her, he was Jewish and had come from obscurity (Bernhardt's mother had been a prostitute) to achieve a high place in the theatre. How could she resist Sam's doelike eyes and his quick, soft voice, especially after he made her the best financial offer she had ever received, the astounding sum, as Lee would later report, of eighteen hundred dollars a day for a season of two hundred performances? "We figured our contract with Madame Bernhardt would net us but little profit," Lee remarked dryly.[26] Bernhardt was Lee's equal in money matters: she insisted on being paid before her performances, in gold whenever possible, and as Lee was later to enjoy repeating over the years, she pretended to be absolutely incapable of English except when it came to discussing her salary. The contract was signed on April 18, 1905.

After Sam engaged Bernhardt for the 1905–1906 season, he mapped out a route in a string of first-class theatres, fully expecting that the Syndicate would block him by pressuring theatres around the country not to book the show. When that is exactly what they did, Sam asked his star if she would consider appearing in skating rinks, circus tents, open-air theatres, and town halls. As Sam must have known it would, such a tour stirred Bernhardt's sense of adventure.

Though he had been acquiring theatres swiftly, in the spring of 1905 Sam had not yet succeeded in matching the Syndicate house for house in the important cities. Nonetheless, he was beginning to make a decisive assault on their stranglehold. In addition to his original cluster of theatres in upstate New York and the nucleus of six houses he had taken over in New York City, he had picked up theatres in cities located along a major railroad route: the Columbia in Boston, the Teck in Buffalo, the Colonial in Cleveland, and the Garrick Theatres in Chicago and St. Louis. Acquiring the lease on the Duquesne Theatre in Pittsburgh in May 1905 was particularly significant to Sam. A theatre in a new, well-placed city, in open competition with the Syndicate-controlled Alvin, notably enriched his circuit. Klaw and Erlanger tried to block Sam's lease, threatening to blacklist the theatre's owners if they signed with Sam. Sam responded by doing what the Shuberts would always do in a tight spot—he instigated a lawsuit, claiming restraint of fair trade.

Ordinarily, Sam might have permitted lawyer William Klein to go alone to Pittsburgh to represent his interests in the Duquesne, but he felt the theatre was so crucial to his expansion that he wanted to be on the spot himself. With Klein and Abe Thalheimer, one of his Syracuse partners, Sam took a night train from New York to Pittsburgh to be at court early the next morning. Although Sam wanted a drawing room, he settled for an upper berth in a sleeping car when no other accommodation was available. Shortly before two o'clock in the morning on May 11, 1905, his train collided with the ammunition car of an army transport train heading east. Whether the combined speed of the two trains caused them to sway dangerously close to one another or whether the track gave way slightly was never determined; but as the two trains thundered past each other, a baggage car carrying high explosives smashed against the passenger car in which Sam and his colleagues slept. The explosion ripped open the side of the Pullman and ruptured the steam line running the length of the carriage, scalding Sam's hands and his body from his waist down to his feet.

In later years, William Klein claimed to have pulled Sam from the burning train and then arranged for him to be taken to the Commonwealth Hotel in Harrisburg, and it's a part of Shubert lore that Klein's heroism earned him his lifelong post as Shubert counsel. Klein himself was badly scarred by the flames, however, and it was actually Abe Thalheimer and a local mill boy named Charles Germer who helped Sam. The seventeen-year-old Germer brought Sam a chair and, as was the common practice, covered his body with grease to ease his pain. After Sam had been taken to the hotel, he asked for the boy to be brought to him, and according to an account in the *Syracuse Journal* of May 13, 1905, Sam "placed Germer's hand in his and would not permit the youngster to leave his side. He demanded the young man be kept near him; and when he sank into his last sleep, his hand rested on that of the stranger who had hastened to assist him." John Shubert maintained that for the rest of his life Germer received a monthly check from the Shuberts.[27] The *Syracuse Journal*, however, reported on May 20 that "the family have sent for the boy, and will give him a position in one of the Shubert enterprises—he will have every opportunity to make his way in the world." There is no further record of Charles Germer.

Amazingly, despite his fatal burns, Sam was able to call newspapers from his hotel at 5:00 A.M., three hours after the accident, to report, "Abe Thalheimer saved my life; he carried me across burning cars into the woods, while explosion after explosion occurred. I am pretty badly hurt myself. My legs are burned and I have suffered great pain."[28] His mother, two of three sisters, business associates, family physician, and J. J. (who traveled from Chicago, where Sam had put him in charge of Shubert interests) went immediately to Harrisburg. Lee was in London for the opening of the Waldorf Theatre; J. J. reassured him by telegram that Sam was in no danger. But by the late afternoon of May 12, it was clear that Sam's frail body could not withstand the trauma it had received, and J. J. cabled Lee that Sam's condition had become critical. That night, Sam died.

"Not since the death of Augustin Daly have theatre circles appeared so agitated," the *New York Times* reported. "Men whose business interests were directly opposed to those of Sam Shubert moved silently about, showing on their faces the sorrow they felt. Many there were who did not always think as Sam Shubert thought . . . but not one word has been raised in protest against the general praise of his earnestness, his energy, and his shrewdness."[29] In his brief career, Sam had established himself at the head of the class of the new breed of financial buccaneer rapidly overtaking the theatre. The public expression of respect for his achievement and of sorrow for his untimely death was enormous; the family received more than five thousand telegrams, which Lee, J. J., and Syracuse business associate Joseph W. Jacobs acknowledged in an open letter published in newspapers on May 16. Both the Shubert apartment at 222 West Seventy-ninth Street and

Temple Emanu-El, where services were held, were flooded with hundreds of floral wreaths. Even Abe Erlanger sent one, and even Erlanger, at least publicly, realized it was prudent to speak well of Sam. John Shubert claimed that Erlanger later told Lee he would have attended the funeral, "only he felt so bad that he stayed at home."[30]

When Lee received word of Sam's death, he collapsed and had to be placed under a doctor's care. Profoundly shaken and disoriented, he worried over whether to remain in London for the scheduled May 22 opening of the Waldorf or to return to New York for the funeral, but his doctor ordered him to stay where he was. With Lee in London, David ostracized (still in Syracuse), and Catherine Shubert and her daughters helpless with grief, J. J., the last and so far the least of the Shubert brothers, became acting head of the family. "Our family was broken in spirit, our dynamic personality was gone," J. J. recalls in his memoirs. "Our lawyer was in the hospital [where he remained for six months], our booking manager [Thalheimer] thought we were through and took an engagement with Erlanger's office. But life must go on, and in four weeks we had to begin mending the wreckage. It took us a month to realize what had happened."[31]

During that month—before they, as J. J. put it, "got their second wind"—there was wide speculation that without Sam, the moving spirit behind the Shubert enterprise, the Shuberts were surely defeated. Observers were skeptical that Lee and the still relatively unknown J. J. would be capable of realizing Sam's dynastic dreams. As the *Syracuse Journal* reported the day after Sam's funeral, "The consensus along Broadway was that Lee and J. J. would be content to conduct the dozen or so theatres under their control now" and thereby withdraw from competition with Klaw and Erlanger.[32]

In his will, written two years earlier, Sam named Lee as his successor and sole executor and directed that, after the payment of his debts and funeral expenses, all his property should go to Lee. "I make this provision well knowing and directing that he will act fairly and honorably toward our sisters and mother [no mention of David or J. J.] and that he shall never leave them in want but will maintain them in their proper station and sphere in life."[33] Sam left an estate of nearly one-half million dollars, including one hundred thirty-two thousand dollars in insurance policies. It is another Shubert myth that Sam's insurance saved the empire, but though his liquid assets were limited, Sam was hardly destitute. Theatre leases had both Sam's and Lee's names on them; their Syracuse backers were not suddenly penniless; and J. J. had about seventy thousand dollars in an upstate savings account. While Sam's insurance policies certainly helped, they were not the determining factor in the Shuberts' survival.

The test the Shuberts faced—and as Sam's will indicates, the "Shuberts" now really meant Lee—was psychological rather than economic. Lee, who up to now had played only a supporting role, was suddenly confronted with the steepest challenge of his life: could he continue Sam's grand plans, protecting what Sam had built up so far while also extending the Shubert reach? Lee did not, and would never, have Sam's charm, which had been so crucial to their success. But could he, in his own way, convince theatre owners, producers, actors, and the Syndicate that the Shuberts without Sam were still a formidable operation? To survive, Lee all at once would have to become impresario and financier, a man for all theatrical occasions. The question Lee Shubert had to consider in the agonizing month after Sam's death was not did they have the funds to continue but were he and J. J. shrewd enough and tough enough to complete the battle against the Syndicate that Sam had begun?

Sam had not adequately prepared his brothers for command—inability or unwillingness to plan for an orderly succession was to be a family fault, one that was to have nearly fatal consequences. Yet Sam couldn't have progressed as rapidly as he did without his brothers' help. Lee and J. J. were trusted lieutenants if not quite equals. As the business grew, however, Sam depended more and more on Lee: Lee is there on the crucial visit to Richard Mansfield and in London for the opening of the Waldorf. Yet Sam allowed Lee little real authority of his own. A characteristic note of brotherly disapproval saturates Sam's July 13, 1904, letter to Lee in London about the Waldorf. "Be careful and see everything is correct in the lease. You know you are not too well versed in legal instruments. Therefore, if possible arrange it so that the lease can come over here to be looked over, make it binding however before you do so, as we would like to have Klein go over it. I think it is an excellent proposition and like the idea very much, so do not let it fall through."[34]

If Lee was in second place, J. J., the brother who had more than once beaten up saintly Sammy when they were kids, was a very distant third. Sam called Lee down to New York but kept J. J. in the hinterlands. J. J. was always in charge of provincial operations, first in Rochester, then in the upstate New York circuit, and later in Chicago, where he supervised the outfit's expanding midwestern interests. Perhaps Sam was ashamed of his pugnacious, red-faced younger brother, as he had been ashamed of his uncultivated, un-American parents and sisters;[35] but J. J. was nonetheless an active and necessary component of Sam's empire building.

One of Lee's shrewdest maneuvers immediately following Sam's death was the way he exploited Sam's memory. Suppressing whatever private anger he felt at his younger brother's high-handed, autocratic treatment of him, he began at once to make Sam an idol he worshiped for the next fifty years. Sam was raised to a mythic place as the all-knowing older brother, the family's untainted mentor.

Sam had led the way, and now, in May 1905 and forever after, it would be Lee's job, and J. J.'s job too, to pursue Sam's goals according to the high moral example Sam had set.

Lee constructed an image of Sam that gave the Shubert dynasty the aura of immaculate conception, and over the years Lee repeatedly invoked the purified image of his dead brother as a shield against his own and the Shubert empire's misdeeds: if this great business was established by a man like Sam and has continued to be conducted in his spirit, can you really believe the things our enemies are saying against us? "The Shuberts were very well thought of in the beginning, because everybody liked Sam," Larry Lawrence, the last Shubert to head the Organization said in June 1990, repeating the shibboleth that had been handed down across the generations within a family that had precious little family feeling.[36]

3

Lee and J. J., Front and Center

*S*ometime in the second week of June 1905, so the story goes, about a month after Sam's death, his brothers crossed the street from the Shubert offices in the Lyric Theatre to pay a visit to Abraham Lincoln Erlanger at his headquarters atop the New Amsterdam Theatre. They carried a contract Sam had signed with Erlanger in which, in return for payments made to Erlanger, the Shuberts were promised first-class theatres for their touring attractions. Lee and J. J. had come to inquire if, in view of Sam's death, the contract was still valid. Glancing over the paper that Lee handed to him, and then taking a hard look at the two young men fidgeting in their chairs on the other side of his oversized desk, Erlanger paused dramatically before announcing, in his characteristic growl, that he never honored contracts with dead men.

Did this brief meeting really take place? J. J. told John that it did and boasted that Erlanger's dismissal only strengthened their resolve to continue Sam's fight.[1] The three participants all behaved entirely in character, and such a meeting could have happened and in the way J. J. described—but not in June 1905 because at the time of his death Sam had already launched an all-out war against the Syndicate. The challenge he left his brothers was to pursue the battle rather than to seek a truce. Earlier, upstate and in his first few years in New York, Sam had negotiated with Erlanger; like everyone else at the time, Sam had had no choice but to do business with the Syndicate and on the Syndicate's terms. Unlike most other managers, however, who lacked his fearlessness and ambition, Sam had devised ways of outwitting Erlanger and was adept at recovering from Erlanger's broken promises.

For two years, in the face of Erlanger's growing belligerence, Sam had not only held his own but had prospered. At the time of his death, he was well on his way to realizing his goal of building a circuit to match the Syndicate's, a circuit in which he would present his own productions and provide a haven for an increasing number of producers seeking refuge from Erlanger's monopolistic practices. But now Sam was dead; his brothers were in charge; and Erlanger, like most of the theatre community, was unimpressed. The most powerful man in the American theatre did not feel threatened by the yahoos from across the street. Despite the remarkable resilience his young adversaries had already shown, Erlanger had not yet learned how dangerous it was to underestimate a Shubert.

"The Syndicate thought with Sam dead, that was it," John Shubert reflected.

After all they didn't know Lee too well, and I doubt if they had even heard of my father. [Up until Sam's death, J. J. had had no involvement in Shubert operations on Broadway.] They knew Sam was the spark plug, and so while Sam's death was a tragedy, which set the Shuberts back three or four years, it could have been a blessing in disguise. It might have been the reason that made Abe Erlanger and Klaw forget about the Shuberts and let them get moving.[2]

Whether or not Lee and J. J. actually sat in Erlanger's office one month after Sam's death, Erlanger and the Syndicate he represented were the greatest obstacles the remaining Shubert brothers had to confront. To claim the inheritance Sam had left, they would have to pursue the war against Erlanger that Sam had begun in a small way at the Bastable Theatre in Syracuse in 1897 and that had erupted into a full-scale contest in 1903. They would have to fight Goliath with vigor and cunning, and they would have to win or face the extinction of their brother's dream of building an empire of their own.

It became part of theatrical widsom, both at the time and later, that if only Erlanger and his colleagues had been men of better quality, capable of fair play and of honoring a policy of live and let live, the Syndicate might have endured. The old, pre-Syndicate way of booking and routing clearly needed to be regularized, and centralization in the age of trusts was the inevitable corrective measure. As J. J. (or more likely a scribe in the Shubert press office) wrote in the August 14, 1909, issue of the *Saturday Evening Post*, expressing the opinion of many businessmen in the theatre, "A centralized booking office is a worthy and laudable enterprise." What the Shuberts and many others objected to was not the idea of the Syndicate but the character of the men who ran it, not the power that a centralized agency unavoidably bestowed but the systematic abuse of that power by the avaricious Syndicate leaders. J. J.'s argument, echoed by many, was that, on the one hand, the Syndicate had organized the theatre on a sounder business basis than it had ever been before and, on the other, through the moral blemishes of its ringleaders, inflicted potentially lethal wounds.

Yet it was precisely the Syndicate's blatant misuse of its power that helped Sam and then his brothers move forward. From the moment the Syndicate was founded at the start of the 1896 theatre season, it began to extract money from producers and theatre owners on a slippery, sliding scale that mocked the ideal of regularization under which it had assumed power. Almost immediately Erlanger's rapacity—"he was a great mathematician who could divide a whole into as many quarters, eighths, and halves as he wanted," as J. J. notes[3]—incited rebellion. His methods created a demand for a seemingly fearless dragon slayer, a role Sam was both physically and temperamentally equipped to fulfill. Because Erlanger and his cohorts were so easy to demonize, Sam and then his brothers could masquerade in the early years as brave young leaders fighting for an open, democratic theatre.

From the start, the Syndicate received a chorus of boos. "The incompetent men who have seized upon the affairs of the stage in this country have all but killed art, worthy ambition, and decency," the celebrated actress Minnie Maddern Fiske said.[4] The influential critic Walter Pritchard Eaton accuses the Syndicate of reducing "theatre managers everywhere to the status of janitors."[5] Bringing to the surface the anti-Semitism that simmered beneath many attacks on the trust, critic William Winter writes that "The Syndicate, with its serpentine, blood-sucking tentacles, is an incubus" comprised of "six Hebrew theatrical speculators."[6]

Early protests against the Syndicate lacked the focus, stamina, and capital that Sam and his brothers were to bring into battle. Harrison Grey Fiske, the patrician publisher of the *New York Dramatic Mirror*, the leading theatrical paper, was the first in the field. He led the print war against the Syndicate but was stymied by the Syndicate's threat of blacklisting. In March 1897, Fiske sent out sixty-five letters to managers asking for their views about the Syndicate and received only six replies. Fiske's own determination to expose the trust was strengthened when, one day in the autumn of 1897, Al Hayman stormed into Fiske's office demanding no further mention of the trust in the *Dramatic Mirror*. "What the Syndicate does is my private business and no concern of the theatrical profession or the public," Hayman fumed. When Fiske assured Hayman that the paper would continue to report on the actions of the Syndicate, Hayman screamed, "You go and do that and I'll kill the *Mirror*, break you, and drive Mrs. Fiske from the stage."[7]

In January 1898, Joseph Pulitzer's *New York World* joined Fiske in attempting to reveal Syndicate abuses. "Have you not systematically and persistently practiced fraud and deceit on the public?" a *World* editorial inquired of the trust. "Have you not repeatedly sent out inferior companies, falsely representing them as the original casts of New York successes? Have you not repeatedly advertised actors as playing in these companies who in fact at that time were playing in other and distant cities?"[8]

In December 1898, led by Richard Mansfield, a group of prominent actors organized the Association for the Promotion and Protection of an Independent Stage in the United States. In addition to Mansfield, stars like James O'Neill, Francis Wilson, Nat Goodwin, and Mrs. Fiske, as mentioned earlier, made curtain speeches warning audiences of the newly formed trust and promised to play only in independent theatres. But as Francis Wilson pointed out, the warriors in this conflict were unevenly matched: while the Syndicate brought to the battle expertise in business and a united will to drive independent actor-managers out of the field, the actors who opposed them were "nervous, sensitive, temperamental people to whom, as a rule, matters of business were distasteful, and especially to whom the thought of organizing to protect an art, their art, as mechanics organize to make employers unhappy, was repellently objectionable."[9] When Mansfield withdrew, protesting that it would be a mistake for artists to band together and thereby to descend to the Syndicate's level, the actors' opposition movement was effectively terminated. In record time, actors who had proclaimed the urgency of remaining independent flipped over to the enemy, either out of fear or because they were seduced by sweet Syndicate contracts. Soon only two major performers, Wilson and Mrs. Fiske, remained outside the Syndicate's domination. Maintaining that his choice was either to starve or to leave the country, Wilson too capitulated; and with great bitterness, he cut a deal with Sam Nixon, "a vain little person . . . who could squeeze more juice out of a business orange than any man I have ever met." Wilson regretted that he was "obliged to appeal to any one at all for the privilege of pursuing my profession," but he was especially galled because he was forced to surrender to "these people, scarcely once removed from aliens," when he had "several generations of American ancestors" behind him.[10]

While publishers, local managers, and actors had preceded Sam into the fight, it was Sam and then his brothers who were the only ones to prevail. Sam cunningly began the war by reversing the Syndicate's methods. The Syndicate flourished on an economy of shortage; it did not build new theatres, believing that fewer theatres insured fuller booking and larger audiences. Sam, on the other hand, leased and built theatres by the dozens. Where the Syndicate, for the most part, financed themselves, Sam, from the beginning, depended on outside capital. Against great odds, Sam had remained in the field; and where other anti-Syndicate factions had splintered, he had continued to expand his field of operations in the face of Erlanger's increasing efforts to block him. Now his brothers had to take up the battle for the others in the theatre who were not able to fight for themselves.

In the crucial 1905–1906 season, when Lee and J. J. were on their own for the first time, they followed the pattern that Sam had already established. Financed largely by a group of outside investors, headed by Cincinnati Republican city boss and magnate George B. Cox and Congressman Joseph L. Rhinock of Kentucky, they inaugurated an aggressive building campaign. That first year, they added eighteen new theatres to the Shubert chain. Later they received the support of wealthy New Yorkers like Sam Untermyer and Andrew Freedman. "We had a few good friends," J. J. remarks in his memoirs. One of these good friends, E. C. Potter, "who built the Lyric Theatre for us with Reginald De Koven, helped us when we wanted to incorporate our business. Potter was instrumental in getting people interested." When Sam S. and Lee Shubert, Inc., was set up in August 1905 just as Lee and J. J. were ready to launch their first season without their leader, "we had four million dollars fully paid in," J. J. notes. "That meant we could go ahead."[11]

Lee and J. J. needed productions and stars to fill their expanding theatre chain, and here again Sam helped save them. In 1901 David Belasco had signed with Klaw and Erlanger for a road tour of *The Auctioneer*, a play Belasco had cowritten as a star vehicle for David Warfield. In his eagerness to promote Warfield, who was not yet well known outside New York, Belasco had to make heavy concessions to Klaw and Erlanger for a first-class route, turning over 50 percent of the profits. Further, Belasco agreed to sign the contract with a man named Joseph Brooks. In 1903 Brooks found out that Belasco was secretly sharing in the royalties as cowriter and filed suit against him. Belasco in turn exposed Brooks as a dummy partner whom Klaw and Erlanger were using to hide the agreement from the other Syndicate partners. Belasco filed a countersuit against Klaw and Erlanger, demanding an accounting of their profits on *The Auctioneer*. Belasco was the first major figure to challenge the Syndicate in court, and with his priestly collar, his pious demeanor, his air of having been woefully wronged, and the cheering support of the press, he was superbly cast as a moral crusader, St. George intent on slaying the theatrical dragon. While the perpetually dyspeptic Erlanger frowned and hung his head and glared at the spectators, Belasco, the pluperfect ham, expertly worked the crowd.

After the trial (which ended only a few days before Sam's death), Belasco was exultant. "Haven't we given that gang of grafters a shake-up?" he enthused in a letter to a friend. "It cost me a lot of money—but thank Heaven! I had it to spend, and could unmask them. If I have done a wee bit of good in helping to clear away the rubbish, I am more than rewarded."[12] Although Belasco had exposed Klaw and Erlanger's ruse and had thereby driven another wedge into the gang of six, the judge concluded that the contract Belasco had signed with Brooks was binding.

Before the trial, Sam had had the foresight to sign Belasco for the coming season—the Belasco contract was to be Sam's last great gift to his brothers. Belasco's presence on their slate brought Lee and J. J. a prestige they desperately needed and also helped them attract other important figures who had been burned by Erlanger. The Syndicate chief was so threatened by Belasco's name appearing at the top of the Shubert roster that he made Lee an offer Lee was only too pleased to reject. "Mr. Erlanger said if I'd break my contract with Belasco he would give me anything I wanted," Lee reported to the *New York Dramatic Mirror* on July 22, 1905, "and if I did not, no Shubert attraction would play a Syndicate house. I refused to be dictated to and there the matter stands."

Equally persuasive in gaining prestige and sympathy for the remaining Shuberts was the 1905–1906 Sarah Bernhardt tour Sam had arranged in April. The spectacle of a legendary performer forced by the greed of the Syndicate into appearing under canvas and in skating rinks generated marvelous promotional opportunities and unheard-of profits, and the tour became a public relations bonanza for both the young producers and their star. (As Lee noted in a March 11, 1922, interview in *Billboard*, "The difference between regulation theatres and our circus tents gave us handsome financial returns.") No theatrical event since P. T. Barnum's cross-country tour of Jenny Lind in 1850 had inspired the same kind of commotion. "The most remarkable tour ever played in this country," trumpeted the *Theatre* in May 1906 about the Shuberts' presentation of Bernhardt. "The receipts have been colossal, the size of the auditoriums unprecedented," the report continued. "Up to April 7, the sixty-two-year-old star has traveled 14,441 miles, playing daily, sometimes twice a day. Her receipts have averaged $4000 nightly; in Kansas City [in a special roundtop the Shuberts ordered built for the occasion, with a spread of 150 feet and a 4,500-person seating capacity] the Shuberts collected the largest single night's receipts in history—$9,984."

Channing Pollock, head of the Shuberts' press department, flooded newspapers and magazines with items about the tour. He reported the record-breaking grosses ($36,000 for a week in Chicago, $70,000 for two weeks in New York) when Bernhardt ended the tour at the Shuberts' flagship, the Lyric. He spiced gossip columns with trivia: Bernhardt has preserved her youth even better than Lillian Russell; the most important functionary in the star's entourage is the man who takes care of her dogs; with a dozen policies on her life, Bernhardt carries more insurance than any other performer. In his memoirs, Pollock proudly claims to have invented a story that has become theatrical legend: "There are still thousands of people who believe the Divine Sarah toured Texas under canvas. As a matter of fact, she gave only one performance in a tent." But once was enough—Pollock exploited a photograph of Bernhardt standing outside a tent in Dallas, where she played Camille to an audience of eight thousand, to create the impression that she was forced into tents repeatedly. "The story that this wicked monopoly prevented our finding a playhouse roof to cover a great actress, and drove art to the shelter of clowns and elephants, not only won headlines for her but sympathetic partisanship that was more valuable," he observes.[13] That Lee and J. J. were able to follow through on the grand tour for Bernhardt that Sam had set in motion was a clear sign that they were equal to their brother's legacy.

Headed by Bernhardt and Belasco, and capitalizing on other contracts Sam had made, the impressive 1905–1906 Shubert lineup included Shakespearean actors Edward H. Sothern and Julia Marlowe; Minnie Maddern Fiske; Caroline Carter, or Mrs. Leslie Carter, as she was known; DeWolf Hopper; and Eddie Foy; as well as Mrs. Patrick Campbell and Arnold Daly in repertory. At the beginning of the season, the Shuberts had thirty theatres, and by the end the list had grown to a circuit of more than fifty. And as they held onto their winning streak, they continued to swell their talent roster with other defections from the Syndicate. In their first season without Sam, the remaining boys from Syracuse triumphed.

Lee and J. J. were heroic neither by temperament nor by demeanor, but in their conduct of the theatrical wars in the first year after Sam's death, they achieved a heroic stature. Notably lacking their brother's appeal and his mask of gentility, Lee and J. J. had difficult personalities. "They believed that being tough and making people fear them was a success formula," John Shubert said. "And they trusted no one—you always have to remember that about the Shuberts: they trusted no one."[14] Their leader gone, they entered the field swinging; and off and on over the next one and one-half decades, they proved superb warriors. In the degree and breadth of their victory over the Syndicate, they may even have exceeded Sam's epic vision.

Over the summer of 1905, as he recovered from the shock of Sam's death, Lee began to assume the role of Shubert CEO he was to occupy for the rest of his life. Dour and tight, with sharp eyes that scrutinized friend and foe alike, Lee was the front-runner who kept his younger, hotheaded brother in the background as much as possible. The rivalry that was to boil up over and over again in the coming decades was already simmering.

For now, however, as they continued to fight the war Sam had started, they presented a united front as they enjoyed a public relations victory of a kind they were never again to achieve. Shrewdly, following Sam's model, they presented themselves as "the champions of liberty and freedom against tyranny and oppression," as Alfred Bernheim writes. "They were battling for the weak against the strong, and for art against commercialism. The war that ensued was one in which the arms and munitions consisted not only of theatres, productions and money, but of propaganda as well. And the Shuberts put over this propaganda to perfection. It was swallowed hook, line, and sinker."[15] They prosecuted the war on an astutely named Open-Door policy, linking themselves to the battle cry of American expansionism in the Far East. "Down with monopoly" was their slogan as they led the fight for what they called an independent theatre. They were the advocates of fair play and competition, promising a theatre in which profits could be enjoyed by many rather than horded by a self-chosen few. They wanted to be—and were perceived as—the voice of the people, intent on disturbing if not actually unseating royalty.

In strengthening their iconography as Davids come to slay Goliath, they were once again helped by Sam, who in April 1905 had established a paper called *The Show*. Edited by Channing Pollock, the paper provided a rooting section for the Shuberts and their independence movement. "Any greed in the conduct of theatre must directly concern the person who patronizes theatre," began a typical editorial on October 10, 1905. "It is always the lay public that suffers from monopoly and that therefore should be strongly partisan in any effort to do away with it. The playgoer who cannot witness a performance of *The Music Master* or *Leah Kleschna* because a certain body of men dislike Belasco or Fiske ought not to be 'uninterested.' " Surveying the openings of the independents in the 1905–1906 season in its May 1906 issue, the *Show* enthused that "no one familiar with things theatrical can help admitting that this is the crème-de-la-crème of players, plays and playhouses in America. If the Independent movement has accomplished so much in a little less than a year, what will it have done five years from now?"

In October 1906, the Shuberts sold the *Show* to a corporation and no longer had any direct interest in it, but their first venture in print had been a definite success. Circulation had risen steadily, up to an impressive seventy-five thousand by August 1906, and the experience proved the effectiveness of the written word in molding public perception: the *Show* demonstrated to Lee and J. J. that propaganda could be a useful weapon, a point they were to remember a few years later.

Helped by the *Show*, the Shuberts' stance as mere foot soldiers in the battle for an independent theatre was widely accepted because other anti-Syndicate forces needed to see them that way. And while it was, in part, calculated public relations to present themselves as being on the side of the angels, at least at the beginning they were. It is naive to think that the Shuberts' primary concern was protecting other people's rights or other people's chances to make money, but their early sloganeering may well have contained some sincerity. At any rate, the Shuberts were never again to appear to be as likable and as valiant as when they first took up the battle Sam had left unfinished.

As proof of their new stature, at the start of the 1906 season, Lee and J. J., along with a partner, Max Anderson, took control of the largest theatre in the world. Located east of Broadway on Sixth Avenue and spanning the entire block between Forty-third and Forty-forth Streets, the Hippodrome had a massive facade that resembled a fortress out of the *Arabian Nights*. Inside and out, the theatre's architecture was a riot of Moorish, Spanish Renaissance, and classical motifs.

Outside, fluted columns framed either side of a huge Roman arch on top of which was an elephant head; inside, elephant heads appeared throughout.

Neither the theatre nor its shows were a Shubert invention. The Hippodrome, which opened on April 12, 1905, was built by Frederic Thompson, an architect, Thompson's partner, Elmer S. Dundy, and John W. "Bet-a-million" Gates, a promoter and financier who backed them. In 1902 the three had opened Luna Park, an amusement center at Coney Island, and originally they had conceived of the Hippodrome as a way of bringing the spirit of Luna Park to Broadway. Thompson, the visionary of the group, planned to produce one-of-a-kind theatrical spectacles on the theatre's vast stage, which at 110 feet deep and 200 feet wide covered a greater area than a dozen regular-sized theatre stages, while two circus rings could be placed on the apron. On this monumental playground, Thompson intended to build wondrous new worlds, complete with lakes, waterfalls, moonscapes, Arabian bazaars, and Oriental palaces.[16] The Hippodrome's "entertainment for the masses" were overstuffed carnivals mixing the circus, vaudeville, musical comedy, extravaganza, pantomime, and ballet.

Although the first two shows were successful, Bet-a-million Gates thought Thompson and Dundy were a couple of spendthrifts who weren't producing high enough profits. It had cost Gates $1.5 million to build the Hippodrome, and the theatre required a gross of six thousand dollars a day merely to break even; to run at a profit, it would have to be managed more tightfistedly. In June 1906, Gates fired the theatre's founders and turned the operation over to the leaders of the expanding Open-Door movement, Lee and J. J. Shubert. Coming a little over a year after Sam's death, Gates's offer was a major tribute. Under Shubert stewardship, the theatre began to show increasing profits and within a year was clearing almost eighteen thousand dollars weekly.

It was Lee who managed the books. He cut prices—$1.50 bought the best seat in the house—without forsaking the grandeur audiences had come to expect from Hippodrome extravaganzas. Most Shubert-backed shows at the Hippodrome played to virtual capacity twice daily (in those pre–Actors' Equity days, there were fourteen performances a week) for forty weeks a year.

When the Shuberts presented their first Hippodrome production, on November 28, 1906, a whopping three-part extravaganza, they proclaimed that their "munificent managerial policy" had resulted in "a scenic and sartorial equipment more complete and colossal than anything ever before attempted in the annals of theatre history." "Startling," "stupendous," "gorgeous," and "amazing" were some of the critical reactions to the big new show.[17] Part 1, called "Pioneer Days," was a Western featuring a Ghost Dance performed by a large band of genuine Sioux in war paint and feathers and an attack on a stagecoach, with a last-minute rescue by troops and cowboys, accompanied by thunderous war cries and gunshots. Part 2 was a two-ring circus, with tumbling clowns, gaily costumed aerialists, and what was to become a specialty of the house, a procession of elephants. Part 3, "Neptune's Daughter," a romantic extravaganza in three scenes, was the pièce de résistance that introduced the theatre's water tank, a mechanical marvel the Shuberts were to claim as their exclusive property.

With cracks of lightning and buckets of rain, the storm at the end of scene 1 of "Neptune's Daughter" shook the building and threatened to engulf the audience. In scene 2, the fishing port of the first scene was now viewed from the ocean. Scene 3, set at the bottom of the sea in the palace of King Neptune, featured the water tank that was to become the trademark of the Shubert reign. As it rose up from below the apron to represent the ocean, King Neptune and a bevy of mermaids swam into view. The spectacle concluded with a ballet in which hundreds of chorines representing a variety of fish were costumed in every color of the rainbow. For ten minutes, this gigantic corps de ballet danced behind a gauze curtain; when the gauze curtain was lowered, and the richness of the scenery and the costumes was fully revealed, the first-night audience erupted into waves of applause that competed in volume with the storm that had split the heavens in scene 1.

Because the Hippodrome had its own in-house staff of directors and designers, Lee and J. J. functioned as overseers rather than as creative participants. For Lee, who had little interest in Hippodrome spectacle anyway, the setup was entirely satisfactory, but J. J. had plans to produce Hippodrome-like entertainments of his own, and his frustration mounted as Lee forcibly prevented him from taking a more active part in assembling the shows. Backstage, J. J. became extremely unpopular. One January night during the second Shubert season at the Hippodrome, J. J. went to the theatre to ask for four five-dollar prop bugles for use in a show he was producing at the Casino. The next day, when the instruments did not arrive, J. J. in a rage demanded an explanation from the stage manager, Arthur Voegtlin. "I don't take orders from you," Voegtlin said, adding, "We don't recognize you in the Hippodrome." "You'll recognize me after I'm through with you," J. J. bellowed. "Oh, go to hell," Voegtlin shouted. This time J. J. didn't use his fists—he went to see Lee instead. And together the brothers went over to see Voegtlin, who informed them that he, not they, was the Hippodrome's "moving spirit." On the spot, Voegtlin and stage director William J. Wilson, who sided with Voegtlin, and a musical director were fired. Wilson and Voegtlin brought a breach-of-contract suit against the Shuberts. In court Voegtlin said he would refuse J. J.'s request for the property bugles if the request were made again and that he would use force if necessary. The judge said that J. J.'s request was proper and that the plaintiffs were guilty of insubordination; he dismissed the suit.[18] (On October 14, 1909, after three years of J. J.'s tantrums, Max Anderson resigned his comanagership of the Hippodrome. He told the *Morning Telegraph* that he was leaving because he could no longer stand J. J.)

Despite backstage contretemps, the up-and-coming Shuberts and the world's largest theatre proved to be made for each other. Shubert-produced spectacles at the Hippodrome were exactly what they should have been, giddily overscaled festivals of sound and light and papier mâché. Sometimes their shows had an uplifting theme, as if the Hippodrome were a secular temple; but most of the time the opulent illusions created on the huge stage were a technological display, put on to prove that it could be done. Deliriously excessive, this was people's theatre for people dazzled by special effects. The Shuberts had the skill to turn the Hippodrome into a profit-making institution and the sense to bail out when the era of the superspectacle was over. On May 21, 1915, Lee offered a prize of one thousand dollars for the best practical suggestion for "a novel and ingenious utilization" of the Hippodrome's great tank. On June 8, he announced their departure, correctly assessing that Hippodrome extravaganzas could not compete with the greater literalism of moving pictures, just then beginning to tell feature-length narratives.

"The Shuberts squeezed [the Hippodrome] dry," writes the theatre's historian, Norman Clarke. "[They] ran it into the ground, and left it a physical wreck. Some of their shows were moronic . . . some were clumsy monsters too sluggish to pick themselves up and move, and some were sadly tasteless. But most of them were wonderful."[19]

If Lee and J. J. began their second season without Sam by taking over the Hippodrome, they ended it with an even greater tribute to their stamina. In April 1907, Abraham Lincoln Erlanger asked them for help. Because the Syndicate was short of attractions to fill theatres, Erlanger decided to produce vaudeville. In venturing into vaudeville, however, he would be confronting a monopoly that was even mightier than his own, for by 1907 B. F. Keith and E. F. Albee had transformed big-time vaudeville into a virtually impregnable fortress. With his customary bluster, Erlanger dismissed the competition: "I went up against Keith before, and he is an easy mark."[20] Privately, though, he realized he could not launch his invasion with Syndicate strength alone, and so he invited Lee to join forces with him. And not for the first or last time, the Shuberts decided to sleep with the enemy. Together the erstwhile opponents formed the grandiosely titled United States Amusement Company. In the agreement Lee hammered out with Erlanger, the Syndicate was to receive 51 percent of the profits, and Erlanger was to be in charge of all booking. When Lee signed with Erlanger, the war with the Syndicate was suspended.

The titans of the legitimate theatre joined together, however, proved no match for the veterans of vaudeville, who "had given a lifetime of study to the business, and had things systematized in a manner not surpassed by a national bank," as theatrical impresario M. B. Leavitt writes.[21] Keith, who had originated the idea of a vaudeville circuit, was the good guy in the partnership, "a combination of clodhopper and con artist,"[22] and "generally beloved by people in the amusement world."[23] Albee, a robber baron of the classic mold and "infinitely more hardheaded and aggressive than Keith,"[24] was among the most despised figures in the history of American theatre.[25] The first palatial theatre for their upgraded vaudeville, Keith's New Boston, had opened in that city on Easter 1894, and since then they had built a chain of lavish theatres and had acquired a roster of top performers they treated like indentured servants. As protectors of their realm, they proved invincible.

Early in 1900, in reaction to Albee's tyranny, vaudeville performers formed a union called the White Rats. Albee's response, on May 29, 1900, was to found the United Booking Office, a centralized booking agency, which provided performers with consecutive routes and managers with assured programs. Like the Syndicate on which it was modeled, the UBO regularized the booking and routing of the far-flung vaudeville circuit while also guaranteeing hefty profits to the middleman and the virtual enslavement of everyone else. A performer paid 10 percent of his or her salary to the UBO. Albee's quest to consolidate power and to eliminate competition was greatly strengthened six years later when F. F. Proctor, Keith's former rival, joined forces with the Keith–Albee combine; and a year later, when other vaudeville managers Oscar Hammerstein, Percy Williams, and F. Z. Poli also entered the fold, Keith and Albee were the unassailable godfathers of American vaudeville. When Keith died in 1914, his obituary cited the UBO as "probably the greatest consolidation of money and power in the entertainment world which ranks with the most important of America's industrial combinations."[26]

It was this machine that Erlanger decided to take on, and as surely he and the Shuberts realized, the odds against competing successfully were monumental. Is it possible, however, that Erlanger and the Shuberts entered the tournament with the intention of losing it? Albee called the new competition "a flea bite" but was nonetheless threatened enough to offer the United States Amusement Company three million dollars to quit vaudeville. "I'm going to make those guys give us seven million. They don't know the show business and I will teach them a trick or two," Erlanger boasted.[27] But once again the Genghis Khan of the legitimate stage was undermined by his arrogance, and as it turned out the United States Amusement Company was bought out not for millions but for two hundred fifty thousand dollars, with the UBO assuming all unexpired talent contracts and stipulating that neither Erlanger nor any of his partners was to attempt to enter vaudeville for a period of fifteen years. Behind his partners' back, Erlanger tried to get a personal exemption from Albee's ukase but to no avail.

In April 1907, Erlanger had announced his assault on vaudeville with a great blare of trumpets; by January 1908, he and the Shuberts had retreated from the field. As the United States Amusement Company was being battered, Lee and J. J. faced another major upset in London where their Waldorf Theatre continued to lose money. Associating the Waldorf with Sam's death, as Sam had died the week the theatre opened, Lee as often as possible sent J. J. over to conduct business with the fainthearted British manager who had been hired to represent them. J. J.'s usual response was to throw up his hands. "The theatre is absolutely impossible and I am afraid that my trip here will be a failure and no one wants this theatre if we gave it away for nothing," he wrote Lee in a May 22, 1906, letter.[28]

In August 1907, Lee had begun a long and complicated legal procedure to extricate himself from the jinxed theatre "I don't want another theatre in London, you can be sure of that," Lee told the *New York Times* on August 12. Lee and J. J. would continue to travel regularly to England and the Continent to scout for shows, but they did not venture again into British theatrical real estate until the late twenties, when they gained control of five London playhouses. Unlike the genteel Charles Frohman, however, the Shuberts were never to become major West End producers—the gruff Shubert tone did not play well in London; and to the Shuberts, British reserve was both inscrutable and unnerving. "There is more work than you can imagine in getting this theatre opened," Lee had complained to Sam from London in a May 1905 letter, "besides being in a strange country and not knowing their ways."[29]

When the United States Amusement Company was dissolved, the temporary entente between the Shuberts and the Syndicate came to an end as well. An uncertain truce remained in force through 1908, but by early 1909 a second theatrical war erupted. In this series of skirmishes, which were to last until 1913, Lee and J. J. occupied a distinctly different position from the one they had held after Sam's death. Lee was clearly the front man who handled all the major negotiations, while J. J. was in charge of the firm's out-of-town activities, but both were perceived as hardened infighters who had achieved a balance of power in the face of their adversaries. Indeed, by the end of 1910, the Shuberts were widely recognized as a second Syndicate.

As the second war began to heat up, the theatrical map changed on a daily basis as theatre owners, producers, and stars shifted allegiance from one side to the other. In April 1909, both David Belasco and Harrison Grey Fiske defected to the Syndicate. Ever the opportunist, Belasco returned to the Syndicate because Erlanger offered him better terms than Lee was prepared to. His flip-flop did more damage to him than to the Shuberts: in jumping ship, after for so long having presented himself as a Syndicate victim, Belasco opened himself to ridicule. "His crown of thorns lay crushed beneath his crumbling pedestal," according to Sam Weller, a contemporary journalist.[30] But Fiske's leap to the opposition did prove far more troublesome to the Shuberts and the Good Samaritan image they were still trying to project. Fiske's motives had always seemed relatively free of the taint of self-interest; he was the first and—apart from Sam—the most persistent Syndicate challenger. Yet now he had chosen to join up with the gang of six. According to Alfred Bernheim, and many other contemporary witnesses, Fiske's departure indicated that "the Syndicate was now the lesser of two evils. There was no more independent movement for Fiske to cling to—there were only two Syndicates."[31]

Lee Shubert slyly hailed his loss of Belasco and Fiske as a sign of how far the Open-Door policy had advanced. "Two years ago when we arranged a working agreement with the Syndicate, Klaw and Erlanger were most unwilling to book Mr. Belasco's attractions and Mr. Belasco refused to play in any houses owned or controlled by Klaw and Erlanger," he reported. "It is really gratifying to note the tendency toward a general letting down of the bars."[32] Privately, Belasco became a dirty word to the Shuberts, and John Shubert claimed that, even when they had been partners, Lee and J. J., unlike Sam, had never trusted or liked him. "He was a cheap phony that wore the minister's collar, dressed in black and was a real whoremaster. He screwed any kid who came up for an audition. He was just a dirty old man, and a dirty fraud."[33]

As the Shuberts lost important allies like Belasco and Fiske, they gained the Liebler Company, one of the largest producing organizations in the country; producer William Brady ("Brady was a drunk, and my uncle and father used him for our own purpose," John said[34]); and, crucially, a large block of about two hundred theatres in the Midwest that had seceded from the Syndicate, thereby opening up a Shubert route to the Pacific. Spurred by the Midwest acquisition, Lee sent J. J. to secure theatres in important Coast cities from Los Angeles to Seattle—and for the first time, the western circuit got a taste of the theatrical wars. The Shuberts also picked up circuits run by Julius Cahn and Mose Reis, which included about 150 theatres in New England, Pennsylvania, and Ohio.

For the first time, Lee and J. J. had a good route of one-night stands. Without these small-town theatres, Shubert routes often had inefficient and expensive leaps between big-city engagements. Previous Shubert attempts to lure small-town theatres away from the Syndicate had not been successful, largely because the Syndicate offered a roster of continuous bookings the Shuberts could not then guarantee. Since the Shuberts had begun to seduce producers and stars away from the Syndicate with more generous contracts than those of the Syndicate, the Syndicate had fewer attractions and could not always keep the one-night-stand houses fully stocked. As a result, regional managers began to feel neglected, and sometimes on their own, sometimes in a group, they began to decamp from the Syndicate to join the Open-Door network.

By the spring of 1909, the Shuberts could claim to have a truly national circuit. "We are in a position to book offerings for forty weeks from New York to San Francisco without requiring assistance from anyone in any way," a triumphant J. J. announced in the May 22, 1909, *New York Dramatic Mirror.* "Any man who wants to make a production is in a position to get what time he desires." In other words, the Shuberts were now a self-sufficient entity, in every way the equal of the Syndicate. Yet Shubert propaganda continued to insist that, as J. J. affirmed, "We have not formed a Theatrical Trust to beat the Theatrical Trust. All we have done, in our recent so-called fight against the Trust, is to tell theatre owners that if they don't want to take Klaw and Erlanger shows, to take ours."[35]

If during the second theatrical wars the Shuberts quickly established parity with the trust in booking and routing, they pulled far ahead of their opponents as producers. With the single exception of Charles Frohman, the Syndicate had a meager track record as producing managers. Sam Nixon and Fred Zimmerman produced infrequently and unadventurously, and Al Hayman presented only about half a dozen plays in all. The one major success Klaw and Erlanger could claim was *Ben Hur,* which, as J. J. maintained, they "forced upon the small theatre managers for ten years at percentages which virtually meant giving up the entire gross receipts. It is too large for the average theatres, inasmuch as it employs a chariot race that demands a treadmill. Klaw and Erlanger compelled the managers to go to this extra expense, circused the show, and in most instances lost on the transaction."[36] "Erlanger kills almost every play that he puts on himself," journalist Norman Hapgood wrote. "He bullies everybody; nobody dares answer back and yet they know that his interference means certain death."[37]

In his abbreviated career, Sam had been a shrewd commercial producer -imported farces and musicals with lush scenery and costumes were his specialties—and now Lee and J. J. were determined to carve their own identities as showmen. Like Sam they were not content merely to be landlords and money changers; they wanted to fill the theatres of their mushrooming empire with productions of their own.

Here too, as in most everything else, the two brothers split, both as to the kinds of shows they wanted to present and the styles they were to cultivate as Broadway impresarios. Most of their more than five hundred productions were billed as "the Messrs. Shubert present," but in fact Lee supervised the straight shows—the dramas and comedies—while J. J. was in charge of the firm's musical offerings. "Producing was the biggest sore spot between them. There was never a rivalry between them as regards bank accounts or real estate or legal problems, but producing a show was something else again," John said. "Father often ridiculed Lee's producing activities. 'Lee can't tell a proscenium from a men's room,' he would rail periodically. And, 'Lee should have been a ticket broker—what the hell does he know about putting on a show?'

"Lee never had a feeling for the theatre; my father did, and so did Sam," is the way John defined the difference between Lee and J. J. as producers. "If it hadn't been for Sam, I have a feeling Lee wouldn't have been in the theatre at all," John speculated. "Lee might have been a very good, oh, let's say, small-time money lender. That business he knew. He invented money in his own mind. He knew it backwards and forwards."[38] The battle between the brothers over who was the better producer was the only one J. J. was ever to win.

Right after Sam's death and for a number of years to come, Lee actively discouraged J. J. from producing. When J. J. insisted, Lee allowed him to supervise the musicals at the Casino; and when these proved unsuccessful, Lee felt vindicated in confining J. J.'s creative urges to this one theatre. Lee himself superintended all the major productions that appeared under the Shubert banner for a good five years after Sam died; and as he gained confidence as a Broadway producer, he followed closely the model Sam had set. Like Sam, he immediately began to shop abroad for plays and players. He regularly bought properties, musicals as well as straight plays, that were the current hits in London or the Continent. If the show was in English, he imported an entire production (which was possible in pre–Actors' Equity days); if it was in another language, Lee had it translated and adapted to Broadway tastes. Importing hit shows was a way not only of playing it safe but of saving money, especially on foreign-language pieces. Typically, Lee bought foreign-language plays at a bargain price and for a lump sum with no royalty participation for the original author. The initial translations often had to undergo additional tinkering before the language sounded like American English, and Lee would have the satisfaction, in those days before the Dramatists Guild or the enforcement of copyright laws, of getting two or three writers for the price of one. The adapters were hacks—Shubert hired hands who had no union to support them—and could be bought off for a modest flat fee. If a translated show became a hit, the producer was the only one to see a profit.

Lee's early foreign purchases included British and French comedies and melodramas (by long-forgotten, never-celebrated authors) with quaint titles like *Mr. Preedy and the Countess* (1910), *The Three Daughters of M. Dupont* (1910), *Bunty Pulls the Strings* (1911), and *Oh, I Say* (1913). The first "serious" American play he produced was *The City*, the last work by the enormously popular Clyde Fitch, who was departing from his usual line of well-made comedies of manners. Lee promoted the play as if it were an artistic landmark, but when *The City* opened at the Lyric Theatre at the end of 1909, sensationalism rather than literary distinction made it a smash. Telling a familiar story of country virtue corrupted by urban wickedness, *The City* treated such then-taboo topics as illegitimacy, incest, and drug addiction. On opening night, when an actor playing a dope fiend shouted, "You're a goddamn liar!" the audience erupted, and the drama critic of the *New York Sun* was one of several spectators said to have fainted. Lee Shubert had his first homemade dramatic hit.

Unlike his brothers, Lee had no illusions about being a director or about his ability to work with others in a creative capacity. He was a strictly hands-off producer, a Maecenas who delegated creative authority to the people he hired. He knew how to finance shows and how to book them, and more often than most producers, he could pick which ones would make money. He didn't know, and didn't need to know, how shows were created. As early as 1910, in an article for the *Green Book*, published under his byline (though written by a press agent), Lee spelled out his version of how a commercial producer should operate.

Neither I nor my brother has been able to attend to every detail in the rehearsing of every one of the fifty-odd productions we have made during the current season. But we have superintended all essentials. Not a single dress rehearsal takes place without my presence. Why should the theatre manager be expected to oversee every detail or to be his own stage director throughout rehearsals? Is not the owner of a metropolitan paper or magazine able to put his own individuality into his publication even though he must hire a corps of editors to handle the mass of material? I have never been distinctly and specifically a stage director and yet, if I were not able to judge and direct my stage managers and when necessary, make changes, how could I continue in the business? If all the men who produce on a truly large scale altered their tactics to those of a Belasco putting out only the work he can stage himself, what would the public do for amusement?[39]

While Lee was proud to be a commercial producer in the tradition Sam had established, he also had a taste for "the finer things," theatrically speaking. His commitment to art was to be intermittent and rarely more than half hearted, but nonetheless he tried to cultivate an image as a businessman with a tinge of highbrow taste. J. J., in marked contrast, detested classical theatre and never displayed any interest whatever in serious new plays. If a show didn't have music, he wasn't interested.

In 1908, just as his first truce with Erlanger was coming to an end and as he was trying to establish his own identity as a producer, Lee was appointed the business manager of an important venture called the New Theatre. Plans for the New Theatre had taken root in 1906 among a group of the wealthiest men in the country. It was their intention to endow a repertory theatre that would be run along the lines of the state theatres of Europe; and as a repertory house immune from the compromises of the commercial stage, the New was expected to provide the nucleus of an American national theatre. The program was to be divided among the classics, opera, and native plays of merit that would be unlikely to receive a commercial production. Included among the New's founders were John Jacob Astor, August Belmont, Henry Clay Frick, Elbert H. Gary, Otto H. Kahn, J. Pierpont Morgan, William K. Vanderbilt, Clarence Mackay, and Harry Payne Whitney—the cream, in short, of New York's Four Hundred, none of whom knew anything whatsoever about running a theatre.

To superintend the magnificent edifice their millions would build, they appointed two men of unmistakably patrician bearing: Winthrop Ames was to be the director, John Corbin the literary manager. To look after the money, they chose Lee Shubert. Both Ames and Corbin were Harvard graduates and to the manor born. Ames was a scholar, as well as a practical man of the theatre, who had headed a stock company in Boston that was generally regarded as the best in the country. Before his appointment, Corbin had been a drama critic for seven years. Ames, with his long, angular face, clearly belonged to the horsey set of the American upper crust; Corbin, wearing glasses and with rounder, softer features, would have been central casting's choice for the role of placid scholar. Lee was the bull in this china shop. How had he earned what the *Cleveland Plain Dealer* called "the highest and most coveted honorary position in the entire field of the drama?"[40]

When his appointment was announced, William Lewis, the editor of the Syndicate-backed *Morning Telegraph* demanded to know what Lee Shubert's qualifications were.

> What do intellectuals like Ames and Corbin find to talk about with Mr. Shubert? At present the two plays under his production attracting the most notice are *The Blue Mouse* and *The Mimic World*, with the Salome Dance 'starred' and advertised as 'The Salome That Out-Salomes All Other Salomes.' Certainly Mr. Morgan, Mr. Mackay and their associates do not purpose permitting their Home of Art and Culture to be made the center of Blue Mice and 'Salomes.'[41]

Lee may not have had the same tone or belonged to the same clubs as the New Theatre founders but he was in their company because by 1908 he had become an acknowledged expert in theatrical finance. His appointment was, in fact, another major indication that he had escaped from Sam's shadow to claim a place of respect for his own accomplishments. "The capital invested in the New Theatre and represented by the Founders is practically unlimited, and we can afford to give the public the best," Lee announced loftily in the *New York Dramatic Mirror* on September 12, 1908, a year before the theatre opened. "The Founders have given the three directors practically carte blanche in the working out of the plan. With every possible means at our command, our one ambition shall be to offer such artistic performances as will surprise the public and defy the competition of any ordinary commercial theatre." Nonetheless, Lee hastened to add, the New Theatre will not "injure" the commercial theatre but instead give it "a direct impetus"; its success can only mean "the immense enlargement of the theatregoing public."

When the New Theatre opened at Central Park West and Sixty-second Street on November 8, 1909, to a resplendent society audience, the onstage performance of *Antony and Cleopatra* seemed almost beside the point. Designed by John Merven Carrère and Thomas Hastings in a monumental Italian Renaissance style, the theatre's Indiana limestone exterior and its vast, gilded auditorium bespoke wealth and prestige. Built at a cost of over two million dollars, a record sum for the time, the theatre was hailed as "the most complete and beautifully appointed playhouse in the English-speaking world."[42]

Despite its vast financial reserves, its magnificent setting, and its three capable directors, the New Theatre was a two-season casualty. The enterprise failed for a number of reasons, easy to spot in hindsight. The founders, who were the pillars of the Metropolitan Opera House, had chosen Heinrich Conreid, the Met's director, to advise the architects in designing the auditorium, and the horseshoe shape he recommended was a disaster from both an artistic and a public relations point of view. To accommodate the ring of twenty-three founders' boxes, which circled the orchestra, the upper levels of the house were too far from the stage. The boxes themselves became a focal point, the platform on which the founders and their families could see and be seen—a phenomenon Walter Pritchard Eaton, the theatre's most powerful critic, denounced as an "utterly undemocratic social display" unfitting in a theatre "loftily announced as 'national' in scope and 'educational' in intentions."[43] For all its architectural grandeur, the New quickly developed a reputation as a dilettantes' folly, a toy of the rich that the rich soon tired of. The theatre's scale made it unfit for intimate dramas or for realistic plays of any size, and many critics felt that the poor acoustics doomed any kind of spoken drama.

Although it was to be a resident stock company adhering to a strict no-star policy—and as such an antidote to the star mania that gripped the commercial theatre—the New immediately reversed its stated policy. *Antony and Cleopatra* was a star vehicle for the wrong stars: at the time, Edward H. Sothern and Julia Marlowe, the country's leading Shakespearean actors, were both too stout and too mature to strike the sexual sparks their roles demanded. Furthermore, as stars of the old school accustomed to directing themselves, Sothern and Marlowe were ill-suited to the democratic methods of repertory.

In its first season of twenty-four weeks, interspersed with grand opera produced by the Met, the New presented eleven productions: four classics—*The School for Scandal, Twelfth Night,* and *The Winter's Tale,* in addition to *Antony and Cleopatra*—and seven modern plays, including Henrik Ibsen's *Brand* and John Galsworthy's *Strife.* All but two were the work of foreign authors, and only one American play, Edward Sheldon's *Nigger,* described in the New Theatre program as "a play of today treating of the social and economic condition of the freed Negro," was truly American in subject. At the end of the season, Lee Shubert organized a tour of eleven weeks that played in Shubert houses in fifteen cities for audiences totaling 170,000. Twelve baggage cars carried scenery, props, and electrical effects, as well as the one hundred people needed to stage the productions.

The second and final season included Shakespeare (*Merry Wives of Windsor*); the American premiere of a British success (Sir Arthur Wing Pinero's *Thunderbolt*); a stage version of a literary classic (*Vanity Fair*); and Maurice Maeterlinck's fantasy *The Bluebird.* Lee valued the mandarin pedigree that his association with the New Theatre and its founders conferred, but he always had his eye on the gate. Despite his genuine if unformed interest in serious theatre, he was even more interested in exploiting the New as another possible source of revenue for the burgeoning Shubert empire. When *The Bluebird* caused a stampede at the box office, Lee was in a privileged position and he snapped up the production for his own Majestic Theatre. At the height of the first season, when there had been a gap in the schedule, Lee booked a purely commercial play he owned called *A Son of the People,* which starred John Mason, an actor Lee had under contract, and featured not a single member of the New's acting roster. During the second season, he shoveled a Shubert warhorse, *Old Heidelberg,* into another gap and was again accused of using the theatre as a commercial house run for the Shuberts' benefit.

"The New Theatre has been used as an easily moved pawn in the Shubert theatrical chess game," the *Morning Telegraph* griped on March 4, 1910, this time Shubert-baiting with more than a little justice.

> The New has given Lee Shubert, its learned and elegant business manager, a personal dignity not easily acquired as an impresario of *The Blue Mouse.* It has been an outlet for his quiescent stars and an inlet for many of his favored performers. It has brought him into contact with Wall Street in the most approachable and genial form of Wall Street. He has used the New to advertise him and his in every way he could. A number of the Founders have a financial interest in his various enterprises.

The unholy alliance between the house of Shubert and the houses of Astor, Morgan, et alia piqued the scorn of others besides the pro-Syndicate *Morning Telegraph*. Typical of Lee's bad press is the response of an independent chronicler, George Creel, in the *Denver Post* on January 7, 1910. "The New has simply been used as a tryout for Shubert people and productions. The Shuberts were the last people in the world that should have been permitted connection with an enterprise that called for courage, intelligence, and artistry. They are the most commercial of managers and responsible for much of the rottenness that marks the present stage."

As early as March 1910, the *Morning Telegraph* reported rumors that Lee's tenure at the New was in danger. The following February, before the second season had concluded, Lee along with Winthrop Ames, resigned. At the end of the second season, when the theatre was over four hundred thousand dollars in the red, the founders jumped ship. More out of guilt than conviction, they announced that the New Theatre would relocate to less formidable quarters, a theatre, which would seat no more than twelve hundred, to be constructed directly behind the Hotel Astor on West Forty-fourth Street. When, inevitably, they withdrew, Lee Shubert, on the spot and smelling a good deal, purchased the site from them and built two theatres there in 1913. Those two theatres, the Shubert and the Booth, and the private roadway the Shuberts shared with the Hotel Astor (which was to become known as Shubert Alley), have been ever since the geographical center of the Broadway theatre district.

During and soon after the time he was associated with the august New Theatre, Lee tried to achieve recognition as a major producer of serious new plays. On April 18, 1910, he presented Russian actress Alla Nazimova in the American premiere of Ibsen's *Little Eyolf*. Lee had for several years been courting the dark, exotic, sensuous actress (who is often said, inaccurately, to have introduced Konstantin Stanislavsky's "method" style of acting to America). In 1906 he had presented her in English in matinee performances of three Ibsen plays. Lee was bewitched by the actress, and there were unsubstantiated rumors of a romantic involvement. Nazimova, however, was bisexual and surrounded herself with a Sapphic entourage (in 1919 she produced a film version of Oscar Wilde's *Salomé* with an all-gay cast and crew) and so it is unlikely she returned Lee's ardor in any serious way.

To present her in *Little Eyolf*, Lee built an elegant, intimate theatre on Thirty-ninth Street, which he named in honor of the new star whose career he hoped to mold. Nazimova's performance palpitated with quicksilver shifts of mood and a neurotic subtext, and her rich, dark voice quivered with emotion, but the play was by and large rejected. The *Theatre* called the play "tedious and unnecessarily offensive" and "suitable for library reading only."[44] The *Evening Post* called it "dreary, unprofitable, and obnoxious" and warned Nazimova that she "must venture upon higher things."[45]

On February 5, 1911, for reasons she never made public (inferior scripts and inebriated stagehands Lee assigned to her), Nazimova jumped off the Shubert bandwagon to sign up with the Syndicate's Charles Frohman, a far more illustrious producer than Lee and one, moreover, with a track record for handling divas. "Mme. Nazimova already had agreed to sign with Mr. Frohman when the Shuberts christened their 39th Street Theatre after her," the *Morning Telegraph* reported on February 6. "They offered her enormous inducements, even proposing a weekly salary of $1500 and 50% of the profits. But the actress could not be persuaded to stay with the Shuberts—she knew when she had had enough." Certainly one to hold a grudge, Lee immediately stripped Nazimova's name from the theatre, and for the rest of its short, sixteen-year-life, the house was known simply as the 39th Street.

Shortly after *Little Eyolf* opened, Lee negotiated another prestigious contract. In London for one of his buying expeditions, on the day after he saw Harley Granville-Barker's acclaimed production, he signed papers for the American premier of George Bernard Shaw's *Fanny's First Play*. Lee had presented Shaw's *Widowers' Houses* at the Herald Square on March 7, 1907, and was hoping that, if he scored a hit with *Fanny's First Play*, he would be in a position to forge a long-term relationship with Shaw. He could then claim the kind of literary partnership Charles Frohman had with Sir James M. Barrie, author of *Peter Pan*. Despite an excellent production (Lee imported Granville-Barker to direct a company of skilled British actors), *Fanny's First Play* had a disappointing run, and Shaw never again entrusted Lee with one of his plays.

Attracted once again by a glittering foreign reputation, Lee in 1913 helped German director Max Reinhardt produce *Sumurun*. Lee took no credit for his financial assistance. At this point in his career, art plus profits was the formula Lee was seeking; but the next time he won attention as a producer, in August 1913, it was not for presenting Shaw or Ibsen but for a show called *The Lure*, a lurid tale of white slavery set in a bordello. Several newspapers, in addition to the Shubert-baiting *Morning Telegraph*, accused Lee of offending public morals and of endangering the public welfare. After the police raided the theatre on September 2, Lee defended the show as "artistic" and as contributing to "social welfare in exposing a seamy, factual side of life."[46]

When a grand jury began to investigate the possibility of closing the play, Lee stepped forward to say that he would have the show rewritten. In a placatory letter, written by William Klein and signed by Lee, he contended that "personally I adhere as firmly as ever to the view that the play performs an important public purpose and that its withdrawal will be a distinct loss but I refuse to be placed in the position of offending the sense of propriety of even a small minority of serious people who take a different view."[47]

During the time that Lee was trying to build his reputation as a producer (and at the same time suppressing J. J.'s attempts to expand his own producing activities), the second theatrical war escalated. This time printer's ink was the primary ammunition. For years after the Shuberts sold the *Show*, the Syndicate-controlled *Morning Telegraph* had an open field of fire on Lee and J. J. personally and on their Open-Door policy. "The Shuberts get Eureka Springs!" chortled the *Morning Telegraph* on January 15, 1907, adding with typically clodhopping irony that "nobody knows the geographical location, except that it is in Arkansas. The Shuberts will send all their principal attractions to Eureka next season—if they can find it." "The Shuberts abandon the South," blazoned a *Morning Telegraph* headline on February 18, 1908, "and find themselves without a theatre from Washington to New Orleans and their promises to corral the theatre business raise a laugh." As an acid test of the Shuberts' mounting misfortunes, the *Morning Telegraph* periodically reported Shubert conversions of first-class theatres into burlesque, stock, or motion picture houses. "As a result of Shubert activity and the Open Door movement, the motion picture and burlesque craze is spreading over the country like an epidemic," the paper gloated on November 19, 1909. "At the present rate of growth of the Shubert 'circuit' there will be twice as many burlesque houses by the end of the season as on September 1, and motion picture houses will be as numerous as Shubert stars with a grievance." The *Morning Telegraph* persistently lit into a Shubert touring show, a cheesy musical called *The Queen of the Moulin Rouge*, as proof positive of the firm's degeneracy. "The show was attacked in Birmingham," the *Telegraph* announced on October 7, 1910. "The lavish display of the female form is made to catch the men and decency is thrown to the winds. The show was disappointing to all but the Negroes in the gallery."

Frequently, the attacks became personal. The *Telegraph*'s drama editor and chief Shubert watcher was a Wolf (first name Rennold) who wrote a slew of both signed and unsigned articles in which he excoriated the Shuberts for every conceivable offense, from their sartorial and grammatical infractions to their putative profession as purveyors of pornography. "The Shuberts interest me," he intoned from a typically Olympian height on November 10, 1909. "They appeal to me because I am curious to study all forms of man and all phases of his intellectual advancement or otherwise."

In self-defense, Lee and J. J. started publishing their own theatrical weekly. When the first issue of their *New York Review* appeared on August 29, 1909, they began to attack the Syndicate in print. The opponents fought much of the second theatrical war hurling almost identical accusations in the same no-holds-barred style. Each side regularly smeared the other as buffoonish, smut-peddling incompetents who were about to be all washed up in the theatre business.

Just as the Shuberts from the beginning had fought the Syndicate without ever quite admitting a war was on, so they launched their *New York Review* with a double masquerade—first, that they themselves had no connection with the paper and, second, that the paper was founded in an open-minded spirit to give everybody "an even break." Lee and J. J.'s names appeared nowhere on the masthead. Milton Wolf, married to the Shuberts' sister Dora, and Emmanuel Klein, who worked for the Shuberts and who moreover was Shubert attorney William Klein's brother, were listed as president and secretary-treasurer, respectively, but they were figureheads with little or no responsibility in the day-to-day management of the paper. Sam Weller, a former Rough Rider, was the editor, and he brought to journalism the same gusto that had made him an apt partner for Theodore Roosevelt. Weller reported directly to Lee and J. J., who maintained a firm if anonymous grip on the paper's policies.

"This paper will see both sides," the first issue promised. "It will not be the child of an alliance." No sooner was it declared, however, than the paper dropped its neutral pose to display the rancorous partisanship it would pursue: "Great combinations have grown up in almost every industry. But in no industry more than that of supplying amusement to vast millions of worn but buoyant people has the rapacious hand of monopoly gone unfettered." Under the democratic slogan that "there is room for everybody," the Shuberts used the *New York Review* to make sure that there would be plenty of room for the Shuberts. Dutifully obeying as always the Old Testament injunction of an eye for an eye, and plainly infuriated by the years of abuse the *Morning Telegraph* had aimed at them, the Shuberts came out swinging. Meeting the *Telegraph* on its own level, the *New York Review* called the Syndicate and the *Telegraph* itself a threat to public morals. "One of the stated purposes of the *Morning Telegraph* is to purify the drama," a September 4, 1909, *Review* editorial began. "Think of a sewer purifying a mountain stream, of garbage sweetening the family food chest, or of thugs and gamblers giving spiritual uplift to a camp meeting." "Ever since the Syndicate proclaimed itself the coming censor of the American stage and nobody paid any attention, it started off on another tack, to allow attractions playing Syndicate theatres to inaugurate as vile and as loathsome methods of theatre advertising as could possibly be devised," an editorial proclaimed on August 15, 1910. "The forces of imperialism have been beaten soundly," Sam Weller wrote on June 25, 1910, in one of the *Review*'s periodic premature obituaries for the Syndicate. "The Theatre Syndicate is no more. It may have a nominal legal existence, but its old ability to do harm—to crush, and to curse and to crucify—is dead, never to rise again. The victory of the Open Door is a victory for the personal manhood, business energy, and commercial acumen of the Messrs. Shubert."

Like the *Morning Telegraph*, the Shuberts' house organ lobbed down-and-dirty personal attacks. "C. F. now stands for Complete Failure," a *Review* headline on July 11, 1910, stated. "Charles Frohman has been an upright and industrious man according to his own mistaken lights. While canny little Aby [Erlanger] was raking in the coin from all sides and risking practically nothing, Charley Goat risked much and has little. He's a well-meaning dupe. It is high time for his friends to put him in some safe barnyard." The *New York Review* often gave their archenemy Rennold Wolf a taste of his own methods. On January 3, 1910, the paper ran an interview with Wolf's estranged wife, living in Italy in illness and poverty, who had had to sell jewelry when her baby became ill and died. "My husband wouldn't send me any money, yet he draws a salary of $10,000 a year from the *Morning Telegraph* and in addition is paid $75 a week by Abraham Lincoln Erlanger for acting as his errand boy and companion," she attested.

Many of the most hard-hitting articles in the *Review*, both signed and unsigned, were written by the Shuberts' dreaded press agent, a man with the intimidating name of A. Toxen Worm. "Little Aby, a modern imitation of Old Canute, the King who couldn't make the waves roll back," a vitriolic attack on "Aby" Erlanger, was Worm's first article, published on September 12, 1909. Worm's gruff style helped to create the aura of fear that the Shuberts began to inspire during their pursuit of the second theatrical war. Known as the Great Dane because of a fifty-inch waistline, Worm was brusque and hot tempered. *Variety* called him "one of the most unpopular publicity procurers in the history of the craft."[48] Worm once forcibly kicked out of his office a man who had posed as a reviewer from the *Washington Times* in the hope of getting free tickets. When a musician insulted Shubert star Julia Marlowe, Worm started a riot in the pit when he sat on the heckler with the full force of his enormous weight. When he represented the Shuberts in Chicago in 1912, two papers refused Shubert advertising because they would not deal with Worm. And at the end of his tenure in July 1919, he sued *Variety* for $100,000 for the statement that, as general press agent for the Shuberts, he had embroiled his employers in an unprecedented number of battles with the press. Worm did not collect.[49]

By 1913 the *New York Review* was a vital part of Shubert enterprises, bringing in advertising revenue and offering a ready-made vanity press; and even when a second truce with the Syndicate was signed at the beginning of the 1913–1914 season, Lee decided to keep the paper running. If the Syndicate for a time was no longer an enemy, the Shuberts had many others they could embarrass in the *Review*. The paper was not only a Shubert showcase but also included columns on opera, politics, the history of the theatre, vaudeville, cars, and sports; it also featured interviews with current celebrities and the latest theatre news from London and Paris, police gazette items on local crimes, and increasingly broad coverage of the expanding motion picture industry, all written in a slangy, hard-boiled tabloid prose. Not until 1931, when the Shuberts were facing a second great struggle for survival, did the *Review* become a luxury the firm could no longer afford.

For years the *Morning Telegraph* had gleefully reported J. J.'s flareups, but no previous J. J. item was as newsworthy as the *Telegraph*'s headline on January 10, 1911, which exposed him as a married man who had kept his marriage a secret since 1906.

> It is not every man who can develop a household with a regularly established family as unostentatiously as Mr. Shubert, who had been generally regarded as footloose and without the matrimonial trammels. It could not have been because of his stage connections that quiet was preserved, for Mr. Shubert is no matinee idol and his marriage or otherwise would cut no figure, either in the Open Door theatre circuit or elsewhere. And if Miss Catherine Mary Dealey is the happy bride, as she has long been suspected to be, then she has overcome a proverb: a woman can keep a secret.

Three years earlier, on March 30, 1908, the *Telegraph* had noted that Miss Dealey was J. J.'s frequent companion at restaurants and theatres and rode with him in the Shubert automobile, "a distinction no other young woman is known to have enjoyed. Broadway has heard with an interest it makes no effort to conceal that Jake Shubert is in fact engaged to be married, or is already married. But he denies it." Even after the birth of his son, John, on December 13, 1908, J. J. continued to behave to the world at large as if he were unmarried, and he hid his wife and infant son in an apartment at 471 West End Avenue. Despite its vigilance, the *Morning Telegraph* exposed J. J.'s curious charade more than three years after John had been born.

J. J. first met Catherine Mary Dealey backstage at the Casino Theatre in the spring of 1906. What brought them together was stickball, a form of baseball played on New York streets with a sawed-off broom handle for a bat and sewer tops taking the place of bases. No evidence exists of any Shubert ever having played the game; still, it has its place in their history. During a stickball game in an area in the far west Forties then known as Hell's Kitchen, a ten-year-old named Jackie Dealey was killed when an out-of-control grocer's wagon ran into him as he was standing in the "outfield." His family, staunch Catholics, plunged into deep mourning; and like everyone else in the family, Jackie's sister Catherine Mary dressed in full mourning clothes—black shoes, black stockings, black dress, black hat and veil, and a black armband, a detail that was to have a lasting impact on her life. Catherine Mary's cousin Jimmy Dealey, who worked as a stagehand at the Casino Theatre, invited her to attend a party celebrating the one hundredth performance of the theatre's current attraction, *The Social Whirl.*

Although the Shubert sons did not inherit their father's religious fervor, the family did make a practice, in the year following Sam's death, of attending Friday night services at Temple Emanu-El, where they recited Kaddish. After attending services on the night of the Casino party, J. J. continued to wear a wide mourning band on the left sleeve of his jacket as he walked down to the theatre. "When Catherine Mary went with her cousin Jimmy to the Casino, she expected nothing," John said, "and in the long run, maybe that's what she got."[50] The fact that accompanying her cousin to the Casino was Catherine Mary's first night out since her brother's death several months earlier, however, gave the pretty young woman an air of becoming shyness; and J. J., on the lookout as ever for attractive, non-Jewish women, immediately noticed her as she stood backstage near the fly ropes. The inexperienced visitor watched a short, ruddy-faced fellow walk toward her; and as he approached, she saw his hard blue eyes sweep up and down from the hem of her dress to her strawberry hair and then slowly descend again, in a gaze of naked sexual appraisal that, as she told her son John in later years, embarrassed her and made her entire body tense. She relaxed a little, however, when she noticed the black armband the man wore: as mourners, clearly they had something in common.

When he introduced himself as J. J. Shubert, the name at first meant nothing to the cloistered young woman; it was only when J. J., seeing her blank expression, explained to her that he and his brother operated the Casino that she became animated. Like all the women the Shuberts were to become infatuated with, Catherine Mary Dealey had the looks and figure of a chorus girl: seventeen-inch waist, striking profile, dazzling porcelain skin, and upswept hairdo popularized by the fashion illustrator Charles Dana Gibson. Though Catherine Mary later claimed that she was in fact a Gibson Girl, no evidence exists that she ever was. However, though she was later vigorously to deny it, soon after she met J. J. she appeared in the chorus of several Casino musicals.

Two months after their backstage meeting, J. J. Shubert and Catherine Mary Dealey were secretly married. Only their families knew, and neither family was pleased: to the Dealeys, Jewish J. J., despite his money, was a most unsuitable husband for a devout young woman who had been schooled in a convent; and to the class-conscious Shuberts, Catherine Mary was common, a pretty Gentile very

much from the wrong side of town. Her father, Patrick Dealey, was a former sa-
loonkeeper who became a whiskey salesman and was killed in a brawl in a Cincinnati tavern. The Dealeys' initial resentment against their Jewish son-in-law sof-
tened when, within a year of the marriage, J. J. gave jobs to many of his wife's
relatives.

Catherine Mary was never to enjoy cordial relations with any of her husband's family except for her father-in-law, David, who, perversely, as if once again
declaring his distance from his estranged wife and children, accepted the Gentile
everyone else in the family despised. John recalled,

> I know that when my grandfather came to visit us, he would go out into the
> kitchen and my mother would bring copper pots, dishes, and silverware out
> of a locked closet—these would only be used for David's cooking. I think one
> of the reasons he split up with my grandmother was that he thought he was
> being double-crossed, that she was mixing pots on him. But he trusted my
> mother, who was never religious, or a first-class Catholic any time after she
> married my father. He felt she had the integrity, that she wouldn't try to dou-
> ble-cross him. Like all of us, I guess, he was very, very suspicious of every-
> body.[51]

J. J. may have wanted to keep his marriage a secret so that he could continue
to masquerade as a carefree man-about-town. Even in this early period, before
they became the undisputed rulers of Broadway, both J. J. and Lee mixed sex and
business. Their approach to sex was the same as it was to everything else: too
much was never enough. They owned more theatres, employed more performers,
produced more plays, and probably bedded more chorus girls than any other producers in the history of the American theatre. They were as voracious and insa-
tiable about sex as they were about money. Intensely homely, they nonetheless
from early on exuded the sex appeal of the conqueror, and they grasped at sex as
if it were their right, the tribute that beauty owes to power. For decades they were
untiring sexual athletes, every bit the "whoremasters" they accused others of
being.

Becoming a husband and a father while continuing to entertain many chorus
girls did not blunt J. J.'s ambition to surpass Lee as a producer. Both of his brothers
had tried to squelch his creative itch: Sam had kept him out of New York entirely;
and after Sam's death Lee put him in charge of their out-of-town affairs and regularly sent him on the road as a troubleshooter. J. J. watched from the sidelines as
Lee negotiated with Erlanger, oversaw the financial management of the Hippodrome, and garnered prestige by his association with the New Theatre. The one

area where Lee allowed J. J. a measure of creative control was at the Casino, where he supervised a series of routine musicals and revues. By 1910, J. J. was determined to have a theatre of his own, where he could at last prove himself to Lee and to the Syndicate, who continued to regard him as the "other" Shubert, the one who repeatedly lost his temper.

In later years, J. J. liked to tell the story of a walk he took up Broadway one day in the spring of 1910. At the corner of Fiftieth Street, then well beyond the northern limits of the theatre district, he stopped to look at the American Horse Exchange and decided on the spot to go inside to watch the horse auction then in progress. On the flat first floor, heavily sprinkled with sawdust, the horses were trotted out before each sale began. In a raked balcony above sat the men who bid on the animals. One glance and J. J. knew he wanted the space for a theatre. When he learned who the landlord was, he was not at all taken aback—the Shuberts had never been intimidated by the wealth or power of others. Instead he took a carriage down to Wall Street to ask if he could have an appointment with William K. Vanderbilt and was told to return the following day. At the meeting, J. J. asked Vanderbilt how much he would want for the Exchange; Vanderbilt said he would not be interested in selling—his grandfather had set a family policy of never selling land—but he would be happy to rent the Exchange to the Shuberts for a reasonable sum. J. J. offered forty thousand dollars a year for forty years. Vanderbilt accepted. Buoyed by a sense of victory, J. J. suggested they dispense with lawyers and merely sign an agreement on the back of an envelope lying on Vanderbilt's desk. The two men shook hands, and J. J. left, elated by the prospect of his new theatre.

J. J. then had to convince Lee that a theatre way uptown at Fiftieth and Broadway was a good idea. Lee railed against the location—at the time, he was watching the New Theatre, located even further uptown, flounder during its first season—and questioned the practicality of building a theatre out of a horse barn. On an expedition to the site with J. J., he pointed out the forlorn tenements, carriage factories, carbarns, and empty lots that surrounded the Horse Exchange. But J. J. was adamant, and for once he prevailed: he was determined that this was going to be *his* theatre, designed according to his own specifications, where he would produce opulent musical shows.

To transform the Vanderbilt horse barn into a resplendent playhouse, J. J. hired a famed architect, William Albert Swasey. Swasey removed the stalls, drains, harness rooms, and dirt-floor arena of the Horse Exchange and built a theatre which had the joyful, light-filled atmosphere of an English garden. Latticework, trellises, trailing flowers, and an artificial sky of blue created an appropriate ambience for the kind of show J. J. intended to produce.[52]

In this version of the founding of the Winter Garden Theatre, J. J. is a vigorous, decisive, forward-looking hero. Acting on his own, he takes what he wants. The facts of the matter, however, are a little different. As with everything else in his life, J. J. had to fight for control of the theatre. Originally, the Winter Garden was to have been built for vaudevillian Lew Fields, who had been in business with Lee since 1906. For several years, Fields had been staging highly successful summer revues at the Shuberts' Broadway Theatre, and the Winter Garden was to have been a year-round showcase for the kind of lavish revue Fields had become adept at. By December 1909, when plans for the Winter Garden were first laid, Fields was an acknowledged revue maestro who had his own team of first-rate choreographers, scenic designers, composers, sketch writers, and performers. Fields had the experience, the prestige, the lingering affection of audiences who cherished memories of the shows Fields had put on with his earlier partner, Joe Weber, at their Music Hall, as well as the friendship of Lee Shubert. J. J. had none of these assets. The musicals J. J. had been supervising for over five years at the Casino had been poorly received for the most part and had failed to bring in the kind of money Fields's shows generated. More than once, Fields had been called in to doctor an ailing J. J. show.

But despite Fields's superior position, J. J. was determined that the Winter Garden would be his. When Fields and Lee first began to plan a theatre along the lines of an elegant Continental music hall, J. J. was a minor player. But he knew Fields was vulnerable—indeed, Fields began as a Shubert partner; but through unwise money management, he became increasingly indebted to Lee and ended up a Shubert employee, working hard to pay off what he owed. Where the Shuberts were experts in cutting and trimming, Fields was a big spender who paid high salaries to his employees and spared no expense in giving each of his shows the best possible production value. Over the summer of 1910, plans for a fall opening for the Winter Garden proceeded as Lew Fields was on tour; J. J. began writing sharp letters to Fields, warning him that his show was overproduced and overstaffed. Where Lee had been tactful with Fields, J. J. was brusque; he demanded that Fields cut down the size of his chorus, and he missed no opportunity to remind Fields who was boss.

Also during Fields's absence, J. J. deliberately contradicted some of Fields's plans for how the auditorium should be configured. When he returned from his tour, Fields was furious. In November, when the notoriously hardworking Fields collapsed from physical exhaustion, J. J. was ready to step in. At first Fields denied that there was any rift and said that the Winter Garden would open under his supervision as planned. But on January 1, 1911, Fields announced that he no longer had an interest in the Winter Garden.

In this decisive battle, J. J. had succeeded in shoving Lew Fields offstage and claiming the spotlight for himself. Fields had always trusted Lee, who had lent him money and at times had forgiven some of his debts and at other times had extended the repayment period. Now he felt betrayed as Lee watched passively while J. J. insinuated himself into the Winter Garden. "Not surprisingly, Fields came away puzzled and hurt by Lee's behavior," Fields's biographers, Armond and L. Marc Fields, write. "Giving Lee the benefit of the doubt," they observe, "perhaps Fields saw it as proof that blood is thicker than water."[53]

When it opened on March 20, 1911, the Winter Garden was in the shape of a flattened ellipse with a seating capacity of 1,200 in the orchestra, 400 in the balcony, and 150 in the side boxes. The house was both unusually wide and unusually shallow, so that any seat afforded an intimate view of the stage. In width, depth, and height, the stage itself was second only to that at the immense Hippodrome. "New York's latest plaything is a very flashy toy, full of life and 'go' and color, and with no end of jingle to it," the *New York Times* waxed, adding that "Broadway's latest temple of Folly is like a roof garden brought to the ground floor."[54] If the cold grandeur of the New Theatre represented Lee's aspirations toward art, the Winter Garden embodied J. J.'s populism.

Although the Shuberts had taken over other theatres like the Casino and the Hippodrome that had specific house policies, they had not yet built a theatre where they themselves originated the policy—their Forty-second Street Lyric Theatre had not become the home of "native American opera" Sam had hoped it would. In pushing so forcefully for the Winter Garden, J. J. envisioned exactly such a theatre, a Shubert-built "temple of Folly," which would become home base for Shubert revues and extravaganzas that could then be packaged for tours to Shubert theatres throughout the country. Nonetheless, J. J.'s plans for his new theatre were hardly original; the kind of show he would produce was a blatant attempt to emulate the revue format Florenz Ziegfeld had inaugurated with his *Follies* two years earlier.

J. J. was Ziegfeld's first and most tenacious competitor, but neither he nor anyone else would ever be able to match Ziegfeld's sense of color and form, his eye for stage tableau, and his taste. To this day, the Ziegfeld name evokes the silken glamour of the American revue style in its heyday. "Ziegfeld had a bit of education, and he had what was known as class," lyricist and Ziegfeld contemporary Irving Caesar recalled. "No one was really taken in by the Shuberts, who were not held in high esteem and were often referred to as 'S. H.' and his brother 'I. T.'"[55]

When J. J.'s revues at the Winter Garden began to compete with the *Ziegfeld Follies* at the New Amsterdam, the Shuberts tried to discredit Ziegfeld in their *New York Review.* "Florenz Ziegfeld is soon likely to have the anguish of knowing that Anna Held is playing in Shubert theatres. Sad, indeed, it will be for Ziegfeld to see his long time meal ticket [and former wife] earn a fortune for someone else, especially in the Shubert theatres," the paper gloated on November 5, 1912. The

next month, on December 8, an editorial tried to account for the failure of the
Follies of 1912:

> Is it because of the presence in it of [black entertainer] Bert Williams? Not-
> withstanding Williams' natural ability as a comedian and his undoubted in-
> telligence white people even in the north are revolted by the commingling of
> negro [*sic*] men and white women on the stage. The idea certainly is revolt-
> ing to self-respecting Caucasians and its continuance will undoubtedly bring
> widespread discredit upon the theatre. No one is particularly astonished,
> however, that Ziegfeld is the one manager who exploits the condition on
> Broadway. It is in line with his policy of going to lengths to which no others
> would demean themselves.

Privately, as John Shubert reported, both J. J. and Lee "thought Ziegfeld put
on very good shows, but they also knew that he screwed every girl that ever came
into the office. He used four-letter words around women, which is something we
never did. Ziegfeld would insult a girl as she walked in the room. He was a whoremaster, a pimp—I mean, a man who would rape someone on the desk."[56]
    Even if J. J.'s Winter Garden productions never displaced Ziegfeld as Ameri-
ca's preeminent master of revue, the theatre J. J. fought so hard for turned out to
be a success. The Winter Garden was to become the Shuberts' flagship, truly a
theatre they could call their own. John claimed that, once the theatre hit its stride
by 1913, it was "the most successful theatre the Shuberts ever had. There were just
packed houses constantly."[57] (And long after there were no further Shubert revues
to fill its wide stage, the Winter Garden has continued to be a singularly lucky
house for the Shubert Organization. Since 1982 it has been the home of Andrew
Lloyd Webber's *Cats*.)
    J. J. opened his theatre with a two-part program that combined variety, spec-
tacle, musical comedy, and operetta and had a running time of well over four
hours. "Bow Sing," the one-act faux Chinese opera that opened the evening, made
a nod to high culture J. J. was not comfortable with, while the second part, "La
Belle Paree," was the kind of show for which he had built the theatre. J. J. promoted the show and the theatre as authentic recreations of "the Continental idea
of *Variété*." "There is no place like this in your home town," explained a "note to
the visitor" in the opening program. "You must come to New York to see it. It's
the American version of the gay life in Paris, Berlin, London, Vienna. Ballet—
Spectacle—Musical Comedy and European *Variété* features all under one roof."[58]
To ensure the Continental ambience, J. J. cast a Mademoiselle Dazie, a prima

donna ballerina *assoluta* (and an American who had changed her name when she went to Europe to study) as the star of "La Belle Paree."

Prophetically, it wasn't the "foreign" star who captivated the first-night audience at J. J.'s Continental variety but a homegrown singer named Al Jolson, who late in the evening appeared in blackface to sing "Paris is a Paradise for Coons." An embarrassment now, the song, with a melody by Jerome Kern and lyrics that rhymed "coon" with "June" and "noon," was the comic highlight of the show, with Jolson as Erastus Sparkler, "a colored aristocrat from San Juan Hill, cutting a wide swath in Paris," playing opposite a hefty comedienne, Stella Mayhew, as Eczema Johnson, a mulatto maid.

Gauging audience response, as he was to do on many overlong Winter Garden opening nights, J. J. trimmed the show, moved Jolson up to an earlier place on the bill, and allowed him to address the audience. "Lots of brave folks out there," Jolson joked, after the not-so-favorable reviews had come out. "Either that, or you can't read. Come to think of it, after the reviews we got, there's a lot of brave folks up here on the stage."[59]

Basically, J. J. would present two kinds of musicals at the Winter Garden: those with and those without Al Jolson. Both were lavish; both featured stages full of chorus girls, many changes of elaborate scenery, and one or two spectacular special effects. The ones without Jolson were straight revue and were J. J.'s attempts to compete with Ziegfeld; the ones with Jolson weren't quite like any other musical theatre offering before or since.

Al Jolson remained with the Shuberts from his debut at the Winter Garden opening in 1911 until he left to make movies in 1926; and when his short-lived celluloid career began to founder, he returned to the Shuberts, as he had promised he would. Jolson was the one great star for whom the Shuberts can take credit, and the Jolson cycle that J. J. produced at the Winter Garden, along with the Sigmund Romberg operettas he produced in the teens and twenties, constitutes the Shuberts' most enduring theatrical legacy. Jolson may not have been "the world's greatest entertainer," as the Shuberts in time began to bill him, but he was an authentic phenomenon of American show business in the first half of the twentieth century.

Aggressive, omnivorous, and seemingly tireless, Jolson and the Shuberts were a good match. "Jolson could stand up to them because he was as tough and distrusting as they were," lyricist Irving Caesar remembered. "And he could drive as hard a bargain."[60] No matter how many times they fought over money and other contractual matters, they always reconciled; the Shuberts and their prize star had a gruff mutual respect for each other as poor Jewish boys who had made it to the top in a rough-and-tumble business. "Jolson was the only performer who could stick with my father and uncle because he was as strong as they were, emotionally and moneywise," John said.[61]

Professionally, "the Shuberts worshiped at Jolson's shrine," producer John Kenley said, "and they helped to give him that superiority complex he had."[62] But personally, like apparently everyone else who knew Jolson, they had powerfully ambivalent feelings about him. "They had great affection for Jolson," John said, "and they also hated and distrusted him." Nonetheless, Lee and J. J., who as a rule did not become personally friendly with business associates, accepted Jolson into their peculiarly close-knit yet riven family circle. Jolson, in effect, became something of a surrogate father to John and spent more time with him than J. J. did. John said,

> Al was very, very good to me when I was a youngster. He took me down to Atlantic City with him whenever he went on a trip for the weekend. My father trusted me implicitly within his care. Al, of course, always tried to have fun. He'd try to see if I'd take a few drinks, or smoke a cigarette, or try to get me in bed with some gal. Then he took me over to [actress] Lenore Ulric's house, when Belasco was keeping her. Al was banging Ulric on the side, and he used to bring me over to these things, and sit me in the outside room, while he'd go into the next room with Ulric.[63]

In time, however, John's feelings about Jolson began to change. "Jolson always poked fun at me," he said. "He constantly needled me, and I just got to loathe him. Once I kicked him in the shins, and the dye from the suit got into his shin bones, and he was very, very badly off. He had to be operated on."

"Jolson was a detestable man," said Janet Cantor Gari, Eddie Cantor's youngest daughter.

> Whenever he came to dinner I hid in my room. I couldn't bear to be in his company. He was a mean man, and as a kid I could just feel it. He was gruff and aggressive and felt children should be seen and not heard. He scared me; so did Groucho Marx, another very mean man. My parents didn't gossip about show people, but once my mother said, "Oh that Jolie, what is he doing to that poor, sweet, innocent Ruby Keeler [then Mrs. Jolson]? He's so jealous that he has her followed."[64]

"Jolson was always for Jolson," Irving Caesar said. "I knew him as well as you could know anyone. When he needed you he made you a friend; he knew how to be pleasant. But he always did what he wanted—he just had to have his own way. I was with him once in Washington, his hometown, and he took me with him when he visited his father. The old man was listening to *Amos 'n' Andy* and didn't want to be interrupted. 'You come once a year and you're interrupting my show,' he snapped."[65]

Even those who despised the *man* were in awe of the *entertainer.* "My father did not like Jolson personally, but as a performer he thought Jolson was God," Janet Cantor Gari said.[66] "With Jolson, the talent was just there; you can't explain it," as Irving Caesar observed. "It's like a fellow being born with a lisp or a hunchback."[67] "I distrusted and in the end sort of hated him, but I could feel his greatness; I guess anybody could," John Shubert said.[68]

For contemporary audiences, Jolson's performing genius is hard to gauge. Jolson's work on film and records does not contain the full measure of his impact, which was released only on stage as he kibitzed with the crowd, working them up to the frenzied admiration he came to depend on. Although Jolson has earned a permanent place in film history as the star of *The Jazz Singer*, he was an uncomfortable screen actor. The blank, staring camera intimidated him, and its silence could not empower him the way a live audience did. Onstage at the Winter Garden, Jolson was an incorrigible extrovert who specialized in breaking the illusion of reality that most films create—what old-timers remember about the Winter Garden shows are the spots when Jolson would step out of character to ad-lib about the news of the day, to poke fun at J. J. or Lee, and to sing songs that had no connection to the show, songs that, in a sense, were "just for them." Taking the audience into his confidence with his improvisatory chatter, and singing the songs they requested, Jolson performed with an ad hoc wit and aplomb that are not needed in the movies. Caught in close-up, Jolson looks surly and scowling—the camera revealed a dark streak in his personality that remained hidden on the stage.

A second barrier in assessing Jolson's stature is the fact that he achieved his greatest renown as a blackface minstrel. J. J. first saw Jolson perform in blackface as an end man in Lew Dockstader's famed minstrel troupe.[69] (One of Dockstader's scouts, Charles Wilson, had discovered Jolson in a small-time vaudeville theatre in Little Rock, Arkansas, where he hired Jolson on the spot.) J. J. pried Jolson away from Dockstader and raised his salary from $90 to $125 a week. "My father wanted Jolson for the opening show at the Winter Garden, but he did not want Jolson to perform in blackface," John said. "But on the first night of the show out of town Jolson got the jitters and put on the blackface because he had almost never worked without burnt cork. With blackface he was back in his element, doing what he had done in the Dockstader show."[70]

Blacking up gave Jolson a feeling of being protected onstage and also connected him to his private sexual impulses. "Jolson screwed Negroes; that was his kick," as John put it. "He'd go up to Harlem before an opening night, to a whorehouse, and they'd close the whole place just for him."[71] "He had sex with blacks before going onstage," Irving Caesar said, "but I only learned that after Jolson died."[72]

"Blackface didn't mean then what we read into it now," Janet Cantor Gari said. "Jolson and my father and the other performers who appeared in blackface were not trying to insult blacks; they were trying to emulate minstrels. Bert Williams, who appeared with my father in the *Ziegfeld Follies*, was a light-skinned black who had to blacken up before going onstage."[73]

Jolson and Cantor, the two greatest blackface performers, were both Jews who believed that in wearing burnt cork they were forging a bond between two oppressed peoples. But whether conscious or not, racism stains the art of the blackface minstrel, who both appropriated and condescended to the black musical heritage. As Gus, the blackface character Jolson played in most of the Winter Garden shows, he appeared as a servant who ogled girls from the sidelines as the bland, handsome white heroes claimed all the romantic conquests—in blackface, Jolson was allowed to do no more than parody (white) sexual desire. To a 1990s theatregoer, more sensitive to racial slurs and stereotypes than a Winter Garden audience in the teens or twenties, the traditional iconography of Jolson in blackface—eyes popping and outlined in white, white-outlined mouth opened in a broad grin, gloved hands raised fervently as he balances himself on one knee—looks like a parody of a black man soliciting white approval.

If blacking up defused Jolson's sexuality, it did not erase his Jewish identity. The son of a cantor, Jolson was a distinctly Jewish jazz singer who sang with tears in his voice; his soaring intensity married cantorial sonorities to the strident pitch and bracing tempo of Broadway razzmatazz. With his trademark cry and the vibrato that lined even the most upbeat Broadway anthem with an emotional urgency, Jolson converted show music into primitive psalms. As a jazz singer, Jolson was pickled with schmaltz, and it was in fact the specifically ethnic root of his style that endeared him to J. J., who was not remotely religious but often had strong responses to Jewish performers. Among his Winter Garden regulars, his own favorites were Jolson and Jewish dialect comedian Willie Howard. Night after night, J. J. would drop in on a Jolson show and stay to the end when the star would come out "as himself" and take requests from the audience. According to John, "He'd stand at the back of the orchestra, out of sight, and applaud wildly, with tears streaming down his face."[74]

When Jolson stole the opening night show at the Winter Garden, J. J. pretended he wasn't surprised. But he stubbornly adhered to his original notion of presenting Continental *variété*, or music hall, and his next headliner was not Jolson but a French import, Gaby Deslys. Though forgotten today, Gaby Deslys was a popular European star before she became even more famous as the siren who cost the king of Portugal his throne. After the scandal erupted in 1911, J. J. went to Paris to urge Gaby to come to America under his personal supervision. He promised her the starring spot in the show that was to open his second Winter Garden season. Before she would consent to make her New World debut, Gaby demanded four thousand dollars a week plus traveling expenses for her entourage, a special allowance for costumes, and ten thousand dollars down. Following Shubert policy, J. J. signed her up for a period of time—she was contracted for three tours over a three-year period—rather than for a specific show. Each year her weekly wage was to rise by a thousand dollars. Although Gaby seemed to have outsmarted her producer, J. J. boasted, "I'm paying her $4000 a week when I can gross $20,000. That means with $6000 running expenses I can clear $10,000. She's cheap at the price."[75]

Once again imitating Ziegfeld (who had enjoyed great success early in his career promoting Anna Held, another saucy French performer), J. J. knew what he was buying—notoriety and sex appeal and very little talent. Gaby's singing and dancing were rudimentary, but her thick accent was delightful; her big gray eyes seemed to drink in the admiration of the audience; she had a round, doll-like face and a lissome figure she enjoyed displaying. In effect, J. J. paid her an astronomical sum for exhibiting lingerie. In *The Revue of Revues*, in which Gaby was the headliner and Jolson a featured player, she made her entrance wearing a long green and gold opera coat and a towering black feather, and what she said or sang or even danced was not as important as her alternatingly excessive or skimpy wardrobe.

In the next Winter Garden offering, *Vera Violetta* (November 20, 1911), Gaby and her dancing partner, Harry Pilcer, had a sensuous *pas de deux* called "the Gaby Glide," but once again it was Jolson who stopped the show—in a supporting role as a blackface waiter who burst into song at the slightest encouragement. Gaby raged as night after night Jolson seduced the audience. After his two scheduled song spots, "Rum Tum Tiddle" and "That Haunting Melody," a George M. Cohan interpolation, the house regularly demanded encores.

Following *Vera Violetta*, J. J. at last realized that Jolson was his ticket to success at the Winter Garden, and in the next revue, *The Whirl of Society* (March 5, 1912), he finally placed Jolson front and center. In this show, Jolson for the first time appeared as Gus, the blackface servant he would play in all his subsequent Winter Garden extravaganzas. Jolson was at last the star; but, as in all his Winter Garden specials, J. J. gave the audience much more than Jolson for their money. *The Whirl of Society* was a three-part show that began at 8:30 and came down at 12:15. In "A Night with the Pierrots," Jolson appeared stage right as Bones, an end man in a minstrel show, responding wittily to the interlocutor center stage and sparring with Tambo, seated at stage left. In traditional minstrel-show fashion, the jokes were interrupted by song and dance specialties; the olio highlight was a ragtime burlesque of *Sumurun*, with Al as the hunchback and Stella Mayhew as Sumurun, and included a ragtime sextet based on *Lucia di Lammermoor* with Jolson and Jose Collins, a big star at the time. (Jolson never again shared the Winter Garden stage during one of his numbers.) Act 2, in which Jolson was introduced as Gus, was a mild burlesque of the recent visit to America of a royal couple, the duke and duchess of Connaught—typical of the Jolson specials to follow, the plot was there only for the star to doctor or to disregard whenever he wanted to, just as the score, by Shubert workhorse Louis A. Hirsch, was jettisoned whenever Jolson interpolated new songs he'd become enthusiastic about. Act 3, "Sesostra," a musical drama with operatic touches played straight, was another misplaced attempt to force opera-house trimmings onto the Winter Garden stage.

Later in 1912, when J. J. sent Gaby and Jolson on tour in a cobbled-together revue called *The Social Whirl*, Jolson openly chafed at having Gaby billed above him at five thousand dollars a week—only Sarah Bernhardt, receiving seven thousand for her entire company, was higher paid. Jolson and Gaby were Winter Garden stars one last time, for *The Honeymoon Express* (February 6, 1913), which was also the last time in his career Jolson appeared with another headliner. Fanny Brice had a supporting role, and Jolson made certain that it remained one; to become a star, Brice had to leave Shubert for Ziegfeld. (Later still, sensing that Gaby's moment on Broadway had faded, J. J. sent her out on tour until her contract expired in 1914. First she appeared in *The Little Parisienne*, in which her costar was Evelyn Nesbit-Thaw, notorious for her marriage to a murderer. And in an equally slapdash confection, *The Belle of Bond Street*, Gaby's costar was Marion Davies, who was to enjoy her greatest fame as the mistress of William Randolph Hearst. In New Haven, Yale students threw tomatoes at both women.)[76]

During the summer of 1912, when J. J. discovered that Ziegfeld was to postpone his new edition of the *Follies* until the fall, he rushed his first *Passing Show* into production. From the beginning, J. J. intended his *Passing Show* to be an annual revue, which he would present in direct competition with Ziegfeld's annual edition of his *Follies*. J. J. opened his show with "The Ballet of 1830," a European import set in the world of Parisian artists; and like all the other attempts in the early days of the Winter Garden to graft opera and ballet onto the revue format, this one too failed. The show didn't hit its stride until part 2, the *Passing Show* proper, billed as "a kaleidoscopic almanac in seven scenes presenting the comic aspect of many important events, political, theatrical and otherwise."[77] There were twenty-five original songs, one Gilbert and Sullivan number, and five dances, including the "Kangaroo Hop" and the "Philadelphia Drag." In what was to become the fashion of the house, no composer received credit for any song; if at all, composers' names were listed at the top of the program. Louis Hirsch wrote most of the score, which had the usual uncredited interpolations, in this case by Earl Carroll and Irving Berlin, who contributed "Ragtime Jockey Man." The cast was young and eager and talented: Charlotte Greenwood, a remarkably agile, long-legged comedienne with a rustic, cheery manner; Trixie Friganza, a slapstick co-medienne whose big moment, and the showstopper, came when, in a comic sketch set in a harem, she fell backwards into a pool; Willie and Eugene Howard, Jewish comics from vaudeville (Eugene was the straight man, Willie the screwball who spoke with a Yiddish inflection); and Harry Fox, who introduced a song called "Ida" that didn't become a standard until Eddie Cantor revived it.

The Passing Show featured burlesques of current theatrical hits and, of course, chorus girls (more zaftig than current taste would allow) arrayed in cos-tumes that were gaudy, eccentric, and seductive. The chorus in flimsy outfits sur-rounding Trixie Friganza in a huge headdress with plastic fruit draped around the crown typified the house style, sartorially speaking. Each Passing Show would pro-duce at least one stunning set or special effect, a mise-en-scèene to make the audi-ence gasp or applaud, and on this first venture the set to ogle was an arched harem with two dozen bathing beauties draped and undraped around a swimming pool. Receding Moorish arches created a remarkable illusion of depth, and on the wide stage an ensemble of fifty-seven managed not to look cramped.

Another special feature of The Passing Show was the runway, first used for The Whirl of Society and to become a renowned Winter Garden fixture until a 1923 renovation removed it. Jolson liked to claim that he talked J. J. into building a runway, that he had had to overcome the boss's objection to ripping out seats, but in fact J. J. had quite willingly installed the runway for the opening part of The Whirl of Society, "A Night with the Pierrots." Jolson didn't use the runway in that show; it was christened by a ten-minute procession the chorus made from the back of the house to the stage. "The Winter Garden is no place for a man with a weak heart," Charles Darnton observed in the New York Sun in a January 11, 1914, review of Whirl of the World, which highlights J. J.'s true motive for building a runway. "The chorus, not the musical play, is the thing to look for at the Garden of Girls. Pretty little things brush past you, while others walk right over you. It is only at the end of the performance that these sirens of the boardwalk go too far by be-coming so—let us say Oriental—that you feel every little movement of theirs isn't wholly above criticism." "The girls come absolutely within your grasp," Alan Dale noted in the New York World in his review of the same show. "You could stretch forth your hand and seize 'em. Troops of 'em, bevies of 'em, galaxies of 'em, hordes of 'em, masses come prancing across a sort of peninsula separating stage from auditorium. They wore full evening dress modern style and slowly crossed the auditorium so you could see how full the evening dress—wasn't."

A big, generous, eye-filling revue (produced for ten thousand dollars), The

Passing Show of 1912 set the pace for J. J.'s annual series. It ran from July 22 until the end of November; and then, as he was to do for most of his Winter Garden shows, J. J. sent it on a tour that lasted until the following summer. The second *Passing Show* opened on July 24, 1913, and the same performance cycle was repeated.

By the end of the 1912–1913 season, J. J. had firmly established the house policy that was to prevail at the Winter Garden for the next dozen years. Embarking on a rigorous schedule, he produced as many as three or four new revues a year while also preparing two or three revues for the road. He hired a permanent staff of writers, designers, costumers, and composers, and he and his scouts canvassed vaudeville shows in New York and across the country. Overseeing operations at the Winter Garden, J. J. had finally staked out an important place for himself in the family business.

As J. J. settled into his role as the Winter Garden's undisputed captain, Lee negotiated another truce with Erlanger. "The Great Theatrical War is Ended— Shuberts and Klaw and Erlanger Reach an Agreement," the Shuberts' *New York Review* announced on February 15, 1913, this time reporting the news with some accuracy. Never to be charged with understatement, the paper declared that the peace treaty between the long-standing adversaries "will go down in theatre history as one of the epoch-making accomplishments of [this] great business."

Lee Shubert and Abraham Erlanger sat down together because each could clearly benefit from an armistice. By early 1913, the road had shrunk significantly— motion pictures had already become a major threat to the theatre's hold on the nation's entertainment needs. There had been too many times in recent months when a Shubert attraction had competed directly against a Klaw and Erlanger attraction in towns and smaller cities that could no longer profitably sustain two first-class houses. It became apparent to both camps that reducing competition would increase their profits. They signed a booking agreement on theatres in Chicago, Philadelphia, Boston, and St. Louis. At least in theory, both pledged to amend their bad behavior of the past, agreeing to refrain from such piratical practices as luring productions and stars from each other, booking plays against each other, and snatching theatres. Each firm was to maintain its separate identity. Erlanger and Lee would select the most popular playhouses and turn the others over to movies and vaudeville (they had been barred from vaudeville, but they could lease their theatres to independent producers). Profits from the theatres would be pooled. Although the agreement was broken intermittently when one side would accuse the other of having violated one of the terms, peace was maintained because the rivals had reached a balance of power they were satisfied to preserve. In January 1915, the two sides selected the best theatres in a number of other cities that could support only one first-class legitimate house. Reducing the number of playhouses lightened the burden of finding shows to present in them—both groups had been guilty of presenting shoddy wares to keep their theatres open.

Although the Shuberts wished to present themselves as the clear victors, Klaw and Erlanger "were *not* brought to their knees—far from it," Alfred Bernheim notes.[78] What the treaty signified was that the Shuberts had attained bargaining parity with the Syndicate—in essence, they constituted a second Syndicate. If Klaw and Erlanger had not exactly been trounced, they were also never again to be as powerful as they once had been, while the Shuberts were only to amass ever greater strength. What was becoming apparent as early as 1910 and what was now incontestable was that the Shuberts were far from liberators, as their original propaganda had cast them. Even their colleagues realized that they were conquerors, and as Bernheim writes, "When they reached their objective they closed the open door to shut out the supplicants from the benefits that were supposed to be across the threshold."[79]

Lee Shubert in Syracuse, 1880s, already carrying himself like a man of destiny. Reprinted, by permission, from the Billy Rose Theatre Collection, White Studio, The New York Public Library for the Performing Arts, Astor, Lenox and Tilden Foundations.

Sam Shubert, ca. 1900, in a typical portrait pose modeled on his idol David Belasco. Courtesy of Evelyn Teichmann.

Theatrical Syndicate chief Abraham Lincoln Erlanger, the Shuberts' fiercest and longest-lasting adversary, ca. 1900. Reprinted, by permission, from the Billy Rose Theatre Collection, White Studio, The New York Public Library for the Performing Arts, Astor, Lenox and Tilden Foundations.

J. J., the third Shubert, casting an ambivalent glance at his son, ca. 1934, when John joined the family business. Reprinted, by permission, from the Billy Rose Theatre Collection, White Studio, The New York Public Library for the Performing Arts, Astor, Lenox and Tilden Foundations.

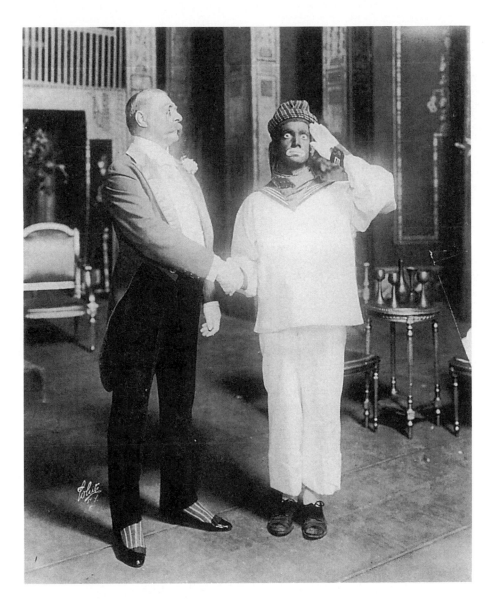

Al Jolson in blackface for his signature role of Gus, a wily lord of misrule. With Laurence D'Orsay in *Robinson Crusoe, Jr.*, Jolson displays a typical wide-eyed grimace. Reprinted, by permission, from the Billy Rose Theatre Collection, White Studio, The New York Public Library for the Performing Arts, Astor, Lenox and Tilden Foundations.

Frank Carter and the pirate girl chorus in *Robinson Crusoe, Jr.*, 1916. The pirate ship was recycled for many later extravaganzas. Reprinted, by permission, from the Billy Rose Theatre Collection, White Studio, The New York Public Library for the Performing Arts, Astor, Lenox and Tilden Foundations.

Competing with Ziegfeld: the harem scene from *The Passing Show of 1912*. Note the runway projecting over the orchestra pit—at some point during each Winter Garden revue, scantily clad chorus girls walked on it directly into the audience. Reprinted, by permission, from the Billy Rose Theatre Collection, White Studio, The New York Public Library for the Performing Arts, Astor, Lenox and Tilden Foundations.

In this 1911 sheet music cover, the Shuberts are promoting their new flagship Winter Garden Theatre rather than Al Jolson, who had not yet become "the world's greatest entertainer." Reprinted, by permission, from the Billy Rose Theatre Collection, White Studio, The New York Public Library for the Performing Arts, Astor, Lenox and Tilden Foundations.

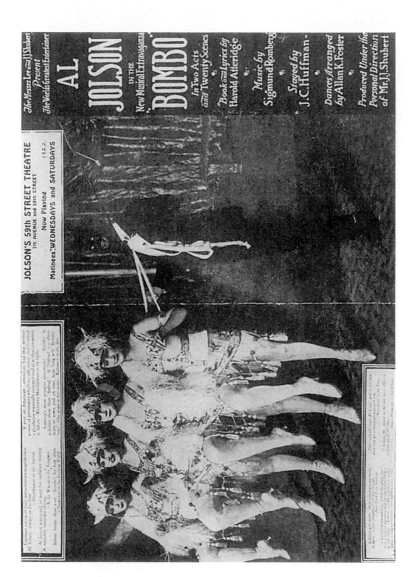

Al Jolson leers at the chorus in the ad for the 1921 extravaganza *Bombo*. Reprinted, by permission, from the Billy Rose Theatre Collection, White Studio, The New York Public Library for the Performing Arts, Astor, Lenox and Tilden Foundations.

The candelabra chorus on display in a production number in *The Passing Show of 1923*. Erotic fantasies of this kind earned J. J. a reputation as a flesh peddler. Reprinted, by permission, from the Billy Rose Theatre Collection, White Studio, The New York Public Library for the Performing Arts, Astor, Lenox and Tilden Foundations.

Olga Cook and a prim chorus in *Blossom Time*, 1921, the all-time Shubert box office champion. The frilly set and costumes were typical of Shubert operettas. Reprinted, by permission, from the Billy Rose Theatre Collection, White Studio, The New York Public Library for the Performing Arts, Astor, Lenox and Tilden Foundations.

The male chorus performing a Sigmund Romberg march and arranged in a typical wide-stage lineup in *My Maryland*, 1927. Reprinted, by permission, from the Billy Rose Theatre Collection, White Studio, The New York Public Library for the Performing Arts, Astor, Lenox and Tilden Foundations.

The 1930s ushered in a new house style for Winter Garden revue. Bea Lillie as Lady Peel, looking svelte in the smart 1935 revue, *At Home Abroad*. Reprinted, by permission, from the Billy Rose Theatre Collection, White Studio, The New York Public Library for the Performing Arts, Astor, Lenox and Tilden Foundations.

Fanny Brice, a Ziegfeld star, in her "Baby Snooks Goes Hollywood" sketch in the Shubert-produced 1934 *Ziegfeld Follies*. Rodney McLennan, *left*, and June Moxon, *right*, both give their full attention to the star. Reprinted, by permission, from the Billy Rose Theatre Collection, White Studio, The New York Public Library for the Performing Arts, Astor, Lenox and Tilden Foundations.

Carmen Miranda, the Brazilian Bombshell, featured in the Shuberts' hit revue *Streets of Paris*, 1939. Reprinted, by permission, from the Billy Rose Theatre Collection, White Studio, The New York Public Library for the Performing Arts, Astor, Lenox and Tilden Foundations.

Lee Shubert, untypically smiling, photographed on-board ship in the late 1920s as he was embarking on a buying expedition in Europe. Courtesy of Evelyn Teichmann.

Lee's chosen successor, nephew Milton Shubert, honored by FDR in 1942 for having coproduced *This Is the Army*. Courtesy of Evelyn Teichmann.

John Shubert, the sole direct heir to the Shubert empire, in a childhood painting hung over the fireplace in J. J.'s apartment atop the Sardi Building. Courtesy of Evelyn Teichmann.

John Shubert, *right*, 1949, standing uncomfortably with his Uncle Lee. Reprinted, by permission, from the Billy Rose Theatre Collection, White Studio, The New York Public Library for the Performing Arts, Astor, Lenox and Tilden Foundations.

John Shubert as the head of the firm in the late 1950s. Courtesy of Evelyn Teichmann.

A candid shot of J. J. Shubert napping, on holiday in Florida, ca. 1952. Courtesy of Evelyn Teichmann.

Lawrence Shubert Lawrence, Jr., 1967, trying to look as if he is in charge. Courtesy of Evelyn Teichmann.

Lawrence's right-hand man, Howard Teichmann, ca. 1967, in the book-lined office that he inherited from John Shubert. Courtesy of Evelyn Teichmann.

A party at "Eckie" (Mrs. John) Shubert's country home, summer 1964. Eckie is embracing Alvin Cooperman, the Shubert booker early in Lawrence Shubert Lawrence, Jr.'s regime; behind them are Howard Teichmann, his wife, Evelyn, and (wearing a hat) Lawrence's mother. Courtesy of Evelyn Teichmann.

4

∿

Power Plays

When the Shubert Theatre, named in honor of Sam, opened on West Forty-fourth Street in the fall of 1913, Lee and J. J. moved into offices on the third floor. Lee had a commanding view of the street from his circular corner office; J. J.'s office was down the hall in the back. Lee referred to both the third and fourth floors as "my offices"—a pointed reminder that in 1913 J. J. was not yet a full partner. In addition to the offices of the two bosses, there were rooms for secretaries, telephone operators, and casting directors, as well as a kitchen, a dining area, a bedroom, and a bathroom equipped with a reclining barber chair on which Lee had a shave every evening at six. The ornate rooms hidden behind the offices were expressly and exclusively Lee's. There was also a two-story ballroom, which was used for auditions of actors, singers, and dancers—no one recalls Lee Shubert holding formal parties in that room. As in the offices of other producers who worked above the store, there was also a panel that when opened allowed Lee or J. J. to look down onto the Shubert Theatre stage.

From 1913 until his death forty years later, Lee held court in the small circular office that looks out over Shubert Alley and that is still the hub of the present-day Shubert Organization. By the time he took possession of the office, Lee Shubert had become the single most powerful man in the American theatre. It was the custom of the house that anybody who wanted to could secure an audience with Lee. "If he were alive and you were writing this book, Lee would have been happy to see you," his grandnephew Lawrence Shubert Lawrence, Jr., told me. "He'd have asked you what you needed from him, and he'd have kept his word to you. He would have followed through on whatever it was he promised. J. J. would also have talked to you, but he would have kept you waiting for hours, he would have given you grief, and altogether he would have made your life miserable."[1] "Lee and my father saw everybody, whether it was a stagehand or a chorus girl," John said. "They never closed the door. It was part of their success formula: if anybody comes in with any kind of a deal, you listen to him. You never know. You might get a tip, you might get a bit of advice."

On the job, Lee conducted business in a terse, deadpan manner. "He never encouraged informality of any kind—he called everyone 'Mr.' and demanded the same formality in return," John said. "My father was definite about that too. They were called either Mr. Shubert, or to distinguish one from the other, Mr. Lee or Mr. J. J., but never simply Lee or J. J. My father would have exploded if anyone dared to call him Jake."[2]

A photograph from Lee's childhood, taken in Syracuse when he was no more than eight or nine, reveals the remarkable containment and self-possession that were to be his major weapons throughout his career. With one arm draped over a wrought-iron fence, the boy stands proudly and gazes into the distance as if beholding his great destiny. Thin lipped, with hooded eyes already heavy with suspicion, he has a masklike face that is startling in one so young. Lee maintained his mask throughout his life. With his slanted eyes, he was often referred to as a Jewish Buddha. Lee's visage, also likened to that of an Eskimo and a wooden Indian, was famously frozen; and with age, his expression became increasingly stony and increasingly resistant to interpretation. Sunbathing was his favorite pastime, and the rays he absorbed whenever he could—in an open car, at a baseball game, in Miami Beach on frequent visits to Florida, or taking the daily sunlamp treatments to which he became addicted—cracked his skin.

"He looked like a cadaver with a shot of Adrenalin," was the vivid way Viola Seff Goldberg, whose husband, Manny Seff, was a Shubert press agent in the thirties, remembered Lee Shubert.[3] "His eyes were opaque," Agnes de Mille recalled. "He was always on guard. I never saw him in a 'civilian' moment. He was intense, smallish, and looked like a beetle. I saw him often over the years, and he would nod with no expression whatsoever. I hope my face revealed no expression either, because if I had dropped my vigilance what would have been revealed would not have been pleasant."[4]

His increasingly wizened poker face, his hard, sharp, unyielding eyes, and his curiously high, thin, piping, womanish voice, which retained a faint trace of a European accent in moments of anger, instilled fear in supplicants and underlings. "I was plain scared of Mr. Lee," office worker Abner Klipstein recalled, with a slight shudder, fifty years later. "He had a stern, brown face; he was very severe looking."[5] Lee assumed his hard look for all business dealings. "Even close friends did not escape 'the look' when a deal was in the air," writer Garson Kanin remembered.

> Lee came to our house frequently for lunch. On one such occasion, around 1:45, Mr. Lee looked at his watch and said he had to go, he had appointments at the office. It wasn't until he was gone that I realized one of his appointments was with me. Ruth [Gordon, Kanin's wife and an actress and writer] and I got into a taxi and went to Shubert Alley. We were ushered into Mr. Lee's office. His face was absolutely stony, and this was just after he'd been to our home. I said, "We're looking for a theatre," and he sat there with his hands to his nose, with a hard look in his eye, after having been a charming guest in our home only twenty minutes earlier.[6]

Lee Shubert ruled a vast business for nearly half a century precisely by his ability to control himself and others. By the time he began to receive visitors in his room above the Shubert Theatre, Lee's office style was firmly set. The four following firsthand accounts of visitors who made the pilgrimage to Lee's aerie provide a glimpse of his behavior. The interviews range over many years, but Lee's iconography is unvarying.

Playwright Ruth Goetz entered Lee's inner sanctum in 1926, when she was "a bright fifteen-year-old." Her father, a producer named Randolph Goodman, was a friend who had asked Lee to talk to his daughter as a special favor.

> I was shown into this tiny office, which had nothing showy about it. I had expected something grand. Mr. Lee spoke so quietly, which also surprised me. He was dressed simply but well, in dark clothes. And I remember he had nice shoes. He was not in any way an ostentatious man. He had a manservant who brought in coffee. I had gone there because my father had asked him to teach me about the stock market. "I think you should learn about it, it's a good business for a woman," Lee told me. He said that he traded every week. He explained how the market works. He was very businesslike, very clever though undereducated, and there wasn't a wasted word. After his "lesson," he said, "Buy me some telephone rights." The office was stunned that Mr. Lee would have me buy telephone rights for him, but he had taught me well, and he knew I could do what he asked me to.[7]

"Lee saw everybody, and he was always cordial," actress Barbara Barondess remembered.

I had performed for J. J. in the revues and musicals he produced, and by 1928 I didn't want to do any more of those, where I'd have to appear half naked and have my family come to see me. I wanted to be a real actress, and so I went in to see Mr. Lee, who was in charge of the dramas, and told him so. He looked at me, in that hawkeyed way he had—he was a tough baby, all right— and on the spot he made a decision. "Go over to the Music Box, ask for the director, and tell him you are to replace the ingenue lead in *Topaze*." He told me he knew I could play the part. I had come at just the right time: he was furious because the ingenue currently playing the part hadn't told him she was pregnant. I was in *Topaze* for two years.[8]

"When I was production assistant to George Abbott in *What a Life*, in which I also created the role of Henry Aldrich, I asked Mr. Abbott if he would consider giving the show to the cast," Ezra Stone recalled.

Mr. Abbott worried about his royalties and so did the playwright; but I got the cast to agree to work for minimum for two weeks. This was after a year, and the show was starting to slip. We were at the Mansfield (now the Brooks Atkinson), a Shubert house. I asked for an appointment with Mr. Lee, our landlord, because I wanted a break on the rent. He knew I was related to David Feinstone, who was longtime general manager of the Shubert theatres, and I thought that might help my case. I had never met Mr. Lee before I saw him that day in his office. He was a little man, and all you saw over his desk were just the tight face and eyes. No expression. None at all. He was gentle but firm. He gave me the crying towel. "We don't own the theatre, we only lease it. It's in trust to a widow." His fingers started to drum on the desk. "The winter will be over soon, Mr. Lee. Please take down the rent when you turn off the heat." He thought it over for a minute, and I could feel the wheels going. Then he said, "Yes," and as he gave a little smile, his lip curled.[9]

"In 1943, I went to see Mr. Lee about booking a show of mine, *Bright Lights of 1944*, on tour," producer Alexander Cohen said.

You didn't need an appointment. You went to see Jack Morris in the reception room. Morris, a crusty old bastard—no charm there—would bark, "Whaddya want?"—and then he'd take in your name to Mr. Lee. Mr. Lee never denied me. When I went into his circular office, a cubicle whose contours followed the curve of the building, he called me "Cohen" and encouraged me to call him "Mr. Lee." I told him that I wanted a theatre for my show. He asked me to tell him what it was about. *Bright Lights* took place in Sardi's, where the portraits on the walls, which had always captivated me, came to life. The waiters were played by [Joe] Smith and [Charlie] Dale, in their last Broadway appearance. The show wasn't any good, but there *was* an idea there. Mr. Lee said, "You have to take this show out of town. Get hold of Jules Leventhal, and he will show you how to take a show out of town."

Mr. Lee was a rough diamond, and he had no sense of humor. The thing about him was, you'd go in and say, "Mr. Lee, I have a show, may I have the Booth Theatre?" and he'd say "yes" and buzz a cheap gold button—that was Jack Morris, who'd follow Mr. Lee's orders. Mr. Lee's answers were instantaneous, and his word was inviolate. You only got two words at a time. He never held forth on anything but his business. I met him only in his office. I never saw him in public. When I was general manager and coproducer of *Make a Wish* at the Winter Garden in 1953, two or three times a week I'd give my figures directly to Mr. Lee; he liked me to drop down with the statement, late at night, where he would be working in the office, and he'd analyze the statement—which seats were selling, which ones weren't. He'd make curt observations, like "Close it!" He could tell I wasn't doing well. "You need some money, Cohen?" He buzzed Jack Morris and said, "Give Cohen ten thousand dollars." I paid that back to him after he died—he'd been dead several years before I could pay it back. Nobody ever asked me for it. There was nothing attached to it. When I had the ten thousand, I gave it to the Shuberts.[10]

Day after day, year after year, decade after decade, "Mr. Lee" received the multitudes in his circular warren—people who wanted a job or a theatre, people who had ideas for shows and wanted to produce and direct and act in them. And after listening to his supplicants, the decisions Lee made often had an absurdly significant impact on what shows theatregoers on Broadway and across the country were given the chance to see. The interviews rarely lasted longer than a few minutes, as he took the measure of each visitor in quick, deft, intuitive strokes. If he didn't want to give a petitioner even those few minutes, he would meet him in the foyer and conduct him to an exit door rather than into the office. Radiating authority, Lee Shubert splendidly enacted the role of a theatrical deal maker, the Donald Trump of his day.

On the job, he was all business, an unfazable potentate. After hours, there were human touches. "In the office he maintained this wooden Indian face, but after six he'd nance around doing terrific imitations of people who had been to see him and of celebrities," office worker John Kenley remembered. "His best imitation was of Jean Cocteau—he'd prance around doing Cocteau, but he'd keep that stony face; he rarely smiled. It was very amusing, and most unusual."[11] Lee's takeoffs on Joseph Jefferson in *Rip Van Winkle,* whom he had seen as a boy in Syracuse, and of Richard Mansfield in *Old Heidelberg* were also skillful and frequently requested at parties. "When he wasn't in the office, Lee was social and warm, bursting with charm and show-business anecdotes," Garson Kanin said. "He loved opening nights and being around a lot of people."[12] And when he was out on the town, he was among the best-dressed men in New York. With his rich, quiet, dark clothes—the ideal wardrobe for a modern man of destiny—he looked like a tailor's model from head to toe.

Near his office, Lee had an elegantly furnished boudoir, reserved for leading ladies and promising ingenues, and a shabby, spartanly furnished room with a single couch where he met chorus girls and soubrettes. "Everybody knew about Mr. Lee's five o'clock girls," Alvin Klipstein said. "On matinee days, one girl from the Shubert show downstairs would go up to Mr. Lee's office, and there'd be one less chorus girl for the curtain call."[13]

"Lee and Willie Klein entertained chorus girls at lunch once a week," lyricist Irving Caesar said. "They'd give the girls ten dollars each, and the girls made them happy."[14] "Mr. Lee was discreet; Mr. J. J. was coarse and didn't give a damn," Shubert press agent Sol Jacobson recalled, "but they both believed in mixing sex and business."[15]

"What they did to those girls wasn't fair," according to Agnes de Mille. "If you didn't sleep with them you didn't get the part. The Shuberts ran a brothel: let them sue me."[16]

When the Shuberts moved above the Shubert Theatre, Lee put J. J. in a three-office suite in the back. Close by but not quite an equal, J. J. was still the "other" brother. And despite the fact that J. J.'s Winter Garden revues were making money, Lee refused to grant him a full partnership. For that J. J. had to wait until after their beloved mother died on November 30, 1914. "One of Catherine Shubert's last wishes had been for her sons to make peace," John recalled. "When Lee, right before their mother's funeral, saw J. J. take a razor and rip each of his vests over the heart as a sign of mourning, he was moved to honor Catherine's request by offering J. J. the partnership he had earned: henceforth, the Messrs. Shubert would mean Lee and J. J."[17]

For the next eleven years, the already-estranged brothers worked side by side above the Shubert Theatre. During this period, Lee conducted a united-front campaign. On June 7, 1914, in a rare public display, the brothers posed together for a photograph for the *New York Times* upon their return "from a foraging trip to Europe for new plays and ideas theatrical." "My brother is me, and orders that come from him are the same as if they came from me," Lee announced to the *New*

York Morning Telegraph on June 2, 1915. J. J., however, continued to embarrass Lee by behaving in the explosive manner newspapers loved to report.

On June 19, 1916, J. J. was arrested in New Haven for striking Francis Hartley, a Yale student. "We had been getting our new show into shape out of town, and when we were catching the train back to New York some intoxicated students swarmed around the girls, and Hartley grabbed one of them. I hit him when he refused to let go," J. J. told the *New York World.* The Shubert showgirls corroborated their employer's story, and J. J. was released.

"My father was not above punching somebody in the nose who got out of line," John admitted. "He wouldn't think of talking to them. He'd hit them first. He hit many a nice person. A guy named Robertson, a big, heavyset singing juvenile, got frapped by my father. Size didn't bother him. My father was sort of an emotional bully with a heart of gold; my uncle, who was a great diplomat, on the other hand, was cold and hard."[18]

During the teens, J. J.'s worst fight, and the one to cause Lee the most discomfort, was brewing closer to home. J. J.'s wife, Catherine Mary, had retired from the chorus in 1908, several months before John was born, but she continued to be stagestruck. In 1915 she convinced J. J. to let her take over the job of costume designer when he fired his chief designer, Melville Ellis, after a bitter quarrel. But Catherine Mary, who was to have a lifetime of bad press, did not fare well. "She has saved more money on tights than Mr. Ellis ever did—hardly any of the girls wear tights," the *Chicago Tribune* noted on June 12, 1915. "Hardly any of the girls wear anything from trunklets to toes but a sprinkling of rice powder and there is a new gown without any back to it that really is an economic wonder." After her designs had received other scalding notices, Catherine Mary, with the help of her husband's press office, responded in a syndicated article that appeared in the *New York World* on November 11, 1915.

I didn't think the costumes were going to create such a furor. They could not be worn at a religious revival, and while some of them are daring I feel they are very artistic. With the war we can no longer go to Paris for the stage thrill and for that reason I saw no grounds why a little Parisian atmosphere should not be injected into our own shows. I now expect to design the costumes of all the Shubert theatrical productions. I find it more pleasant to work than to sit home doing nothing.

But Catherine Mary's hope for a career in the Shubert factory proved to be short-lived. On May 14, 1916, J. J. published a notice in the *New York Times* stating that he would not be responsible for any debts incurred by his wife; and two months later, on July 26, 1916, Catherine Mary served her husband with a petition for divorce. The marriage that had begun in secrecy now unraveled with public denunciations.

It had lasted ten years, but the marriage had soured long before the couple separated. J. J., who like Lee was in essence married to the family business, proved an inattentive, largely absentee husband and father, and Catherine Mary was well aware of his ongoing trysts. She regularly accused J. J. of sleeping with chorus "sluts"; he would respond by saying she should know, since she had been in the chorus herself.[19] To help her endure the stress of being Mrs. J. J. Shubert, she had begun two habits that were to last a lifetime, heavy drinking and clinging possessively to her son. Many nights, John recalled, he would burrow into his pillow to drown out the sounds of his parents' warfare—his mother's screams, his father's curses, smashed plates, a flurry of blows.

In her divorce suit, Catherine Mary named three women as corespondents. "I don't believe the women named in the divorce action were guilty," John said. "There had been many gals before my mother—my father was very well liked by the ladies, and they all liked him—and during the divorce case he was tried for past crimes." Catherine Mary accused J. J. of having contracted syphilis as a result of frequent meetings with prostitutes; under oath, J. J. countered by swearing that John was not his son but the bastard issue of one of his wife's numerous affairs.[20]

For Lee, who valued decorum and privacy and wanted to cloak Shubert enterprises with a veneer of dignity, the bitter cross fire between his brother and sister-in-law was mortifying, and he brought in his lawyer, William Klein—"a tall, thin, steel trap," according to John[21]—to put a stop to it. When Klein could not convince either J. J. or Catherine Mary to relent, he had the case moved from New York to Buffalo, managed to exclude the press, and arranged for the details of the proceedings to be sealed by court order. In Buffalo early on Saturday morning, February 10, 1917, a highly unusual time for a court to convene, a certain Judge Marcus, a friend of William Klein, heard testimony from both sides and quickly rendered his verdict. Marriage between the litigating parties was dissolved; the defendant was to have visitation r᷄ ᷄hts and privileges; the plaintiff was to retain custody of their child and to receive from the defendant the sum of $100,000, payable at the rate of $7,500 per annum. Even in 1917, seventy-five hundred was clearly not a generous settlement, particularly when the husband was a man of great wealth, and accepting the settlement turned out to be the worst decision of Catherine Mary's life—unless she counted her marriage to J. J. as an even greater error. Between them, they were to fight the terms of the divorce for the better part of their lives. Years later Catherine Mary told John that Judge Marcus had warned her to back off because J. J. intended to "clobber" her if she didn't. She also told

John that if she hadn't accepted "the cheap alimony" from "that dirty stinker" John might have been "as illegitimate as hell."

"Their divorce had been a bitter ordeal," John recalled, "and the ensuing years only widened the breach. They never saw or spoke to each other and to me they displayed a violent hatred of each other."[22]

In his business life, however, J. J. was doing splendidly. His annual *Passing Show* had become a box office if not always a critical hit, and his Jolson shows seemed a license to print money. "After *The Honeymoon Express* [1913], Jolson did one show about every eighteen months for my father, and he did about ten of them in a row," John recalled, inflating the number. "Jolson's shows were all pretty much the same, where he portrayed the comedy character of the friend of the hero, always in blackface."[23] Starring Jolson and no one else and mixing revue, musical comedy, and extravaganza, *Robinson Crusoe, Jr.* (February, 1916), *Sinbad* (February 14, 1918), and *Monte Cristo, Jr.* (February 12, 1919) filled the Winter Garden for months. After a summer vacation Jolson insisted on, the shows would go on tour in the fall. On the road, the shows were billed as "direct from the Winter Garden, starring the world's greatest entertainer." Like his bosses, Jolson was more than willing to milk a show for every last cent, and his tours were remarkable for their length and for the number of weekly performances. "The ten performances Jolson gave of *Robinson Crusoe, Jr.*, in two cities within five days is a world's record," the Shuberts' *New York Review* gleefully reported on January 6, 1917. "On Saturday, December 30, he gave three performances of the show in Cleveland, at 10 A.M., 2 and 8, whereupon he immediately left for Chicago on a special train, where on Sunday night, December 31, he gave an 8 P.M. and a midnight performance, and on New Year's Day gave two shows."

Robinson Crusoe, Jr., was a Winter Garden extravaganza in two acts and ten big scenes, with Jolson supported by a company of two hundred. Book and lyrics were by Shubert stalwart Harold Atteridge working with Edgar Smith, and the music was by Sigmund Romberg, another Shubert day laborer (working under protest), and Joseph Hanley. The contemporary opening scenes, in the ballroom and arbor of Hiram Westbury's summer home, introduced a good-looking, flavorless actor, Claude Flemming, as Hiram and Jolson in his traditional blackface persona as Gus, a chauffeur and wily servant whose theatrical ancestry can be traced back to Roman comedy. A dream transported the characters to the world of Daniel Defoe's *Robinson Crusoe*, with the swell becoming the eponymous hero and Gus transformed into his trusty sidekick, Friday. The five remaining scenes of act 1 were divided between Crusoe's island, with its haunted forest, and the cabin and deck of the *Skull and Bones* (pirate ship), stocked with a crew of pirate beauties, billed (on tour) as, variously, "dozens of dainty, darling, dashing, dimpled Dresden doll divinities," and "glittering galaxies of gorgeous, glorious, gladsome girlies mirthfully monopolizing the mad, merry hours and the ten tremendous tumultuous scenes of *Robinson Crusoe, Jr.*"[24]

After starting out in the Ozlike Silver City, the much-briefer act 2 returned to the "real" world, the arbor and ballroom at Westbury Towers. With its fiendish blackface cannibals, its happy Hottentots, and its strutting minstrels, the show was awash with racial stereotypes that reached back to the antebellum South: even in 1916, *Robinson Crusoe, Jr.*, was distinctly premodern.

Twenty-seven musical numbers were distributed over its ten scenes; act 1, scene 1 alone had eight musical spots. Five specialty dances were presented: "Spanish ballet," "Hunter's Fox Trot," "Fast Steppers' " routine, "Happy Hottentots' strut," and "Minstrel Days," which featured many of the cast of hundreds. Surprisingly, Jolson occupied only a small part of the mammoth musical menu. The non-Jolson numbers were more or less integrated into the story line, but Jolson, the king of interpolators, never shared the stage when he sang, doing exactly as he wanted from performance to performance. In the first scene, he sang "Way Down upon the Swanee River," a Stephen Foster traditional, and in the third scene he performed two numbers billed in the program simply as "Songs by Al Jolson," which meant that he treated his audiences to an ever-changing musical feast.

Sinbad, the 1918 Jolson show, was cut to the same two-worlds formula: a contemporary setting, an enclave of privileged whites, the North Shore Country Club, where Jolson made his entrance as Gus, a caddy; and a dream world the show flipped into, in which Gus was reincarnated as Inbad, a busybody porter. Among the exotic locations "in the perfumed East" were the Palace of Sinbad and a Grotto in the Valley of Diamonds; prudently, J. J. recycled the pirate ship from *Robinson Crusoe, Jr.*, into the "Good Ship *Whale*," while Crusoe's island was reborn as the isle of Eternal Youth.

Jolson performed only five of the twenty-three musical numbers. In his first scene, as Gus looked for barbed wire to knit the kaiser a sweater, Jolson sang "Rock-a-bye Your Baby with a Dixie Melody" and "Take the Night Boat to Albany," and in act 2 he sang "Sí Sí Señor"—not exactly a tight fit with the show's Oriental framework. After *Sinbad* had already opened, Jolson interpolated "Swanee," adding forever another song to his most-requested list. "[George] Gershwin, a great pianist, and I wrote 'Swanee' in about ten minutes," Irving Caesar said.

> The words just came to me as though I had them all my life. I write very fast. It was the same way I wrote the lyrics for "Tea for Two": Vincent Youmans played the first four bars for me, which is all he had. He played it twice, I wrote my lyric on the spot and thought it stank and told him I'd write him a new

lyric in the morning. But then the lyric stayed. Gershwin and I wrote "Swanee" for Jolson, who heard it for the first time in Bessie Bloodgood's whorehouse, where we were his guests. He went wild over it and put it into *Sinbad* right away.[25]

Jolson was offstage for all the production numbers, which included a snake dance, a butterfly ballet, a jazz spot called "Raz-ma-Taz," and the "Bedalumbo," a new dance concocted for the show, in an era when new dance steps were all the rage. The show had more of a plot than ever before at the Winter Garden: with a choice of three suitors, the heroine selected a humble cobbler over a king and Sinbad. Although its populist thrust underscored Jolson's image as the people's voice, the book was primarily an excuse for a succession of opulent tableaux. *Sinbad* was advertised as "a bomb of beauty," but Jolson's songs and his low-comedy character clashed with the Oriental fantasia. "Al Jolson was starred—just why it is hard to say," Frank J. Price wrote in his February 15 review in the *New York Telegram*, adding that "It is a great pity to spoil a series of spectacles as picturesque and beautiful as art and a lavish expenditure of money can make them with a setting so bizarre and out of place, so incongruous and repellent as negro [*sic*] comedy that it would have been considered cheap and inadequate in a Bowery variety theatre of thirty years ago."

While J. J. was commanding the Winter Garden, Lee laid plans to build Broadway as we still know it. Following Sam's example, Lee continued to anchor the Shubert empire in real estate. Beginning in 1916, during the prolonged truce with the weakening Syndicate, Lee drew up plans for a group of theatres on West Forty-fourth and West Forty-fifth Streets, which would tip the balance of power in New York permanently in the Shuberts' favor. Clustered around the two theatres Lee had constructed in 1913, the Shubert and the Booth, the new houses—the Bijou, the Broadhurst, the Morosco, and the Plymouth—were to form the core of a new theatre district. "The best thing that ever happened to my father and uncle was their farsightedness in realizing that the theatre center would be in Forty-fourth to Forty-seventh Streets on the west side of Broadway," John said. As early as 1906, in fact, already imagining themselves as the master builders of a new "uptown" Broadway, the Shuberts had begun to buy property in the middle of those blocks; and while theatres were being built on Forty-second Street by such producers as Archibald and Edgar Selwyn and Sam H. Harris, the Shuberts were one step ahead of the competition. Starting at Forty-fourth Street, they bought up brownstones 150 feet in from Broadway and 150 feet in from Eighth Avenue, from Forty-fourth Street up to Forty-ninth Street. "They never went into Fiftieth, even though the Winter Garden was at Fiftieth and Broadway," John said. "I don't know why they stopped at Forty-ninth; I should have thought that my father, because of his sentimental feelings for the Winter Garden, would have forced going on to Fiftieth, but he never did. And they never went below Forty-fourth, although they had owned the Lyric on Forty-second, where they made a lot of money. It was a psychological quirk that they skipped Forty-third completely."[26]

Lee built the theatres with outside capital raised from the core of wealthy investors, continually augmented, that had bankrolled the Shuberts from the beginning.[27] The Shuberts didn't own all the theatres outright, but they had an interest in virtually every house built north of Forty-second Street. They were Broadway's chief landlords, with an array of investments in real estate so vast and deep that the Shubert Organization continues to thrive. "The Shuberts are primarily real estate operators," John noted. "They always believed you had to put money into the land, into bricks and mortar. One of the things that helped them survive was their real estate without any mortgage on it. I would say that only two-thirds of the money is in theatrical real estate—the rest is in very choice, nontheatrical real estate." (Among other prime properties, the Shuberts own thirty-two thousand square feet on Seventh Avenue and Fifty-ninth Street, the site of Gerald Schoenfeld's luxury apartment; a half block on Fifty-fourth and First; extensive nontheatrical real estate in Boston; and all the land around the Broadway Theatre between Fifty-second and Fifty-third Streets.)[28]

As the house architect for their new empire, the Shuberts hired Herbert J. Krapp (1883–1973), who had worked in the office of Henry B. Herts and Hugh Tallant, the designers of the Shubert Theatre; working on his own, Herts designed the Booth Theatre. Having studied at the École des Beaux-Arts in Paris, Herts and Tallant brought back to New York a deep knowledge of French design, which became the leading motif in all their theatres. In 1903 they designed two still-standing theatres, the Lyceum and the New Amsterdam, which are stunning showcases, respectively, of the beaux-arts and art-nouveau styles then current in Europe. With their almost palpable *horror vacui*, both theatres exude a swaggering intensity. Following changing trends, their designs in 1912 for the Shubert and the Booth have a more conservative classical thrust. The Shubert exterior has a restrained, Venetian-inspired facade, called at the time Venetian Renaissance, which harmonizes with the adjacent Booth. Inside, the Shubert features a series of exuberant but conventional mythological scenes and high-relief ornamental plaster panels, while the Booth has a more unusual Tudor motif, with dark wood paneling, which gives the theatre the intimate, homey look of a British manor house.[29]

When the Shuberts launched their massive building campaign in 1916, they hired Krapp rather than Herts and Tallant because, Krapp's daughter Peggy Elson claimed, the latter were morphine addicts.[30] Working for the Shuberts, Krapp became Broadway's principal architect; he designed twenty-one playhouses, fourteen of which are still in use. Unlike Daniel Frohman, for instance, whose single theatre, the Lyceum, announced his taste, the Shuberts were more interested in quantity than in quality, and as a result Krapp's designs have a corporate, mass-produced quality.

The Shuberts built most of their Broadway houses in a period of brisk expansion that lasted from 1917 to 1923; their last New York theatre was the Krapp-designed Ethel Barrymore, built in 1928. Krapp's Shubert theatres, including the Plymouth (1916–1917), the Broadhurst (1917), and the Morosco (1917), are typically severe and unrelieved on the outside and have interior designs often unrelated to the outer coating. Reflecting J. J.'s tastes—and it was a measure of his success at the Winter Garden that Lee allowed J. J. to have any say at all in the design of the new Shubert playhouses—the auditoriums are characteristically Adamesque, a neoclassical style based on the work of the eighteenth-century designer Robert Adam. Shubert interiors tend to favor garlands, floral and foliate motifs, cupids, and angels. Based on English, French, Italian, and Spanish patterns of the Renaissance and the eighteenth century, Krapp's decor enfolds theatregoers in an Old World aura. His interiors, which set the models for theatrical architecture throughout the country, create a dignified atmosphere—a world apart—in which to see plays and musicals.

Building Broadway was a major Shubert power play, one that secured their empire in "bricks and mortar." Their will to conquer was also reflected during this same period in their increasingly high-handed treatment of any individual or group they regarded as being in opposition. With their brigade of lawyers at their side, the Shuberts had an active enemies list to which names were continually added.

The first round of a recurring battle between the Shuberts and critics, one or two of whom were always on the in-house hit list, began on March 17, 1915, when a comedy called *Taking Chances* opened at the Shuberts' 39th Street Theatre. Like many Shubert plays of the time, it was an adaptation of a foreign work, in this case a German piece about a bank robber with lovely manners and dynamic sex appeal. The show was a flimsy star vehicle for Lou Tellegen (Sarah Bernhardt's former leading man), who had to convince the audience he was a devastating lady-killer. The woman he conquers was played by Carlotta Monterey, who was to become far more famous for her nontheatrical role as Mrs. Eugene O'Neill. *Taking Chances* was standard commercial fare; and with so many other plays and musicals on their agenda, surely the Shuberts could not have expected very much from it.

The only favorable review the play received came from the Shubert-run *New York Review*. There were six mixed notices and eight downright pans, the most dismissive being Alexander Woollcott's in the *New York Times*. Enraged, Lee

barred Woollcott from all Shubert theatres. Woollcott's was hardly the first negative notice a Shubert production had received, but evidently by 1915 Lee felt cocky
enough to challenge the power of the press. The ensuing legal battle between Lee
Shubert and the *New York Times* exploded into a national issue. In court Shubert
attorney Max Steuer criticized the judgment of the paper in employing Woollcott,
then a young man just out of college and not the eminent town crier he was to
become in the twenties. "If this is cause for censure," asked the *Chicago Vaudeville
Breeze* on April 20 of that same year, "what about the Shuberts, who employ girls
who are new to show business for important roles in their Winter Garden shows
when they strike Chicago? Ought the Shuberts not to be forced to employ competent artists in their shows?"

The Shubert lawyer also argued that no daily paper would pass judgment on
the quality of goods in a department store. ("But should a theatre put itself on
the same level as a department store?" huffed the *Theatre* in its April 1915 issue.)
And, most specious of all, Shubert counsel invoked a quid pro quo policy, in effect
claiming that, in view of the large amount of advertising the Shuberts placed in
the *New York Times*, the *Times* critic should tread softly on Shubert products. "We
claim the right to exclude anybody who pursues a business that is inimical to
ours," Steuer concluded, coming to the heart of the matter.[31]

At the end of the first round, Woollcott and his employers won. The Shuberts
filed an appeal and hired a new lawyer, Charles Tuttle, while papers throughout
the country rallied behind the *Times*. Astonishingly, the court of appeals reversed
the decision of the lower court. "The Shuberts had enough political influence to
induce the courts to dissolve the injunction so that *The Times* critic is again outside the barrier," the *New York Times* reported on April 14, 1915. "The exclusion of
Alexander Woollcott is effective for a considerable time to come. Our courts hold
that a theatre is a private place and that the manager may exclude whom he
pleases. Our civil rights law, however, makes it a penal offense to exclude any person on account of his race or color. Apparently in New York a negro [*sic*] has more
rights than a white man."

After a year of bitter warfare, with the Shuberts refusing to advertise in the
New York Times and with Woollcott barred from their theatres by court order, Lee
declared a truce: Woollcott would be welcome in any Shubert theatre. Practical as
ever, Lee did not rescind the ban as a matter of conscience but because he realized
that not advertising in the *Times* was bad for business. Besides, he felt he had made
the point that the Shuberts could and would cause trouble for carping critics.

As with critics who had minds of their own, the Shuberts resented actors who
didn't abide house rules, and Shubert history is scarred by both small-scale skirmishes and epochal clashes with disobedient performers. "Actors were his pet

peeve," John commented about his father.[32] J. J. had made a number of headlines by socking, slapping, chasing, and swearing at stars and chorus girls. A typical, widely reported fracas occurred on March 23, 1911, when J. J. fired a showgirl named Peggy Forbes after a matinee, accusing her of quarreling with other members of the chorus and thereby disrupting backstage decorum. Miss Forbes, a grandniece of President Zachary Taylor, then said, "Mr. Shubert, are you a man or are you a monkey?" With that, she later claimed, J. J. struck her on the mouth and on both sides of the face. The feisty Miss Forbes took J. J. to court; J. J.'s defense was that Miss Forbes had stuck him with a hatpin, and he was only defending himself. Miss Forbes could not produce any witnesses who saw the incident her way, and J. J. produced several witnesses, all Shubert employees, including an assistant stage manager, a prop man, and seven chorus girls who swore that Miss Forbes had indeed gone after their boss with a hatpin.[33] Another well-documented run-in took place on September 16, 1914, when Lew Brice, a notably small, attenuated-looking comic, took a drink to quiet his stomach trouble and then became too ill to perform. Enraged, J. J. punched him out, according to the *Morning Telegraph*.

Though he was more subdued, Lee would never qualify as a patron saint of actors either. To both Shuberts and to many of their representatives, actors were a necessary evil. "We didn't fire actors, they left us," John admitted. "Contrary to popular impression, the Shuberts did not break contracts or toss people out; most of the time it was the other way around. People left. People like Marilyn Miller, who started with them, left. Vivienne Segal, who started with them, left. Eddie Cantor left. Mae West, Fanny Brice, Fred Astaire, the Three Stooges left" and became famous under the sponsorship of other producers.[34]

Impresario Morris Gest, walking out of Sardi's with Shubert press agent Max Gendel, "pointed his finger at Lee's office across the street, where Lee as usual was working late," Gendel remembered, "and he said, 'Every union in the theatre was started because of that man.' "[35] While this is an exaggeration, it is fair to say that the Shuberts' consistent mistreatment of actors in the first two decades of the century provided significant inspiration for the actors' strike of 1919, which gave birth to Actors' Equity Association. "The firm was notorious for its abuse of actors' rights," Alfred Harding writes in *The Revolt of the Actors*, his definitive history of the formation of Actors' Equity.[36] The Shuberts were by no means the only managers to clash with actors, but they were the most powerful and most of the grievances voiced by actors were aimed at them.

On April 16, 1910, *Harper's Weekly* reported that the Messrs. Shubert had added professional matinees at which actors employed in other shows could see performances without charge. "This is a rank injustice," *Harper's* claimed, because the Shubert actors were required to perform without pay even though "every stage hand, lightman, orchestra musician and ticket-taker, being a union laborer and not a mere artist, receives full payment."

In May 1911, the Shuberts informed Jack Hazzard, an actor in one of their shows, that he was "unsatisfactory." Claiming he had been fired without cause, Hazzard took his former employers to court; six and one-half years later, the court of appeals upheld the Shuberts, concluding that managers did not have to demonstrate "good faith" in rating an actor's work but could dismiss an actor for being "unsatisfactory" if they so decreed.[37]

In April 1913, dancer-singer Kathleen Clifford was given only half her salary for performing four Sunday concerts at the Winter Garden. She sued the Shuberts for $450; with astonishing gall, the Shuberts maintained that they did not have to pay because their contract with Clifford was illegal—at the time, Sunday performances were in violation of the city's ordinance. (The Shuberts tried to circumvent the blue laws by calling their Sunday shows "sacred" concerts, which meant that the show, typical Winter Garden variety, might contain a religious song.) The court sustained the Shuberts, prompting an outcry about Shubert payoffs. Clifford persisted, bringing her former bosses to court a second time. In this round, the Shuberts were ordered to pay the performer five hundred dollars, and for a time they canceled their "sacred" concerts.[38]

In August 1913, actress Olga Nethersole sued the Shubert Theatrical Company for $31,644.97, claiming the Shuberts had induced her to come to America by offering her a two-year contract that they abruptly terminated at the end of her first (obviously disappointing) season. Nethersole's attorney, Joseph M. Hartfield, called Lee Shubert "a very wicked man" who would not recognize a moral obligation "if he met it on the highway labeled." Remarkably, Lee disavowed the contract, arguing that the Shuberts "would never consent to a contract with a sole star clause . . . sole stars are a great danger to a manager because they tie him down to a single line of plays."[39] What he meant, of course, was that he was opposed to sole star contracts for stars who could not bring in high enough grosses—the Shuberts, after all, negotiated a series of contracts with Al Jolson, one of the greatest "sole stars" in American show business.

When comedy team Gallagher and Shean tried to break their contract in 1914, the Shuberts insisted the defendants were "novel, unique, and extraordinary." Continuing to work for the Shuberts was apparently so grim a prospect that the actors were forced to fall on their sword: Ed Gallagher and Al Shean claimed that, in fact, they were "terrible and replaceable."[40]

The Shuberts did not hide their disdain for actors who did not do as they were told. "It is time that legitimate producers and vaudeville managers get together and prevent actors from holding the whip hand over them," a typical editorial in their *New York Review* announced on November 2, 1912, calling for the formation of a united front to combat the "arrogance" of actors. "The way [managers] are bidding against each other for the services of successful performers has so added to the vanity and ambition of actors that their attitude has become intolerable. Other managers help them break contracts: Joe Coyne was helped by Charles Frohman to break his contract with the Shuberts; Bert Williams broke with [F. Ray] Comstock and Gest and found Ziegfeld and Abraham Erlanger ready to stand behind him."

Abuse against actors had steadily escalated since the formation of the Syndicate in 1896. Actors were no longer members of the family, as they had often been in the days when the independent actor-manager was responsible for his company. Now they were hired hands who comprised only a fraction of the entrepreneurs' big picture. Traditionally actors rehearsed for two weeks without pay, but the Shuberts were known to stretch that period to ten or twelve entirely uncompensated weeks. An actor named John Goldsworthy, under contract to the Shuberts for two years, rehearsed fifty-seven weeks without pay and played twenty-two weeks without pay.[41] Until matinees were added, actors normally played six performances a week, but the Shuberts regularly scheduled extra performances without pay, and their contracts frequently contained a clause stating that the number of performances would be decided by "the custom of the theatre." The Shuberts set a record when they ordered fourteen performances in a single week of a touring edition of *The Passing Show of 1916*, for which no extra pay was allowed. Other grievances, directed primarily but not exclusively at the Shuberts, included the fact that actors could be dismissed "without cause," that they often had to pay their own transportation, and that in some cases they were expected to provide their own costumes.

To combat the mistreatment that had become systemic after the Syndicate and then the Shuberts had won unprecedented managerial power, 112 actors formed the Actors' Equity Association (AEA) in June 1913. The president of the new organization was Francis Wilson, the comic-opera star and firebrand who had been one of the Syndicate's most determined foes. But as Wilson admits in his memoirs, the new organization had no force (indeed, it was to be six years before Equity became a full-fledged union). "The real struggle of Equity was with actors who had to be educated as to the necessity of organizing," Wilson writes.[42]

Unlike any other branch of the theatre, actors had always been reluctant about banding together. "The most recent attempt of actors to unionize is doomed to failure," the *New York Review* trumpeted on June 28, 1913. "Such a league must stand on absolute equality. It is quite absurd to suppose that any actor would admit that any other actor is his equal. In no other profession or art do egotism and jealousy show themselves more luridly." Moreover, Wilson and his cohorts had to fight a thorny three-year battle, beginning in 1916, to become affiliated with the American Federation of Labor. It was AF of L policy to grant one charter in each field, and the White Rats Actors International Union, the vaudeville union, already held the charter. The AF of L would not alter its policy; and the White Rats, though crippled by their war with the formidable Vaudeville Managers' Protective Association, stubbornly clung to their charter. Equity leaders persevered nonetheless.

Recognizing that this group of actors intended to continue to fight for their rights, regardless of the odds against them, Lee Shubert was instrumental in 1916 in forming the United Managers' Protective Association; and as Equity continued to swell its membership roster and its leaders became increasingly outspoken, he began to run scared. As always the boss's feelings were reflected in the *New York Review*. On April 8, 1916, the paper asserted that actors on the whole are against unionizing "on the ground that the friendship of managers is worth more than the doubtful support of union laborers. Managers and actors have artistic results in common to work for and it is necessary that actors work in harmony with managers to get those results."

By the beginning of the 1917 season, Lee saw that it was in his own interests to adopt a conciliatory tone toward the band of rebellious actors. On October 2, along with other officers of the United Managers' Protective Association, he met with Equity delegates to negotiate the first standard minimum contract for first-class productions. Both sides called the contract the start of an "era of harmony," but within three weeks the new era was over when the outbreak of the third theatrical war reduced the standard minimum contract to a side issue neither the Shuberts nor the Klaw and Erlanger forces were interested in honoring.

Equity continued to gain strength, and in April 1919 Lee helped organize a new group, the Producing Managers' Association (PMA), to fight Equity's insistence on a basic week of eight performances. Lee was instrumental in forming the Actors' Fidelity League, a company union to represent the actors in their shows. Vaudevillian and musical comedy star George M. Cohan headed the union; Al Jolson was one of the few stars to stand with Cohan against Equity, which was organized in part to protect actors against such abuses as the ten performances a week and the three performances a day Jolson regularly worked.

Sam Harris, PMA president and Cohan partner, announced that managers intended to deal with actors individually instead of through Equity. At this point, the White Rats finally surrendered their charter; and with the support of the AF of L, Equity did what the producers had confidently expected that it never would: on August 5, 1919, its members struck. The strike lasted for thirty days, spread to eight cities, closed thirty-seven plays, and prevented the opening of sixteen others.

Since "every indication seems to show that the Shubert Theatrical Company is principally responsible for the unreasonable refusal of the managers to enter into any conference with the AEA," Equity enlisted its allies, the stagehands and the musicians, to walk out on all Shubert productions and theatres.[43] The Shuberts sued Equity, claiming strike damages of one-half million dollars. They did not collect.

Reeling from a nationwide strike and outnumbered by Erlanger factions within the PMA, Lee Shubert untypically found himself jammed between a rock and a hard place. He instructed Shubert attorney Levy Mayer to inform the Erlanger group that the managers had no chance to win and that to continue the strike would only mean greater losses. The PMA raised up a white flag. On September 6, 1919, representatives of both sides met at the St. Regis Hotel to settle. For the actors, it was a long-awaited triumph: Equity won the terms it asked for, under an agreement that was to last until June 1, 1924. For the managers, and particularly for the Shuberts, capitulating to the enemy under fire, it was a moment of shame. "Contrary to all expectations, it was the actors who stuck together and the managers who cracked under the strain," as Alfred Bernheim notes.[44] And as Alfred Harding writes in his history of Equity, Shubert representatives at the peace conference "were not there to delay any possible settlement, but to save what they could—themselves if nothing else."[45]

The Shuberts signed a truce with Equity, but it was an agreement they did not intend to keep. They continued to attach to their contracts riders that defied the projections of the basic agreement. Contracts for *Maytime*, *The Passing Show of 1918*, and *Cinderella on Broadway* required nine performances with no extra pay; *The Passing Show of 1919* required nine performances plus unlimited, unpaid rehearsals; for the road tour of *Florodora*, there were no contracts at all, and if Equity members requested one they were given their notice. Equity members who applied for jobs were refused, while others who claimed to be non-Equity were hired. The Shuberts had instructed company managers to require actors to deny their Equity membership; company managers claimed they had "written orders from the office to get rid of actors insisting on Equity requirements."[46]

In the teens, during the same intense period in which the Shuberts were building Broadway, producing a record number of plays and musicals, and fighting critics, actors, and unions, Lee became involved in the rapidly expanding motion picture business. "To the Shuberts, film was always a stepchild," historian Kevin Lewis said.[47] Lee, in fact, never had any interest in films, unlike J. J. who was an avid moviegoer; that Lee entered the movie business was another sign of the Shuberts' unstoppable acquisitiveness.

"At its best the motion picture in its most highly developed form can only be a reproduction," Lee pontificated in the November 1913 issue of *Theatre*. In *Photoplay* of April 1915, he spoke even more negatively about the burgeoning new medium. "I believe that actors of both sexes damage their commercial value by appearing in picture plays," he said. "Nowadays when a legitimate manager presents an actor in an expensive production he is likely to find that the actor is simultaneously and flamboyantly featured in a movie at 5¢ and 10¢." Even after Lee entered the film business, the *New York Review* continued a firm antifilm policy. "The scenario of the ordinary picture as a rule is about as crude and stupid a concoction as can be imagined," a September 25, 1915, editorial declared. "As a literary creation it is in the kindergarten class."

Even if Lee did not personally care for movies, he recognized the medium's moneymaking potential. From virtually the beginning of their careers, the Shuberts had shown short films as novelty items in their upstate theatres that specialized in revue and vaudeville. In 1908 Lee had helped finance a former penny-arcade operator named Marcus Loew, who planned to build a chain of film houses. In 1913, however, when the theatre business fell into a nationwide slump, the Shuberts resisted converting their theatres into film houses. Instead they joined with William Brady, Lew Fields, and a switch-hitting Marcus Loew to present first-class stock plays at a 10–20–30¢ price scale in thirty cities of the East and Middle West. They hoped to attract patrons who had defected to the movies. By the end of 1913, however, failing to attract the hoped-for crowds, Lee capitulated and began to book films into a number of his legitimate houses.

To service those theatres and others, Lee went into partnership with William Brady to form the Shubert Feature Film Booking Company. Early in 1914, Broadway impresarios David Belasco, John Cort, and Oliver Morosco joined with the Jesse L. Lasky Feature Play Company to present film reproductions of their stage works; and spurred by their example, on June 12 Lee announced his intention of launching a film company to record selected Shubert stage properties. With a partner, Jules Brulatour, Lee constructed a studio called Paragon, located in Fort Lee, New Jersey.[48]

Also on June 12, Lee announced a merger between his Shubert Feature Film Booking Company and the World Film Corporation. Like Lee's company, World at first had only released films, but once it was united with the Shubert Film Company, it began to produce films as well. Again Lee's partner was Brady, whom Kevin Lewis called "a blowhard Irishman over whom the Shuberts held the upper hand."[49] And Lee's general manager was Lewis Selznick, the father of David O. and Myron. A brilliant producer with important connections, Selznick, whom Lee could not control, was abrasive, and he and Lee clashed repeatedly. In October 1916, Lee persuaded Brady that Selznick had to be fired—"the worst thing the

World directors could have done," according to Kevin Lewis. "[Selznick's] sons never forgave the industry for ruining their father."[50]

Once he had dismissed Selznick, Lee was unable to find a suitable replacement. He himself was too busy with his vast theatrical empire to attend closely to World. Although part of his reason for venturing into production was to find an extended life for his theatrical properties, only a few, such as *Trilby* (1915) and *Old Dutch* (1915), were actually filmed. Lee remained a World director until he resigned on December 1, 1918. The company suspended all film production in 1919.

"The big Shubert shows and stars were simply not signed up by World," Kevin Lewis said. Shubert cheapness may have doomed the company to attracting only second-rate players. It's possible to read between the lines of William Brady's announcement in the January 13, 1917, issue of the *New York Review* that World will not make "specials with $100,000 stars, necessitating big fees from exhibitors and increased prices at the box office." World failed not only because Lee was distracted but also because most of its movies weren't very good. "What doomed World was its lack of real film stars, and its poor choice of material," according to Kevin Lewis. "An inordinate number of films starred the same people in the same stories. Many of the films were smothered under a mass of plots and subplots and were merely sensational."[51]

His misadventures with World were not Lee's final flourish in the film business. In July 1919, Lee and Al Woods, then at the height of his popularity as a producer of Broadway potboilers, became partners with Samuel Goldwyn. As at World, the venture was announced as a film showcase for Shubert stage properties. Goldwyn in fact was far more attracted to Shubert theatres where he could show his films and which he badly needed to be able to compete with studios that owned theatres. "Very few Shubert-owned plays reached the screen . . . [and] for the most part, suggestions by Lee Shubert were rejected," Kevin Lewis observes.[52]

Goldwyn fought his board as frequently and as virulently as Lewis Selznick had, and like Selznick Goldwyn was booted out. He was, of course, by no means finished. When Goldwyn Pictures foundered, Lee (who served on the board of Loew's) talked his old friend Marcus Loew into buying the forty-acre Goldwyn studio, which was to become Metro-Goldwyn-Mayer, the most gilt-edged of the major studios in Hollywood's Golden Age. "Loew wanted to know what would be gained by combining with a company that was in worse condition than his own," Lee Shubert recalled. "I explained that the Goldwyn company had certain assets which if handled properly would prove of great value, one of which was the picture rights to *Ben Hur* which was then in the process of production and which alone (and finally did) prove the financial salvation of all concerned."[53]

In 1929 Lee under pressure sold his shares of Loew's stock—"the end of their long involvement with Loew's."[54] "Getting frozen out of MGM and being removed from the board of directors was something that almost killed my uncle," John said.

> He couldn't get on with the others. He knew the old pioneers too long before to get along with them and to live with them. The Shuberts in the movie business is a rather unpleasant thing to talk about. The smart boys in Hollywood took them to the cleaners. We were invited by Warner Brothers to get involved with them when talking pictures came out. They thought one of the ways of getting us and getting Jolson to work for them would be to bring us and Jolson in. So we got involved but my uncle got cold feet. He sold his Warner Brothers interests quickly, after a few months, which was good because the Warners are like anybody else out on the Coast. They're good when it's all their own money, but when it's an outsider's money they don't care.

"Don't get involved in things you don't know" was a Shubert motto, according to John. "You only know legitimate theatre, you stay with it. They always believed, 'Shoemaker, stick to your last.' But they were always tempted."[55]

As Lee was expanding and protecting the Shubert empire, J. J. became an important producer of a kind of musical show different from those offered by the Winter Garden. Located across from the Casino Theatre at Thirty-ninth Street and Broadway was a German American restaurant specializing in heavy beer steins and heavier luncheons and dinners that was one of J. J.'s favorite spots. It was a place where ladies had to unlace their corsets after eating and men had to open their vests and unbuckle their belts. The decor was Teutonic gloom: high, dark wood panels surmounted by mahogany molding of gingerbread design. On the far wall, the Stars and Stripes were crossed by the imperial German colors, and on either side of the flags were photographs of Wilhelm II. Beneath the one-sided patriotic display, a six-piece musical ensemble played airs meant to aid diners' digestion.

J. J. particularly enjoyed a pianist who played melodies whose national origins he couldn't place. One day early in 1913, he asked who had composed the music. The pianist, Sigmund Romberg, informed him that he was playing traditional folk tunes from Hungary, his homeland—music that schoolchildren sing, peasants dance to, and Gypsies play on violins and mandolins. Romberg admitted, however, that he embellished the original folk melodies by adding notes and changing pitch and rhythm. Impressed, J. J. hired him.

At the time, J. J. was trying to duplicate the success of *The Merry Widow*, an operetta with a ravishing score by Franz Lehár that represented the height of the Viennese style in its most sweeping, most arioso, and most elegant incarnation, which had opened on October 21, 1907, at the New Amsterdam. "We always regretted we didn't have *The Merry Widow*—the opposition struck it rich on that one," John said, "but we acquired Lehár's work toward the end of his life—all except the early ones that Henry Savage, the *Widow*'s lucky producer, did."[56] As decisive a hit as *H.M.S. Pinafore* had been in 1879 and having as marked an impact on the American musical theatre's inferiority complex, *The Merry Widow* inaugurated a vogue for Viennese operetta that lasted until the Great War, when the style began to seem suspiciously Germanic.

The robust melodies, the faraway settings, the star-crossed romances of the Viennese mode appealed to J. J.'s highly developed theatrical sweet tooth. He wanted to cash in on *The Merry Widow* craze with a hit operetta of his own, but he also genuinely loved the genre's silvery music and dewy romanticism. For seven years after *The Merry Widow*, he had Shubertized a series of European properties in a vain attempt to repeat the success of a rival. And by the time that J. J. signed Romberg to his first five-year contract, the producer had already established an operetta division that was run in similar fashion to the musical factory he had set up to service the Winter Garden.

"My father would buy a foreign show, in Paris or Berlin, Budapest or Vienna, and then have it adapted." John said.

You got a composer, and it didn't matter who it was in those days. Except Victor Herbert [who wrote all his most successful shows for producers other than J. J.], there weren't too many greats around. My father would give the foreign piece an American adaptation—what used to be called *My Beautiful Girl in the Woods* was suddenly called *Hello, Lola!* for American consumption. There were at least twenty boys in Berlin, Vienna, Budapest, turning out the stuff once a year; my father would get somebody to doctor up the scripts and bring in a fellow from Tin Pan Alley to goose the lyrics. Then you'd add a couple of American tunes, or you'd buy a song from José Padilla in Spain and shove that in. Nobody cared. There was no author's society or Dramatists Guild, everybody got paid, though you didn't pay anybody too much money. And so, one after another, the operettas were formed. There were always five or six in production, composers in one room banging away, and then an author in another room cutting and patching, and seven or eight rehearsals going on around town. We had fourteen rehearsal halls right down the block from the office on West Forty-fourth Street.[57]

When *Blue Paradise* opened on August 5, 1915, at the Casino Theatre, J. J. finally had an operetta bonanza. The original script, which J. J. had purchased in Vienna from Otto Eirich (who later sued J. J. for money owed), was by Leo Stein,

The Merry Widow's librettist. It tells of a young Viennese man who returns home after making millions in America, only to discover that the woman he loved has become a shrew and that the Blue Paradise, the inn where he fell in love with her twenty-four years earlier, no longer exists. In this bittersweet story of an unconsummated romance, the music of gay Vienna is the Proustian madeleine that evokes a memory of the idealized past. Edgar Smith Americanized the original libretto, and J. J. had two composers add to the eight original songs by Edmund Eysler that were retained: Leo Edwards wrote two new numbers, and Romberg contributed eight. The most hummable of Romberg's songs was "Auf Wiedersehen," composed in the florid style that was to become his hallmark. When at the end of act 1 Vivienne Segal, an out-of-town replacement for the leading lady J. J. fired, sang the song in a duet with the hero she is about to lose, she stopped the show and at eighteen became a Broadway star.

Both before and after the success of *Blue Paradise*, J. J. also exploited Romberg as a hired hand for the Winter Garden. Just as J. J. had stubbornly refused to promote Al Jolson to the top of the bill at the Winter Garden for over two years, he took even longer to allow Romberg to write the soaring ballads, stirring marches, and gliding waltzes that were to earn him his place as a king of American operetta. Instead, J. J. put his composer to work contributing songs for the bread-and-butter summer and fall Winter Garden revues and for the Jolson specials, in which the scenery, the chorus line, or Jolson's interpolations upstaged Romberg's work. The composer chafed at having to provide tangos, fox-trots, rags, ballroom dances and hurdy-gurdy tunes for opulent revues, but he complied, hoping that his boss would finally reward him with the chance to write a complete operetta score.

In addition to simply wanting to extract as much work as he could from Romberg, J. J. was well aware that a Viennese pastry like *Blue Paradise* appeared at an awkward time, and he decided to keep his composer's gemütlichkeit under wraps as long as the war lasted. J. J.'s biggest wartime musical was *Robinson Crusoe, Jr.*, a homemade Jolson show with Romberg, under orders, disguising his Austro-Hungarian musical accent. J. J. had a modest success with *Her Soldier Boy* (December 6, 1916), a Viennese operetta with a score by Emmerich Kalman, with added songs by Romberg, but the producer's wariness can be gauged by the way he tampered with a show called *My Lady's Glove* by Oscar Straus. Anticipating anti-German sentiments in his audiences, J. J. ordered the show's locale changed to France; and to soften growing resistance to European operetta, he introduced a gimmick in which chorus girls handed out pieces of chocolate to the crowd. The show closed after only sixteen performances anyway.

Romberg had to wait two years after *Blue Paradise* to make his Broadway debut as a full-fledged operetta composer. But the show, *Maytime*, which opened on August 16, 1917, might never have happened if the composer hadn't threatened to break his contract. Except for his songs for *Blue Paradise*, Romberg's contributions to J. J.'s shows had been either critically ignored or scorned for being derivative, tinkly, and anonymous—Alexander Woollcott wrote that Romberg "knows a good tune when he hears one."[58] The composer had been branded a Shubert lackey, a Broadway hack who wrote to the boss's specifications. Yet both J. J. and his employee knew that writing background music for production numbers was not the measure of Romberg's talent, and Romberg finally demanded an opportunity. Sensing that this time Romberg's threats were not idle and that audiences might be in the mood for a romantic operetta whose Viennese origins were concealed, J. J. gave in. He instructed a staff writer, Rida Johnson Young, who was almost as hardworked as Romberg, to Americanize the settings and characters of a Viennese play he had bought before the war.

Mrs. Young's libretto mined the bittersweet vein of lost romance—the pattern set by *Blue Paradise*—that became Romberg's and the Shuberts' special niche. In four acts, which span the years from 1840 to the turn of the century, *Maytime* chronicles a romance that did not take place between a young woman with money and a young man without it. Banished by parental decree at the end of act 1, the young man goes off to South Africa to seek his fortune. A generation later, his former love is desperately unhappy, married to a man of her own class who is a gambler, while the spurned, adventurous hero has become a millionaire. In their final meeting, thirty years after the perfect springtime of their youth celebrated in act 1, the rich old man rescues his childhood sweetheart from poverty. In the last act, their romance is "consummated" vicariously through their grandchildren, who fall in love and marry.

An ideal platform for Romberg's brand of Austro-Hungarian schmaltz, *Maytime* gave him a place in a still-new American musical tradition that included the works of Reginald De Koven, John Philip Sousa, Victor Herbert, and Rudolf Friml. His succulent score, which includes "Will You Remember?" a ballad that has become an operetta standard, teems with waltzes and lullabies, a Gypsy song, a mazurka, a ragtime number, a Spanish dance, and a "coon" dance called "Jump Jim Crow." The musical variety, the spectacular dance and production numbers, and the nightclub setting for act 2 underscore the fact that, despite its Viennese accent, *Maytime* was American operetta edging toward American musical comedy. Still worried about anti-German reaction, J. J. insisted that *Maytime* emerge from the Shubert factory as a Broadway show rather than as a foreign light opera. Romberg wrote separable musical numbers judged solely by their tunefulness, and the only musical repetition he used was reprising "Will You Remember?" at three climactic moments.

Overproduced and impure in its genre, *Maytime* nonetheless did exactly what J. J. wanted it to: it appealed to audiences during wartime. The story of a romantic bond that endures across generations proved comforting to soldiers about to be shipped overseas and separated from their fiancées or wives. J. J.'s marriage of cleverly disguised Viennese operetta and Winter Garden revue was so great a success, in fact, that a second company opened across the street from the original—a Broadway first.

Even after Romberg's first major success, J. J. continued to punish his staff composer with piecework assignments for *The Passing Show* and Jolson extravaganzas, and it wasn't until four years later that he allowed his employee another chance at a full operetta score. Yet despite the overwork, the frustration, and the ingratitude, Romberg alone among the top Broadway composers remained with the Shuberts. Why? If Jolson lasted with the Shuberts because he was as hardened as they were, Romberg continued for exactly the opposite reason: he was an easygoing, warmhearted man with a zest for working hard. And for all their clashes, he and J. J. were united in their love of operettas set in Ruritanian never-never lands. "Romberg was very nice to work with, and he loved working, as if he couldn't get enough of it," Irving Caesar said.

> He loved to eat too, and he'd say to me in his thick accent, "Now, Caesar! We will have a big, good lunch and then we write some songs." Tunes came easily to him, the way words come easily to me. I've been rhyming since I was a child at the Settlement House on the Lower East Side. Jews are natural rhymers. Romberg, who was also Jewish, played the piano well; he had the tune, and then I added the lyrics. He was easy to write for, because if there was a word for every note he'd say that it was all right, it fits.[59]

After four years of calm, the third and final theatrical war erupted in December 1917. If the United States entered the World War to fight the German aggressors, the Shuberts were clearly the aggressors in this small war. According to Klaw and Erlanger, the Shuberts violated the terms of the 1913 agreement by booking first-class attractions into the Chestnut Street Opera House in Philadelphia (the agreement had limited first-class productions to the Forrest, Garrick, Adelphi, and Lyric Theatres) and by announcing their intention to build a Shubert Theatre in that city. In other offensive actions clearly designed to break the 1913 pooling agreement, the Shuberts also took over the Wilbur and Plymouth Theatres in Boston and the Studebaker Theatre in Chicago. Within a few days, the pooling arrangement between the two trusts was also severed in St. Louis and Baltimore. Lee Shubert broke the peace because he knew he could win a new war. This last war sputtered to a final, decisive victory for the Shuberts late in 1921, when "unfavorable conditions throughout the country induced the enemies to bury the hatchet."[60] Both sides suffered from the widespread slump in business that affected the national economy from 1920 to 1922. The 1921 season was a calamity for both Broadway shows and those on the road; and outside of New York City, only movie and vaudeville houses were showing any profits. The peace treaty consisted of a booking arrangement covering all the theatres in the country outside New York, with Shubert plays booked into Erlanger houses when convenient, and vice versa.

At the end of 1921, when for the last time Erlanger smoked a peace pipe with Lee Shubert, the original Syndicate had shrunk to the Abraham Erlanger Amusement Enterprises, Inc. Charles Frohman had died on the *Lusitania* in 1915; Sam Nixon and Fred Zimmerman had dissolved their partnership in 1913 and, like Al Hayman, were retired; and in 1919 Marc Klaw had split acrimoniously from Erlanger. They dissolved their booking partnership and Erlanger gradually assumed Klaw's interests. Between 1920 and 1922, the litigious pair filed a battery of suits and countersuits against each other. The initial break had been precipitated when Erlanger in a tantrum had fired Klaw's son (Joe), but wounds had been festering for years. After having spent his professional life working damage control in the wake of Erlanger's explosions, Klaw at last broke his silence and accused his erstwhile colleague of a number of financial double crosses: acquiring an interest behind his back in George C. Tyler's production of *Clarence*, a big hit; colluding with Ziegfeld in cheating him of his share of the profits of the *Ziegfeld Follies* and the *Midnight Frolics*; claiming interest credits on excess profits of over $216,000 to which Klaw said he never consented.

When Erlanger died on March 7, 1930, he left nearly $3.1 million in debts, after having amassed an estate of over $75 million in his prime.[61] And as always in the Shuberts' dealings with this titan with the bulldog face, they snatched the last laugh. In 1932 they purchased the Erlanger Theatre on West Forty-fourth Street, which the mogul had erected as a monument to himself; and in a gesture of friendship to England (and a gesture of animosity toward their ancient sparring partner), they renamed it the St. James, as it is still known.

"All forms of sons of bitches they referred to him as," John Shubert recalled as the way his father and uncle talked about Erlanger. He was "their prime hate." But John remembered as well that his elders also "respected" the man who had fought so long and so vigorously to keep them out of show business. When (according to John) Lee commented that he would "miss" Erlanger, he was doubtless sincere. "Erlanger was a mean, cruel, vicious, dangerous man," but then, according to many people, so were the Shuberts, and if, as John said, his father and uncle condemned Erlanger "with an air of respect and even a little admiration," it was the respect they had for their own warfaring ways. The Shuberts and Erlanger were alike in regarding theatre as a form of jungle combat; and for warriors who maintained a keen taste for a fight, an adversary as cunning and as durable as Erlanger would indeed be "missed."

> They admired the fact that Erlanger didn't have weaknesses. He only had a weakness for a girl. They never referred to him kindly, but they never really laughed about him either, even after he was virtually dead in the business and we had subsequently combined with his nephew, a man named Bergman. In fact, I still [1960] get along with Mrs. Erlanger. She's the head of the Red Cross in my particular area, and I see that we do our collections through her.[62]

5

The Long-Distance Runners

O nce they finally knocked out the Syndicate, the Shuberts devoted the rest of their careers to protecting their great power. They were reluctant to divide the spoils with anyone else, including family, and they never properly trained a successor. Garson Kanin recalled being with his wife, Ruth Gordon, in Shubert Alley sometime in the 1950s and running into Lee. "When Ruth and I saw Lee leaving the Shubert office well after eleven, Ruthie asked, 'Why do you need to work so late, Mr. Lee? After all these years, don't you have enough?' Lee gave Ruthie and me a long, wistful look, then said, 'How much is enough?' "[1]

It's the question Lee and his brother spent their lives trying to answer. In the process, they became theatrical overlords on a scale that will surely never be matched. In 1921, when they claimed a final, decisive victory over the Theatrical Syndicate, they were at the height of their power just as the American theatre itself was beginning a period of unprecedented vitality. As Europe recovered from the Great War, the American economy (despite a temporary dip in the early 1920s) prospered; and as the nation's most active and firmly entrenched theatrical producers, the Shuberts were ideally placed to make a killing. Lee and J. J. were twin colossi who rode the rails to an empire estimated in 1929 to be worth well over four hundred million dollars.

"In their prime Lee and J. J. had total power," Agnes de Mille said, wincing.[2] "People were scared shitless of both of them," said Dorothy Terolow Reissman, who worked for them in the forties when they were past their prime.[3] To ensure their "total power," or at least to maintain the illusion of having it, they developed a tough-guy image that clings to the Shubert name to this day. "The Shuberts became a nasty household word only because we never took anything lying down," John said. "We always had a law firm at our elbow, and nobody ever started anything, or did anything, which we weren't prompt to jump upon and sue immediately. We have actually sued more people than have sued us."[4]

"The Shuberts sue"; this was their primary weapon, the threat that in any dealings with the firm hung in the air like the sword of Damocles. The Shuberts sued not only as a response to a supposed grievance but as a matter of policy: they sued quite cold-bloodedly. "Suing was part of the success formula," John continued. "My father and uncle sued if they felt they had the slightest color of interest that might be violated. Suing was part of how they kept hold of the power they had won in their fight with the Syndicate." "If you dared to sue them, they'd come back at you with ten, twelve, twenty lawyers, and because of their 'understanding' with many judges, they'd almost always win," said a former associate, speaking anonymously. "That's why people were afraid of them, and that's why many people—grown men, powerful in their own right—quake at the mention of their name still."[5]

"I would say conservatively that I could always remember at least five important lawsuits every year," John said.

> Suits to do with running a place of public assembly—someone has tripped down the stairs, a woman has had a miscarriage in one of your theatres—and suits over real estate closings. Big lawsuits—I would say there would be one every eighteen months, on which an awful lot of money would be riding. Our lawsuits were often against music publishers. We sued every music publisher in one form or another who tried to copyright the songs of our shows in their own names and then tried to pick up renewals in their own names. We sued authors all the time. We sued the Dramatists Guild, to find out whether or not all the provisions of its contracts could be enforced under the existing laws; we wanted to find out what type of organization it really was. We sued actors. So many actors used to jump our contracts and go to Hollywood, and I don't blame them. They had better offers. We didn't break contracts—we were too smart for that; actors broke contracts with us. Mr. Lee was always willing to settle quick; my father, though, as a matter of principle, sometimes wouldn't settle at any price; he'd battle it right through to the finish. Our batting average was very high.[6]

Inevitably, Shubert lawyers have been a continuous presence in the Shubert saga. Like the godfather's consiglieri, they were always there, hovering in the background, occupying an unobtrusive but significant part of the negative space surrounding the central figures of Lee and J. J. "Years before it was general custom, they believed it was important and necessary to keep a lawyer at your elbow," John said. "The lawyer was our own lawyer, and it was almost a captive law firm quite like we have today. The lawyer loved being the Shuberts' attorney, and he would bring a suit at the drop of a hat on anything."[7]

The lawyer most frequently and for the longest period at the Shuberts' elbow—and probably the chief supporting player in Shubert history—was William Klein (hired by Sam in 1900 and with him in his fatal train accident in 1905). Klein remained the Shuberts' indispensable chief counsel, lawsuits at the ready, for forty-five years. Whenever the Shuberts were under fire, it was Klein who wrote and even sometimes delivered house policy. Working for the theatre's long-running sovereigns, Klein had the distinction of becoming the chief architect of much of American theatrical law.

William Klein was "a tall, craggy-faced, rather homely man," recalled Miriam Krengel Pulvers, who worked in his office for seven years in the thirties. "He would look in the mirror and exclaim to others in the room, 'What an ugly b . . . I am,' and then laugh. He had very little hair left and quite a long nose. He liked to think he had a good sense of humor, and was quick on the repartee. He had many friends, including Judge Samuel Rosenman (who wrote Franklin Delano Roosevelt's speeches), Surrogate Delehanty, and Judge [Joseph] Crater."[8]

Dorothy Derman, who worked in the Shubert legal department as a stenographer in the late thirties and early forties, remembered that "if you got in Klein's way he tore you to pieces. He was very tough. He always dressed beautifully; he was certainly no Prince Charming, but sartorially he was splendid, whereas J. J. dressed like a slob at all times. Klein always sparkled, and he walked with an important gait. He had a brother, Jacob, who worked in the office, but William was the brains."[9]

Lee Shubert spent more time over the years with William Klein than with anyone else. The two played gin rummy together, traveled to Miami together, and as men-about-town entertained chorus girls together. Mrs. Pulvers recalled that Klein had a closet full of perfumes in his office. "When the showgirls came to visit him (he was a bachelor of course!), they would leave with gifts. Although it could not be proven, we all thought he would give them cash, especially if they were hard up."[10]

To outsiders Lee and his lawyer seemed to be the best of friends, but John Shubert felt otherwise.

I don't think Klein ever really liked Lee too much. They were inseparable— Lee needed Klein, he absolutely depended on him—but he also made practical jokes that were cruel. Lee always kidded Klein about his looks, and Klein naturally resented it. My father did the same thing. Sam was the one Klein had great affection for. I think Klein was the fellow on whom Lee took out everything he had wanted to say to other people earlier in the day and felt he couldn't. Lee was always very, very careful in his business deals with people, very circumspect; he'd never get familiar, he would never say anything sarcastic. He might say it later on, but never to their face. So he took it all out on Klein, and Klein, like Pollyanna or Happy Hooligan, kept sticking out his head to get hit every night at dinner. Lee would always accuse Klein of being cheap and taking him to cheap restaurants, or kid him that he was homely, and that that's why he had ended up with such a homely-looking girl the night before. He would always accuse Klein of cheating when they played gin rummy. It was agony to be with them and to hear this constant ribbing— maybe Klein was fascinated by Lee's personality, but Lee certainly kept pouring it on and Klein kept taking it.[11]

The other long-running guardian at the Shuberts' gate was their press agent, Claude Greneker. While Klein and the other lawyers helped build the Shuberts' image as titans one dared not cross, Greneker and his staff tried to counteract their bosses' reputations as litigious lethal weapons. But the press department was more successful in selling Shubert shows than in creating affable show-business personae for the Shuberts themselves.

"Grennie [Claude Greneker] was a courtly Southern gentleman, the antithesis of what you'd think of as a press agent," said Sol Jacobson, who worked for Greneker in the late thirties. "He was well-read and cultivated."[12] Henry Senker, who also worked for Greneker, agreed. "He was a secretary of state type—very dignified, very reserved, very conservative, and very icy."[13] Greneker had started with the Shuberts in 1911, when J. J. placed him in charge of publicity for the new Winter Garden Theatre. His first assignment was to conduct an extensive publicity campaign for French import Gaby Deslys, about whom he wrote stories of her jewels and her love affair with the king of Portugal. In 1919 Greneker replaced the notorious A. Toxen Worm as the head of the Shuberts' press department. Unlike Worm, Greneker was a diplomat whose policy, according to John, was "to keep all the critics and theatre columnists in good spirits."[14]

"He was an ideal company man," Sol Jacobson remembered.

His interest was in the empire: "What does Mr. Lee want?" He never really revealed what he thought of the Shuberts—he was too discreet. He was not a mere employee, but really an adviser. He was an executive, not a working stiff. He was given full powers over the press department, so much so that we almost never saw the Shuberts—it was Grennie we worked for. He read scripts;

he went to auditions; the Shuberts would buy into other people's shows on his say-so. And he looked after their properties as well as their plays.

In addition, he often served as a buffer between the warring brothers. "He would have two phones on his head," as Jacobson recalled. " 'Yes, Mr. Lee,' he'd say into one. 'Yes, Mr. J. J.,' he'd say into the other."[15] Abner Klipstein, however, told me that Greneker was "Mr. Lee's man. He was really a confidant of Mr. Lee, and disliked by Mr. J. J."[16]

Tall, stately, well-spoken, and nonethnic, Greneker presented a facade of class the Shuberts lacked, and he was often their official spokesman. Despite their prominence, Lee and J. J. never overcame a reputation as yahoos who had much more money than taste; both brothers were extremely uneasy public speakers, and they preferred to have Greneker or Klein meet the press in their place. Like Samuel Goldwyn, the Shuberts became famous for misspeaking. "It's Omar of Khayyáam," Lee is said to have corrected an actor during a rehearsal. When informed that the actor had in fact spoken the name properly, Lee improvised, "Take out the 'of'— the act is running a little long." Interrupting a rehearsal of a new play by Augustus Thomas, Lee turned to the playwright and said, "There, right there is the place I want you to insert a witty line." After a pregnant pause, Thomas turned to his producer and asked, "For instance, Mr. Shubert?" "There's only going to be one captain on this ship, the director . . . and me," J. J. is alleged to have announced to the large company of a Winter Garden revue. "Softly, play on only one string," J. J. admonished the violin section during a rehearsal when he thought they were too loud.[17] After Jay Gorney's song "Brother, Can You Spare a Dime?" became a hit in a Shubert revue, J. J. asked the composer to write more songs. "Only this time, not so sorbid."[18]

That these stories and many others in the same vein gained currency indicates that people derived pleasure and comfort from ridiculing the Shuberts. Lee and J. J. were uncultivated men who had achieved awesome power, and attacking them in an area where they were vulnerable may have helped defuse the widespread resentment their hardball tactics aroused. Mocking the Shuberts as lack-wits who spoke a mongrel brand of English may have been an attempt on the part of the have-nots and also-rans to even the score against the longtime champions. Whether or not the Shuberts actually said the dumb things they were accused of, a lot of people in the theatre clearly wanted to believe that they did.

Like the bosses for whom he often spoke, Claude Greneker put in full days, from early each morning often until after frequent midnight conferences in Lee's office. Abner Klipstein recalled that one of his jobs was to gather all the morning newspapers on the days after a Shubert show had opened and to leave them outside Greneker's door at 25 Central Park West. Greneker would "digest the reviews, and then send his analysis to both Mr. Lee and Mr. J. J." Greneker became such an astute judge of the critics that he could predict "with uncanny accuracy" how each one would be likely to react to a new Shubert offering.[19]

"Greneker was so good at his job that the Shuberts could be removed," recalled Viola Seff Goldberg, whose husband, Manny Seff, worked for Greneker in the thirties. "However, Greneker had a crazy wife, whom I got to know very well. Lillian had ideas, a lot of them, but they didn't have much to do with each other. She was a sculptress; she had an invention for 3-D scenery made of papier mâché; she believed in saints and had a friend studying to be a saint; and later she went into the manikin business."[20]

The Shubert brothers were different in almost every respect except in their absolute dedication to their business. In a literal as well as a figurative sense, they lived over the store, putting in heroic hours for more than half a century. Midas in his cubicle, Lee had a nightly ritual of poring over the receipts for every Shubert theatre on Broadway and for the road shows (Broadway grosses were phoned in; road grosses were telegraphed). Most nights as well he held midnight conferences with his top aides. Even in his final years, he regularly worked sixteen hours a day, and then with a vigorous stride, which seemed "impossibly fast for one of his age and size,"[21] he took late-night or early-morning walks that could last until 4:00 A.M.

"My father and uncle came to the office every Sunday of their lives," John said,

> except in the summer when, in earlier days they'd meet up in the country to talk and work. Saturday we always had a full day's work here—until we stopped producing, when we cut down to a half day. But from force of habit my father still kept coming down, and Mr. Lee always came to the office on Sundays, even after the producing days were over. In fact, just before he died, he always made sure of hitting the office on Sundays, when he would schedule appointments to meet producers, talk about terms, future plans, new shows. Their business was their entertainment, and it kept them constantly interested. For both of them, their office was really their home.[22]

Despite the vast size and complexity of their business, and despite the lawyers and factotums like Klein and Greneker who were crucial to its operation, Lee and J. J. to the ends of their lives made certain that they and they alone remained in ultimate charge of all Shubert enterprises. Sharing the responsibilities and the profits, the brothers between them ran the Shubert shop. "The Shubert Organization consisted of Lee and J. J.," John said. "They were the two men at the top of a rather peculiar pyramid. The executives underneath them—even the top fellows like Klein and Greneker—were actually minus or blank. There were no executives that really helped them, because nobody except them ever really had any authority. Or if they did, after a while they were out."[23] Klein and Greneker lasted as long as they did precisely because they played according to house rules, confining their power base to their own particular departments while always deferring to the two men at the top. Except for Lee and J. J., everybody else—including their two nephews, Milton Shubert and Lawrence Shubert Lawrence, Sr., who worked for them for decades, and John Shubert as well—was an employee without tenure.

In the twenties, as in the teens, when the Shuberts were in full stride as the sovereigns of the commercial theatre, Lee evidently could not resist any deal that might broaden his base in the entertainment business. When the temporarily weakened economy in 1920 caused vacancies in a number of Shubert playhouses, Lee in association with some of his partners at Goldwyn Pictures once again attempted to invade vaudeville. (Counting his brief 1913 assault in defiance of the agreement he, Erlanger, and Albee had signed, this was actually Lee's third try to break the vaudeville monopoly.) Lee denied rumors in the spring of 1920 that the omnivorous Shuberts were preparing a new plan to form a vaudeville circuit. "The rumors are rubbish," E. F. Albee was quoted as saying in the *New York Times* on May 11, 1920. "We have no intention of entering each other's fields."

On January 25, 1921, Lee announced that Shubert Advanced Vaudeville would be launched at the beginning of the fall season. Incorporated for twenty million dollars and covering more than twenty cities, Shubert Advanced Vaudeville was designed to end Lee's losing streak. Although J. J. had far more feeling than Lee for vaudeville as an entertainment form, J. J. refused to have anything to do with his brother's recurrent efforts to puncture Albee's fortress. He figured it was a lost cause; and for once, J. J. had greater common sense than Lee on a business matter.[24]

Because vaudevillians were prized for their split-second timing and their complete command of the stage for the few minutes they were on, Shubert talent scouts had been raiding vaudeville circuits for years to sign up performers for the Shubert revues at the Winter Garden. ("Shubert Winter Garden vaudeville—8 acts of the world's finest," is the way a Shubert vaudeville show was advertised for a 1921 tour.) By 1921 the Shuberts had a corps of first-rate vaudevillians under contract—Lew Fields was still their star—and they certainly had access to plenty of first-class theatres. But once again, Lee could not defeat the still-mighty machine Albee commanded from his office above the Palace Theatre. When the vaudeville shows for the Fox and Stanley theatre chains (which were to have become part of the Shubert enterprise) pulled out, Lee discovered he did not have enough acts to fill his circuit, and he had to add films to provide a full evening's entertainment. The policy alarmed Lee's partners from Goldwyn Pictures.

Caught between motion picture interests and the Albee octopus, Shubert Advanced Vaudeville teetered. Lee, however, bristled at rumors that he would soon be selling his vaudeville interests. "The report is nonsense," he snapped to a *New York Times* reporter on February 5, 1922. "We are adding to our circuit all the time, and by this time next year we hope to have about thirty-five theatres in as many cities." But "by this time next year," Shubert Advanced Vaudeville had disappeared.

As he was preparing his vaudeville campaign early in 1921, Lee was also a principal in the continuing power plays that erupted between producers and the new actors' union. On January 12, 1921, charging them with repeated violations of the September 6, 1919, basic agreement, Equity requested that the Producing Managers' Association drop the Shuberts. Reacting to Shubert abuses, Equity leaders began the fight for a closed shop, which would ensure that in any company in which there is an Equity member all members of the company must be Equity members in good standing. "One of the chief reasons why the Equity shop is a necessity is that since the combination of the Shubert and Erlanger interests there is no longer any competition in this country in the booking of theatres," Equity President John Emerson said. "The booking of theatres in this country is a practical monopoly, to all intents and purposes controlled by one man, and that man is Mr. Lee Shubert."[25]

Equity's demand for a closed shop precipitated another standoff between actors and the PMA, but this time Lee made certain he would not be bruised in the cross fire. In September 1923, he approached Emerson, saying that he was willing to concede an Equity shop so as to avoid another strike. A revival of ill will between the Shuberts and the diminished but still-contentious Erlanger faction within the PMA, however, forestalled an early settlement: if Lee Shubert was in favor of a closed shop, Erlanger and his minions were determined to be against it. At his final appearance at the PMA, Lee tried to persuade the other managers that "a fight with Equity would be the mistake of their lives—that in Equity there was unity, while in the PMA it was every man for himself."[26] When Erlanger wouldn't budge, as Lee suspected he wouldn't, Lee called a meeting in his office the next day, April 30, 1924, to form the Managers' Protective Association. The new group elected Arthur Hammerstein president (though Lee was running the show) and proceeded to negotiate a contract with Equity.

In an ironic flip-flop, dictated entirely by self-interest, Lee Shubert was now an Equity ally arrayed with actors against the intransigence of the Erlanger-dominated PMA. In exchange for a victory without a fight, Equity backed off, for a time, from its demand for a 100 percent Equity shop: not less than 80 percent of all casts should be composed of Equity members, and none of the other 20 percent should be members dropped or expelled from Equity. Stubborn to the end, Erlanger and the remaining PMA members refused to accept the closed-shop provisions; and so, when the basic agreement expired on June 1, 1924, a strike began. Only seven productions were affected. The strike limped along for seven or eight weeks, but the fight was really over by July 6. On October 20, the PMA along with its company union, the Actors' Fidelity League, expired once and for all.

Lee had skillfully managed to convert another defeat for producers into the appearance of a personal victory. He had not only outwitted Erlanger one last time and won credit for adopting an uncharacteristic prounion stance, he had also proven he was the kind of fellow who changed direction rather than stepped on the gas when he saw a brick wall up ahead.

For a brief period after the 1924 agreement with Equity, the Shuberts moderated their traditional antiunion fervor, but it revived when with mounting dread they watched dramatists begin to mobilize into a coalition. In 1917 when a group of playwrights had presented a standard dramatic form contract to managers, Lee Shubert had said he would sooner close his theatres than sign. "Managers will treat with authors individually and in no other way," he stated, adding that it was simply "good business for a manager to get the best and most he could." [27] Encouraged by Equity's victories, playwrights continued to agitate for a minimum basic agreement contract. They charged the Shuberts with a variety of abuses: variable royalties, late payments, and arbitrary script changes without consultation, as well as placing a stable of writers on a house salary with no royalty interest and holding manuscripts indefinitely. On April 27, 1926, after five months of concentrated effort, during which all scripts were withheld from the market, the first five-year Minimum Basic Agreement was approved. The Shuberts were the only managers who refused to sign; a year later, they relented.

From 1905 to 1930, when Lee was most active as a producer, theatre was a bustling business. Shows didn't need to run more than a few months in New York to return a profit, and even a New York flop could be advertised on the road as "direct from Broadway" and become a hit. Lee presided over a theatre of quantity in which plays and musicals were frankly regarded as merchandise. In effect, Lee operated like a movie mogul of the studio era, supervising an entertainment factory as he supplied a steady stream of products to his own theatres. Imitation and repetition were built into the system, and most of what was produced was routine. But the system—the Shuberts' as well as Hollywood's—did not inevitably stifle or expel the truly talented.

The decade of the twenties was the Golden Age of the American theatre, a time when artistic experiment and writers of genuine literary distinction invigorated Broadway. Led by the towering example of Eugene O'Neill, a group of American playwrights were bringing American drama into the modern age. While no other writer of the period was as ambitious as O'Neill, either stylistically or thematically, many strong voices were heard for the first time. Sidney Howard, S. N. Behrman, Philip Barry, George Kelly, Robert Sherwood, Paul Green, Maxwell Anderson, George S. Kaufman, Elmer Rice, Marc Connelly, George Abbott, and John Howard Lawson, among others, wrote fresh, challenging plays on American subjects. However, Lee Shubert's productions of original American works that reflected the postwar spirit—works fashioned in the shadow of O'Neill, as it were—were startlingly few, as he continued to present his usual quota of presold properties consisting of West End farces and melodramas, revivals of hits from the past, and adaptations of best-selling novels.

The Detour (August 23, 1921) was Lee's major bid in the twenties as a producer of serious literary drama. Before this play, its author, Owen Davis, had written more than one hundred fifty Bowery melodramas cut to the same crude formula. "The old melodramas were practically motion pictures," Davis writes in his memoirs.

> One of the first tricks I learned was that my plays must be written for an audience who, owing to the huge, uncarpeted, noisy theatres, couldn't always hear the words and who, a large percentage of them having only recently landed in America, couldn't have understood them in any case. I therefore wrote for the eye rather than the ear and played out each emotion in action, depending on dialogue only for the noble sentiments so dear to audiences of that class.[28]

In *The Detour*, language counts at least as much as the stage pictures Davis had had such vast experience devising. Written in the style of the "new" realism introduced by O'Neill in his 1920 drama *Beyond the Horizon* (this time it is the heroine rather than the hero who is an idealist and potential artist drained by a squalid existence on a farm), *The Detour* may be ersatz O'Neill but it is an honorable play nonetheless. "One regrets one's sneers at Mr. Davis' previous tawdry ineptitudes," reported the *Evening Post* on August 24. "No matter how bad Mr. Davis has been heretofore his performance last night condones his past. And it should be noted as well that the Shuberts have taken a real step forward as serious producers."

Despite the praise, *The Detour* ran for only forty-eight performances. And, typically, Lee lost his author, who decamped to rival producer Sam Harris for his next serious play, *Icebound*, another gloomy study of a rural family. To Lee's dismay, the show had a respectable 170-performance run and won the Pulitzer Prize for 1922–1923. Though Davis returned to Lee for two more tries to establish himself as an important playwright of the American rural scene, both were unsuccessful.

While it too had a brief and unprofitable run, Lee was able to claim the credit for producing (on his own) the first play by a major American writer. Ben Hecht's 1923 play *The Egoist* (December 25, 1925) is about a playwright with words on the brain who seduces women with talk and then retreats when it's time to pounce. For all the neo-Shavian sparkle of much of its dialogue and the scintillating performance of the Viennese actor Leo Dietrichstein, then under contract to Lee, *The Egoist* lasted only forty-nine performances—a crucial defeat for Lee in his on-again, off-again attempt to become a producer of stature. Hecht took his next play, coauthored with fellow journalist Charles MacArthur, to producer Jed Harris, at the time a Shubert foe, and the result was *The Front Page*, a crackling fable about the newspaper game and an endlessly revivable popular and critical success of the kind Lee was never to have.

"Lee helped us out with money on *Coquette* [1927], even though it wasn't his kind of show," George Abbott remembered. "It was a romantic tragedy, not his field, but I was grateful for his assistance and I respected his judgment. He did produce *The Fall Guy* [March 10, 1925, a comedy-cum-melodrama Abbott had cowritten with James Gleason about a clerk who becomes the patsy for bootlegging heroin dealers], which was much more in his line." Set entirely in a drab apartment, the minor play was an authentic example of American verismo in which the characters speak in a racy vernacular twang. *The Fall Guy* was a hit, but Lee lost Abbott, who became his own producer and later joined up with other producers.[29]

In 1924 Lee, without credit, assisted Ray Comstock and Morris Gest in presenting Max Reinhardt's production of *The Miracle*, a major theatrical event of the twenties. "Lee knew about how much Reinhardt was respected in Vienna and Berlin, and that he did very, very good artistic things on a repertory company basis," John said. "Over here with *The Miracle* Reinhardt threw money right and left recklessly. He was very unbusinesslike. Oh, I don't know, we felt that really he was a phony; we always felt he was like Mr. Belasco, a big fake."[30]

Lee was equally scornful of the Theatre Guild, the preeminent producing organization of the post–World War I decade. Organized in 1919 by Lawrence Langner, the Theatre Guild was America's first successful art theatre, a group that in many ways took up the agenda defined by Lee and his associates at the New Theatre ten years earlier. Throughout the twenties and thirties, the Guild produced distinguished, mostly Continental plays unlikely to have received regular commercial runs. To Lee Shubert, however, the Theatre Guild was "a longhaired bunch of jerks, dangerous, and dishonest to a certain degree. Lee didn't like Lawrence Langner," John said.

> I guess it was his English accent—Lee always thought he was a phony-baloney. We thought they were damn fools for stopping the selling of their subscriptions. When they got to some 30,000 people, they stopped it in New York. Toward the tail end of the Depression, the Guild lost everything, including their theatre; it was only at that point that they became very pro-Shubert. We bailed them out, and the Guild was loyal to us only because they threw in their lot with us.[31]

If Lee disdained Reinhardt and the Theatre Guild as "longhairs" who valued art over money, he nonetheless had notions of his own about "serious" theatre. And in the twenties, as he had periodically since 1905, he strayed from his usual turf as a maestro of boulevard confections to present oddities that often came wrapped in a religious or supernatural aura. J. J. scorned these curios—plays like *Peter Ibbetson* (1917), in which two lovers meet only in their dreams because the hero is in jail—and dismissed them as "Lee's folly."[32] But to Lee, the unconventional productions that cropped up throughout his career were evidence that he had a sensitive side, that when a play touched him he could be an art-theatre enthusiast like Lawrence Langner, and that his name was not, as his detractors claimed, Lee Shylock.

Of all his supernatural dramas, *Death Takes a Holiday* (December 26, 1929) was the one he was most proud of. This was another Shubert translation, with hired hand Walter Ferriss working from the Italian original by Alberto Casella. A parable in which Death disguised as a prince resides in the castle of an Italian count to learn why mortals fear him, the play was received either as a shimmering poetic fantasy or as an airy pseudophilosophical bore. *Death Takes a Holiday* was Lee's idea of the perfect marriage between commerce and art, and he kept it running until it found an audience. (He revived it during the Depression doldrums of 1931 only to discover that its day had already passed. Paramount bought the rights and turned it into a Hollywood art picture in 1934.)

In the same period in which he nurtured *Death Takes a Holiday* into a hit, Lee presented Ethel Barrymore whom, as John said, "he was just crazy about," in a play that seemed like a Theatre Guild reject. Another Lee Shubert import, translated from the Spanish of Gregorio Martínez Sierra by Helen and Harley Granville-Barker (Lee did not Americanize this one), *The Kingdom of God* inaugurated the Shubert-built Barrymore Theatre on December 29, 1928, named for the actress. When Lee was soft on an actress, as he had been on the equally strong-willed Alla Nazimova, he more or less allowed her to do as she pleased. For the regal

"Miss B," he even participated in the kind of public relations pageantry both he and J. J. avoided as often as possible. To dedicate her theatre (though, in fact, the new playhouse belonged to her in name only), Lee presented Ethel Barrymore with a lifetime key to the star dressing room. A distinct look of discomfort underlay Lee's usual deadpan as photographers gathered to snap pictures of this nonevent.

The Kingdom of God was a tour de force for the autocratic star, who directed herself (under the name E. M. Blyth) in the kind of adore-me role that was her stock-in-trade. As a sister of God devoted to the poor, she aged from nineteen in act 1 to twenty-nine in act 2 to a lame seventy in act 3. Barrymore performed in the hushed, tremulous tone she affected to indicate quality, and as usual surrounded herself with an inferior company. In April, Lee presented Barrymore in a play of her own choosing called The Love Duel, a sophisticated drawing-room comedy of the sort her fans expected. (This time Barrymore played opposite a superb actor, Louis Calhern). After the Broadway runs, Barrymore took both shows on the road for a lucrative eighty-week tour.

The star's hold over Lee—her ability to cloud his own judgment—was apparent in the next show she convinced him to produce at "her" theatre. In Scarlet Sister Mary (November 25, 1930), Barrymore and the entire company of white actors appeared in blackface. Playing a lusty woman over a twenty-year period, from her tardy wedding to the day her first child dies in her arms, Barrymore maintained her unwaveringly genteel demeanor. As Margot Peters, Barrymore's biographer, writes, "Some small still voice should have warned Ethel not to attempt blackface or a [Gullah] dialect." The show expired after thirty-four performances, yet Barrymore's influence on Lee was so great that she convinced him to send her on tour where, as Peters notes "the reaction was the same: 'Why did Miss Barrymore do it?' "[33]

If Lee missed out on the theatrical highlights of the Roaring Twenties, and if his own limitations prevented him from nurturing the careers of significant new writers, he nonetheless made it possible for theatregoers to see many plays. A number of them succeeded in their modest goal of providing a decent evening's entertainment. (Given the intimidating economics of present-day Broadway, there are, alas, no Lee Shuberts at work—no producers, that is, who can afford to put on play after play, season after season.) Neither in the twenties nor at any other time in his career did Lee achieve a distinct profile as a producer, however. Although he coveted the prestige of being a commercial producer with taste, his focus was on the financial and practical aspects of running his empire.

For J. J., however, producing continued to be his primary activity. By the twenties, his musical theatre factory for operettas, as well as revues, was firmly in place. His Winter Garden programs gave the Messrs. Shubert an identity that none of Lee's straight plays ever did; and under J. J.'s watch, the Winter Garden became a synonym for a particular kind of bright, racy, musical smorgasbord: a Shubert kind of show presented in a Shubert kind of showplace.

For all the non-Jolson Winter Garden shows, J. J. provided the same basic blend: burlesques of popular plays, which were a staple of an older style that stayed in the Shubert lineup longer than in any other producers' revues; comic sketches, usually with an ethnic flavor, another throwback to an earlier tradition; production numbers on the runway, featuring chorus girls in partial undress; scenic grandeur and multiple changes of scenic backdrops; dance specialties that reflected current fads and attempted to start new ones; and songs, which for the most part were not noted for originality, usually composed by a consortium of often uncredited Shubert employees. Critics quickly spotted J. J.'s formulaic approach. Reviewing *The Show of Wonders* in December 1916, the *Theatre* complained that "for the twentieth time the Shuberts have changed the show, or at least the title, at the Winter Garden. You would scarcely realize that anything is new, however." But the Shuberts were hardly the first or the last purveyors of popular entertainment to rely on minor permutations of a successful model; and in catering to an audience of Winter Garden regulars, J. J. managed to keep his revue showshop in operation for almost two decades—a nice run.

To fill his theatre's stage with revues year after year, J. J. in effect ran a theatrical sweatshop. He had his own in-house team, many of whom toiled on the operettas, as well as the revues. Employees worked under five-year contracts that were to become the model for the seven-year contracts of the film studios. "In his prime [in the late teens and twenties] my father was probably the most prolific and successful producer in the world," John claimed. "And he was impossible to live with. He was riding the horse real high, and I don't think he got on with anybody, including the staff who worked with him. Many times he ran after J. C. Huffman, his house director, who carried a cane, was about six feet, and weighed two hundred pounds, and a great athlete. There was a lot of footwork those days." [34]

Despite J. J.'s truculence, his frugal salaries, and the prodigious amount of work, he held on for decades to the key members of his musical production staff. Except for Sigmund Romberg, none became well known; they remained anonymous craftsmen who fulfilled the assignments J. J. handed out.

Writer-lyricist Harold Atteridge was the poet laureate of the Winter Garden who wrote thousands of sketches and lyrics. A tall, slender midwesterner with a direct gaze, a crooked nose, and a twisted smile, Atteridge moved to New York from Chicago with the peculiar dream of becoming a staff writer for the Shuberts. After persistent attempts, he finally succeeded in obtaining an interview with J. J., who admired his breezy lyrics and hired him to write several numbers in *Revue of Revues*, the second Winter Garden show.

Atteridge, who really wanted the job he was to keep for the rest of his life, was a skillful populist who became adept in giving the Winter Garden audiences what they wanted and what they came to expect. "They are looking for catchy words, something that can shock them into laughter, and dancing, but most of all they want sensationalism and scenic effects, and they want speed," he said in a 1915 interview in the *New York Review*.[35] "What they are going to like later on, nobody knows, but that's what they want now." Because Winter Garden revues had topical material and often included travesties of contemporary shows, Atteridge as the self-appointed vox populi had to keep up with the times. He developed into an avid newspaper reader and saw all the new plays each season. "You know your public by keeping beside it, by eating with it, by smoking and drinking and laughing with it."

Atteridge admitted that his job above all required the ability to write quickly and on demand. "I get my orders from J. J. and I obey like a soldier," he said. "If there's a noise going on like a boiler factory, I have to go on just the same." Atteridge boasted that he could write the lyrics for a song in under an hour and that he could finish a sketch in under two. A Winter Garden show, he pointed out, was "unlike the writing of a straight musical comedy. There are many more details; there are more principals for whom parts and songs must be arranged." Like a juggler, "a revue writer must consider the balance of elements—performers, singing, dancing, dialogue, comedy, drama, spectacle—without letting any one outweigh the others. The first forty years as a Winter Garden librettist are the hardest," he quipped.[36]

Seven or eight weeks in advance of the first rehearsal for the latest revue, Atteridge would meet with J. J. to plan a tentative skeleton of sketches and musical numbers. With the cast and chorus already engaged by J. J., and with a plan of scenery and lighting effects already mapped, Atteridge's job was to mold material to the performers. "In shaping a piece to fit a personality one has to go through many of the careful observations that a tailor follows in cutting a suit to measure," he said. "Willie Howard, for instance, has a fast, snappy way of talking while outwardly he remains in repose. This means that those who surround him must talk slowly and give the light and shade in order to supply contrast. Al Jolson is a speed dynamo and the whole cast must be built up in order to maintain the speed he sets. Though he leaves the stage for a moment we dare not relax."[37]

Atteridge served composers with the same combination of modesty and expediency. "We can't always observe the best metrical principles, because our method varies with the composer," he pointed out. "Sigmund Romberg writes his music first and we must shape the lines to fit it afterwards and in other instances we have topical subject matter and force the lines to fit the idea."[38]

His self-effacing service-with-a-smile attitude continued into the four-week rehearsal periods (the chorus, under a dance director, usually rehearsed for six weeks), when he was expected to cut, paste, stitch, and add until the last minute and sometimes beyond it. For each Winter Garden show, Atteridge typically would write lyrics for about thirty-five songs, at least ten of which would be cut during the rehearsal period. Often on the first day of rehearsal, he would have five times more spoken material than would actually end up in the show on opening night. Atteridge attended every rehearsal, where he would take suggestions from the director, the leading performers, and the composers. Sometimes, because of the topical nature of much of the material, he had to make changes to keep the show fresh.

Because Winter Garden productions opened in New York without an out-of-town dry run, the dress rehearsals (of which there were usually three or four, and to which the public was invited) could last as long as five hours. It was during and after these marathon evenings that J. J. would have his famous tantrums; and as he chopped a show down to an endurable length, he often ordered Atteridge to supply new material. Then, as Atteridge claimed with an imperturbability that surely accounted for his long run, "if a comedian wants a couple of minutes of zippy business or gags I step once more into the breach."[39]

Atteridge's steady competence in the line of fire provided the backbone for J. J.'s revues. Never crumbling in the face of his boss's eruptions or Jolson's egomania, Atteridge certainly seemed to be the right man for the job, yet he was an alcoholic who died in 1938 at age fifty-one from cirrhosis of the liver.

As general stage director for the Shubert Organization, J. C. Huffman lasted almost as long as Harold Atteridge, was almost as prolific, and just as anonymous. He too worked both sides of the street, switch-hitting between Winter Garden extravaganzas and Shubert operettas. He directed all of the Shuberts' biggest hits and every one of the Jolson vehicles that played the Winter Garden. By the time he retired in 1927, to write monographs on stagecraft that were used in college theatre departments in the thirties and forties, he had directed nearly two hundred shows, a Broadway record, nearly all for the Shuberts. Huffman became established on Broadway as a director of dramas; but after he signed on in 1911 as the house director for the Shuberts, musicals of all types became his specialty. In the teens and twenties, when he seemed to work nonstop, producers rather than directors got most of the credit for revues: Julian Mitchell directed most of the *Follies*, but Ziegfeld's name was on the marquee, and Winter Garden programs alerted patrons that the "entire production was under the personal supervision of Mr. J. J. Shubert."

Speed, efficiency, and composure in dealing with his irascible boss were the job requirements, and these the tall, good-looking bachelor certainly possessed. Because J. J. fancied himself a director, he often interfered with Huffman's work and, as John reported, blowups were frequent. Yet Huffman lasted because he was not a perfectionist; at rehearsals he'd often be slumped in an orchestra seat, giving the performers their head and interrupting only to correct a blatant error. Like Atteridge he learned to stand by quietly during chaotic dress rehearsals when J. J. typically discarded or rearranged much of his work; and after the times when he did challenge J. J., clearly neither held a grudge. Huffman's relaxed attitude allowed him to direct as many as five shows a season for New York and another five or ten Shubert road companies, for which he had the assistance of two subordinate directors.

In a rare interview, Huffman offered some trade secrets and a defense of his métier.

> The popular idea that the work of the stage director in producing a modern revue is lowbrow stuff is all wrong. It requires more technical ability, thought and artistic talent to successfully stage a Winter Garden production than it does to put on any high class drama. A true revue consists of hundreds of little farces or travesties strung together without any definite or sane connection. It goes from one climax to another and each must be properly led up to and this makes a lot of rearrangement; on the success with which he does this work the production stands or falls.[40]

Huffman had agreed to the interview to publicize the latest *Passing Show*, whose trump card was a sensational scenic effect, the bombardment of a city by a zeppelin airship. "The effect was devised by Mr. Shubert and myself during rehearsals," Huffman reported. "We used nothing we did not have in stock in the scene loft and prop rooms." As if reconsidering his statement, Huffman ended with the kind of self-effacing gesture that kept him on the Shubert payroll for decades. "Mr. Shubert really deserves the entire credit for devising it."[41]

Beginning with *Sinbad* in 1918, scenic designer Watson Barratt worked on more than three hundred productions for the house of Shubert. He was still on staff in 1954 for *The Starcross Story*, the last offering to be presented under the banner of the Messrs. Shubert. In addition, Barratt found time to design at least three hundred sets for other producers. "He was a neighbor of my mother's and I got to know him rather well," Agnes de Mille recalled. "He delivered sets; I don't suppose he was a real artist: how could he have been, with all that work? But he *was* a nice guy, which made him a misfit in the Shubert organization."[42] Barratt had been a successful magazine illustrator, and J. J. thought his colorful style was just the touch he needed at the Winter Garden. He called Barratt in for an interview and after a brief talk convinced the illustrator to become a scenic designer. In effect Barratt became J. J.'s general art director, the man who not only designed the settings but also supervised lighting and frequently selected costumes.

J. J. hired Barratt to compete with Joseph Urban, the extraordinary designer Ziegfeld had hired in 1915. Born in Vienna in 1872, Urban was trained as an architect and was influenced by Jugendstil, impressionst, and pointillist artists. He came to America in 1912 to design sets for the Boston Opera Company, where he introduced elements of the "new stagecraft" from Germany, such as light and shadow to create mood and deep focus and platforms to provide contrasts of scale. His vibrant colors and the spare, sinuous lines of his sets wrapped the *Follies* in a frame of sophisticated European modernism, at once elegant and ethereal. Urban's sets often created a visual unity for the entire show: the 1915 *Follies*, for instance, was known as the "Blue *Follies*," with a color scheme arranged around a sky blue that critic John Corbin described as "a deep and magic blue; velvety in texture, yet suggesting limitless regions of heaven. It is a symbol, if you wish, of the Mediterranean . . . and it dominates the successive scenes with a sense of imaginative unity only less pervasive, compelling, than that of music."[43] Urban also introduced in-one staging, where the forestage is used for intimate solos or to cover scenic changes: the alternation between forestage and inner stage, between intimacy and spectacle, allowed for architectural variation and a flowing, unbroken rhythm. Lush, airy, and tinged with romance, Urban's designs for Ziegfeld evoked an idealized world of pleasure.

Once again J. J.'s attempt to outdo Ziegfeld was doomed; Barratt's cloyingly sweet work delivered the sense of opulence then mandated for the musical stage, but it lacked the delicacy of Urban's art-nouveau swirls and curves and his luminous palette. (Barratt's settings ended up warehoused in the Shubert shop, which in the forties became the theatrical equivalent of the Salvation Army. The Shuberts rented out old scenery as a way of continuing to earn money on their initial investment, and in the process Barratt's formerly fresh and lavish backdrops became increasingly threadbare and laughable as they trundled along a circuit of regional and community theatres.)

Like the other longtime Shubert minions, Barratt had prodigious capacities for working long hours under tense circumstances. In 1934, for J. J.'s summer season at the St. Louis Municipal Opera, the largest outdoor theatre in the world, he designed the settings for twelve operettas in twelve weeks for a stage comparable in size to that of Radio City Music Hall. Two nights a week, J. J. would hold all-night rehearsals, and for the other five nights Barratt could count on no more than five hours of sleep. Barratt, however, claimed that, compared to the many sets required for each Winter Garden revue, this job was "easy."[44]

Albertina Rasch choreographed many musicals and revues for J. J.; but unlike the other longtime staffers, she consistently talked back. As a result, her tenure was notably brief. Madame Rasch was too ambitious to remain for long under J. J.'s thumb. She was a savvy entrepreneur who billed herself as the creator of the American ballet; established a ballet school, which promised students "an open sesame to any production where real and artistic dancing is required"; and branched out to choreograph for the Keith–Albee vaudeville circuit where, she liked to boast, "the whole of America has been treated to a sight of her dancing acts."[45] "I didn't think anything of her work," Agnes de Mille said. "She had been classically trained and was a dancer at the Met, but all she did was put her dancers on point and had them all dance alike. Like Ned Wayburn [who also worked for J. J.], she sent rows of girls spinning. She moved her dancers from one edge of the proscenium to another, as if they were in *Swan Lake*. (She was a delightful hostess, however, when she was married to [composer] Dimitri Tiomkin.) She was made of iron."[46]

From almost the very beginning, J. J.'s musical factory was enlivened by the presence of casting director Ernest Romayne "Ma" Simmons, who joined the firm in 1912 and remained on the staff until neither J. J. nor Lee was an active producer. Ma Simmons auditioned almost every singer and dancer who ever appeared in a Shubert show, and his decision could make or break the career of a young performer. "At my audition for the 1929 Shubert operetta season at the Jolson Theatre, Ma Simmons had to listen to over five hundred people," Ethel Lynne remembered. "I wasn't Equity; I saw an open call listed in the paper and so I went along with all the other hopefuls. You sang a scale, and if Ma Simmons liked you, you were chosen."[47]

"He was a homosexual with outrageous proclivities who always had a scarf wrapped around himself," Agnes de Mille recalled. "I wonder what the Shuberts paid him. The boys in the chorus were certainly safe from the Shuberts, but I doubt if they were safe from Simmons."[48] "We'd slap you if you said 'Ma' in front of us," John Kenley, who was one of the boys in the chorus in a 1925 revue, told me.

> We regarded him highly. He was five feet by five feet, dumpy and wide, and looked like Queen Victoria. He was a brilliant pianist who had accompanied Madame Lillian Nordica for fifteen years before he joined the Shuberts. J. J. didn't think that much of him, at least when I was in the Shubert office in the thirties; he was getting tired of him. I always thought it was ironic that J. J. had me play piano for him, when there was a great pianist right next door.[49]

J. J. discharged Simmons in the mid 1940s, when Shubert production had dwindled to a trickle, but Lee kept him on the payroll and paid for Simmons's hospitalization in the last year of his life. Simmons died on March 7, 1954, aged eighty-nine; "J. J. had him buried in a Jewish cemetery even though he wasn't Jewish," John Kenley recalled.[50]

With his creative team in place, J. J. prepared three and sometimes four revues a year for the Winter Garden: an edition of *The Passing Show*, which traditionally opened in the summer; a fall or winter revue, with such generic titles as *Whirl of the World*, *A World of Pleasure*, and *Show of Wonders*; and a Jolson show, which typically opened in February. For twelve years, with an occasional gap or alteration, this remained the Winter Garden house policy, up through the last edition of *The Passing Show*, which premiered on September 3, 1924. Even with his hard-working in-house staff, however, the only way J. J. could produce so many revues was through a process of standardization. Titles, settings, production numbers, and personnel rotated, but the basic format for each seasonal revue was preordained—Winter Garden revues were a mélange of movable parts that could be easily recycled.

Before a show opened, J. J. was lax about the order of acts or the overall length. He waited for audience reaction during dress rehearsals before deciding which turns to trim or eliminate and which ones to build up or to reposition. After years of experience, his sense of pacing was often astute. Unlike Lee, J. J. craved recognition as a creative artist. He resented that his own work was hidden under the "Messrs. Shubert" credit—until 1933, Lee had no hands-on participation in any Winter Garden show—but his program billing, "entire production under the personal supervision of Mr. J. J. Shubert," came to haunt him, for that is how critics labeled him, as a supervisor rather than a creator. The only good notices J. J. could count on were the ones in the Shubert-controlled *New York Review*. ("If some of the old-time showmen like P. T. Barnum and the elder Kiralfy could come back, they'd be amazed; they never dreamed that such speed, pep and spirit could be put in a production as J. J. put in," a typical "review" with no byline enthused.[51]) Independent observers typically toasted J. J.'s energy rather than his creative gifts. "In rapid succession J. J. Shubert supervised *The Show of Wonders* at the Winter Garden and *Follow Me* at the Casino," reported the *Chicago Herald* on January 1, 1917.

> Then in Baltimore with *Her Soldier Boy* he produced new situations, revised others, quickened the action, laid more emphasis on dramatic possibilities, caused new comedy contrasts to balance an occasional note of pathos. In Washington he spent two days putting speed into *The Passing Show of 1916*; then he was off to Chicago where he prepared *A World of Pleasure* for a tour of the South and Southwest, the first time a Winter Garden show has ever toured the South.

Perhaps unwittingly, John offered some clues about his father's artistic limitations.

> He got his musical education from hanging around the theatre. He was interested in the length of music because of the timing—timing between the change of an actress's costume. You need a verse and two choruses before the other actor can make his change. Things like that. How long did it take to change scenery? We were always forever cutting down the amount of stagehands. We figure the verse, the chorus, and the reprise of a number—you'd save ten stagehands in the carpenter department.

If J. J.'s interest in music was distinctly more pragmatic than aesthetic, so was his attitude toward what came between the musical numbers.

> My father had a habit of injecting vaudeville acts in the weak spots of the usual musical comedy. That had been his formula for years, ever since in three days' rehearsal out of town he had changed a musical comedy into one of the most successful revues of all time by throwing everyone out of the cast except Jack Pearl and hiring Flo Baker and Irene Santley to give added comedy, singing, and star billing to the venture. If it had worked once so well, he thought, why not continue to strengthen any type of musical show by injecting first-rate specialties?[52]

"You never knew when J. J. would show up out front or backstage, at rehearsals, in town or out," a former employee told *Variety*'s Bob Russell in 1964.

> He followed the *Passing Show* all over the map just to stand in the back to watch Willie Howard. He'd laugh til the tears streamed down his cheeks—the greatest tonic in the world for a lonely man. Yet he wouldn't let Willie Howard see how amused he was—he'd tilt his head downward and stomp away in a sulk. He was a tycoon with a genius for production and business who would have given millions to have had the creative gift.[53]

In the twenties, as J. J. continued to supervise his increasingly formulaic Winter Garden seasons, encouraged by the reception of *Blossom Time* on September 29, 1921, he also expanded his operetta department. As *Das Dreimäderlhaus*, the show had been a wartime smash when it was first produced in Vienna in 1916. A Hungarian company was launched with notable success and other companies toured the war-torn Balkan states. The show ran for two years in Germany, closing only after postwar Germany headed into an economic tailspin. As *Lilac Time*, it ran for three years in London and, as *Chanson d'Amour*, for two years in Paris. Naturally impressed by these statistics, J. J. bought the American rights and assigned Dorothy Donnelly and Sigmund Romberg to undertake a drastic revision that became the Americanized *Blossom Time*.

Like *Maytime*, J. J.'s first operetta gold mine, the new piece was about a romance that does not happen, only this time the theme was unrequited rather than interrupted love. The hero of *Blossom Time* is Franz Schubert, short, squat, and doomed to romantic frustration, who loves a pretty young woman who loves someone else. Spurned, Schubert expresses his submerged and powerful yearnings through his music, forcing Romberg to adapt "the immortal music of Franz Schubert" rather than composing his own. Purists felt that reworking Schubert to fit the narrative demands of a saccharine operetta was sacrilege and sneered at Romberg's synthetic arrangements of the "Serenade" and "Ave Maria" and his use of a theme from Schubert's *Unfinished* Symphony for a waltz called "The Song of Love," which became the hit number reprised throughout the show. The purists, however, had little effect on ticket sales. *Blossom Time* became one of the most lucrative properties in theatrical history, an all-time Shubert blockbuster.

"It's a toss-up between *Blossom Time* and *The Student Prince* as the most successful single production the Shuberts ever had," John said.

> At one time, there were six companies of each of them out. *Maytime* had six companies too, but the show never reached the potential of *Blossom Time*, which is virtually three small sets with a cast of twelve. They were getting the same prices for that as they would for *The Student Prince* and *Maytime* with a chorus of twenty-four or thirty-six people. It was cheaper to run, and the *Blossom Time* companies were just slot machines that paid off week after week, year after year.[54]

The show ran a year at the Ambassador, while a second company opened at the Century. For months the two companies played to standing room only. The original company went to Chicago for a year and then returned to New York. Through the summer of 1923, *Blossom Time* played in two theatres (the Shubert and the 44th Street) across the street from each other. One season the Shuberts sent nine different companies on the road. And so it went, year after year after year. For fear it would be forever lost to the stage, the Shuberts never sold the property to the movies, and the work remains the only show from the old days that continues to be licensed by the Shubert Organization.

The Shuberts revived *Blossom Time* in New York in 1924, 1926, 1931, 1938, and 1943, though in a sense these weren't revivals because the show had never been out of production. Each time, critics agreed that the show was hopelessly old-fashioned and irresistibly entertaining. Only the comic relief was attacked: but were the comic subplots and the dialect comics of operetta ever endurable? Acting like the custodians of sacred writ, the Shuberts allowed no new jokes or routines to be added or, alas, none of the old ones to be excised. When J. J. "revived" the show for the last time in New York to launch a wartime tour, it was greeted by Robert Garland as "undiluted escapism of a deeply nostalgic, picturesque sort,"[55] and by H. T. P. as "an old-fashioned bouquet, quaint and lacy."[56] Immune to the emerging temper of the theatrical twenties, *Blossom Time* had been distinctly old-fashioned when it opened in 1921. Lilting and serene, the show played right through the Roaring Twenties, the Depression, and the Second World War. Not a season passed between 1921 and 1943 when there wasn't at least one production on the boards of Shubert houses. Because *Blossom Time*, unlike *Maytime*, made no concessions whatever to "modern" tastes in music, in time it won the approbation of critics opposed to the increasing use of jazz on Broadway and earned for the Shuberts rare and unexpected prestige—as sponsors of classical music on the Great White Way. "The richest musical score of any operetta ever presented, and a surcease from jazz and like assaults upon the ear," cheered Brooks Atkinson, a disaffected reviewer, on the occasion of the show's 1931 "revival."[57]

After *Maytime* had become a hit in 1917, J. J. had punished Romberg with four years of piecework assignments for *The Passing Show* and Jolson extravaganzas; and after *Blossom Time*, the loyal, harried composer still did not receive deliverance from his Winter Garden chores. Romberg's next assignment was *Bombo*, the pinnacle of the top-heavy Jolson vehicles, which opened a week after *Blossom Time* at a new Shubert theatre his producers had named in honor of their number one attraction. In the past, Shubert taste in theatre design had been restrained, but appropriately enough the house built for Jolson was a gaudy combination of Empire and Renaissance styles with bright red accents throughout. "The theatre is vast, comfortable, and hideous," the *Daily News* pronounced.[58]

Bombo matched its flamboyant surroundings. Once again a Jolson special floated on a dream in which, this time, the story of Christopher Columbus is retold. Jolson's Gus becomes Columbus's servant, Bombo, the life of the party who sees to it that his handsome white master (Forest Huff, another bland Shubert contract player) can claim his historical and romantic victories. It's Bombo who persuades Queen Isabella to finance the voyage to America, offers encouragement to the explorers when they grow disconsolate, and settles matters with the West Indian natives. And as always he speaks in a racy, contemporary argot, a distinct brand of Broadway wit. He informs Columbus, for instance, that no pinochle was played on Noah's Ark because Noah "sat on the deck." Asked which comes first, Rosh Hashanah or Yom Kippur, Bombo responds, "I don't know. I haven't played the races for a year."

When he made his entrance opening night, greeted by five minutes of tumultuous welcome, Jolson walked to the edge of the stage, leaned over, and confided to the audience that the high prices were not his fault but J. J.'s. At the end, when he came out for his usual chat, he had a word of greeting for Governor [Nathan L.] Miller in the proscenium box and a word of farewell for the old Winter Garden first nights.[59] More than ever, Jolson played *against* the show—his character was a clever Mr. Fix-it who put Columbus's affairs in order, but Jolson himself was a self-appointed lord of misrule who subverted the plot whenever he felt like it. And more than ever before, he injected a note of sexual mayhem, so that the specter of miscegenation haunted *Bombo* in more suggestive ways than in the earlier Gus shows. Ducking in and out of the show with a priapic gleam in his eye, "Al Jolson is like some demonic sorcerer of humor, some Dionysiac worshipper of mockery," as Kenneth Macgowan wrote.[60]

Some nights he'd ask the audience if they would rather hear him sing or see the rest of the show; and when he received the answer he expected, he would dismiss the cast, have the curtain lowered, and sing as long as he and the audience could endure. In the two-act, twenty-scene extravaganza he had five songs, none of them by Romberg, much to Romberg's mounting irritation. Jolson sang perched on a little platform over the conductor's desk that literally, as well as symbolically, thrust him away from the show and toward the audience. In the first act, he sang Southern songs; in the second, bowing to audience demand after opening night that he reveal his sentimental side, he performed a tear-stained, showstopping "April Showers." Later in the run and on tour, he interpolated "Toot Toot Tootsie!" and "California, Here I Come."

"A tremendous amount of costly scenery was trundled laboriously on and off the stage in the brief intervals when Jolson is resting in the wings," Alexander Woollcott complained. "There are some of us plagued by the notion that if about half of the fortune spent on these ornate accessories had been spent on a comedian or two and a few good singers the new musical would have been more entertaining."[61] But then it would not have starred Jolson, who was resigned to sharing the stage with elaborate sets and costumes (which this time included tons of ostrich feathers) but couldn't tolerate human competition.

During the run of *Bombo*, as Romberg was stewing over the routine assignments J. J. kept handing him, J. J. also for the first time seriously offended Jolson. Although Jolson and J. J. had had many skirmishes over money, the only feud that had heated up to dangerous levels had been in 1912, when—alarmed that Jolson's success in "La Belle Paree" would embolden the star to raise his price—J. J. had threatened to blacklist him unless he signed on the Shuberts' terms. Further, J. J. had promised he would promote Jolson's brother, Harry, if Al would not cooperate. ("Jolson hated it when his brother used the name 'Jolson,' " John Kenley recalled. "That wasn't their real name, and Al felt his brother was only trying to cash in on the reputation he had earned as a star."[62]) Jolson had agreed to the new contract, a generous fifteen hundred dollars a week plus a percentage of gross receipts, though as always Jolson was enjoined from playing anywhere else, and the Shuberts had immediately demoted Harry from the star spot he was then filling opposite Gaby Deslys in *The Revue of Revues*. "We'll keep him in, but we'll have to cut some of his routines," J. J. assured Al.[63]

During *Bombo* J. J. charged Jolson four hundred dollars for costumes. Jolson claimed the costumes, which were from the Shubert shop, had cost only fifty. He was deeply insulted and promised that he would not do business with the Shuberts again once his current contract was up. While hardly unprecedented, this example of Shubert bookkeeping was remarkable: surely J. J. could not have imagined that Jolson, who gave as good as he got, would have disregarded the four-hundred-dollar bill. With his longtime agent, Louis "Eppy" Epstein, Jolson thoroughly examined all Shubert statements. "Jolson couldn't be appeased, no matter how hard my father tried," John said. "Jolson insisted he would not return [for the 1921–1922 season] and so J. J. had to find a star replacement."[64]

As if he had been anticipating a break with Jolson, or perhaps as a ploy to threaten his greatest star, J. J. had hired Eddie Cantor in 1920. "After the 1919 actors' strike, Ziegfeld didn't speak to my father for several years," Janet Cantor Gari said. "My father had tremendous respect for Ziegfeld, who in fact had always treated him well. When Ziegfeld asked him why he was striking, my father told Ziegfeld that other producers hadn't treated actors well and that it all needs to be down on paper."[65] When J. J. offered Cantor star billing in a new revue, the then-unemployed performer accepted eagerly.

J. J. sent Cantor out in 1920 as the headliner in a seventy-week road tour of the Shubert circuit. The opening night of *The Midnight Rounders* in Philadelphia was a trial by fire. "This night would decide whether I could be a star," Cantor later writes. Screaming for immediate changes in the order of acts and making on-the-spot decisions to cut material and performers, J. J. was in high gear. "Kill the next scene. Reverse the dance numbers and put in the specialty after that. The next four songs are out. Call Eddie!"[66] Three times during the show J. J. asked Cantor to stall—to keep the audience laughing—while backstage J. J. ordered last-second changes of scenery. Cantor's ad-libs proved so successful that they became a set part of the show.

Recycling some material from *The Midnight Rounders*, *Make It Snappy* opened on April 13, 1922, at the Winter Garden as J. J.'s feud with Jolson continued. It was a showcase for J. J.'s new star. "Al Jolson now has a rival," the *New York Sun* reported the next morning, providing sweet music for the Shuberts. In a series of sketches, Cantor was a cowardly applicant for a job as a policeman, a harassed tailor, and a put-upon cabdriver. He performed a takeoff on Rudolph Valentino's sheik and had two sets of songs; not until 11:30 did he appear in burnt cork with his white gloves and white-rimmed spectacles. As in the films he was to make for Samuel Goldwyn in the thirties, Cantor enacted his own version of the schlemiel; rolling his eyes to express dismay and to underline double entendre, he played hypochondriacs, fall guys, and sissies.

A forerunner of Woody Allen, Cantor with his Yiddish inflections in song and speech was also following in the tradition of Ned Harrigan and Tony Hart, of Weber and Fields—he was, after a fashion, a dialect comedian who voiced the complaints of urban (Jewish) audiences. Cantor had the gift of gab: "He liked to lecture, and would have been a rabbi if he hadn't been a performer," his daughter claimed. Both in his puns and malapropisms and in the mayhem he created through his body movements, he also had a touch of the Marx Brothers. With Cantor, J. J. was hoping to appeal to the same constituency that Jolson and the Howard Brothers spoke to, a wised-up Jewish audience that enjoyed seeing its foibles and preoccupations—food, sex, money, and health—burlesqued. He was an easier, more genial performer than Jolson, and unlike Jolson he was a deft physical comic (this and his willingness to move away from his ethnic image earned him a longer career in movies than Jolson had). But Cantor was no match for Jolson as a singer. Where Jolson's voice soared and throbbed, Cantor put over a song with gyrations, interpolated dialogue, and over-the-top rolls of his eyes. But Cantor too achieved an extraordinary rapport with audiences. "My father always said there is no such thing as a bad audience, you just haven't got 'em yet," Janet Cantor Gari recalled.[67] "Jolson was way above Cantor as a star," Irving Caesar said, "but unlike Jolson, Cantor was generous to his costars and was easy to get along with. I liked him very, very much. Everyone did."[68] ("When my sisters and I put together reminiscences for a possible book, publishers rejected the material as too treacly," Janet Cantor Gari told me. "What were we supposed to do, say we hated him? We didn't.")

It was J. J. rather than Ziegfeld who made Eddie Cantor a star, but after *Make It Snappy* closed, Cantor returned to his former producer. Cantor respected Ziegfeld far more than he did the Shuberts, and the Shuberts never had the same feeling for Cantor that they did for Jolson. "A dirty, cheap little actor," is how John Shubert summed up his elders' reaction.

My father always told the story of what Cantor did in Pittsburgh when they were out of town with *The Midnight Rounders*. Cantor went regularly to the little Jewish delicatessen around the corner from the theatre. When my father went in a few nights later the fellow said, "Oh, you're Mr. Shubert with the Eddie Cantor show. I'll make you the same deal I made for Mr. Cantor."

"What's that?" "You get all the company to eat here, and I give you your meals for free." That was a yardstick of the man. A great performer, they respected him, he made money for them, but they couldn't forgive him for being cheap.[69]

Cantor made the same complaint against them. When he discovered a production cost of nineteen hundred dollars for glue on one of his statements, he swore he would never work for J. J. again. He never did.

With Cantor returned to Ziegfeld and Jolson remaining angry, J. J. had no big star to headline a revue, and so he attempted to create one, a strategy that almost never worked for either him or Lee. A singer named Georgie Price had caught J. J.'s eye at a Sunday night Winter Garden concert, and J. J. took him in as a member of the family, inviting him for dinners and Sunday breakfasts. But as J. J. was preparing Price for the big time with a thousand-dollar-a-week contract, Lee made peace with Jolson. Even though the Winter Garden was J. J.'s arena, Lee always stepped in to fix problems or to soothe employees J. J. had snapped at or roughed up. And as always, Lee knew when to end a war—he realized that the continuing standoff with Jolson was simply bad for business. With Jolson back, the Shuberts figured they didn't need any other big stars demanding hefty paychecks, and Price became superfluous. J. J. decided he would force Price to cancel his contract. First he gave him third billing in small print in *Spices*, a Winter Garden show that opened on July 6, 1922, and was to have launched his stellar career. With Mae West starring, Price did little more than lurk around the edges of a few production numbers—in blackface. When *Spices* closed after six months, J. J. assigned Price to the road tour of *The Passing Show* and this time overworked the performer, still holding out the promise of a star spot at the Winter Garden. Price appeared in thirteen scenes, sang eight songs, and did a monologue. J. J. gave him a tiny dressing room, the smallest available at each theatre on the tour and the one farthest from the stage. And since Price's contract stated that he "would travel as directed by the management," on this grueling tour of one-night stands J. J. made Price travel in boxcars—with the scenery.

After thirty-six weeks on the road, Price lost fifteen pounds and developed an ulcer. His last round with the Shuberts was over a show that J. J. had promised would be Price's bid for Broadway stardom. During the Detroit tryout of *A Night in Spain*, J. J. performed his customary reshuffling, at Price's expense and also at the show's. By this point, J. J. was openly furious with Price, who had demonstrated more resilience than J. J. had expected and who, moreover, had continued to urge both him and Lee to honor the contract they had signed with him. J. J. slashed Price's songs and sketches, reducing him to a featureless bit performer in a revue he was originally to have headlined. When the show was about to open in

New York, Price used a ploy Jolson had fallen back on in contractual disputes: he developed a sore throat. Price left town for a week. When he reported to the theatre with his lawyer, carrying medical affidavits claiming he was ready now to go to work, he was barred. William Klein, on the Shuberts' behalf, charged Price with breach of contract. Summoned to Lee's office, Price said he wanted the twenty-six weeks' salary still remaining on his contract. Lee wondered how that would be possible since J. J. would not allow Price anywhere near any theatre the Shuberts ran. But Price had an ace up his sleeve in the form of a photostatic copy of a check to him drawn on a Shubert charity-fund account, and Price threatened to show the check to government authorities. After consulting with Klein, Lee issued a check to Price for twenty-six thousand dollars, ending the contract, as well as his history with the Shuberts. Unlike many performers who left the Shuberts in high dudgeon, Price did not go on to become a superstar under other managers. He did play the Palace and for a brief period was a vaudeville headliner, but by the end of the twenties, he left show business for a career as a Wall Street broker.[70]

Jolson returned to the Shubert orbit on January 7, 1925, when *Big Boy* opened at the Winter Garden. This time Gus was a stableboy who rides the eponymous horse to victory in the Kentucky Derby; instead of an exotic locale, scenic excitement was provided by galloping horses on a treadmill, the first time in twenty years the old showstopping device from *Ben Hur* had been seen on Broadway. Though Jolson joked with the house, maintaining his mutinous image by remarking opening night that, with all the eleven-dollar seats he had sold, J. J. must already be showing a profit on the production, the script this time afforded him moments of pathos, which he played straight; and, as never before, the Negro spiritual and the mammy songs on his musical program fit the show's setting.[71]

Twice Jolson had to interrupt the run of the show with laryngitis rumored to be serious enough to end his career. J. J. accused Jolson of only pretending to be ill, but a battery of doctors asserted that Jolson was indeed unwell. J. J. was forced to close the show, though he did draw up a contract with Eppy for Jolson to appear for a month in the 1925 edition of *Artists and Models*, scheduled to coincide with the Winter Garden's fifteenth anniversary. Jolson joined the revue on March 21, 1926, for a sizable ten-thousand-dollar weekly salary and a percentage increment if grosses exceeded a specified amount. Jolson stayed on for a fifth week. At his last performance, April 24, 1926, which was also to be his last appearance at the Winter Garden, Jolson kidded his boss by saying that J. J. had given him a story that failed to raise laughs so that he wouldn't have to pay him as much money next season; and when a reporter accused him of being "delicate" because he had had to close *Big Boy*, Jolson responded by asking, how could he possibly be "delicate" when he had worked for the Shuberts for fifteen years?[72]

By fall Jolson was well enough to reopen *Big Boy* (which was placed at the

Shuberts' 44th Street Theatre rather than at the Winter Garden). On his entrance, he received a record nine-minute ovation and was cheered each time he appeared for a new scene. He added two new songs, "Miami" and "Nobody but Fannie." Though he lived for another twenty-five years, *Big Boy* was to be Jolson's last major hurrah on Broadway. After the usual post-Broadway tour of the show, Jolson departed for Hollywood to make *The Jazz Singer*.

A month before Jolson returned, J. J.'s other star workhorse had given his boss another operetta hit. As always Romberg had been toiling dutifully if unhappily in the sweatshop, writing songs to J. J.'s orders. After *Bombo* J. J. forced Romberg to write the score for *The Blushing Bride*, a mélange with "a tinge of vaudeville, a shade of revue, a color of burlesque, a hue of musical comedy, a suggestion of concert, and a tincture of the devil himself."[73] Uncredited, Romberg wrote songs for a revue called *Dancing Girl*, which reopened a refurbished Winter Garden minus its runway. He also contributed a few numbers each to the 1923 and 1924 editions of *The Passing Show* and the 1924 and 1925 editions of another J. J. series, *Artists and Models*, and he supplied interpolated songs for two of J. J.'s Viennese operetta imports.

Romberg did not win a permanent reprieve from the Tin Pan Alley side of the Shubert workshop until *The Student Prince*, which opened at the Jolson Theatre on December 2, 1924. If J. J. had had his way, however, the show wouldn't have opened at all. Even after *Maytime* and *Blossom Time* the producer still did not trust the musical and theatrical instincts of his star composer, even in another Shubert operetta in which the hero, a prince who must choose duty over love, doesn't get the girl, a waitress at a tavern. When he saw the show out of town, J. J. was appalled: the score seemed too heavy, almost operatic in its romantic and emotional intensity; he saw no reason for the enlarged male chorus (thirty-six in the original) Romberg had insisted on for the show's drinking and student songs; he regretted the absence of a female chorus line; and he hated the unhappy ending, in which the prince parts forever from his true love. It was as if J. J. had completely forgotten *Blossom Time*, in which a thwarted romance and no chorus line had spelled box office gold. Fulminating, J. J. threatened to jettison both the composer and his score. Romberg and his lawyer promised that if he did that they would sue. On Lee's advice, J. J. backed off.[74] After the male chorus won universal approval, J. J. made a practice of inserting augmented male choruses into a number of his later operettas. Ads for later productions of *The Student Prince* promised that "the student chorus will set you a tinkling and lift you from your seats" and that "the company of 150 includes the famous student chorus of 60 male voices."

J. J. may have been especially sensitive because *The Student Prince* was based on *Old Heidelberg*, which Sam had convinced Richard Mansfield to appear in as the opening attraction at the Lyric Theatre. J. J. in a sense was now testing himself against the idealized figure of Sam: under his watch, could he make lightning strike a second time?

Romberg, of course, had been correct to insist on doing the show his way. With its lush, unapologetically sentimental score, which includes "Golden Days," "The Students' Marching Song," "The Drinking Song," "Deep in My Heart, Dear," "Serenade," "Just We Two," and "Nevermore," *The Student Prince* presented the composer at his silvery peak. The original production received the best reviews of any Shubert show ever. Even George Jean Nathan, no fan of either the Shuberts or operetta, liked it. Arthur Hornblow wrote that it was "of transcendent worth, beautifully sung, acted, staged, and costumed."[75]

Like *Blossom Time*, *The Student Prince* became a Shubert evergreen whose popularity overrode changing trends. At one point during the same season, nine companies traversed the nation's theatres. For twenty-five years, the show held the stage; and once J. J. was assured the well had finally run dry, he sold the rights to MGM, which released a film in CinemaScope and color in 1954. (In 1927 MGM had made a silent version, released as *The Student Prince in Old Heidelberg*.)

At the beginning of 1925, with *The Student Prince* launched as one of the biggest hits of the decade and his breach with Jolson healed, J. J. was at the peak of his success. Although J. J.'s operettas and revues brought in substantial amounts of money, for which Lee of course was grateful, Lee also resented and envied his younger brother's track record. Despite a public charade that all was well between them—a charade Lee had been orchestrating since they had moved into their offices above the Shubert Theatre in 1913—their mutual animosity had continued to fester. In the summer of 1925, while J. J. was on one of his regular shopping expeditions in Europe, Lee moved his brother's office across the street onto the sixth floor of a new Shubert building at 234 West Forty-fourth Street. This sudden and aggressive act was clearly a signal to J. J. that, despite his success as a musical impresario, Lee was still the firm's CEO. When he returned, J. J. at first was enraged, but then he realized that Lee had in fact given him the opportunity to create a duchy of his own. J. J. bullied the architect of the new building—John claimed that J. J. physically threatened the man—into adding six more stories into his design so that the building would be higher than the Shubert Theatre. He had the architect build a penthouse, which included a living room almost the entire width of the building, a dining room with a stained-glass skylight, a library, a master bedroom, dressing rooms, two baths, a kitchen, servants' quarters, and a terrace facing Forty-fourth Street. When the architect protested that there would hardly be enough room for a terrace, J. J. persisted, adding that the terrace needed only to be wide enough for a couple of chairs and an awning. "I want to be able to sit out there and look down on my brother across the street," he said.[76]

Once J. J. moved into the building (known as the Sardi Building in honor of the ground-floor restaurant it houses), the split between the brothers had a physical manifestation. For the rest of their lives, they worked across the street from each other, employing a go-between, usually John, to carry messages back and forth. Rarely, if ever, did either man venture into the other's domain.

"J. J.'s apartment was garish beyond words," playwright Ruth Goetz recalled. "It was designed on a grand scale, and was elegant, I suppose, according to the taste of the time."[77] Garson Kanin said that "Mr. J. J. had a charming apartment with lovely rooms."[78] Whether the decor was "garish" or "charming" was, of course, in the eye of the beholder; what the penthouse signified unmistakably, however, was that its owner was a man of consequence. Heavy and ornate, the style was distinctly baronial, with Louis XIV furniture, a wrought-iron door from a Venetian palace, Syrian furniture inlaid with nacre and ivory, and a fountain. The bathroom was equipped with a battery of electric heaters and a roomy armchair where J. J. did most of his play reading (because heat in the Sardi Building was turned off late at night and on Sunday, and it would not have been possible to heat J. J.'s apartment without heating the entire building, an expense J. J. did not wish to incur).

J. J.'s offices six floors below were another matter. Like Lee's circular cubicle, the place where J. J. conducted business was disarmingly modest. Where Lee's round tower had an elegant severity, J. J.'s suite was close to being downright shabby; and over the years, the mise-en-scène became increasingly down-at-the-heels. It was harder to gain access to J. J.'s office, which was more moated than Lee's; but once you got in, J. J. was much less guarded. Where Lee remained hidden behind his unflinching mask, J. J. vibrated with anger or enthusiasm and was incapable of sustaining Lee's brand of terse office politics.

J. J. was king of the hill when he first moved into the Sardi Building, but his fortunes as a maestro of revue and operetta soon thereafter began to slip. From 1912 until after the Great War, the *Follies* and *The Passing Show* had been the only annual revues; but at the start of the Jazz Age, a crop of new annuals appeared. Their topical satire and syncopated music gave the new shows an up-to-the-minute flash that made Ziegfeld's stately showgirls and tableaux begin to seem a little stiff jointed. As always the Shuberts kept a close watch on the competition; and to keep up, J. J. began to branch out beyond the Winter Garden, with often disappointing results.

The George White *Scandals*, supervised by a former hoofer, featured more dancing and modern music than any other revue. "Georgie White was a tough little dancer from Canada, who worked for us before he split off to do his *Scandals*," John said. "My father couldn't accept him as a hoofer, and resented his later success." Sam Harris and Irving Berlin produced *The Music Box Revue* at their Music Box Theatre (co-owned by the Shuberts and built for revues). "Sam Harris was a loudmouthed bum; Father told me he was dangerous and not to be trusted," John reported. "Irving Berlin is a dangerous, annoying little man who doesn't belong in show business, he belongs up in Tin Pan Alley with the publishing stuff," John said, expressing family consensus. Earl Carroll's *Vanities* was the naughtiest of the annuals. Perversely, the Shuberts respected Carroll, a producer with a peep-show sensibility and a seedy private life. "For some unknown reason, in spite of all the bad publicity—Carroll served a term in prison for bootlegging and he got written up for bathing girls in gin and for the wild parties he held on stage after the openings—my father and uncle always spoke very nicely about him," John recalled. "There was never any of the gossip I ever heard around on the outside, about what a peculiar character he was. They thought he was a very good businessman. They especially started respecting him when he built the Earl Carroll Theatre [an art-deco masterpiece, in fact] for himself up on Fiftieth and Seventh Avenue."[79]

Presided over by John Murray Anderson, *The Greenwich Village Follies* was more intimate and irreverent than the uptown revues. At the tiny Greenwich Village Theatre in 1919 and 1920, Anderson produced and directed two shows, which had a naive, homemade quality. Early in 1921, J. J. (who conducted the revue wars with typical Shubertian fervor as he and his lieutenants raided the talent of other producers' revues) signed Anderson and relocated his *Follies* uptown. Well aware that Anderson was a more skillful revue director than any of the Shubert in-house staff, J. J. allowed him to create the kind of stage pictures that had won him acclaim in the Village. Critics noted Anderson's "glories" of color and form and movement and cited a scene with pirouetting figures in silver and black, which might have come to life from an art-nouveau etching by Aubrey Beardsley. "Nothing since the revue form first appeared has resembled this amazing combination of Picasso, Puvis de Chauvannes, and Rube Goldberg," Alexander Woollcott wrote about the Shuberts' uptown *Greenwich Village Follies*, which opened August 31, 1921, at the Shubert Theatre. But to Anderson's arresting designs, J. J. added a third-rate Jolson imitator named Al Herman, who performed in blackface; a singer named Irene Franklin whose brassy, strutting style warred with Anderson's delicate touch; and retained James Watts, a female impersonator, who had been the weakest element in the downtown edition of 1920. "Dismal, vulgar dialogue and touches of bad taste mar an otherwise beautiful show," Woollcott concluded.[80]

Five more Shubert-backed *Greenwich Village Follies* followed, but each new entry retained less and less of the original quality. Under J. J.'s supervision, a downtown show became increasingly uptown, and indistinguishable from other slick revues of the period. Anderson departed in a huff after the 1925 edition. The last of the series (April 9, 1928) was an entirely in-house production with settings by Watson Barratt, book by Harold Atteridge, and direction by Shubert foreman J. C. Huffman. Opening at the Winter Garden, the show was no different from the other regulation Winter Garden revues of the time.

J. J. created the Palais de Danse, a cabaret atop the Winter Garden, and the Century Promenade, later renamed the Casino de Paris, atop the Century Theatre (which had originally been the New Theatre and which J. J. now ran like an uptown Winter Garden). Modeled after the rooftop theatre at the New Amsterdam, where Ziegfeld presented his series called *Midnight Frolics*, neither Shubert spot for late-night revelry developed the cachet of Ziegfeld's original.

Another of J. J.'s revue series, *Artists and Models*, had five editions, which spanned the twenties, beginning with a notorious debut at the Shubert Theatre on August 20, 1923. More than any other show, it was *Artists and Models* that earned J. J. his reputation as a flesh merchant. If J. J. had installed the Winter Garden runway to bring patrons and chorus girls in closer proximity than they had ever been before in a legitimate theatre, he began *Artists and Models* as a ruse to inject nudity onto the revue stage. Written and designed by members of the Society of Illustrators, *Artists and Models* had twenty-four scenes in two acts, including a burlesque of *Rain* called "All Wet," Samoan dancers, a ukulele specialty, a pictorial survey of popular magazines, vaudeville comic Frank Fay, acrobatic dancing, and a blackface comedian. But it was the sensation of bare flesh that accounted for the then-record-setting 312-performance run. "The chorus girls broke the American record by appearing with simply a slim wisp of chiffon above the waist," according to the *New York American*. "Never before in an American revue has a similar degree of nudity obtained," the report continued. "Before, virtually unclothed performers have stood immobile or been shaded in dim lights—here they marched and danced in the full glare of the footlights."[81]

For the remainder of the twenties, J. J.'s revues often struck blue notes. The nadir of the rowdy, hurly-burly Shubert revue style came with two shows starring Texas Guinan, the raucous, bull-faced mother abbess of the Jazz Age nightclub, famous for her "Hello, suckers!" greeting. *Gay Paree* (1925) and *Padlocks of 1927* were rough-and-ready attempts to sustain audience interest in a faltering genre. The high point of *Padlocks* was when Texas orchestrated a confetti fight between the cast and the audience.

In the "all new" *Gay Paree* in 1928, the chorus appeared in cat costumes as they raised their hands in a pawlike gesture; carried fake bulldogs; dressed as baby grand pianos in peekaboo Greco-Roman slips; were spread-eagled on a huge fan, wearing risqué, two-piece bathing suits. For a Baghdad sequence, phallic-looking minarets and towers were strapped to their heads. *The Great Temptations* (1926) featured a Viking chorus of scantily clad women carrying spears and helmets; chorus girls pinioned on three spreading butterfly wings; and a production number with thirteen women in elaborate floral dresses and headgear in which the real women and the fake flowers seemed to merge in a bizarre organic unity.

In these late-in-the-day revues, J. J. provided fuel for feminist rancor. Sexual display, always a part of the revue format, had been elegant, stately, and witty in Ziegfeld's shows and in many of J. J.'s earlier revues as well; but at the end of his run as a sultan of revue, J. J. seemed to be expressing his own lusty fantasies through an iconography that had become increasingly crude and depersonalizing. The way he presented the chorus in these later shows seemed to confirm J. J.'s reputation as a legendary poacher.

Irving Caesar recalled that "once during a rehearsal at the Winter Garden J. J. turned to me and boasted that he had had every one of the chorus girls."[82] Abner Klipstein said that "at rehearsals Mr. J. J. would put his hands on the breasts of chorus girls: everybody knew about him and the chorus girls, even I did and I was young. There were two sets of chorus girls, tall ones and short ones, and they all played up to Mr. J. J."[83] "J. J.'s job was taking care of the chorus," singer Dorothy Seegar remembered. "I felt safe because I wasn't in the chorus."[84] Yet singer Ethel Lynne told me that she "didn't dare go near J. J. He was wild and if you attracted him he went after you. The same went for his brother."[85] Jewish actress Barbara Barondess felt safe from both Shuberts.

The Christian producers were out for Jewish girls, and the Jewish producers wanted the shiksas. They didn't feel guilty this way. (I only had trouble with William Brady, a drunk, but I talked him out of it.) Anyway, I was too intelligent and ambitious for the Shuberts. When I auditioned for a Jolson road show J. J. was in the auditorium looking over the girls very, very carefully. I didn't want to go on the road so J. J. put me in *Gay Paree* in New York. I wasn't tall enough for a showgirl so J. J. put me with the shorter ones and had us all strapped onto the curtain in the shape of a fan. I was the one in the middle. We wore practically nothing, and this was before bikinis. I went to complain to J. J. "If I'm going into the theatre," I told him, "I want to speak lines and not go on the road or be in a Winter Garden revue." The Winter Garden shows weren't legit; the speaking theatre was legit. "My family wouldn't stand for it," I told him. "I'm a Barondess—Brandeis was part of our family." "You're pretty proud of it, aren't you?" he snapped.[86]

Dorothy Terolow Reissman, who was a Shubert road player in the early forties, did not feel that J. J. exploited the chorus. "They were hard-bitten bitches, for
the most part, and going on the casting couch was nothing to them. In that business you need either a strong stomach or a strong back."[87]

If the quality of J. J.'s revues began to falter after 1925, so did that of his operettas. Try as he did, he was unable to produce another operetta made to the order
of *The Student Prince*. Despite their battles over that show, however, Romberg
continued to work for J. J., composing the score for a 1925 operetta called *Princess
Flavia*, which was based on *The Prisoner of Zenda*. The new show represented J. J.
at his height as an impresario of expensive operetta bonbons. Having learned
Romberg's lesson about the effectiveness of massed chorales, he hired a chorus of
two hundred, and the show, hailed by Robert Coleman as "the loudest in Chris-
tendom," was universally praised for its vocal ensembles and finales.[88] Far from
being branded with their later reputation as cheapskates, the Shuberts in 1925
were lauded for their munificent operetta spectacles. "When we tell you it has been
staged by the Shuberts you will realize it has been done lavishly, artistically, and
stupendously," cheered Coleman, who was not on the Shubert payroll, in the *New
York Mirror*. "During the last three seasons the Shuberts have developed a type of
opéra comique which may easily become our national musical expression," he
continued, concluding that *Princess Flavia* is "the Shuberts' latest and greatest
pageant."[89]

The scenic high point of act 1 was a forest with great trees bearing a colorful
tapestry of autumnal foliage; at the back was a raised roadway over which the
thundering chorus of soldiers made their entrance in bright uniforms and shin-
ing helmets. The pièce de résistance in act 2 was a palace setting of tapestries,
arched doorways, crimson damask hangings, and a broad sweep of stairway leading up to a background of brilliantly illuminated stained-glass windows. Opening
night cheers brought Sigmund Romberg, director J. C. Huffman, and musical conductor Alf Goodman to the Century stage. "Only the innate modesty of J. J.
Shubert prevented his appearance," reported the *New York Review* on November
10. Despite the notices and the bewitching settings, *Princess Flavia* had a disappointing 152-performance run, an indication that the kind of operetta J. J. favored
was beginning to lose its hold on the general public.

After the show opened, Romberg finally made good on the threat he had been
issuing for years—he broke from J. J. What made the rupture especially hard for
J. J. was that Romberg left to work for J. J.'s perpetual nemesis, Florenz Ziegfeld.
The Romberg–Ziegfeld collaboration turned out to be a goofy low-comedy spectacle called *Louie the 14th* in which Ziegfeld's sumptuous three-hundred-thou-
sand-dollar production overshadowed Romberg's unmemorable score. For his
next show, the composer approached a new team, Laurence Schwab and Frank

Mandel, and worked with Otto Harbach and Oscar Hammerstein II, as well as Mandel, on the book and lyrics for *The Desert Song*, the Romberg operetta that has had the longest theatrical life. When it opened at the Casino Theatre on November 30, 1926, starring former Shubert star Vivienne Segal, J. J. was only the landlord. (Romberg worked with the same creative team on another canonic operetta, *The New Moon* [1929].)

Amazingly enough, with a promise of creative independence, J. J. lured Romberg back to the Shubert stable following *The Desert Song*, but the shows they collaborated on from 1927 to 1930 were derivative operettas in what seemed to be an increasingly outmoded style. *Cherry Blossoms* (March 28, 1927), based on a moldy potboiler in the Shubert catalog, was a kind of light-minded *Madame Butterfly*. Into another romance that ends unhappily, Romberg mixed Eastern and Western musical signatures and employed the Japanese stage technique of using chroniclers who recite the action that occurs between the acts. Next, based on an 1899 play by Clyde Fitch, came *My Maryland* (September 12, 1927), a Civil War operetta about the legend of Barbara Frietschie.[90] *The Love Call* (October 24, 1927) was based on *Arizona*, the Augustus Thomas Western that had been the first hit at Sam's first theatre in New York. *Nina Rosa* (September 20, 1930) was a romance set in the Peruvian Andes.

Of these only *My Maryland* had a substantial run. Produced in the shadow of Kern and Hammerstein's *Show Boat* (1927), the genre's first American masterwork, the late Romberg–Shubert operettas were musically and thematically reactionary. Despite the shifts in the theatrical weather vane, J. J. and his composer continued to repeat themselves, concocting overstuffed operettas with exotic settings, romantic misalliances between royalty and commoners, and clodhopping comic subplots. *Nina Rosa*, the one show in this late group not based on an earlier play, was in fact the most imitative, with J. J. once again trying to match a Ziegfeld success—this time the model was Ziegfeld's 1927 Latin horse operetta, *Rio Rita*, a tremendous hit. J. J. hired Ziegfeld's star, Ethelind Terry, and the same choreographer, Busby Berkeley, whose dance numbers added musical comedy flash. With its café and hacienda scenes as backdrops for dances and musical specialties, with its native religious festivals, whipping scenes, hidden Inca caves, and last-minute rescue, *Nina Rosa* was the last go-for-broke musical extravaganza J. J. was to supervise.[91]

Though Romberg was to return to J. J. one last time many years later, *Nina Rosa* effectively marked the end of their long association. John Shubert cited Romberg's departure as the beginning of his father's decline as a musical impresario.

After Romberg, the music of J. J.'s theatrical endeavors continually moved downhill. My father was plagued by a fast snow job performed by a no-talent named Morry Rubens, a bad piano player, who had come to us first as a rehearsal pianist, and who ultimately worked himself up into hiring all the house musicians for our theatres. Then, to compound the felony, he made himself the number one composer, dragging down a substantial salary.

Regardless of Romberg's having substantially contributed to J. J.'s success, John (unfairly) remembered Romberg—who remained loyal to the Shuberts despite the overwork and the ongoing frustration of not always being permitted to do what he could do best—this way: "Romberg was a phony, a workman for my father, who used to hand him the scores of shows he had bought in Europe. Romberg would steal music from European folk tunes, but like Jerry Kern he had that God-given gift of putting the notes in the right rotation, and making a thirty-two-bar chorus out of a traditional eight-bar theme."[92]

Though even earlier in the twenties J. J.'s brand of operetta had been considered old-fashioned, his shows were still able to hold their own against brash new musical comedies like *Lady, Be Good!* and *No! No! Nanette!* In the healthy, vital theatre of that decade, there was room for all kinds of musical offerings, from the Old World picture-postcard operettas J. J. preferred to lavish, witty revues to jazz-based musical comedies with contemporary settings. J. J., however, rarely ventured into book musicals in the modern mode. The only hit he manufactured in the musical comedy vein was *Sally, Irene, and Mary* (September 4, 1922), a concoction about three Lower East Side Irish girls who become Broadway stars, a shameless rip-off of three successful Cinderella musicals. The Shuberts coproduced one of the major contemporary musicals, George and Ira Gershwin's *Oh, Kay*, but only for the road and for a return engagement of sixteen performances at the Century. (The producers of the original 1926 show had been Alex Aarons and Vinton Freedley.)

Just as the important dramatists of the 1920s worked for producers other than the Shuberts, the significant new Broadway composers, the ones who created the modern Broadway musical comedy, also went elsewhere. "All the great composers worked for J. J. at one time or another, but they never lasted," John admitted.

George Gershwin was a rehearsal pianist for us. They liked Gershwin, even though he did only one show for us, *The Show Is On*; he did some of the numbers with his brother Ira, whom they also liked a great deal. (They knew George was a fairy. Other people didn't believe it.) They didn't work with [Richard] Rodgers and [Lorenz] Hart because they were the only team who remained distinct and didn't sell their songs piecemeal in the early days. Everybody else sold, and every composer worked with many lyricists; Gershwin worked with maybe ten different lyricists. Vincent Youmans was a rehearsal pianist for us. Both Lee and J. J. had a great liking for Youmans and felt sorry for him because he had consumption from the first day he came in the theatre, but they thought he was a damn fool. When he finally did his own producing he threw away his money ridiculously.

Although the Shuberts were involved with Jerome Kern early in his career, when Lee helped Elisabeth Marbury put on a series of intimate, now legendary musicals at the Princess Theatre, that relationship too did not survive. "Kern was a tough little English kike who looked down his nose at my father and my uncle," John said. "He was real hot to handle. They knew Kern from those days when he was difficult, and they never used him later on. Kern went over to their rival, Ziegfeld, who produced Kern's greatest success, *Show Boat*. Kern hated them as much as they hated him, and so he and they never got together after 1919."[93]

Despite the changes in musical theatre throughout the twenties, J. J. remained stubbornly devoted to the fashions of an earlier period. In effect he became a self-appointed custodian of a superannuated Broadway form, the sugar-spun operetta that took place somewhere over the rainbow. In 1929, with the help of his nephew, Milton Shubert, J. J. supervised an operetta revival season that featured many of the major prewar operettas he wished he had produced originally. The season included *The Chocolate Soldier*, *Sweethearts*, *Mlle. Modiste*, *Naughty Marietta*, *The Fortune Teller*, *Robin Hood*, *The Merry Widow*, *Babes in Toyland*, and *The Prince of Pilsen*. "We were a true repertory company," said Ethel Lynne.

> While we played one show, we were in rehearsal for the next one. Each show ran two weeks. We did *Babes in Toyland*, which had 150 in the cast, three times a day, with a 10:30 A.M. milkman performance for the children. Milton Aborn was our director, an elderly gentleman who wore half a high hat—he would call us his "crabs" and "lobsters." The Shuberts never directed—this was Milton Aborn's baby, and we were called the Aborn Opera Company. We specialized in Victor Herbert's work.[94] Following the season at the Jolson Theatre we went on the road with *Babes in Toyland* for forty weeks. Milton Shubert started the tour with us, and came out on the road from time to time. He was the money man, nothing more.[95]

Although J. J.'s loyalty to an operetta tradition he loved is one of the most endearing aspects of his career, in the thirties and forties it was also one of the activities that would help earn both brothers their growing reputation as theatrical antediluvians.

In their long heyday, which spanned over two decades, from 1905, when they took over from Sam and carried the first war with the Syndicate into high gear, up to the stock market crash of 1929, the Shuberts regularly presented a dozen or more shows each season in New York while sponsoring double that number on tour. At their peak, in the teens and twenties, they were the most active and powerful producers and theatre owners in the world. For more than twenty years, the boys from Syracuse were the czars of American entertainment, the principal suppliers of theatrical goods to millions of theatregoers throughout the country. Knowing well how little they knew, they never presented themselves as innovators or tastemakers. Instead, they were Broadway's most indefatigable imitators, who copied the successful shows of other producers. In a perhaps not-so-strange way, their intellectual and cultural limitations had kept them on an even keel with the popular tastes of their time—as producers of commercial entertainment, they did not condescend to the general public whose patronage they sought, and for the most part they presented shows they themselves wanted to see.

But the signs of their eventual decline began to appear in the twenties, when the American theatre at long last liberated itself from European models to discover a voice (or rather many voices) of its own. Other producers appeared who had a deeper, surer sense not only of literary values but also of the theatre's ability to reflect the spirit of the times. The Shuberts had never been noted for their modernity; and as the American theatre made artistic gains throughout the twenties, both Lee and J. J. began to seem and to feel increasingly out of touch. Their once-fabled ability to gauge popular taste and to cater their wares to satisfy it began to wither. After the crash, show business was never to be quite the same for the Shuberts or, for that matter, for anyone else.

6

All in the Family

*T*he crash affected the theatre a little later than it affected most businesses," John Shubert claimed. For a couple of seasons after the stock market tumbled, the Shuberts behaved as if indeed they had remained unscathed. During 1929–1930, they mounted twenty-one productions. In 1930–1931, their offerings swelled to an impressive twenty-three productions. And the following season, thirteen new productions were unfurled under the Shubert banner.

And as other producers like Al Woods, Charles Dillingham, and the Selwyns lost their money, it was the Shuberts who either bailed them out or paid for their funerals. "The other fellows, when they became secure, they had a good time, they spent carelessly but not the Shuberts; we never stopped cooking," John said. "In the late twenties other producers entrusted their business to men who didn't give them the right shake or advised them badly. We buried Dillingham out of the Astor: one of the great men of all times—I think we spent eight hundred dollars on his funeral."[1]

The Shuberts may have thought they could ride out the deepening Depression—they had decades of sound business practices behind them and a sizable precrash nest egg that had not been depleted entirely. But in fact the Shuberts were in trouble. As the economic crisis expanded, theatre began to seem more and more a luxury item fewer people could afford. To keep as many theatres open as possible, Lee put on more shows on his own than he ever had before. He revived past hits, including *Peter Ibbetson* and *Death Takes a Holiday*. He allowed Ethel Barrymore to talk him into presenting her and an inferior supporting company in Sheridan's *School for Scandal*. And along with his usual quota of boulevard imports, he also presented Judith Anderson in Luigi Pirandello's *As You Desire Me* and August Strindberg's *Father*. None of Lee's solo shows made a profit.

Even more damaging was J. J.'s track record. Except for the 1929–1930 operetta revival season at the Jolson Theatre, which did well, J. J.'s musical factory had few offerings and no hits. J. J.'s last edition of *Artists and Models* in 1930 seemed like a faded reminder of times past. In desperation J. J. decided to revive *Blossom Time* and *The Student Prince* during the 1931 season.

Lee recognized that to survive they could no longer continue to present the same kinds of shows they always had, but J. J. was still attached to the ancien régime. Yet even he agreed to present his greatest star in a new guise. When *Wonder Bar* opened at the Nora Bayes Theatre on March 17, 1931, Al Jolson did not appear in blackface in a multiscene, cast-of-hundreds extravaganza. Rather, his new show was almost experimental, a tawdry backstage melodrama in an environmental staging. The theatre was converted into a nightclub as tables spilled from the stage into the orchestra. Shedding at last his blackface persona, Jolson, as the host of the Wonder Bar, a speakeasy, wandered out into the orchestra to greet the customers. Issuing welcome in several languages and delivering his dialogue in the staccato style of a movie gangster, Jolson came on like a precursor to Joel Grey's demonic master of ceremonies in *Cabaret*. Whenever he felt the show needed a lift, Jolson inserted his own topical humor and reminded the audience that he was back from Hollywood in a new kind of role but that he was Jolson still. Nevertheless, Jolson adhered to the script more than he had in the old Winter Garden shows, and his character had a seedy, menacing edge his fans didn't warm to. The show's disappointing run unnerved the Shuberts: if even the great Jolson in a modern musical failed to bring in enough patrons to show a profit, times were very bad indeed.

When federal court Judge Francis G. Caffey placed the Shuberts in receivership in 1931, the street was shocked: nobody had expected the Shuberts to go bust, perhaps not even the Shuberts. But despite their hectic roster, the Shubert Theatre Corporation had posted net operating losses of $1,230,000 in 1930 and $1,670,000 in 1931. On October 21, the corporation, which had been organized in 1924 to consolidate all Shubert enterprises and which controlled or had an interest in seventy theatres in New York and other cities, listed debts of $17,109,687. The Irving Trust Company and Lee Shubert were appointed coreceivers to continue the business of the Shubert Theatre Corporation.[2]

"The receivership is the result of two years of Depression," Lee announced grimly in the *New York Times* on October 22, 1931. "The cash resources of the Corporation have been so far reduced that the receivership seemed the only means of conserving the valuable properties and good will of the Corporation for the benefit of its creditors and stockholders." Before October 1929, the corporation had a paper value of twenty-four million dollars; its stock was listed on the New

York Stock Exchange for 85¼, and Lee and J. J. had personal equity in the company of between eight and nine million dollars. At the time of the receivership, the book value had slipped to half that amount—and you couldn't give the stock away with a set of dishes.

Lee was now faced with his greatest challenge since Sam's death had left him in charge of an expanding, unsettled, vulnerable empire. As always no one knew exactly how much the Shuberts were personally worth, but to keep the corporation going, Lee and J. J. put in their own money. On December 3, 1931, Lee claimed to have made a contribution of six hundred fifty thousand dollars; J. J.'s contribution was never itemized.[3]

Stunned by his losses, though as resilient and resourceful as ever in the face of crisis, Lee began to make draconian cuts in his staff. He halved his operating expenses. Jules Murry, head of the booking department, went off the payroll for about six months, and his assistant, Elias Weinstock, handled what few bookings there were. Joseph Gaites, head of production, was laid off. Claude Greneker, long-time head of the Shubert press department, was told to take an "indefinite" rest, and the formerly bustling press office was reduced to one full-time and two part-time employees. Ma Simmons, the veteran Shubert casting director, was also placed on leave for an unspecified period. (Both Greneker and Simmons were back on the job by the following year.) Of the heads of departments, only the man in charge of the theatres was still on the payroll: David Feinstone had moved down from Syracuse with Sam and remained with the firm until his death thirty-five years later.[4]

Throughout 1931 and 1932, as he was struggling to hold on to his business, Lee more heatedly than ever assailed theatrical labor unions. "The theatre alone is still burdened with the same vicious union conditions which were created during the inflationary period," he proclaimed. "If the unions—electricians and stage hands and scenic artists and authors—realize that times have changed, that everybody has to start again from the beginning, then the theatre can come back. Otherwise," he predicted, "there'll be no more show business. It will become as extinct as the dinosaur."[5]

During the receivership period, some independent bondholders in the Shubert Theatre Corporation accused Lee of conflict of interest and both Lee and J. J. of using the corporation's funds to enrich themselves. The aggrieved bondholders demanded an audit of the corporation going back to its founding in 1924. Among the revelations was the buying and selling of the Central Theatre, owned by the brothers, which was sold to the corporation then bought back by their real estate company, Trebuhs (Shubert spelled backwards), which turned around and resold it to the corporation at a profit to Lee and J. J. of fifty thousand dollars. Also uncovered was the fact that J. J. was leasing an apartment above the Central Theatre (where he had installed a mistress) for a dollar a year. Like many other judges both before and since, Judge Caffey treated the Shuberts leniently—he not only asked for no further audits but also extended the receivership period for another six months.[6]

But regardless of friendly judges, staff dismissals, reductions in the number of plays produced, and continued tirades against unions, Lee could not forestall the inevitable. On January 19, 1932, the *New York Times* reported that, to avoid bankruptcy, the Shubert Theatre Corporation would have to raise two million dollars by April. Moreover, the paper predicted, "should a sale of Shubert theatrical properties be forced in the near future, realty values are so shrunken that the mortgages would absorb most of the money." By the end of the year, on December 6, the *Times* reported that the Shuberts looked "washed up. It now seems unavoidable that the Shubert properties will go under the hammer in the process of liquidation. The Shuberts are through producing shows—they have no money left to try further production. During the receivership period, a year and two months, the business has lost $979,000."

On January 10, 1933, the court ordered liquidation. Once again Judge Caffey extended a helping hand to Lee, allowing him to resign as coreceiver so he could become a bidder for whatever was left of the Shubert enterprises. On February 11, 1933, at 10:30 A.M., the Shubert Theatre Corporation was to go on the block. Lee huddled with William Klein, trying to figure out how to take advantage of what was looming as a giant opportunity. He had decided, for once, that he did not want any anonymous angels to help. He asked for and received an extension; and on February 16, he announced a plan to form a new corporation, Select Theatres, which would purchase the properties of the Shubert Theatre Corporation from the receivers.

Assets of the corporation were ordered to be sold on the steps of the county courthouse at 11:00 A.M. on March 17, 1933. The properties were to be auctioned only for bids over four hundred thousand dollars. The estimated book value of the corporation in 1929 had been twenty-four million dollars; in 1933 it was said to be worth $12.5 million. Lee asked for another extension, which was granted, and on April 8, looking dapper, he appeared with William Klein to bid for his own properties. Reporters and photographers were present as the two men walked up the steps of the courthouse, and as usual Lee did not play to the camera. He looked stern and tense, but he was well aware that the drama he was enacting had heroic proportions; indeed he had worked carefully behind the scenes to ensure that the moment would be orchestrated in just this way. According to plan, Lee was the only bidder and his only bid was four hundred thousand dollars. Taking place near the end of FDR's first Hundred Days, Lee's drama highlighted the way the government and the courts were helping rescue big businesses like the Shuberts' and thereby ensure continued employment for many workers who would otherwise be bereft.[7]

The Shubert Theatre Corporation was no more. Risen from its ashes was a new entity, Select Theatres Corporation, with Lee Shubert as president and William Klein, vice president and treasurer. A longtime business associate, M. R. Weinberger, was named secretary. "All the stock is in the hands of the three of us," Klein announced, adding cryptically that "J. J. will not be a moving spirit in the new company."[8] Soon after the new company was formed, Lee offered one-half of the issue of common stock free to the creditors, stockholders, and holders of debentures of the Shubert Theatre Corporation "in the hope that I will be able to repay them in part or entirely for the investment lost in the Shubert bankruptcy. I want the investing public to know that my brother, the other members of my family and myself suffered our share of the losses in the Shubert Theatre Corporation. We didn't step out, leaving the public to bear the burden."[9]

Despite the heavy secrecy under which he operated during the receivership and the lingering suspicion that trailed his bookkeeping practices, Lee Shubert emerged from this life-and-death struggle as the man who had saved Broadway. Not since his early battles with the Syndicate had Lee appeared in so likable a role: against the odds and rising above a possible financial scandal, he had held to his purpose of salvaging whatever he could of the family business. His perseverance and steadiness and his shrewd negotiating saved the buildings that housed the American theatre. During the halcyon twenties, a massive Depression had never figured in Lee's projections for his empire; but when it hit, he was able to maneuver so smoothly and skillfully that it almost appeared as if a Depression and a company reorganization were part of his long-term game plan. In fact, of course, Lee was to preside over a business that was significantly diminished from what it had been in 1929. For the 1932–1933 season, the Shuberts presented only five productions; and for the rest of the decade—indeed, for virtually the rest of their careers—they continued to present only a handful of new offerings each season.

But if Lee Shubert had walked away from his business, the basic hardware of the American theatre might well have been demolished. "Lee carried the theatre through a ghastly Depression," Garson Kanin recalled.

> He held the theatre together, not only in New York but on the road, where he bought failing theatres for a song. It wouldn't have occurred to him to convert his theatres to other uses, even for a profit. Inherent in his makeup he was a shrewd businessman but he also had a genuine love of theatre as an institution, not only as a business. Lee Shubert was stagestruck, and the proof of it is the way he persevered during the receivership period, when he had every inducement to throw his hands up and dismantle the business.[10]

As the man who masterminded the resurrection of America's greatest theatrical empire, Lee Shubert was in his glory—and the glory was all his. As he was honestly trying to save his company (and the American theatre along with it) he was also taking advantage of the situation to stage a familial conquest as well. Not only was J. J. not to be a "moving spirit" in the new company but, by the end of the year, Lee would see to it that J. J. would no longer have the job he had created for himself in 1911.

"Lee told me at the time that he thought my father had lost a lot of his ability as a producer," John recalled. "Lee also resented the fact that my father had always acted as if he owned the Winter Garden. 'We're in a Depression now, the Winter Garden has to make money for us, and I just can't trust your father to do that,' Lee told me."[11] Lee's vindictiveness as always had a personal, as well as professional, basis. He resented that J. J.'s past successes at the Winter Garden had surpassed any of his own producing efforts, and he continued to be embarrassed by J. J.'s tirades, still commanding newspaper coverage (in January 1933, J. J. was forced to pay his former chauffeur five thousand dollars in damages after the chauffeur accused J. J. of striking him).[12]

J. J.'s fall had been foreshadowed since the end of the twenties. By then the lush and ornate revue style associated with J. J.'s Winter Garden spectacles, as well as the *Ziegfeld Follies*, had received a double blow—from the stock market crash and from the new phenomenon of all-talking, all-singing, all-dancing movie musicals, which could create fantasy on a scale the living theatre could not match. The first revue of the thirties (which actually opened on April 30, 1929) had a significant title: *The Little Show*. "Shunning ballyhoo and grandiloquence, it was anything but little in merit and importance," Gerald Bordman writes, "for it really began the long line of smart, superior connoisseur revues that were among the great delights of Broadway in the troubled thirties."[13] On the revue stage, twenties brass and glitter were replaced by a new streamlined format with a topical twist. Lee was willing to adapt to the genre's changes; J. J. was not.

In March 1932, Lee had been appalled by the poor reception of a musical called *Marching By*, a clunky adaptation of a German operetta J. J. had worked on with Harry B. Smith, Broadway's most prolific librettist and lyricist whose career had begun fifty years earlier. In October Lee on his own presented a smart revue in the new mode. The topics in the third of a series written by J. P. McEvoy, *Americana*, included disgraced politician James "Jimmy" Walker, breadline racketeers, the Forgotten Man, and the Kansas farmer, among other Depression-era targets, and it featured a song that became, in effect, the era's anthem, E. Y. Harburg and Jay Gorney's plaintive and haunting, "Brother, Can You Spare a Dime?" "Lee Shubert must have suffered during rehearsals from a good many doubts," Arthur Pollock wrote in the *Brooklyn Eagle* on October 7, concluding that "no musical

show on the American stage has ever satirized with such level-headed and intelligent savagery. It has a virility and an acidulous quality you are never likely to
have discovered in a revue before." Choreographed by such avatars of modern
dance as Doris Humphrey and Charles Weidman, the numbers echoed the astrin-
gent tone of many of the sketches. "They are of a kind not often to be seen on
stages less ambitious than that of Carnegie Hall," Pollock enthused. In one number, ten male dancers dressed as bums were placed austerely against a black drape.
In another, a shaker dance conceived in spartan chiaroscuro, performers in severe
costumes appeared on a simple wooden platform with a stiff-backed chair the
only prop. Even a bathing suit routine, announced in the program as a "water
study," adhered to the sober new tone as eleven dancers in plain-looking suits
formed impressions of waves building and then breaking. This was dance with a
more abstract vocabulary and greater intellectual ambition than any preceding
style of theatre choreography.

Too experimental for Broadway, *Americana* was not a commercial success.
But that Lee and Lee alone produced it was a portent of the surprise he was holding in reserve for J. J.

During this period, J. J.'s problems did not end with the theatre. Late in 1931,
his ex-wife "got into the hands of a very high-class lawyer [the aptly named]
George Gordon Battle, who persuaded her to reopen her divorce suit against my
father," John said. One of many lawyers Catherine Mary was to take as her lover,
Battle persuaded his client she could fight the Shuberts in court and win. Both
John and William Klein urged her to desist, but she refused. "My lawyer is going
to drag that sheeny kike father of yours in the mud until he gives up," Catherine
Mary told John with her usual elegance. In April 1932, a justice of the New York
Supreme Court dismissed Catherine Mary's claim and held that the original 1917
separation agreement was still binding; even though Catherine Mary contended
that she had signed under duress and that J. J. had bribed witnesses, the judge
noted that she had accepted the agreement at the time without making any
charges. Nonetheless, on Klein's advice, J. J. agreed to increase his former wife's
income, though he angrily refused to give her the million-dollar cash settlement
Battle had asked for.[14]

During the summer of 1933, John joined the family business, a move that
might have bolstered J. J.'s seriously faltering position. But perversely J. J. did not
want John to become part of the firm; and once John started to work with him,
he treated him like a competitor rather than a potential successor. John himself
was reluctant to begin a career in the theatre. He was afraid of being compared to
his father and uncle and worried that, like many sons of eminent parents, he
might not measure up. He was also keenly aware that he would be entering the
business against his father's wishes. Yet returning to Harvard Law School, where

he was about to enter his third year, was a more odious prospect than trying his luck in the family trade.

J. J. had often bragged over the years that it was he rather than his brother who had produced the one Shubert heir; but even before John entered the business, J. J. had not treated him like an heir apparent. Absorbed with affairs of state, J. J. had been a mostly absentee father. He and his wife had given their only child a distinctly peculiar upbringing. Because his nouveau riche parents hired only French-speaking domestics, John's first language was French. His first school was the Scudder School for Girls; and as a young man-about-town, John sometimes appeared in drag. At seven, in a photo taken when he was in Venice on holiday with his parents, John has prominent buckteeth and a stupid grin. Surrounded by his parents, both of whom are of Falstaffian proportions, he looks smothered. Only seven when his continually warring parents finally divorced in 1917, John was left with an indelible impression that family life was treacherous. "My parents could agree on absolutely nothing," he recalled, "and I played them against each other. I found out that it worked, that there was a good percentage involved. I don't think I did it maliciously. I think I found out it was the only way I could survive." [15]

A year after the divorce, when John and his mother lived in Long Beach, New Jersey, J. J., who by court order had limited visitation rights, rented a house nearby so he could spend some time with his son over the summer. John was placed in the awkward position of running back and forth between the two houses—good practice for the years he would play the go-between on West Forty-fourth Street carrying notes between his father and his uncle. "The situation in Long Beach was ridiculous," John recalled. "I was supposed to sleep in Father's house each night, but he often wasn't there, it was just me and four servants, and during the day I'd run to my mother's house to spend time with her. That's when I learned to become a diplomat; I couldn't show that I loved one better than the other."

When John developed a touch of consumption, his mother decided to rent an apartment near Van Cortland Park, in New York City, believing the fresh air in the park would be better for him than the sea air in Long Beach. By this point, however, J. J.'s penuriousness was beginning to tell, and the walk-up apartment was far more modest than the cottage mother and son had shared in Long Beach. "The rats in the undeveloped lots nearby were as large as dogs," John remembered.

One day during the year John was recuperating (way uptown beyond the last subway stop), J. J.'s usual check had not arrived on the first of the month. Catherine Mary, in her cups as she was more and more often, ordered John to go downtown to tell his father "how we live." In the kind of furious outburst John was getting used to, Catherine Mary urged the boy to demand more money "from that cheap bastard." And she also warned him not to pay attention to the "whores" who always hung around J. J. When he went to his father's office, he was told that Mr. J. J. was rehearsing the new show at the Winter Garden. John walked up to the theatre and timidly entered the auditorium as J. J. was barking orders to the musicians in the pit. When he noticed John, J. J. stopped the rehearsal and, as he sometimes could, played the role of a loving father. He embraced his son and kissed him on both cheeks. When John explained the situation at home, amending his mother's instructions in a way he hoped would not antagonize his father, J. J. did not hesitate. He pulled out a bulging roll of money and peeled off bill after bill, warning Johnny to "tell that woman I took out of Hell's Kitchen not to spend it all on alcohol."

"Ask my driver out front to take you home," J. J. said, as if issuing an order to an underling. When John entered the limousine, he saw a heavily made-up blond sitting on the far side of the backseat. Instinctively recognizing her as one of the women his mother had railed against, he went back into the theatre to announce to his father, with a bravado no doubt borne of the anger he felt toward both parents for having made him enact such a scene, that he would not ride in the same car with a whore. J. J.'s right fist lashed out in a split-second reflexive action and caught the boy full on the mouth. A moment later, J. J. demanded cold water and bandages from assistants. When he had patched John up, he walked him out to the limousine, now empty except for the driver.

After a year uptown, John and his mother moved back downtown, where they occupied a number of modest apartments. John saw his father only rarely during this period. He became his mother's son, her primary companion and number one bargaining agent in trying to extract more money from J. J. His parents communicated only through messengers. "My father believed in intermediaries," John recalled. "He always used somebody to do his talking for him, but when the chips were on the line he would meet my mother at his lawyer's office—they wouldn't speak directly to each other—where they would decide what to do with me."

With J. J.'s consent, Catherine Mary enrolled John in a Protestant high school, another parental choice designed to incite an identity crisis in their only child. It was there that John cultivated secrecy, which was to become characteristic. "I was the only person with any Jewish blood, and there was a great amount of persecution," John recalled. "I found out it was good not to let them know who I was. I soft-pedaled the fact that I had anything to do with the Shuberts."

John attended one more unlikely school, when he spent a fall semester at Fordham University filling time before he was to start at the University of Pennsylvania in February. At this Jesuit institution, he took Religious Evidence, a course intended for students preparing for the priesthood. When J. J. found out, "he flipped" and accused Catherine Mary of trying to widen the gap between father and son. But John had no thought of becoming a priest; he had merely felt that since he was at a Jesuit college it would be "the normal thing to do" to enroll in such a course. "This was no Catholic plot of my mother's either," John said. "She had been upbraided so severely by her priest when she married a Jew that she gave up the Church and never went back into one for the rest of her life."

Catherine Mary accompanied her son to the University of Pennsylvania, moving into a nearby apartment, where she spent most of her time drinking and entertaining men, usually lawyers. As he was later to do in New York, John began commuting among a number of residences, from his dorm to his mother's apartment to an apartment of his own that he used on weekends. Once he settled down, John was a decent student.

J. J. was the Shubert with the greatest respect for education, and John recalled his graduation from the University of Pennsylvania as the one time he had his father's undivided attention. J. J. went to the ceremony beaming. Next to him was an empty seat where Catherine Mary was to have sat; to escape having to face her ex-husband, she was at home, drunk. After the ceremony, J. J. snatched John's diploma, taking it back to New York, where for the rest of his life it was framed on the wall behind his desk.

J. J. decreed that John should go to law school; and through powerful real estate contacts in Boston, he arranged for John s acceptance at Harvard Law. The grand plan J. J. had conceived for his son—which pointedly did not include taking over the family business—was that after Harvard John would earn a doctorate at Oxford and then enter government service as a federal judge. "My father had very close connections with [Warren G.] Harding and [Calvin] Coolidge, though he wasn't a Republican—he had no political affiliation at all—and he was assured by the leader of the Republican Party that I would be appointed a judge." John went to Harvard because his father wanted him to, but he hated law school.

Because John was following orders, J. J. was generous. He set John (and Catherine Mary) up in a nicer apartment than they had been used to and had furniture from the Shubert warehouse sent up to decorate it. J. J. visited John more frequently than he ever had before. It was during John's first year at Harvard that Catherine Mary reopened her divorce suit. "Being a tough fighter, my father promptly cut off all funds," John said. Now practically destitute, Catherine Mary and John took a cramped apartment in a cheap hotel, which John paid for from his tuition money.

By the fall of 1932, John's second year in law school, J. J. had settled with Catherine Mary and was once again sending her alimony. John moved into an apartment in Cambridge with four other students, while Catherine Mary had an apartment of her own nearby. John later claimed to have graduated from Harvard Law School, but in fact he did not. He left to do what J. J. had never intended him to do.

When John joined the firm, J. J. was working on a new show, a musical called *Hold Your Horses* that was to reopen the Winter Garden in the fall. Plunging at once into a baptism by fire, John became a coproducer, a job for which he was not remotely prepared, and this first experience in show business gave him a preview of what working with his father would entail. (In a 1933 photograph taken at J. J.'s office, John looks callow and beaten as J. J. regards him suspiciously.) Lee knew by now that he did not want J. J. to be involved in the plans for the Winter Garden, but he had not yet officially banished him. Knowing he was on uncertain ground, however, J. J. became more truculent than ever. He barged into rehearsals, undermined John's authority, and proceeded to change the show. "He turned a musical comedy with a strong book into a revue," John said. John was both too inexperienced and too intimidated to defend either himself or the show from J. J.'s bullying; but in the Boston tryout, John's ability for getting along with coworkers emerged clearly. Story conferences were held in John's room rather than his father's. The show's star, Joe Cook, and its book writers, Russel Crouse and Corey Ford, seemed to pay more attention to John than to J. J., who began to make speeches to the company, in effect reminding them who he was. When J. J. had to return to New York, he left the director, R. Burnside, rather than John in charge.

After J. J. left, John called his uncle in New York to complain about how J. J. had treated him. "If you expect to survive in the business, you'd better get used to your father's way," Lee said. "I've had trouble with him all my life." Although Lee was then only a few weeks away from pushing J. J. out of the Winter Garden, he knew that he could never prevent J. J. from continuing to produce shows in other venues. Therefore, if John remained in the business, he would have to learn to cope with his father's tirades. Lee urged John to stay with the show and, in effect, to spy on his father by reporting back to Lee what J. J. did and said. John remained but could not prevent his father from, as Lee later put it, "ruining the Cook show."[16]

When the show opened to disappointing reviews and lackluster business, J. J. tried to convince John that he did not have the skill to be a producer. But Lee used the show's failure as further ammunition against J. J. Indeed, he may well have appointed John to the show in the first place as a ploy to incite J. J. Lee may well have been willing to risk a failure at the Winter Garden to harden his case against his brother.

In the fall of 1933, after the demise of *Hold Your Horses*, Lee was at last in a position to fire J. J. The new, Shubert-backed *Ziegfeld Follies* was being prepared for its January 4, 1934, opening at the Winter Garden, when Lee informed J. J. that he was to have no part in the production or in any other upcoming offering to be presented at the Winter Garden. "Lee told me he was going to do the *Ziegfeld Follies* himself," John said. "He hoped to God my father would keep away from the theatre during rehearsals."[17] J. J. was enraged: Lee's backstage putsch prevented him from savoring the victory of producing his old rival's show. J. J. still had a financial share in the business—a letter of agreement first signed in 1919 and renewed in 1922 made him an equal partner with Lee in company profits—but at least for the moment he was forced to suffer the embarrassment of having his theatre taken away from him. Lashing out at a convenient victim, J. J. demoted John from being a coproducer to the job of overseeing the Shubert shop, thereby placing John in a battle between J. J. and Lee. Furious at how he had been treated, J. J. refused to allow Lee to use the shop's scenery-building facilities for any Winter Garden show.

At his death in 1932, Ziegfeld had left his widow, Billie Burke, heavily in debt. Like everyone else in the theatre at the time, she turned to Lee Shubert for help: would he consider producing a new edition of the *Follies*? For Lee the prospect was doubly appealing—he could claim a sweet victory over his departed rivals, Ziegfeld and Ziegfeld's partner, Abraham Erlanger, and he could have the chance of beating J. J. as a revue impresario. As Lee embarked on preparing a new, post-Ziegfeld *Follies*, a lawyer representing the Ziegfeld estate charged him with using the Ziegfeld name without authorization and threatened to halt the upcoming production. But Lee presented a contract he had signed with Billie Burke and the estate of Abraham Erlanger, dated May 16, 1933, under the terms of which the nearly destitute widow was to be paid one thousand dollars outright and to receive 3 percent on gross earnings, to be shared with the Erlanger estate.[18]

Uncredited, though everyone in the business knew, the Messrs. Shubert in association with Mrs. Florenz Ziegfeld presented a new *Ziegfeld Follies* on January 4, 1934. Ironically, though he was not involved in the production, the new *Follies* looked like a J. J. special. *Variety* called it "a super-revival of the old Winter Garden extravaganzas, the most ornate of the Shubert *Passing Shows*."[19] (The Shuberts presented three other Shubertized *Follies*, with two editions in 1936 and a final entry in 1943.)

In the summer and fall of 1933, as he was plotting to remove his brother, Lee drastically altered the Shubert production portfolio, reducing the number of Shubert-backed shows while increasing his investments in the promising shows of other underfinanced impresarios. He was far too busy for hands-on involvement with the series of new-style revues he projected for the Winter Garden, and so he needed someone to represent him on a full-time basis. To succeed his deposed brother, he chose an obscure man named Harry Kaufman. Kaufman had started out as a sweater salesman in the garment district, where he made it a policy to entertain prospective buyers by taking them to the theatre. Before he went to work for Lee Shubert full time in the summer of 1933, Kaufman had become known on the street as a grassroots critic who loved to talk about the shows he had seen and could back up his opinions on why a show succeeded or failed with his vast, perhaps even record-setting, experience as a playgoer. Once he was installed in the Shubert Organization, Kaufman boasted that from 1910 to 1933 he had seen every show that had opened on Broadway. It was, in fact, in his self-appointed role as amateur critic that Kaufman had met Lee Shubert in the Turkish baths at the Hotel Astor.

After his sweater business folded in 1923, Lee encouraged him to go into the cut-rate ticket business, but Kaufman quickly discovered that he could not compete against Joe Leblang, the cut-rate king. Lee then suggested that Kaufman open a regular theatre ticket office. These were the days when brokers, operating with the instinct and savvy that had been the making of producers like Lee Shubert, often bought large quantities of tickets before a show opened; when their hunches were right, they charged as much as $15.00 for a $5.50 seat. After the ticket business became regulated in 1930 and a seventy-five-cent surcharge was made the legal maximum, Kaufman liquidated his business and became a partner in the Tyson–Sullivan Agency, in which Lee had a substantial interest.

Kaufman maintained to journalist Maurice Zolotow that his agency "never cheated on a single ticket and is one of the few agencies which the League [of American Theaters and Producers, Inc.] has never accused of charging more than the 75¢ advance." A rival broker, however, said that, because of his connection with the Shuberts, "Kaufman murders us, he's absolutely ruthless."[20] Kaufman countered that he was given more tickets to hit shows in Shubert theatres because his was the larger outfit.

Harry Kaufman was an adept meeter and greeter, a man with contacts. Not the least of his social skills was his ability to gain the confidence of Lee, who had never really trusted anyone before. Kaufman often accompanied Lee on late-night walks; conferred with Lee daily in Lee's circular office; went to Europe with Lee; attended Lee at rehearsals and opening nights. When Lee hired him, Kaufman moved into a modestly furnished office on the third floor of the Shubert Theatre Building. He had no title, no contract with the Shuberts, and no annual salary, but he got a piece of the shows he helped produce. Though Kaufman claimed he was "only a sort of Grand Vizier carrying out the orders of an unapproachable Sultan,"[21] Broadway insiders soon knew him as the power behind the throne—the man who dictated policy at the Winter Garden.

As Harry Kaufman was settling into his new job during the fall of 1933, John Shubert quit working for his father to produce shows for the Radio-Keith-Orpheum (RKO) circuit. He supervised tab, or abbreviated, versions of *Artists and Models*; a *Passing Show* built to RKO specifications, which was more RKO than Shubert; and *The Student Prince*. With a sixty-minute running time, the live tab shows played five times a day between film screenings at RKO movie palaces. John worked hard for a meager salary,

> about $100 a week I could keep for myself. My salary was a peculiar thing. At that time I was to give half to my mother—that was her income. As the cost of living increased and her standards seemed to increase, mine went proportionately downward. I ended up living in a small room at the Edison Hotel. Then that was too expensive and I moved to the Windsor. A small room. And then I shared it with my cousin Norman Light and a stage manager, Edward Duryea Dowling.[22]

In the summer of 1934, recognizing how useful John could be to him as his breach with J. J. widened, Lee offered his nephew a job. John already knew what he could expect working for his father, but crossing the street to Lee's side had difficulties as well. "I was scared of the business," John said. "Many times I thought of just quitting, and one of those times was when Lee offered me a job."[23] Catherine Mary, who saw John as her only chance to seize the Shubert millions she coveted, urged him to accept Lee's position. "Lee was always wonderful to me," John sometimes said; other times it was his uncle's coldness he recalled. The points at which Lee was "wonderful" to John seemed to coincide with the times when J. J. was being especially harsh. Lee had succeeded in seizing the Winter Garden from J. J.; in hiring John, he also seemed to be seeking to win the loyalty and affection of J. J.'s son.

Part of John's new job was to accompany his father to Europe and, following Lee's instructions, to see that J. J. did not buy any French costumes or scenery, which he had done in his heyday as a producer of revue, or any Viennese operettas, which, according to Lee, no one in America in the depths of the Depression would be likely to want to see. Nonetheless, J. J. continued to meet with Max Weldey, the top scenery and costume maker in France, from whom he continued to buy material that would then rot in the Shuberts' Greenwich Street warehouse. "Even through the Depression, Father was a sucker for a snow job by the smiling, personable M. Weldey," John recalled. Often John had to report to Lee that he had been unable to prevent his father from buying material for shows that were never to be. John's new job also included reporting to Harry Kaufman.

"Kaufman knew how to court important people," John said. "For instance, at his own expense he had Barney Greengrass's deli send out sturgeon and whitefish and smoked salmon once a week to Ira Gershwin in Hollywood." As a result, Kaufman was able to lure Ira Gershwin to New York to work on a new revue for the Winter Garden called *Life Begins at 8:40*. Using similar methods, Kaufman also secured E. Y. Harburg, Harold Arlen, and Dave Freedman (Eddie Cantor's sketch writer) for the same show.

> Those kind of people wouldn't work for my father. At the time Lee told me that these people might not work for us either, because the name "Shubert" meant all of us, and by then my father had a reputation as being a very tough customer to get along with. The best people shied away from "Shubert." Harry was a super salesman and he had gotten all these talented people to work for us because he had promised them that *he* would be their contact, not my father.[24]

Presented at the Winter Garden on August 27, 1934, *Life Begins at 8:40* marked a partial return to a twenties style. "It has the giant touch of the Messrs. Shubert, and is bigger than all bigness," Brooks Atkinson huffed.[25] An old revue hand from the earlier period, John Murray Anderson, directed, with his trademark opulence and mechanical precision. But there were plenty of new touches as well—in the modern-sounding music by Harold Arlen, the satiric lyrics by E. Y. Harburg and Ira Gershwin, and a fresh cast from which Ray Bolger and Bert Lahr were promoted to Broadway stardom. John Mason Brown, no Shubert fan, admitted that "although the Brothers Shubert have for many years been identified with a type of revue without the sophisticated trappings which of recent season have been gaining favor in Broadway's showshops they have made fortunate and generous use of these trimmings here. The show recalls the smart manner of *Bandwagon* and *Three's a Crowd* [two early-thirties revues, which had been critical and popular favorites]."[26]

For his next show, *At Home Abroad*, Lee was able to sign beloved comedienne Bea Lillie, but only after Harry Kaufman had mitigated her hatred of the Shuberts. She demanded a provision in her contract that J. J. could have no say whatever about the show. Even though it was J. J. who was being slighted, Lee fought to preserve the family honor. "Uncle Lee, substituting anything in place of such an outrageous insult in print, finally OK'd a clause that Harry Kaufman would have full say about the show," John said.[27]

Kicking off the 1935 season at the Winter Garden on September 19, *At Home Abroad* featured music and lyrics by the monarchs of early-thirties revue, Howard Dietz and Arthur Schwartz. This was a theme revue, with a world cruise providing a frame for such splendid performers as Bea Lillie, Ethel Waters, Eleanor Powell, and Eddie Foy, Jr., who each turned up in various guises in foreign countries. Classic numbers still cherished by the genre's connoisseurs included Lillie discoursing on double damask dinner napkins and Waters as a Hottentot potentate. Scenery, costumes, and direction were by Vincente Minnelli, new to the Shubert factory, whose bright colors and airy decor created an enchanting setting for song and dance. Brooks Atkinson hailed the show's "unity of appearance" while saluting its "extraordinary loveliness. Nothing quite so exhilarating as this has borne the Shubert seal before."[28] And *Variety* noted that in the entire show "there's not a bit of nudity, that alone in a Shubert revue being enough to go on the billing."[29]

By the time *The Show Is On* opened at the Winter Garden on December 25, 1936, "many a playgoer must have come to perceive the theatre as the home of the best revues of the period, which it often had been," Gerald Bordman writes, adding, "Indeed, for a while [the Winter Garden] was to revues what earlier the New Amsterdam had been."[30] By this point, Harry Kaufman was publicly recognized as the supervisor of the Lee Shubert musicals. Lee handled the money and helped to select performers, sketches, and songs, but Kaufman had J. J.'s former job as artistic supervisor.

Like *At Home Abroad, The Show Is On* was a theme revue, with show business replacing travel as the focus. Included were attacks on Eugene O'Neill and the Theatre Guild (Shubert bêtes noires), a spoof of John Gielgud's and Leslie Howard's competing Hamlets then playing in New York, Bert Lahr satirizing a Hollywood idol, and Bea Lillie taking off on "Josephine Waters," a burlesque of Josephine Baker's flop appearance in the *Ziegfeld Follies* of 1934, in which the toast of Paris in the twenties had failed to impress New York audiences. Minnelli's sets were once again notable for wit, unity, and subtle pastel coloring. "He has transformed all the material and performances into a luminous work of art," Brooks Atkinson raved.[31]

J. J. was chagrined as one revue after another got the kind of notices his shows had never commanded. As John said, "During the Depression the Winter Garden saved our bacon. Mr. Lee, with my assistance to a certain degree, and Mr. Kaufman's, did seven successful shows which ran through the Depression and saved the firm." As head of the Winter Garden operation, Kaufman exerted an enormous influence on Lee, who, as John noted, "had never really produced musicals before the thirties. And when he had it was the usual fiasco—it was because he was stuck on somebody in them, or he got talked into it. His heart wasn't in it."[32]

Kaufman encouraged Lee to take a more active part in the rehearsal process. Imogene Coca, who worked in several Shubert revues in the thirties remembered that Lee was wonderfully encouraging to her.

I worked for Lee in a revue in New Haven; the first performance lasted until 1:00 A.M., and after the show, as I was walking back to the hotel Lee came up behind me and put his arms around me and said, "At last something happened up there: you were funny, and you're going to be a star." I get a warm feeling whenever I think of Lee's embrace. I wanted to write him a thank-you note but never did: maybe this is my thank you.[33]

Despite Coca's testimony, however, Lee hadn't really mellowed, it was simply that, like practically everyone else, he adored Coca. A rare and notable exception was director John Murray Anderson. "He hated me," Coca claimed. "He staged my dance number, a ballet, 'Afternoon of a Faun,' in one, and put it at the beginning of the show, which was the wrong place for it. It was second-act material. It was one of the best things I ever did, and it had worked until Mr. Anderson came in; Mr. Simmons even told me that they would have spent more money on the set if they had known it was going to be that good." Lee did not come to her rescue, and neither did Kaufman.

While Kaufman was popular with Lee and some of the big stars he brought into the Shubert fold, he earned mixed to scalding reviews from others. "He had more clichés than a Madison Avenue advertising executive, and he held inane production conferences which always resulted in a monologue during which everyone suffered," John recalled. "But he did somehow manage to inspire the best efforts of everyone because he never professed to know anything about show business, except in a general way. He just loved to be around the theatre, and his enthusiasm rubbed off."[34]

"Kaufman was a real bastard, a pasty-faced, obnoxious man," Ezra Stone recalled heatedly more than fifty years after his last meeting with him. Eve Arden remembered Kaufman as the man who handled all the problems Lee Shubert "couldn't or didn't want to solve. [He had] marble eyes and shark's teeth hidden behind his closed smile."[35] "He was unspeakably vulgar," Agnes de Mille said.

He wore a big thick coat and was surrounded by men who were lawyers or who looked like lawyers and who brought girls who sat on the aisles during rehearsals. Working on *Hooray for What!* [a 1937 show supervised by Harry Kaufman] I was glazed with fatigue, apprehension, and fury. It was all enough to tear a person to pieces. I'm not suprised I had a stroke; my only surprise is that it took as long as it did to happen.[36]

If Kaufman's taste brought the Shubert revues of 1934, 1935, and 1936 a sheaf of unaccustomed critical kudos, his judgment began to falter on *Hooray for What!* Out of town, the show had been a sharp satire of the armaments race, a topical musical in the acidulous vein of the Gershwins' *Of Thee I Sing* and *Let 'Em Eat Cake*. But Kaufman allowed the show to become a carnival built around the star, Ed Wynn. Wynn's persona, the Perfect Fool, with his ridiculous clothes, his fatuous giggle, his lisping delivery, and his absurd gadgets and inventions took precedence over the originally tough-minded libretto by E. Y. Harburg, Howard Lindsay, and Russel Crouse and, to her everlasting chagrin, much of Agnes de Mille's antiwar ballet. "In those days you could be fired just like that!" de Mille recalled.

> And when I challenged Kaufman I was fired the next day, along with two of my dancers, Mary Greer and Dorothy Bird. Mary was a beautiful girl, brought up with quality and not an easy lay. Dorothy went off on parties—one of the producers took her out and then gave her a mink (she said it was mingy). She had a milkmaid beauty and became one of the leading dancers with Martha Graham. She was in *Hooray for What!* earning money to eat. After he had fired the girls, Lindsay and Crouse said to Kaufman, "No, you don't," and the girls went back in. I'd been made the football of Vincente Minnelli, the original director, who was also fired. Robert Alton was brought in for the dances—he was not underhanded or crooked and gave me advice about how to get by the Shuberts. The girls trusted him. I had trusted Minnelli, who was very nice. . . . But Kaufman and Lee didn't care about what they did, as long as it made money.

De Mille remembered that Lee was rarely to be seen at rehearsals and that on his infrequent appearances he hovered in the rear of the orchestra surrounded by an entourage of men in raincoats "who looked absolutely sinister. I often had the feeling I was working for the Mafia. Lee Shubert knew nothing about the arts of the theatre, and he had ceded his authority to that dreadful Kaufman. Rehearsals were like a hunt breakfast and I was the fox."[37]

When Lee and Kaufman reopened their hit of the previous season, *The Show Is On*, in the fall of 1937, they pulled a fast one. They recast the show with second-stringers: Rose King for Bea Lillie, Willie Howard for Bert Lahr, among others, and presented it briefly at the Winter Garden so that for the road tour the production could be advertised with the still-potent come-on "direct from Broadway." John Mason Brown grumbled that the "Messrs. Shubert owe it to patrons to remove the notices of the first edition from the portals—they were written with enthusiasm for a very different show. The show is off."[38]

One of the untalented chorines added to the grade-B edition of the revue was a woman named Marcella Swanson. Although no one knew it at the time, she was Lee's wife. He had married her in Berlin on July 29, 1936, and he would manage to keep the marriage absolutely unknown for a dozen years. A tall, cool blond and, like Catherine Mary, a Gentile with chiseled features and a fair complexion, Marcella appeared with her sister, Beatrice, in a number of Winter Garden revues. "She was a cluck who couldn't sing a note but was tall and lovely and looked beautiful in the costumes," recalled Ethel Lynne, who performed with her in the late

twenties. Like Lee, Marcella was remote, and while Catherine Mary spent a lifetime attacking the Shuberts, Marcella maintained the public silence and composure Lee demanded. "She had no *tam* [flavor]," Lynne remembered. "She was
aloof and secretive, and we all thought it was her sister Beatrice who was with
Lee."[39] Office worker Miriam Krengel Pulvers said that Marcella was "vapid-look-
ing and didn't appear to have much of anything on her mind; this may have been
misleading as she was smart enough to catch the prize, to wit Lee Shubert. Un-
doubtedly many others had tried over the years."[40]

"We all knew Marcella was Lee's mistress," recalled William Packer, who
acted with her in 1938 in a play called *Bachelor Born*, "but we received the news
that they were actually married with astonishment. They didn't live together—he
lived in the Century Apartments; she lived in a beautiful apartment at First Avenue and Fifty-ninth Street. I got to know Marcella very well, and she never said a
word about being married." Packer said that he was once playing bridge backstage
with Marcella during a performance and missed a cue. He was sure that Lee would
fire him instantly, "but Marcella spoke to Lee, saying it was her fault, and Lee
never said a word to me."[41]

Once the secret marriage was exposed in 1948, observers had varying inter-
pretations of Lee's behavior. William Packer's sister Annette, who also became
friendly with Marcella, speculated that "Lee couldn't marry her because she
wasn't Jewish and his family, especially his parents, were Orthodox."[42] Yet by 1936,
both of his parents had long been dead; and besides, Lee had only the faintest
religious convictions and no respect for his father's beliefs anyway; to him, Or-
thodoxy was a one-way ticket to the poorhouse. John Kenley offered another explanation.

> Lee had five o'clock girls every day including Saturday, and there was a special
> girl on Sunday. They were sent to him by a Miss Leach, who claimed to be
> the sister of Archie Leach, who became Cary Grant. She sent him two girls
> at five; Lee's lawyer Klein said it should always be two so the girls couldn't
> claim rape. Then Marcella came for dinner; I don't know what was left for
> her, or if she knew. Marcella was sweet and laid back—that was why she
> lasted.[43]

It is likely that Lee pretended to be a bachelor to be able to conduct his daily
trysts without the public appearance of adultery. The "girls" who were sent up to
him may have been more likely to sue or threaten him with blackmail if they had
known he was a married man. Before his marriage, Lee had had a string of pub-
licized affairs with famous women: the Polish opera diva Ganna Walska; a Ziegfeld showgirl named Justine Johnston, for whom he opened a nightclub in his 44th

Street Theatre; the much-married sometime showgirl Peggy Hopkins Joyce, whose choice of mates was always guided by the size of their bank accounts; and Jeanne Eagels, a great stage actress of the twenties. "Jeanne Eagels was the love of his life," playwright Ruth Goetz said.

> Lee once asked me if I had seen *Rain*, in which she played Sadie Thompson, and when I said yes, he asked me if I liked the actress who starred in it, and when I said yes, he got very quiet. It was my father [Randolph Goodman] who told me how much Lee loved Jeanne Eagels; and when my father asked him why he didn't marry her, he said he was afraid if he married her she would want a child and she would die in childbirth—she had been very much a woman-about-town [she was also bisexual]—and he would kill himself.[44]

Though it is unlikely Lee Shubert would have committed suicide for any reason, Jeanne Eagels was in fact doomed: she was a drug addict who died from an overdose in 1929.

As Ethel Lynne said, there were rumors that Lee had had an affair with Marcella's sister. "Beatrice was so much taller and so much more willowy," John Shubert said. "But Marcella had a wonderful personality and honest-to-goodness warmth, and I think Lee realized that she was the girl for him."[45] (John and other family members knew of the marriage.) Since Marcella was willing to hide her marriage and to agree to the financial restrictions that accompanied any Shubert marriage contract, she may well have been "the girl for him." Marcella nonetheless was strong willed. Against his objections—Lee gained nothing from a formal marriage, he did not want children, and he cared not at all for the respectability that being a married man conferred—she had convinced Lee to marry her. Lee realized he cared for her enough to comply—so long as she agreed to keep the marriage secret. It is possible, finally, that Lee was determined to keep his marriage a secret simply because secrecy was an elemental part of his nature. The close-to-the-vest, inscrutable style he cultivated in the office may have become habitual. Lee Shubert was as garrulous as the Sphinx, and he may well have felt that his marriage was nobody's business.

Lee was also said to have had a secret son. In 1927, an appellate court decided he had to pay seventy-five dollars a week to Frederica Bond, an ex-showgirl who charged that Lee was her child's father. Lee denied paternity but agreed to make payments. He also paid Bond's son seventy-five dollars a week, up to the age of twenty-four. Lee, of course, arranged for the settlement to be kept secret, at least until 1942 when Bond sued for continued support. Lee claimed to have paid "woman and child" $116,000 and agreed to pay the child $24,000 in additional funds. But he insisted he was no longer obligated to pay the plaintiff because she was now married. Although this "stipulating provision was omitted by error from the original judgment," payments were to extend for only three years if she married after ten years from the "date of arbitration."[46] In May 1983, Lee's "son" applied for an order permitting him to open a file Lee had managed to have sealed at the time of the hushed-up 1927 settlement. The alleged son, then fifty-seven, notified the executors of the still-unsettled Lee Shubert estate that he was entitled to more money, but the Board of Directors of the Shubert Foundation contested his petition and won.[47]

After Lee banished him from the Winter Garden, J. J. turned his attention to operetta. Each summer he produced a slate of his favorite operettas at the Muny in St. Louis and other large outdoor theatres. He also continued to present an occasional new operetta on Broadway. *Music Hath Charms*, a 1934 show with a score by Rudolf Friml, was J. J.'s attempt to get back in harness after the shame of having been ousted from his home base. Because he felt at the time that he had a great deal to prove—to Lee, to Harry Kaufman, to John, to the theatre community, and not least to himself—J. J. was especially tense during rehearsals, and he had many run-ins with his equally fiery composer. Friml was a "crazy, sex-mad Czech," according to John. "He was a great talent, but he was hard to handle."[48] At that point, J. J. was extremely hard to handle as well. The show the two fought over was doomed. About a young fisherwoman who loves a duke, *Music Hath Charms* had "yesterday" written all over it. "Back to the Old Deal in operetta," Brooks Atkinson griped. "In fact, way back. The Shuberts have not mounted it to improve their reputation for progress in the arts."[49] "It's the kind of new production which is so old-fashioned in its plotting and so exhausted in its attempts at humor it persuades you it must be a revival," wrote John Mason Brown, adding that "we could not help but think back to the other operettas that once were common, and understand why it is that they, like knighthood, are no longer in flower."[50]

J. J. fared no better with two 1937 operettas. *Frederika*, about a village maid who renounces Johann Goethe, revived *The Student Prince* formula. *The Three Waltzes* offered a variation on *Maytime*: the grandchildren of lovers separated in 1865 because of social etiquette make a go of it in 1937. But by then, J. J.'s attention was primarily on his summer productions. In 1936 he had discovered "thievery in the box office at the Muny," as John reported.

We were not on a percentage—we had a guaranteed salary—but my father was outraged. He put a counter on the door to click admissions coming in, and the box office statement he received showed three or four thousand less. He told the mayor of St. Louis, a man by the name of Kiel, after whom they named an auditorium, one night at a dinner party, and the next day my fa-

ther's contract was not renewed. He was determined to get even—he was going to produce open-air shows and ruin them. He was going to take away their
fame.[51]

To help fight his open-air war, J. J. decided he wanted John on his team; and early
in 1937, he asked his son to work for him. Warily, John crossed over to J. J.'s side.

Employing an old Shubert tactic, J. J. tried to clobber the opposition through
sheer quantity. The theatre at Jones Beach, Long Island, was his opening salvo,
followed by a theatre at Randalls Island in the Bronx; the State Fair at Dallas,
Texas; Billy Rose's Aquacade in Cleveland, Ohio; and an amphitheatre in Louis-
ville, Kentucky. Office worker Abner Klipstein recalled that J. J.'s mushrooming
summer circuit began when Fortune Gallo, a small, rotund, ebullient man who
owned a second-rate opera company, "bounced" into the office to ask J. J. to come
in with him on his operations at Jones Beach and Randalls Island.

> To attract customers Gallo wanted to mix Shubert operettas with his operas,
> and J. J. had the operetta catalog and warehouses full of scenery and cos-
> tumes. Gallo had connections with Robert Moses, so it was a trade-off. J. J.
> wanted to bring John into the setup. He wanted John to publish the souvenir
> books, which sold for twenty-five cents and cost five cents. Originally Claude
> Greneker had the concession, but when J. J. found out how much money it
> took in he grabbed it away from him.[52]

Going along with his father's battle plans, John spent the summer going from one
theatre to another. The pace was killing, and John lasted only two years. By the
end of the thirties, J. J. withdrew from the open-air circuit. The Muny, which he
enlisted John to help him "ruin," is still in business.

Working again for J. J., John made the mistake of entering into coproduction
with the Messrs. Shubert on a musical called *You Never Know*, which opened at
the Winter Garden on September 21, 1938. John also cowrote the libretto with
Rowland Lee; the score was Cole Porter's least successful. No longer banished from
the Winter Garden, J. J. worked on the new show. As he had with *Hold Your Horses*
(though this time with Lee's approval), J. J. Winter Gardenized an intimate musical comedy. The show was set in Paris, and J. J. ordered big production numbers
in the Gare du Nord, the Lido, and the base of the Eiffel Tower; and he added
interpolated specialty turns by the Hartmans (a dance team) and by the Debon-
aires (a half dozen six-foot tap dancers). He enlarged the originally small-scale
musical with sixteen dancing girls and twenty-four showgirls. And once again
John stood by, helpless. John also blamed George Abbott, the production's third
director, who during the closing week in Chicago took a blue pencil and "cut the

audience's agony from 2½ hours to 1¾. The audience was grateful to George, but I was outraged at the emasculation of the fairly decent musical adaptation I had co-concocted," John later lamented.[53]

Lee and J. J. took the failure of the new Winter Garden show in stride because on the very next day they opened a production that turned out to be one of their all-time moneymakers—and the last Shubert blitz on Broadway. The Shuberts were in fact silent partners, and at first they had been reluctant ones as well. Persuaded by the enthusiasm of radio pioneer Niles T. Grantland, Lee had gone with John and Harry Kaufman to Philadelphia to see a ninety-minute show that a couple of zany clowns from vaudeville and nightclubs had been playing in minor vaudeville houses for twenty-five years. The next day, in a pronouncement he was to regret, Kaufman (according to John) claimed that the comics, Ole Olsen and Chic Johnson, were "too offbeat" for a Shubert revue and that their show, *Hellzapoppin'*, didn't stand a chance on the main stem. Lee, however, had enjoyed their surreal humor and invited the pair to New York to audition the show on a bare stage for a select audience, which in the event consisted of Niles Grantland, Harry Kaufman, Shubert house director Eddie Dowling, John, Lee, and Lee's entire clerical staff. J. J. surprised everyone by turning up uninvited.

"The chorus line was sixteen gals of different sizes and ages who had been recruited from every tank town that Olsen and Johnson had played in the last twenty years," John recalled.[54] On the stage was one lone pianist; the lights were dim and poorly focused besides; drapes had been carelessly hung; and a half carload of props were dragged out by stagehands who had been rounded up at the last minute and hadn't a clue about the show. There were no costumes, no makeup. "Olsen and Johnson ran through the audition as if it was all a nightmare that wouldn't go away," John said. John remembered becoming "increasingly hysterical" not so much because of the comics' well-worn routines as the bizarre spectacle of curtains opening and closing at the wrong times, of miscued lights, and of Lee and Kaufman looking utterly stone-faced. Except for John, the rest of the audience remained as silent as a tomb.

Olsen, the gaunt straight man, and Johnson, the moonfaced cutup, looked like traveling salesmen gone to seed. Their success was based not on their slender comic gifts but on sheer daredeviltry, their eagerness to rock the house. Like Lee, J. J. saw the possibilities in the threadbare, amateur production they had just endured. "$7,000," he said cryptically when it was over, though he hadn't exactly been asked for any comments, and then he left. Lee understood. "$7,000—we'll take a chance if it can be done for that," John recalled Lee saying. J. J.'s opinion still counted for something after all. Olsen and Johnson put up a matching amount.

Lee and Kaufman brought the production up to Broadway standards. Kaufman persuaded magazine illustrator John Held, Jr., to design ten backdrops and Sammy Fain to compose a brace of new songs. Robert Alton was engaged to choreograph the not-so-chipper-looking chorines, and Mort Lewis and Tom McKnight were hired to spice up the comedy on the promise that their contributions, like the Shuberts', would remain anonymous. John recalled that the director, Eddie Dowling, would sneak into rehearsals at the Imperial and then, making certain that no one saw him, dash for the stage door of the 46th Street Theatre, which was about fifty feet away.

Hellzapoppin' opened at the 46th Street on September 22, 1938, for a total cost of $14,520. Only one hundred seats were sold for the premiere; Shubert employees and their friends were ordered to fill the remaining eleven hundred seats. Audience reaction was exuberant, though among the critical fraternity only Walter Winchell expressed enthusiasm. Winchell's plugs on the radio and in his column turned the show into a must-see attraction; and for one of the few times in their careers, the Shuberts were actually grateful to a critic. At the end of the performance opening night, Richard Rodgers and Sam H. Harris approached Lee with an offer to buy 10 percent of the production for twenty thousand dollars, but Lee reasoned that if these two pros were so excited he'd keep the show for himself.

When *You Never Know* closed after an abbreviated run, *Hellzapoppin'* moved to the Winter Garden. And 1,404 performances later, it claimed the long-run record (at the time) for a Broadway musical. The merely serviceable score by Sammy Fain and Charles Tobias, however, was a minor element in its success compared to the sight gags, the sound effects, the high-voltage interaction with the audience, the belly laughs cooked up by Olsen and Johnson in their first shot at the big time. *Hellzapoppin'*, which has become a synonym for a theatrical free-for-all, was a hootenanny that provided audiences with a respite from sobering news of a world headed toward war.

In a filmed prologue, three political leaders praised the show the audience was about to see: "Adolf Hitler" spoke in a Yiddish accent, "Benito Mussolini" sounded like a Harlem soapbox orator, and "FDR" spouted pure gibberish. The show, however, had no social or political agenda—*Hellzapoppin'* was old-time variety with a touch of burlesque. More than half the performance was conducted in the aisles. Workmen with large ladders trundled through the rows, forcing patrons to rise, and the audience was showered with beans and bursting balloons. A woman in the audience screamed that she had left her baby at the Automat and then rushed out of the theatre. Another woman walked the aisles yelling for Oscar. A stuffed gorilla dragged a lady out of a box seat. A Gentleman Godiva appeared on a horse in the upper balcony. In the most popular running gag, a man walked up and down the aisles in an effort to give a lady a plant she had ordered; with each of his appearances, the plant grew larger and larger; and at the end, the audience could see the man sitting in the lobby next to a small tree as he continued to call out the woman's name. The sounds of pistols, sirens, and firecrackers filled the air. To preserve the fluid structure, Olsen and Johnson added and subtracted routines and gags throughout the run. Giddy, swiftly paced, and cavalierly thumbing its nose at theatrical decorum, *Hellzapoppin'* was 3-D theatre.

"The successful musical shows of the immediate future will be fashioned around laughs and not social significance," Harry Kaufman warned shortly after *Hellzapoppin'* had settled in as a surprise hit. "With a world in turmoil, playgoers want entertainment, want to forget trouble, want to laugh," he announced.[55] Once Olsen and Johnson became Broadway luminaries, Kaufman changed his earlier estimate of them; within the Shubert firm, he assumed the role of their chief promoter and began to claim that he had discovered them and given them their chance to graduate from two-bit vaudeville. (Kaufman and Lee went to bat with Olsen and Johnson on two more shows, *Sons o' Fun*, which opened at the Winter Garden a week before Pearl Harbor was attacked, and *Laffing Room Only*, the last Shubert revue, which debuted at the Winter Garden on December 23, 1943. Both entries were more of the same—madcap, carnivalesque musicals that were part smoker, part burlesque, part revue, part New Year's Eve pandemonium, and more expensively produced than their progenitor. For their revue finale, Lee and Kaufman hired John Murray Anderson, the pacesetting revue director who once again adjusted his style to a new wrinkle in the genre he had helped mold in the teens in Greenwich Village. He gave *Laffing Room Only* a slickness completely absent from *Hellzapoppin'*, but still no part of the Winter Garden was out of bounds for the resident buffoons. Olsen and Johnson climbed up into the boxes by rope and ladder and dropped from and disappeared into the flies. Rabbits multiplied in geometric proportions. A six-hundred-pound bear made a surprise cameo appearance. Furniture collapsed. And, seeming to take on a life of its own, the scenery jumped and swayed.)

After Olsen and Johnson, Lee had one last prize, a performer he discovered on a cruise to Rio de Janeiro. He had been told about her in advance, but he had the sense to recognize that if Carmen Miranda were properly presented in New York she could become a star. He put her into a 1939 summer revue, *The Streets of Paris*, which also featured the Broadway debuts of Bud Abbott and Lou Costello (whom Harry Kaufman found in a burlesque theatre in Newark) and Gower Champion. Miranda came onstage at the end of the first act, outfitted in one of the monumental fruit-laden comic headdresses that were to become her signature, swinging and wriggling her hips, flashing her eyes, rotating her arms, undulating every part of her anatomy, and singing "The South American Way" in her high-pitched yet husky style. A star was unmistakably born.

Since Miranda refused to rehearse at full steam, no one connected with the show except Lee knew what she was capable of. To the rest of the company and to the exasperated director, Eddie Dowling, who could not understand why Lee insisted on giving Miranda and her band the privilege of closing the first act, she seemed listless. Lee's stubbornness paid off opening night in Boston, when Miranda, facing a full house, exploded into action.

Miranda's six-minute number was the hit of a show that had little to do with the streets of Paris. As with Olsen and Johnson, the Shuberts' timing was apposite—Miranda appeared at the start of the Latin American craze that was to sweep through American popular culture in the forties. Although there were dissenters—some Brazilians felt that Carmen sailed to stardom on a shipload of ethnic stereotypes—only a die-hard sourpuss could resist her incandescent smile and her sly, delirious English.

Lee instructed Claude Greneker to promote the hot new star, and Greneker's campaign was to be one of the firm's most blatant and successful promotional efforts. A bonanza of exploitation for a star who loved it, it was something of a last hurrah for the Shuberts as big-time commercial showmen. Ironically, it was Lee rather than J. J. who orchestrated the Miranda madness—Lee who had wanted three decades earlier to have the prestige of heading an American national theatre. There were rumors of an affair between Lee and his Brazilian Bombshell. When Bidú Sayão, a Brazilian opera singer, visited Carmen backstage after a performance, she reported that Carmen told her she ought to meet Lee Shubert, who would be "a wonderful manager for you, too. You don't have to do anything. You just lay on the bed and he does everything!"[56]

Greneker arranged for Miranda to do a radio commercial for Rheingold Extra Dry Beer, to launch a "South American Turban Tizzy" for Macy's Department Store, and to pose for fashion layouts. Shoe stores sold versions of Miranda's trademark platform sandals and department stores across the country sold replicas of her costume jewelry and headgear. Carmen and the Shuberts enjoyed a substantial cut of all the gross sales. Another, more local way in which the Shuberts exploited their new star was in injecting a travesty of her in their concurrent *Straw Hat Revue*. "Mr. Simmons got the idea [for me] to do a satire of Carmen Miranda when the dancer who did a ballet with me in the show refused to do the number," Imogene Coca remembered.

> I had never seen Carmen, so I went to see her show and told her afterwards what we were planning. She couldn't have been nicer. She helped me to parody her, and gave me tips and pointers. I have no ear for foreign language, so her Portuguese came out sounding like a thick stew. But then it was reported in gossip columns that when she saw me perform she was upset. Claude Greneker, the press agent for both shows, said that it didn't matter if the re-

port was untrue—it was good for business. I thought that was terrible. Of course Carmen wasn't upset; she had known I was going to satirize her, and besides she had too much of a sense of humor to be upset.[57]

After Jolson, Carmen Miranda may well have been the Shuberts' greatest discovery. But unlike Jolson, Miranda did not last long on the Shubert payroll. Her original contract gave the prescient Shuberts half of every cent she was to earn on Broadway or elsewhere in the United States; and Carmen, as shrewd about money matters as her bosses, soon rebelled. Abner Klipstein remembered that the star was paid

on Friday night, and she insisted on being paid in cash. She even wanted cash for the three or four checks I had given her early on. I collected cash from the Shubert box offices where they knew me. She didn't know anything about American money, or at least she pretended not to know anything. But she knew what she needed to know. She was quite a character. "You come to South America and I'll give you my sister," she told me.[58]

In 1940, between her appearances in Shubert revues, Miranda went to Hollywood to appear in *Down Argentine Way* for Twentieth Century–Fox, where she told costar Don Ameche about how Lee Shubert was taking 50 percent of all her earnings. Ameche urged her to break her contract, assuring her that she would be better off with a Hollywood agent. He introduced her to his own, George Frank. But Carmen had been made aware that the Shuberts sued anyone who dared to breach one of their contracts. The only solution was for her to buy her way out of her contract with Lee, which Carmen did, though for how much was a matter of dispute. Carmen claimed it was seventy-five thousand dollars, and to accumulate that amount she and her band accepted a grueling, two-week engagement at the six-thousand-seat Roxy Theatre during which they performed nine shows a day. On August 19, 1942, *Variety* reported that Carmen's passport to freedom was sixty thousand dollars; Carmen's Brazilian manager claimed it was one hundred thousand. Whatever the actual sum, it was, for the time, a sizable bundle.[59]

After the Brazilian Bombshell, Lee and Harry Kaufman began to flounder as producers of revue. Relations between Lee and the man who had been at his beck and call for seven years also deteriorated as the quality of their shows declined. "He wanted billing," John said, "and he started becoming too big. He was therefore doomed to extinction by Lee as well as by my father." With a 1942 show called *Wine, Women and Song*, Lee hit the bottom of his career in musical theatre. Coproducing with Max Liebman and I. W. "Izzy" Herk, a burlesque impresario who had been a partner in Shubert Advanced Vaudeville in the twenties, Lee billed the show, desperately, as "a revue-vaudeville-burlesque." *Wine, Women and Song* blatantly ripped off *Star and Garter*, Michael Todd's hot new burly-cue, which had opened a few months earlier. In place of Gypsy Rose Lee and Bobby Clark, the genuine articles who starred for Mike Todd, Lee and his partners substituted an ersatz stripper, Margie Hart, and B-level clowns Jimmy Savo and Pinkie Lee. Accused of being obscene, the show was closed by police order and the theatre where it was playing was padlocked for nearly eleven months. Izzy Herk spent a short time in jail. "J. J. gloated," John said. "He was pleased to see Lee fail after so many years of success in revue, which my father always considered his territory, and he felt vindicated when Lee and his coproducers were hit with the smut-peddler label. He had had his battles with bluenoses, too, with his *Artists and Models* series."[60]

A nightclub entrepreneur named Clifford Fischer was the last fast talker to inveigle his way into the Shubert musical department. Fischer convinced Lee that bringing back old-time vaudeville would be a cheap way of keeping Shubert theatres lit during wartime. The four shows Fischer managed to push through the Shubert turnstile, on all of which he had coproducer credit, were simple, bare-bones vaudeville—bargain-basement theatre at bargain-basement prices of one dollar for matinees, two dollars for evenings. The often appealing performers, including Zero Mostel, Hazel Scott, Hildegarde, Jack Cole, Gracie Fields, and Henny Youngman, used their own material, and the only sets were drops from the Shubert warehouse. *Priorities of 1942, Keep 'Em Laughing, Top Notchers,* and *New Priorities of 1942*, produced between March and September, were last-ditch efforts in a vaudeville format, a format in which the Shuberts had never been successful. After Harry Kaufman died in 1944—"fortunately, or let's say unfortunately, cancer got him before Lee did," John said—Lee never produced another revue.[61]

When Carmen Miranda tried to duck out of her contract with Lee by going to Hollywood, J. J.'s greatest star, Al Jolson, headed in the opposite direction. After a ten-year absence, during most of which he had languished in Hollywood playing second fiddle to his wife, Ruby Keeler (then enjoying an improbable movie success as the world's most leaden-footed tap dancer), Al Jolson returned to a Shubert stage one final time. In his comeback vehicle, which opened at the Shubert on September 11, 1940, Jolson played a radio cowboy on a dude ranch: East meets West in a musical comedy pattern established in 1930 with the Gershwins' *Girl Crazy. Hold on to Your Hats* was more plot driven than the Winter Garden extravaganzas, and there were no interpolations—all of the songs were composed by Burton Lane, with lyrics by E. Y. Harburg. Even with Martha Raye as costar, however, Jolson focused more on the audience than on anything that happened onstage. When he entered by walking to a chair center stage and talking to the audience in the colloquial, topical manner he had made entirely his own, he at once "established his pre-eminence and banished formality," John Mason Brown wrote.

"Jolson spills his public secrets with a breezy surety belonging to a vanished race of vaudevillians," Brown continued. "His eyes shine like two black moons when a gag is coming or an innuendo stands in need of illumination."[62] And at the end, Jolson bounded onto the stage, notifying the audience that the critics had gone home and the show was over, and asking what they wanted him to sing.

As at the Winter Garden, Jolson was both in and out of the show, host and performer, a hero within the play and at the same time a raconteur turning his own life into the stuff of legend. In 1940, Jolson was clearly an old-timer, a reminder of an ebbing show-business tradition, just as the show itself, a patchwork star vehicle, recalled the splashy Winter Garden revues of yesteryear. When the show closed after a disappointing twenty-week run, the longest creative association in Shubert history came to an end. Through numerous battles over salary and a sojourn in enemy country in Hollywood, Jolson maintained his atavistic loyalty to the New York producers who had helped make him a star. His relations with Lee remained remote, but Jolson felt a kinship with J. J. that overrode all their clashes. J. J.'s affiliation with his Winter Garden star was his most notable theatrical achievement: J. J., the "other" Shubert, could claim the distinction of being the sole architect of the Broadway career of one of America's most dynamic entertainers.

The Jolson show, however modest its reception, reminded J. J. of the good old days. Throughout the thirties, both before and after Lee's coup at the Winter Garden, the shows J. J. had personally supervised were critical and financial duds. While Lee had been credited with saving the theatre and was riding high on a series of well-received revues, J. J. had become a Broadway has-been. His appearance and his office reflected his fallen estate. Where Lee was a smart dresser and stained a perpetual brown, J. J. was increasingly rumpled and red faced, and he was paunchy where Lee was lean. "J. J. looked like a fretful caterer specializing in weddings and bar mitzvahs," playwright Arthur Kober remembered.[63] J. J.'s suite of offices on the sixth floor of the Sardi Building had always been disarmingly modest, but after his removal from the Winter Garden they had grown shabby.

In 1934, when J. J. was nursing his freshly inflicted wounds, a young woman named Miriam Krengel answered an ad for a secretary for the Select Theatres Corporation. At that time, the offices were no more than ten years old, but she recalled the place as "old" and "musty" and "unattractive."[64] When aspiring actress Dorothy Tewlow Reissman first went to J. J.'s office in 1941, she was

> surprised at how poor looking it was. When you walked in from the sixth-floor elevator there was an empty room, then a room where a woman named Loretta sat. She was a hard-bitten Irishwoman who scared the hell out of me. She sat barricaded behind her desk. You would say, "Good morning, Loretta."

You wouldn't dare not say hello to her—she guarded the throne. Everybody had to sit out there in that depressing room—nobody just walked in. And you could sit there for hours. There were old-fashioned wooden chairs, and there wasn't a picture or a poster on the walls. There wasn't even a magazine. It was dismal. After Loretta's outer office there was another office, a large dark area where J. J.'s secretary had her desk. Unlike Loretta, Belle Jeffers was very nice. She'd been with J. J. for years and years, and I always wondered how she was able to see to do her work. Then after her office at last you reached the inner sanctum, J. J.'s office, which had a window so there was some light at last. Mr. J. J. sat behind a big desk.[65]

J. J.'s manner was typically as unwelcoming as the appearance of the workplace. On the first day of her job, Miriam Krengel took dictation from "what I considered an old man with a huge cigar in his mouth. He spoke quickly with what I thought was a slight foreign accent. He made no attempt whatever to introduce himself or to add a note of welcome to a new office employee." It was only later that she learned she was working for J. J. Shubert, who was "world-renowned." Miriam Krengel did not last long on the sixth floor. "One day, after working pretty hard, with not much appreciation, Mr. Shubert asked me at six, in a sharp tone, 'Where are you going? There is more to be done here.' He lived in a very large apartment above the offices and I had at least a one-hour subway ride home. And there was no overtime." When she complained to Stanley Yoseloff, the lawyer who had hired her, he suggested that since she had legal experience she might be happier in the Shubert legal offices at 1860 Broadway, working for William Klein. "I went over to Mr. Klein's office, where I felt right at home, and stayed for six years."[66]

"Mr. J. J. had whims, and the office staff had to pay for them," recalled Dorothy Derman, a legal stenographer who worked on the sixth floor in the late thirties.

He'd get up one morning and decide he was going to Europe within twenty-four hours, and he wanted to take a résumé of every single property that belonged to the Shuberts. We would have to work until we had what he wanted. There was no overtime, are you kidding? And we had to work on Saturdays. My husband told me, "I'm not going to work on Saturday, and neither are you." I quit the Shuberts and went to William Morris [Agency], where I didn't have to work on Saturday.[67]

Infrequently represented on Broadway, J. J. kept busy supervising road revivals of *Blossom Time, The Student Prince,* and other canonic operettas like *The Merry Widow*. And more than anything else, it was these revivals that nailed the stakes in his theatrical coffin. Having started out as the Shuberts' out-of-town man, J. J. ended his career in the sticks, overseeing increasingly shopworn replicas of the once-vibrant productions of his beloved gold mines. His retreads became industry jokes, virtual synonyms for shoddy showmanship.

"The old saw among actors in the thirties and forties was that if you worked for the Shuberts you always had a job, you could keep working *The Student Prince* or *Blossom Time* on the road forever," recalled Dorothy Tewlow Reissman. "The productions were so tacky, and they didn't get good reviews. They were laughing-stocks in the business. *The Student Prince* on the road was not to be believed. Everett Marshall was out in the show for what seemed like one hundred years. J. J. decided to bring it in in the war years—it didn't cost him anything; he was using costumes and scenery from his own warehouse, and they owned the theatre."

J. J. cast Reissman for a small role in his 1941 Detroit production of *The Merry Widow*. She told me,

I was Fifi at Maxim's. He didn't even buy my ticket to Detroit, that's how his cheapness came out. The rest of the company had bulk tickets. Even then, so late in his career, he liked to discover people, and he'd change the script around to find spots for them. He never went by the book, but put in all the people he was grooming for stardom. In our show he brought in a ballerina, and thought he was creating another [Vera] Zorina [a ballerina who achieved stardom on Broadway and in Hollywood]. But we could all see the woman had no talent. There was an old man in the show who couldn't remember his lines, and J. J. started screaming at him in front of the entire company. He could be so cruel. But he was a contradiction, as people are. When an actress in the show had to go into the hospital, he paid all her bills.

During the Detroit run, J. J. came out once for a few days and then we never saw him again. We never got much direction. The musical director and stage manager did most of the placing onstage. Nominally, the director was Rowland Lee, who was so mean to us. The whole backstage crowd was gay, and a lot of the chorus. The leads, Muriel Angeles and John Moore, couldn't really hack it anymore. J. J. insulted Muriel Angeles and made John Moore's life miserable. But once you were there you were there forever—J. J. never fired anybody.

"The actors of Shubert road operettas were a special breed," former Shubert press agent Max Gendel said.

Ageless, they could neither sing nor dance. Such performers seemed only to work for the Shuberts. They were cast by Ma Simmons. Some soubrettes of sixty played ingenues. The actors were so well up in their parts they could start the season without a rehearsal. Crooked company managers tried to line their own pockets at the Shuberts' expense. The Shuberts attempted to caulk this leak by planting in every company one of their ex- or future girlfriends who were instructed to write to J. J. everything that happened in every company. They were known to the trade as "litter writers."[68]

As his professional fortunes ebbed, J. J.'s ardor seemed to cool as well. "He had no girlfriends in our company," according to Dorothy Tewlow Reissman.

By that point he no longer had a reputation as a lecher, and neither did Lee. Those funny-looking little men? Come on! The chorus girls never said anything about J. J. He was a portly, white-haired man who was fatherly not predatory. He'd ask me if I was writing to my mother, and once he got annoyed because I was writing to my aunt rather than my mother. He said I could have money if I needed it, and he'd give me tickets to shows. This man never put a finger on me."[69]

"J. J. was like the fairy godmother to me," said former Broadway actress Iva Withers.

I came to New York to study singing in 1943. I first sang at a dingy club on Fifty-second Street; a showgirl came to see me after one show, to say I should try Broadway. She mentioned a singing teacher to me, Estelle Liebling, who taught Beverly Sills. Estelle sent me to see J. J., early in 1944. I was told that if J. J. liked me, he'd pay for my lessons. I passed the audition. J. J. footed the bill for 50 percent of Miss Liebling's students. He didn't want anybody to know, and Miss Liebling said not to tell. J. J. had a decent streak; he may have done what he did for me and others to compensate for past "crimes." Maybe we were a tax write-off. I don't know. And I don't know what Estelle's connection to J. J. was—she was a grande dame, and she was definitely not a procurer. If it hadn't been for those lessons I would never have gotten an audition for Rodgers and Hammerstein. J. J. was so proud when I got the replacement leads in *Oklahoma!* and *Carousel.*

When Iva Withers got a role in *Guys and Dolls*, she received a gracious, wistful letter (dated February 1, 1953) from her former silent benefactor. "Dear Miss Iva: I was very pleased to read in the newspapers that you are replacing Miss [Vivian] Blaine in *Guys and Dolls*. I know you will make good in the part. If I had been producing, as I did in the past, I certainly would have kept you working at all times. Best wishes! J. J. Shubert."[70]

After spending more than eight years going back and forth from Lee's side to J. J.'s side of West Forth-fourth Street, John was determined to claim a greater share of independence. In 1941 he began to produce a show on his own, a pungent political satire by Charles MacArthur about a governor who drops dead in a whorehouse on election eve. Perhaps because *Johnny on a Spot* was a straight show and therefore not in direct competition with his musicals, J. J. this time was helpful. He offered John both moral and practical support during the show's out-of-town tryouts, encouraging John to continue with the project despite extensive rewriting and recasting. The show opened in New York on January 8, 1942, one month after Pearl Harbor, not perhaps the ideal moment for a denunciation of the American political system, no matter how biting or clever. In producing a good show at the wrong time, John continued his losing streak.

Worried about the draft, John made a startling confession to his father. He admitted that since September 20, 1937, he had been a married man. J. J. was "a little astounded" that John had kept his marriage a secret, but like John he hoped that being married might keep him out of the armed services. J. J. had earlier told John to move back in with his mother so that he might be able to "claim a dependent." But John's draft board called him up anyway, and on October 24, 1942, he enlisted. When he and his wife moved to Washington, for the first time in six years they lived openly as Mr. and Mrs.

Following family tradition, John had married a Gentile showgirl, a petite blond of Norwegian descent named Helene Kerttu Ecklund, whom everyone called "Eckie" and who had been a "pony" (ponies are short chorus girls) in several Winter Garden revues. John claimed he had kept his marriage a secret to protect his mother. Since his parents had divorced in 1917, Catherine Mary had become increasingly dependent on him, and he feared she would feel "abandoned" if she learned he had a wife. When Catherine Mary found out about the marriage, a few weeks after John had already told J. J. ("she had heard rumors, and one time in a phone call she asked me if what she had heard was true"), she reacted more calmly than John had expected her to. But once she met Eckie, she despised her.

Like Marcella Swanson, Eckie clearly felt being married to a Shubert was worth the sacrifices she was forced to endure. She had remained in hiding for six years—she and John had lived in connecting rooms at the Hotel Astor, whose manager had kept their secret—and had learned to look the other way as John continued to behave like a carefree bachelor. (Surely John's philandering, along with his desire to shield his mother, and the habit of secrecy he had cultivated since early childhood were motives in concealing his marriage.)[71]

John may have tried to avoid being drafted, but to his surprise, he found army life agreeable. "I don't think I came of age until I was in the army for six or eight months," he said. "The man I first reported to, Marvin Young, said he had never seen anybody so insecure in his life. I was just absolutely confused. I didn't know what I was doing. Young built up my confidence." John produced troop shows on his own and for the first time enjoyed theatre work. Away from West Forty-fourth Street, he discovered that he could take command and that, in fact, he had genuine ability as an executive. Flourishing, he wanted to remain in the army permanently, but both his mother and his father "put up a squawk." Whenever he returned to New York, with often a period of a year or so between visits, he would notice that his father and his uncle were both beginning to fail. In the spring of 1946, J. J., feeling fatherly and trying to reach out to John as he did from time to time, urged his son to come back to work. Reluctantly, on May 3 John left the army and that summer rejoined the business. "I was a changed person," he maintained.[72]

For all his newfound bravado, however, John quickly discovered who was still in charge. "God help our firm if both of us ever die," Lee announced to J. J. at a family gathering in the Edison Hotel Green Room shortly after John's return. John was mortified; his cousins, Milton and Lawrence, apparently used to this sort of abuse, did not visibly flinch. Privately, John later confronted his father. "You and Lee just don't respect Milton, Lawrence, and me," he said. "The second generation of Shuberts isn't wanted around here. You and your brother are too old to delegate authority."[73]

The second generation may not have been as gifted as the founders—they were certainly not as driven or as cutthroat—but they were also consistently undermined. From the time they entered the family business, the elder Shuberts had treated them like hired hands.

Milton and Lawrence, who suffered equal portions of scorn from their uncles, were brothers whose lifelong rivalry paralleled that of their famously feuding relatives. From the first, they seemed destined to be family outcasts. Their mother was Fanny, the eldest of the three Shubert daughters who, while the family was still in Syracuse, married a prosperous merchant named Isaac Isaacs. When Sam summoned the family to New York, Fanny moved with them, leaving her husband and her two sons behind in Syracuse. "She sort of abandoned her husband like her mother abandoned *her* husband," John observed. After a time, Fanny sent for her two sons to join her in New York but also remarried, whereupon she "almost became an outcast," as John remembered. Her second husband, William Weisiger, was "a short, fat, jolly fella, and he just didn't fit in with the serious atmosphere of the Shuberts," John said. "Fanny had a slight accent, but her husband had a very pronounced German Jewish accent. And when he opened his yap, everybody looked daggers at him. He had been a real estate man, and we put him in charge of our real estate department, but he was dominated by Charles Sleece, our head real estate man. He just didn't fit in, which I don't say disparagingly; I always thought he was a pathetic figure."

Unlike her sisters, Sarah and Dora, who remained passive, Fanny was a fighter whose husbands embarrassed the Shubert brothers' attempts to conceal their Old World origins and upgrade their social status. Both her sons changed the name they had been born with because, according to John, "Nobody knew who Isaacs was; nobody in New York had ever seen the boys' father." They took on the Shubert name because they felt they had a right to it and because that was the name that meant something in the theatre. Milton became a Shubert, but Lawrence, as John said, "got a little apprehensive, and a little embarrassed. He feared the idea of carrying the name in the early days and since his father [Isaac Isaacs] had a double name, he gave himself a double name too. He certainly could have gone ahead and used Shubert, but the fact is he didn't."[74]

Milton joined the business at age seventeen in 1918. He began on J. J.'s side, supervising touring companies of hit operettas. He remained with J. J. until the early thirties. After J. J. was deposed, the two became bitter antagonists. Milton moved over to Lee's side, where he remained for the rest of his career. Setting up his own production firm in 1933, Milton began to spend time in London looking for properties. Over the next five years, he presented eight plays on Broadway, routine British imports unable to survive transplantation. In London in 1936, however, he had a hit with *Kind Lady*. With the Group Theatre in 1936, he coproduced *The Case of Clyde Griffiths*, an ambitious departure for the Group, as well as for Milton. Cowritten and directed by Erwin Piscator, from whom Bertolt Brecht adopted many techniques, the play was an adaptation of Theodore Dreiser's *An American Tragedy*. Piscator's brand of political theatre—he mounted the play as a bitter indictment of American capitalism—was anathema to the Shuberts. Milton's attraction to the Group and his support of this particular production were clear indications that his uncles' empire would never become his.

In 1937 Milton joined Warner Brothers as associate producer and true to Shubert form was unlucky as a movie mogul. After two grade-B films, he resigned from the studio early in 1939. His major project of the forties, both before and after he joined the navy during World War II, was an operetta based on the life of Giacomo Puccini—an attempt to duplicate the family's success with *Blossom Time*. But Milton's efforts created a scandal. The American attorney for Puccini's heirs called the project an "outrage—there must be no tampering with the operas." When Milton signed a contract with the Office of Alien Property, located in the Department of Justice, in April 1947, the Dramatists Guild sent a letter of protest to President Harry Truman, claiming heatedly that "such a licensing by the United States Government leaves American culture open to ridicule. Such a precedent can cause grave damage to hundreds of masterpieces of European authors and composers."[75] At the same time, the Committee for a Just Peace with Italy sent a telegram of protest to the attorney general's office. Milton did not produce the show.

Actor-director Ezra Stone got to know Milton well when Milton hired him to work on the libretto of the ill-fated Puccini musical, to be called *Liberté*. "At first Milton had hired Louis Verneuil, the illegitimate son of Sarah Bernhardt, who had had a hit show called *Affairs of State*, to write the book, and Deems Taylor to adapt Puccini and Kay Swift to write the lyrics. When Verneuil died, Milton hired me," Stone recalled.

> Milton took me to Paris for eight days to do research. He was not very bright—a slow thinker. And quite pompous. But he wanted to be liked, and he had an underlying sweetness. I pity him now. He was ineffectual, a poseur, and was living a sham. In Paris I saw him threatened by a taxi driver; he got white. He was a coward, a powerless man.
>
> I began to have the feeling that Lee was using our show to keep Milton out of his hair, to give him a reason to draw a salary, but that he never had any intention of actually producing it. Milton had no creative input whatsoever, but let me do what I wanted. I would bring my work to show him, and he would nod in agreement. He even assigned his secretary to me. He didn't have an office, but seemed to be using Mr. Lee's old apartment, the dining room in the Shubert Theatre Building, which at that time looked like the Addams Family lived there: no windows, a skylight, a grand piano and a nonfunctioning fountain, and furniture that seemed unrelated and that probably came from Shubert shows. Behind the rococo white-and-gold piano were four Rolls-Royce tires wrapped in strips of burlap. One time when I was there, and I will never forget it, Milton laid out a ticket taker at the Cort Theatre who came into the dining room. As the ticket taker stood in his coat, Mr. Lee came in behind Milton and stood there like a ghost. After the ticket taker left, I meekly said, "Hello, Mr. Shubert." Nervously, Milton went into a monologue of explanation, ending with, "You would have said just what I said, Mr. Lee." Mr. Lee, quietly and evenly, and with so much menace, said, "Milton, you dare to compare yourself to me?"[76]

Abraham Grossman, a budding playwright in 1932 (later director of graduate studies in theatre at the University of Denver), recalled a telling glimpse of Milton.

I had submitted a play to the Shubert office. The head play reader was a Dr. Hunter, a kindly, learned man who praised my talent, and said he wanted to see more of my work. But, he explained, he did not think my play was the kind that would move the Shuberts to produce it. He suggested—possibly with a smile on his face—that I speak with one of the Shuberts about their interest in new playwrights. I believe he may even have referred to a particular Shubert, Milton, who, he said, could be found "upstairs," and I could take the elevator, to which he directed me. When it arrived, I got in, and found that it was going downstairs, and there was a youngish man in it. He asked if I was looking for someone, and I explained that I had been directed to Milton Shubert "upstairs." After a moment's hesitation, he said, "I'm Milton." I told him of my contact with Dr. Hunter. After a few seconds he said, "Look at me. Look at me." I thought I obeyed, and looked. But he repeated, "Look at me. Look at me." Then, looking sharply at me, he said, "What do I know? You know who I am? I'm the one who turned down *Abie's Irish Rose* and *Tobacco Road*. So what do I know?" The elevator was not more roomy than a coffin, and it went "down" all the way, and I found myself at a level handy for an exit.[77]

Milton was married once, briefly, in 1930, to a statuesque beauty named Jean Lehmann. The couple had no children. "Milton was a roué; he had sixteen thousand paramours," recalled Ethel Lynne, who was in one of Milton's *Blossom Time* companies. "I didn't dare go near him—my father had warned me about the Shuberts. Milton was very afraid of his uncles."[78] Dorothy Seegar, who appeared in a *Blossom Time* revival on Broadway under Milton's supervision, said "he acted like he was afraid his uncles would fire him if he even told a dirty joke."[79]

In his will, Milton left six million dollars he didn't have to Syracuse University and another phantasmic six million to the Actors' Fund.

Unlike Milton, who tried at various points to make himself useful to both J. J. and Lee, his older brother, Lawrence, wanted no part of the family power plays. At sixteen, Lawrence began as a telephone boy in the Winter Garden box office. In four years, he worked his way up to treasurer and house manager; but he left in 1915 for Philadelphia, where he remained head of Shubert operations until his death on April 17, 1965. "My father hated New York and was content to be in Philadelphia which, as far as Lee and J. J. were concerned, might as well have been Siberia," Lawrence Shubert Lawrence, Jr., recalled.[80] According to Ezra Stone, Lawrence "wasn't ambitious and cared more about alcohol and about collecting books than he cared about the theatre."[81]

Like Milton, Lawrence had no major success as a producer on his own—his uncles didn't want him to. He produced *Hellzapoppin'* in Philadelphia but wasn't given credit after the show became a smash in New York. His diffidence, his lack of creative ability, and his alcoholism kept him out of the loop, and Lawrence was never a threat to either Lee or J. J.

"Lawrence hired me to take over a show, *The Man Who Corrupted Hadleyburg*, based on a story by Mark Twain, that had played originally at the Hedgerow Theatre," Ezra Stone said.

> In the original production, it had been well received, but when we opened in Philadelphia at the Shuberts' Erlanger Theatre we were panned, and Lawrence closed it after one week. When I had been working on the adaptation, he let me do what I wanted—like Milton he had no creative ideas whatever. He was a surly, unpleasant man, and would come staggering into the theatre during rehearsals. But after we got panned he said the book needed reworking and blamed me for the failure. Later I was told that the New York Shuberts—the bosses—had never intended to bring the show to Broadway: it had been a calculated tax deduction.[82]

Lawrence followed the family pattern of marrying outside his religion. Frances Von Summerfield, a former chorus girl who had become pregnant with her only child before Lawrence married her, was a devout Catholic. The marriage soured, but Frances would not give her husband a divorce, though she did grant him a legal separation. Lawrence, Jr., remained close to his mother and was permanently estranged from his father.

For the last twenty years of his life, Lawrence, Sr., lived openly with his mistress, Rosina Malvolti. Joan Lavender, a registered nurse who attended Lawrence during his prolonged final illness and who got to know him and Rosina well, said he was

> a nice man who should have been much more than he was. People knew about his drinking problem, but he was a popular figure in Philadelphia—a local legend, really. He never got the credit he deserved; the Shuberts saw to that. He was relegated to an inferior position, and that infuriated Rosina. His legacy seems to be that he was the guy who left out the dressing room when the Shuberts built the Forrest Theatre—a dressing room had to be built in the building across an alley—and that's a hell of a legacy.

At the time Joan Lavender began to take care of him, Lawrence had retreated from active involvement in the theatre. "His love for the theatre remained, but by then he really didn't give a damn. I was stagestruck, and he enjoyed listening to me rather than talking about the theatre himself." As he had for many years, Lawrence spent most of his time engaged in activities that made him unique in the extended Shubert family: he collected—and read—rare first editions. Lawrence kept a meticulously annotated bibliography. He proudly noted, for instance, that his eight-volume edition in original cloth of *The Autocrat at the Breakfast Table* was "in immaculate state" and called his first edition of O'Neill's *Moon of the Caribbees and Six Other Plays of the Sea* a "mint copy."

After Lawrence died, his common-law wife spent the remaining twenty-six years of her life in increasingly straitened circumstances. "When Mr. Lawrence died, he left her money in his will, but the Shuberts in New York contested the will," Joan Lavender said.

> For safekeeping she gave me the will Mr. Lawrence had made out, favoring her, but I got so scared I gave it to my girlfriend. Rosina fought the Shuberts in court for years. The Shuberts forced her to sell the house where she had lived with Lawrence, and gave her half the money, but nothing else. You'd have thought they'd be grateful to her for having scooped Mr. Lawrence up out of every bar in town for all those years, but they had no family feeling. The last time I visited her she was living in a filthy apartment at the end of a long corridor. The house had "died" and she had become a total recluse—so many people had hurt her that she no longer trusted anyone. Mr. Lawrence's ashes were lying on a desk. She had loved him very much; she'd devoted her life to him, and when he went she had nothing.[83]

If Lee and J. J. were hard on their nephews and on John, they were even more unyielding to more distant relatives. "I don't believe Lee and J. J. felt that charity began at home," John said. "Through the years third, fourth, and fifth cousins showed up, and we always checked to see if they were really related, and the ones who were received employment, usually as doormen. It was a question of finding them a job that gave them from fifty to seventy-five dollars a week."[84] Lucille Lawrence, the widow of one distant cousin, recalled that her husband, Leslie, applied to the Shuberts for a job in 1939; and within a half hour, he was hired as assistant stage manager of *The Straw Hat Revue.* "After the interview Leslie rode down in the elevator with Mr. Lee, who asked him what was the least amount of salary per week he could live on. They settled for twenty dollars."[85]

Norman Light went to work for his cousins in 1917. He managed a number of theatres but wasn't promoted to a high position until his second cousin Lawrence Shubert Lawrence, Jr., appointed him the general manager of Shubert theatres in

1964. "The older Shuberts never gave him a chance," Norman's widow, Marjorie Light, said.

They always treated him like a poor relation, and fired him and then brought him back. They never gave him any money except his salary, and there was no money at all after his death. I'm a nurse and I worked, although Norman didn't want me to. I saved what money we had. "I'm a Light and I don't want to be a Shubert," Norman would say. "The Shuberts may have millions, but I have a gem they couldn't buy," meaning me. I never had any interest in the theatre and I never wanted anything from any of the Shuberts.[86]

After John returned from the army, he soon became aware that Lee and J. J. were still determined to occupy the room at the top. It was clear that where their business was concerned they respected and even trusted each other in a way that pointedly did not carry over to any other member of the family. Despite the personal rivalry that had festered and grown since childhood, they were business partners bound by legal cords of umbilical strength. Lee and J. J. on their own were still the Shuberts, while John and his cousins were employees who served at the pleasure of their willful elders.

If in 1946 J. J. needed to prove to John that he was in charge, he also needed to prove himself professionally competent and relevant. His career had hit bottom the year before when, for the only time, he received a solo producing credit. It was on a show called *A Lady Says Yes*, which in fact had been a vanity production. The author, a plastic surgeon named Maxwell Maltz writing pseudonymously as Clayton Ashley, put up most of the money, with J. J. serving as the front man. A musical comedy (part of the score was by Arthur Gershwin, George's brother) about sexual impotence in which a navy lieutenant travels in a dream to sixteenth-century Venice and China, *A Lady Says Yes* was a bad idea gone totally wrong. It was part *Passing Show*, part Jolson dream-play extravaganza, part operetta, part burlesque, and all mess. "No, no, no, a thousand times no," Brooks Atkinson wailed, offering an opinion J. J. might well have interpreted as Broadway's collective response to his pitiful attempt at a comeback.[87]

Shortly after John's return, J. J. started planning a new operetta he hoped would restore him to popular and critical favor. When the show, *My Romance*, began its long and troubled pre-Broadway tour in Boston in 1947, the score was by an obscure composer named Dennis Agay. "We got raves," recalled Anne Jeffreys, the show's star.

[Boston critic] Elliott Norton loved it, and we did terrific business. After a matinee one day, Mr. Shubert, who had come up from New York, came to my dressing room and said, "Miss Anne"—he always called me "Miss Anne"—"I want you to have dinner with me." I said I couldn't go out, so he had a sumptuous champagne dinner brought in. During the dinner he said, "I have a new piece of music I want to go into the first act tonight. I'm staying over to see this one song and then I'm going back to New York." The song, "No One's Heart," was haunting and had difficult intervals. I told him I could never have it ready by the evening performance. "Yes you can," he said, and that was that. I worked with Mr. Agay on the song over and over. In the scene I wore an ermine muff and I wrote the lyrics out in the muff. The beautiful song stopped the show. "It's in the show, see you next week," J. J. sent word back.

We then went on to Chicago, where J. J. wanted to reopen the Great Northern Theatre. He had put in blue velvet seats and he wanted a big show to go in there. But I came down with pneumonia. "Miss Anne, I'm going to close the show," J. J. said. He kept me on salary, to hold me and also to be nice to me: for both reasons. While the show was closed he came to me and said, "I need more prestige in a composer, and I'm going to have a new score which Sigmund Romberg will write."[88]

J. J. hadn't worked with Romberg since 1930. Both had been out of the theatrical limelight for many years; but for the show he hoped would reverse his decline, J. J. turned to the composer who had given him his three most durable properties.

Based on *Romance*, a 1913 play by Edward Sheldon, the show in fact reprised the collaborators' favorite operetta theme of thwarted love: a prima donna falls for and then leaves a minister, dedicating herself to a celibate life in which music replaces romance. "Frankly, Agay's score was more modern and creative than Rommie's," Anne Jeffreys said.

Some of what Rommie wrote was pretty, but some of it was old hat. I wanted to keep "No One's Heart" and to put Agay's name in the program, but Rommie said, in his very thick accent, "I am Sigmund Romberg and I couldn't have anyone else's music in the show." He begged me on his knees, and he cried. I understood how he felt, I really did. The song was a showstopper and he was resentful. I was mortified, but I can't exist under unhappy circumstances and I finally gave in. Rommie could be charming, but he was very emotional.

My Romance was J. J.'s baby, and it was very important to him. He came often to rehearsals. He and Rommie had some head to heads. They were both old men then, but they were also still fiery and they'd scream and yell. J. J. also would yell at the director, Rowland Lee, a thin, effete man, and a lovely gentleman. J. J. had him on a chain—he was afraid of J. J. but he had learned to roll with the punches. J. J. would never actually sit down and direct, but he'd send back notes. Sometimes he'd yell out to the chorus from the middle of the house: "Mill! Mill! Now mill!" so they wouldn't all be just standing around. He was a showman and his instincts were usually right, if a little extreme.

When *My Romance* finally opened on Broadway, on October 19, 1948, the reviews were among the harshest J. J. or Romberg had ever received. Instead of the vindication they had wished for, they were greeted with their obituaries. "We had a sweet, heartrending show, but operetta was old hat in New York at that time," Anne Jeffreys said.

We ran for three months because some of J. J.'s operetta audiences from the old days came to see us. J. J. was heartbroken. He loved the show; he believed in it; he spent a lot of money on it. In New York he gave us the Shubert, one of his finest theatres. The show's failure helped to break him; it really contributed to his demise.

After the show closed I never saw Rommie again, but I always saw J. J. whenever I was in New York. I loved the old man. I knew of his reputation—how mean he was supposed to be, and how he was supposed to treat women—but he had a kind side, too, a sweet, likable side which he didn't want people to see because then they'd think he was a softie, and he wanted to be known as tough. I had more than a year in *My Romance* all told and the whole time I was proud to be working for a man whose family had done so much for the theatre.[89]

John claimed that, within a year after he rejoined the business, his father and uncle "had split to the point that they weren't talking at all."[90] But surely, as partners in a great business, they would have had to speak sometimes; and given their lack of trust in others and their atavistic secrecy, they couldn't *always* have depended on emissaries to communicate for them. Nonetheless they wanted to create the impression that they did not speak, a charade John was clearly prepared to go along with. Pretending to be at odds on every important issue allowed them leverage in rejecting or raising the ante on potential deals. "I would love to invest in your show, but of course my brother wouldn't allow it"; "perhaps if the terms were better my lawyer could convince my brother to go along with your proposal"— these were strategies both Lee and J. J. frequently employed in the good cop–bad cop scenario they enacted.

In town they may not have spoken to each other, but they did speak face-to-face in the country, as Anne Jeffreys testified.

I visited J. J. in his country house on many weekends, and I was witness to the fact that they *did* talk to each other. I would go out on John's boat, with John and Eckie, while Mr. Lee and Mr. J. J. would sit on the porch all afternoon talking. They may well not have cared for each other, but whenever I saw them they talked to each other in a civilized way. I never saw them screaming. They didn't want anyone to know that they talked: it was a cover-up.[91]

In town, where they wanted to maintain the illusion that they did not speak to each other, John was their liaison. "I ran confidential messages back and forth." John noted that despite their estrangement the brothers spoke the same language, communicating in a kind of code or shorthand. "Each one always seemed to know the other's intention. I got to know their thinking, because they didn't reduce much to writing. They didn't even trust their own lawyers. They both felt they could rely on me. I was never sick, I was never absent. And gradually the power to countersign checks was given to me—they had never delegated this to anybody else."[92]

The brothers' distrust ran appallingly deep, as two events from the decade's close display. On September 4, 1948, Marcella publicly divorced Lee, an action that exposed their marriage for the first time but one that also hid as much as it seemed to reveal. Marcella's public grounds for divorce were that Lee had "humiliated" her by refusing to acknowledge her as his wife during twelve years of marriage. Closely protected by William Klein, who was himself soon to be "divorced" by Lee, Marcella would not answer any questions from reporters about why her marriage had not been made public or about her financial arrangements with a man said at the time to control six hundred million dollars of theatrical, as well as other, real estate. "I've said before and I'll say it again—that I'll never say anything about my romance with Mr. Shubert. If Lee wants to, that's his business—but I don't think he will," Marcella said, clearly playing her role according to Lee's specifications.[93]

Later that fall, in what John maintained was one of the last face-to-face meetings between Lee and J. J., the brothers decided to get rid of the lawyer who had served them for nearly half a century and who, for whatever reason, had tolerated decades of his masters' abuse. When they were getting started in New York at the turn of the century, Klein had witnessed Lee's jealousy of Sam, and Lee may have come to resent Klein as the man who had known him when he was the "other" Shubert, Sam's brother. Given his secrecy, he may also have felt that Klein was simply the man who knew too much. "I think we should change lawyers," Lee announced with characteristic terseness to J. J. and John at a weekend meeting in the country. In the city the night before, during their gin rummy game, Klein had mentioned a 1932 stock transaction in which he and Lee had bought one hundred thousand dollars' worth, half for each of them. The money was lost and Klein still owed Lee fifty thousand. Casually, Lee asked Klein when he intended to pay the money; Klein responded that the statute of limitations had passed and he didn't have to honor the debt. In so brazenly challenging Lee on a money matter, Klein must have known he was playing with fire. Perhaps after fifty years on the job, he figured it was about time he retire anyway. J. J. urged Lee to fire Klein. "I'll do it on Monday," Lee promised. And he did, though publicly Klein was allowed to say he had decided to retire.[94]

Klein was replaced by his partner, Milton Weir, who had joined the firm in the twenties. Like many others, Abner Klipstein remembered Milton Weir bitterly. "He was a phony bum, and Mrs. Weir, a social climber and an anti-Semite, wanted him to change his name, which originally had been Weinstein. He gave in to her."[95] Weir took on Adolph Lund as his partner, and in 1949 Lund brought a young lawyer named Gerald Schoenfeld into the firm.

Lee remarried Marcella in Miami in March 1949, seven months after the divorce, only deepening the mystery surrounding his private life. Friends and associates agree that Lee seemed to love Marcella, and so it is unlikely the divorce had been instigated by an emotional rift. "The divorce happened on account of business in some way," Garson Kanin speculated.[96] "We knew that at the divorce Marcella received a good sum of money—one million was rumored—from Lee," William Packer said. "If Lee died, the Shuberts couldn't contest that money, which clearly belonged to her."[97] Annette Packer developed this divorce scenario further.

> Marcella was sweet and lovable but seemed not to be well informed regarding financial matters, and Lee worried about what would happen to her after he died. Realizing how J. J. felt, and how easily smart lawyers could take advantage of her, he devised a scheme. He told J. J. that his marriage had been a mistake and that he was going to get a divorce. He asked Marcella to divorce him and she "agreed" only if he would give her a million dollars. So she went to Reno, and banked a million outright, in her name only and belonging to her no matter what.[98]

But Marcella's appearance of being financially helpless was as much a pose as her pretending not to be Mrs. Lee Shubert. "Her brother was a stockbroker," William Packer said. "And she invested in the market. She would have breakfast in bed, and read the market news the first thing in the morning."[99] Like all the women who won the heart of a Shubert, Marcella was intensely interested in money.

Another theory about Lee's divorce and remarriage involved the possible disappearance of the Berlin record of the original 1936 marriage. Since most German records were destroyed during the war, perhaps Lee was concerned that he would be unable to verify the legality of his marriage. According to *Variety*, Lee divorced and remarried Marcella "to establish the marriage beyond legal challenge and therefore to protect Mrs. Shubert's interests after his death."[100] If publicly Lee seemed a remarkably aloof husband, privately he was devoted to his wife, as she was to him. Beyond all the machinations surrounding their divorce and remarriage, they seemed genuinely to have loved each other.

Remarrying Marcella publicly may well have represented Lee's acknowledgment that he was growing old.[101] And his example may have convinced J. J. to marry the woman who for thirty years had been his companion. Like Marcella, Catherine Mary, and Eckie, the second Mrs. J. J. Shubert had also been a Shubert showgirl. In 1919 she had come to New York from Huron, Ohio, as Muriel Kish; in 1921, as Muriel Knowles, she caught J. J.'s eye when she auditioned for a place in the Winter Garden chorus. After J. J. hired her, she remained at the Winter Garden for three years and at the same time began dating the boss. It took more than three decades for her to become the second Mrs. J. J. Shubert. "My father and my mother sort of had an understanding at the time of their divorce that neither of them would remarry until I came of age," John speculated. "They sort of used that as a defense."[102] "Muriel had her own apartment for years," recalled Anne Jeffreys. "J. J. loved to go to Paris and whenever Muriel went with him she went under the guise of being his nurse. She was his companion and his confidante for many years—she was very strong with him, though she remained in the background. She was always there when he gave his wonderfully elaborate dinners up at his apartment, which I always called Versailles."[103]

J. J. finally married Muriel late in 1951. He had just had a prostate operation; he was seventy-four; and, like Lee, he felt it was time to put his house in order. After the marriage, he made out a new will and tried once more to create a closer relationship with his son. (Lee had written a new will in 1949.)

Like the first Mrs. J. J. Shubert, Muriel won no popularity prizes. "She was hard-bitten, and like most old chorus girls she looked tarnished," recalled Dorothy Terolow Reissman. "She was neither pretty nor well dressed. They would have big fights; once she threw out all his pills and medication."[104] "Muriel was a matronly housewife with no artistic instincts when I knew her," Iva Withers said. "She was dull."[105] "Muriel was a large woman, and J. J. seemed to be shrinking: they were like Mutt 'n' Jeff," remembered one of John's secretaries, Eileen Kelly. "She was very, very protective toward him. And she was very demanding to the staff. 'I want a pair of tickets,' she'd say, in a voice that meant, 'Do it now.' She wasn't abusive, exactly, but she knew her position and used it."[106]

By the start of the fifties, both Lee and J. J. had clearly begun to feel the passage of time. As producers both were unable to adjust to changing tastes. The failure of *My Romance* indicated that the kind of musical theatre J. J. remained devoted to was not salable even as nostalgia. A strict traditionalist, he had been immune to all the important operetta innovations of the prior two decades. The new musical and thematic terrain that the Gershwins had explored in their satiric political operettas *Of Thee I Sing* (1931) and *Let 'Em Eat Cake* (1933) found no place in J. J.'s portfolio. Even after Rodgers and Hammerstein modernized operetta in the forties, with shows like *Oklahoma!* (1943) and *Carousel* (1945), J. J. continued to take his operetta "straight." And whenever he had presented new shows in the antique mode, he had taken a critical and financial beating.

Lee's tastes were similarly dated. Even after he reorganized the company in 1933, the same kinds of commercial imports, mostly British, that had been his bread and butter in the early days still accounted for a sizable share of his offerings. For the most important development in American theatre in the thirties, Lee had been a landlord only. In 1931 Harold Clurman, Lee Strasberg, and Cheryl Crawford, who worked for the Theatre Guild in the twenties, formed the Group Theatre as a corrective to what they felt the Guild had become, a stodgy outfit favoring Continental art plays rather than dramas written on and set in native grounds. A seminal force in the history of the American theatre, the Group raised the call for a new, vital, impassioned American style of writing and acting. In 1935 the Group's acclaimed productions of Clifford Odets's *Awake and Sing!* and *Waiting for Lefty* raised New York working-class vernacular to the heights of artistic illumination. John said,

> The Group Theatre was a dirty word to the Shuberts. They were thought to be Communists. They had an idea of communal living—its appeal was the heaven that every man or woman, I suppose, would sort of like to get involved with, even though they might not have the courage to do it. I think they damaged their reputation as being wonderful performers and putting on very good stuff because of their nontheatrical activities, which we thought was very bad."[107]

Nonetheless, perhaps because the Shuberts liked Group director Harold Clurman ("we thought he was able, and Clurman was always a sort of friend to the Shuberts," John said), Lee allowed the Group to perform in Shubert houses. The Belasco was the Group's home base. Lee derived sizable returns on *Men in White*, the Group's biggest commercial success, which had a long run in 1934–1935 at the Majestic Theatre.

Reluctantly, Lee had rented the Comedy Theatre for a season to the Mercury Theatre, a company founded and run by Orson Welles and John Houseman. As part of FDR's federally funded Work Projects Administration (WPA), the Mercury posed a threat to the free-market system the Shuberts lived by. "The Mercury Theatre was a Depression type of product that didn't seem to have any class," John said. "Heaven knows it had a lot of wonderful people working for it, but the Shuberts didn't have any respect for anything that came out of the WPA Project. At that time the Shuberts always looked at anything that started not immediately in Times Square as being something that didn't have a real value to the American theatre." [108]

In the last active decade of his producing career, Lee presented two plays by major American writers. Typically, however, his timing was off. A social satirist whose pungent vernacular dialogue has a distinctive musical rhythm, George Kelly (Grace Kelly's uncle) was a prominent writer of the twenties and winner of a Pulitzer Prize for drama. By 1936, when Lee presented *Reflected Glory*, Kelly had been inactive on Broadway for a number of years. A charming, minor play about the theatre that Lee produced as a vehicle for Tallulah Bankhead, *Reflected Glory* did not have the hefty run it deserved. In 1945, six months after *The Glass Menagerie* had opened on Broadway, Lee produced a play called *You Touched Me!*, which Tennessee Williams had cowritten with Donald Windham. The show had a decent run of 109 performances, but Lee was then on his way out; Tennessee Williams was on his way up; and they never collaborated again.

In the late forties, with powerful new plays like Williams's *Streetcar Named Desire* and Arthur Miller's *Death of a Salesman*, the theatre was revitalized. The Shuberts had no part in the major developments of the postwar theatre, however, nor is there any evidence that they wanted to. Toward the director of *Streetcar* and *Salesman*, for instance, they had only contempt. "Elia Kazan is an animal," John said. "A roughneck. He's a fresh punk. He has no respect for anyone, I wonder if he has it for himself. He's a very fine director, I admit. He instills life. He takes an effeminate type of work, like Tennessee Williams's, and gives it that virility that a truck driver would give. But we never wanted to work with him." [109]

If Lee no longer had any stature as a producer, unlike J. J. he did continue to have a place of real importance in the theatre. With increasing frequency since the early thirties, Lee had begun to invest in other producers' shows. *Street Scene, The Children's Hour, The Green Bay Tree, The Time of Your Life,* and *Oklahoma!* are some of the many shows in which he became a silent partner. In the forties, when he was no longer producing regularly himself, there was hardly a hit show in which he didn't have points. It was common knowledge on the street that a producer who needed end money and advice could get in to see Lee, whose financial participation often meant the difference between life and death for a new production. If he was considered passé as a producer himself, if his name above the title had become a liability, when he spoke about a show's commercial chances the street still listened.

His face cracked with age and sun treatments, his voice more high-pitched than ever as he held court in his small circular office, which was still the financial heart of Broadway, Lee had become a theatrical guru, the "Wise Man of West Forty-fourth Street." He didn't have to make creative decisions or assist in shaping a show. He was asked only for his intuitive judgment about whether a finished work would go over. In his busiest period as a producer, Lee had eagerly solicited the opinions of others—from 1918 up to the end of the thirties, the person whose opinion he most valued was his valet, Joe Peters. Called the "Admirable Crichton of Shubert Alley," Peters regularly accompanied Lee to out-of-town and summer tryouts and to Europe. Peters's judgment about a play's commercial possibilities was so often correct as to be uncanny.[110] But by the forties, after a lifetime of playgoing, Lee's own instinct about a show's chances had been refined to a fare-thee-well. And when other producers asked him to invest in their projects, Lee on his own made quick and firm decisions. He never reversed himself once he gave his word. On opening nights, he still commanded respect. When he would take his customary seat on the aisle in the last row—and he would sit nowhere else— "waves seemed to part," as Garson Kanin observed.[111]

By 1950 Lee and J. J. may have been in the autumn of their patriarchy, but retirement was out of the question. Both of them continued to put in long days in their offices. Lee regularly worked until midnight or later, and both were known to go in on Sundays. In a 1950 photograph, Lee looks as fearsome as ever. He stands with Francis Joseph Cardinal Spellman (Archbishop of New York, 1939–1967), unfazed as always in the company of the high and mighty—indeed, he had long been among their number. After a lifetime of physical fastidiousness, he has grown somewhat stout at last. His leathery skin is deeply ridged. His snake eyes look more distrusting and more vigilant than ever, but they also look a little more readable: it is possible to see in them the coldness and cruelty his many enemies attributed to him. These are the eyes of a man who has been far too powerful for far too long; a man contaminated by having had too much of everything.

John Shubert was the heir apparent who had gradually begun to assume greater responsibility, but his father and his uncle still ran the business. "I felt I was just a worker," John said, "doing a good job for him, the man upstairs, the man in the penthouse."[112] In two separate photographs taken on the same day in 1950, J. J. and his son are seated in the same imposing leather chair. J. J., his arm resting on the arm of the chair, sits behind his massive, marble-top desk holding a script and smiling wanly, with a trace of a wince: he's a prosperous executive working hard to appear dignified and relaxed as, tellingly, he averts his eyes from the camera's inquisition. Seated in the same chair and trying to exude authority, John wears a three-piece suit with a vest-pocket handkerchief and smokes. He looks too young to be entirely convincing as a theatrical titan, and there is a remnant of the doltish grin and the buckteeth from childhood. But unlike his father, John looks directly into the camera.

7

∞

The Man in the Blue Serge Suit

At the beginning of the fifties, the Shuberts' empire was under siege. The growth of network television had already begun to transform the nation's entertainment landscape, and attendance at both legitimate theatres and movie houses took an alarming dip. The postwar migration to the suburbs also eroded the potential audience for the Shuberts' center-city showshops. But the Shuberts' most visible opponent was the United States government. On February 21, 1950, United States Attorney General J. Howard McGrath launched a massive antitrust suit against the firm. In a twenty-two-page complaint, the Antitrust Division of the Department of Justice accused Lee and J. J., their partner Marcus Heiman, the United Booking Office, Inc., Select Theatres Corporation, and LAB Amusement Corporation, of "compel[ling] producers to book through their agency, the UBO, exclud[ing] other producers from booking legitimate attractions, discriminat[ing] in favor of their own productions with respect to booking and presentation; and combin[ing] their power in booking and presentation in order to maintain and strengthen their domination in each of these fields."[1] Select Theatres, the corporation formed when Lee reorganized the company in 1933, was the central artery in the Shubert network. The LAB Amusement Corporation, like the UBO, was jointly owned by the Shuberts and Marcus Heiman and controlled only three theatres and was involved in a limited amount of production. The UBO, as the Shuberts insistently pointed out, had been re-formed in 1932 with the express consent of the government—it was one of the measures taken by the courts during the receivership to save the legitimate theatre from extinction. Nevertheless, it was the little-known UBO the government was particularly interested in.

To eliminate competition, the Shuberts had acquired the old, desiccated Klaw and Erlanger booking agency in 1932. Although it was announced as a "merger," the acquisition was more like a takeover that assured the Shuberts a virtual monopoly on out-of-town booking. To head the office, Lee hired Marcus Heiman, a crony from Syracuse and a gruff veteran of theatrical warfare. Heiman had been quite successful at eliminating competition in vaudeville and was most notorious for ignoring an Actor's Equity ruling that overturned the no-blacks policy at Washington's National Theatre when he was president of the Shubert-controlled League of New York Theatres. When the suit was filed in 1950, Heiman argued that the UBO was merely "a service organization for the many theatres outside New York whose managements are desirous of presenting successful plays. The UBO does not fix the terms on which attractions will play in any theatre, but merely acts as a go-between to arrange terms both sides—the producer and the out-of-town theatre manager—will consider fair."[2] What Heiman neglected to mention was that the UBO demanded 5 percent of the theatre's share of the proceeds. The system was so profitable that Heiman became a wealthy man despite his official salary of only five thousand dollars a year.

Eileen Kelly, who worked for John Shubert at the UBO just before it was closed in 1956, remembered that the Shuberts were "in complete control. 'You don't use my Philadelphia theatre, you can't use my New York theatre': that was their typical tactic."[3] According to John, the UBO's fees were "plowed back into the agency to help finance shows for the road."[4] Since the Shuberts owned most of the theatres on the road, they were the beneficiaries of the UBO's practices.

In its first attempt to regulate the theatre business, the government accused the Shuberts of exactly the sort of tyrannical behavior the Shuberts themselves had accused the Syndicate of early in their career. The Antitrust Division charged that the Shuberts were stifling fair trade by controlling "practically all of the theatrical booking in the United States and operat[ing] or participat[ing] in the operation of forty of the most desirable and necessary legitimate theatres in the country."[5] The government asked that the defendants be required to remove themselves from either the booking or the theatre-owning branch of their business and that they be prevented from acquiring interest in any additional theatres. Branding the Shuberts as, in effect, the godfathers of American show business, the charges were serious and threatened to disrupt the way the Shuberts had been conducting their affairs for fifty years.

In response, Lee Shubert came out swinging, once again demonstrating his zest for a fight. "We have operated with an efficiency that deserves the encouragement rather than the criticism of any government agency," he asserted in a press conference the day after the government filed its suit. "If you're successful, you've got to expect bricks sailing through the air," he added. "When the attacks on you end, it means that you're all washed up. Apparently we are still arousing jealous-ies."[6] Milton Weir, Lee's attorney, called the charges "utterly unfounded" and claimed that they would be "completely refuted," adding the pungent comment that "to classify the stage today as 'big business' must come as a surprise. All too regrettably, it has become 'little business.' It is in fact not conceivable that what remains of the legitimate stage should be included in even the most sweeping 'mo-nopoly hunt.' "[7]

In early March, two weeks after the government's complaint was published, Lee traveled to New York from Miami Beach to face his chief accuser, Herbert H. Bergson, an assistant attorney general and chief of the Justice Department's Antitrust Division, at a meeting of the Drama Desk (an organization of theatre critics). Sporting his customary tan and nattily dressed in a Palm Beach suit, the seventy-six-year-old mogul was in a peppery mood and far more voluble than usual. In his high, quavering tone, he responded vigorously to his Harvard-edu-cated opponent, who spoke with a voice that exuded political and moral authority. "We don't want to alarm you, Mr. Shubert, but we win 90% of our cases," Bergson boasted in his sepulchral voice. "I hope we will be among the 10%," Lee answered. "We're holding the bag," Lee argued. "There aren't enough attractions to fill our houses, particularly on the road, and yet the government would like to see more theatres and more owners though there isn't enough product for the houses now in operation."[8] At the Drama Desk square-off, the press was on Lee's side.

Lee seemed unruffled that afternoon, but in fact it was one of the key con-frontations of his battle-scarred career. It was certainly true that, as Lee and his counsel maintained, the theatre had shrunk to a mere fraction of its former size, yet it was also true that the Shuberts, who were by then no longer active producers, nonetheless continued to exert a disproportionate power over what was left of a once-flourishing industry. Their rapacity had long since peaked, but they still owned and booked more theatres than anyone else, and Lee had points in most of the hit shows on Broadway. The Shuberts controlled sixteen out of the thirty-two theatres functioning on Broadway at the time of the suit, and they controlled 90 percent of the theatres on the road. In Philadelphia they held the keys to all four theatres; in Boston six of nine were in the Shubert name.

In a famous article, the acidulous critic George Jean Nathan, who had never been a Shubert lover, mounted a surprising and impassioned defense of the em-battled czars. He suggested that the Antitrust Division had been prodded into its investigation by bitter complaints filed by three independent producers, "two with little or no previous experience in play production and the third a rich play backer to whom the theatre is simply an enjoyable avocation, like grouse shooting or rhumba dancing."[9] John Shubert, however, maintained that Washington had begun to take a close look at Shubert affairs nine years earlier.

When producer Oscar Serlin was planning the road tour for his big hit, *Life with Father,* he bypassed the UBO and went straight to the theatres, thereby avoiding the additional weekly percentage the UBO demanded. "They asked $52,000 to be paid weekly on a percentage basis, and exclusive of the usual house arrangements," Serlin told *Variety* in 1941, adding that he blamed

> the death of the theatre on the shortsighted tactics of the men who control a great many of the legitimate houses and also book many of the attractions. Most prominent of those men are the Shuberts, who can make or break just about any of the small producers. 90% of all scripts are said to go to the Brothers Shubert for appraisal. If a play doesn't appeal to the company, out it goes. If it clicks, the Shuberts take either a piece of the investment or a house percentage—whichever looks more profitable.[10]

According to John, Serlin did far more than simply complain to *Variety*: dining at the White House, he told Eleanor Roosevelt that the Shuberts had interfered with his tour because he wouldn't comply with their UBO terms. "Eleanor Roosevelt is a fine woman in many respects, and probably the greatest feminist of her generation," John said, but "she sold someone in the Department of Justice a bill of goods that the Shuberts and their half-owned United Booking Office constituted a dangerous monopoly." According to John, as a result of the machinery Eleanor Roosevelt set in motion, Federal Bureau of Investigation (FBI) Director J. Edgar Hoover ordered a tap on the Shubert switchboard; placed two of his FBI "operators" into the accounting department of the Select Theatres Corporation; and "combed Shubert wastebaskets."

"For at least seven years before the 1950 suit my uncle had been conducting a one-man battle against the United States attorney general," John said.[11] Although from the beginning Lee's instincts were to fight the government, the lawyers he hired for the occasion advised him to back off. The case was incomplete, however, until 1947, when the government scored a landmark antitrust victory against the film industry. Forced to sever production from exhibition, the major studios were ordered to sell the theatres in which they had shown their own films. The decision eroded the studio system and changed forever Hollywood's financial infrastructure. Flush with his triumph over the movie moguls and bristling with righteous indignation, the attorney general began to pursue his case against the Shuberts with renewed enthusiasm, announcing his intent "to remove the fetters imposed on this business and to make it possible for any person to enter any branch of the business on a fair competitive basis."[12]

A second powerful enemy was Emanuel Celler, a Democratic U.S. representative from New York who was second to none in his detestation of the Shuberts' business practices. Only eleven days before the attorney general released his indictment, Celler announced that he had received from President Truman "a full steam ahead signal" to investigate monopolies. Celler reported that his House Judiciary Subcommittee would investigate the United States Steel Corporation, the newsprint industry, the E. I. duPont de Nemours Company, the soap industry, Pan Am, the whiskey barrel–manufacturing industry, and the Shubert theatrical holdings. Singling out the Shuberts for his sharpest comments, Celler declared that the theatre was suffering from a "Shubert stranglehold. I find it a very malodorous picture. They control 60% of the theatres in New York and 90% throughout the country. They dominate the League [which has had various names but is now known as the League of American Theaters and Producers, the traditionally Shubert-dominated organization founded in 1930 by producers and theatre owners], arrange for the allocation of tickets to their own pet brokers, using kickbacks of all kinds. Theatre people hesitate to testify."

Celler continued, "The Shuberts insist on taking fifty tickets a performance for *South Pacific* [tenanted at the Shuberts' Majestic Theatre]," adding that the Shuberts "get the best seats in the house, for a yearly total of 20,800 for that one hit. Who gets the tickets? What are the kickbacks? I make a guess that the gains taken in by these tickets run into millions of dollars a year, and you can bet all the tea in China no income tax is paid on those tickets. How long must an abused public suffer?"[13]

House seats had become a staple of the theatre business in 1943 after the opening of *Oklahoma!*, an enormous success for which there was an unprecedented demand for tickets. Until *Oklahoma!*, according to John, the Shuberts had no house seats except for "the couple of pair" the treasurer would routinely hold until curtain time, "waiting for the boss to call up." But after *Oklahoma!*, every producer of every hit show exercised a divine right over several dozen pairs of seats for every performance. At first, the house seats were passed along as a courtesy to key members of the production and the theatre owner: but in time, the practice became contractual. The Shuberts were certainly greedy in demanding more than the usual allotment given to theatre owners, but Celler was more concerned with what the Shuberts did with their house seats. The Shuberts claimed they were given, or in some cases sold at box office prices, to "important friends." "There is no steady amount of seats," John said. "It's according to the success of the show and the call. The mayor's office might telephone, or some politician. You have to be able to take care of them."[14] Celler charged the Shuberts with passing along their house seats to brokers and scalpers, who then sold premium-location seats at vastly inflated prices. Since "ice" (reselling tickets to hit shows at high prices) melts, the path of house seats was notoriously difficult for government investigators to trace once the tickets left the box office.

When J. J. accused Representative Celler of making "inflammatory state-ments," he was right on the money.[15] Celler was on the warpath, and his anti-Shubert tirades, followed almost immediately by the attorney general's indict-ment served notice to the Shuberts that they had enemies in very high places. Once again, the Shuberts were positioned for a fight for their lives, only this time they were not saviors but villains—aged barons whose pockets were stuffed with entirely too much lucre.

Just after the government's charges, Broadway, as always in matters that in-volved the Shuberts, was a house divided. The naysayers, however, haunted by their knowledge of Shubert reprisals, cowered under the cloak of anonymity. "The government has a case, but I'd never act again in the legitimate theatre if you used my name and said I attacked the Shuberts," a well-known Broadway actor admit-ted. "My producing days would be over," a prominent producer claimed. "For God's sake don't use my name," a manager pleaded.[16]

Billy Rose, a scrappy entrepreneur who had made a mint in the theatre him-self, came to the Shuberts' defense, arguing that whatever they did was merely business as usual. "Sure they make the best deals they can, but so do I and so does your wife when she buys the weekend pot roast. I can't help wondering how much theatre there would be to stifle if it hadn't been for Lee and Jake," he added, in-troducing a theme that became the rallying cry of Shubert advocates.[17] George Jean Nathan continued to defend the Shuberts. Even if the allegations were true, he wrote,

> I take great pleasure in remarking: So what? The government has spent a year or more and a lot of your and my money in an investigation in the pious belief that the theatre will benefit enormously. . . . The government's chief grump is against the Shuberts' alleged control of play bookings. This might make some sense if there were enough plays to book. Play shortage has been so acute that, in order to fill their theatres, the Shuberts have now and then been forced to put money into outside producers' productions, then demand the producers book them in their theatres. And why shouldn't they?

In his conclusion, Nathan asked the government to "stop to reflect that the vil-lainous Shuberts kept their theatres going in the theatre's leanest and most threat-ened and perilous years when others were crying uncle and scooting out from under and that, if it had not been for them, we would not have had any theatres left for the government now to interfere with."[18]

The government's case against the Shuberts dragged on for six years, dur-ing which time there were significant changes in the Shuberts' legal department.

"When I went to work there in 1949, the lawyer that really was the Shubert lawyer was Milton Weir," Gerald Schoenfeld recalled. "William Klein was ill or away and really did not actively function." After his forced retirement at the end of 1948, Klein and Lee continued to speak to each other, and Lee would sometimes ask Klein for advice on legal matters. "Weir ceased to be the Shubert lawyer at the end of 1953. I was Adolph Lund's protégé," Schoenfeld continued. "I was not really a partner; I did not share in profits or losses with him."[19] After Weir left, Lund asked Schoenfeld to assist him in the antitrust suit. Aware of the gravity of the charges against them, however, the Shuberts hired Alfred McCormack, of Cravath, Swaine and Moore, antitrust specialists. Working alongside Lund, Schoenfeld did all of the legwork of preparing the briefs and running the case, but McCormack was the front man.

In the first round of arguments, on May 31, 1950, Shubert lawyers petitioned that the antitrust suit be thrown out of court on the grounds that the business of producing or booking theatrical attractions is not "trade" or "commerce" within the meaning of the Sherman Anti-Trust Act of 1890. As the Shuberts waited for a response, it became clear that they were facing a major setback. By August 1953, there were rumors that they were planning

> to divest themselves of virtually all of their out-of-town theatre holdings and to discontinue their financial interest in and control of ticket agencies in Chicago, Philadelphia, and Boston, and also to break up the United Booking Office. The government's case against the Shuberts is figured to be overwhelming as regards the monopoly situation on the road. That's why the defendants are agreeing to such sweeping terms in the consent decree.[20]

Lee, however, denied that the Shuberts were "consenting" to anything. "We're going to fight the charges in court," he roared, still the untamed tiger.[21]

Even on the cusp of entering his ninth decade, Lee was up to the demands of the unwanted role thrust upon him. He presented himself as a feisty CEO temporarily under fire by antagonists who simply did not understand his business. And when he stood up to his accusers in a forthright manner, he earned the best press he'd had since the receivership period.

At the beginning of December 1953, Lee spent ten days with Marcella in Miami Beach, his favorite resort, where he could maintain his tan naturally rather than through the sunlamps he used during the long New York winters. As always, a vacation for Lee Shubert did not mean total separation from the shop. He kept in touch with West Forty-fourth Street several times a day and conducted his nightly ritual of examining the grosses for every Shubert theatre.

A few days after returning from Miami Beach, Lee collapsed on the floor of his office. He was rushed to Mount Sinai Hospital, where he complained that his vision was upside down. This was the second episode he had had of distorted vision; the first had come in the spring of that same year, when, for the first time ever, rumors developed along Broadway that the elder Shubert's health had begun to fail. In June, to disprove the gossip, Lee and Marcella went to Europe for ten days, accompanied by Joe Peters, Lee's indispensable valet. During Lee's absence, J. J. developed severe chest pains and was hospitalized. Dismissing his father's illness as hypertension rather than the heart attack it appeared to be, John decided not to call Lee back from Europe. He knew his father would be enraged if he did. However, Milton, once again demonstrating his ignorance of the rules of the game, phoned Lee and urged him to return. Naively, Milton felt it should be possible for the brothers to meet at the hospital, if only for a few minutes. But John knew his father would never consent to such a meeting, especially since relations between the brothers had recently grown more bitter than ever.[22]

After nine days in the hospital, J. J. returned to the office in a virulent mood. He launched into long and increasingly public accusations against his brother. With the heedlessness that had always caused Lee great embarrassment, J. J. began giving interviews to both trade and general papers in which he asserted that, while he had been on the road overseeing shows, Lee had made money from ice and had stolen millions from him. When he returned from Europe, Lee too began to speak out more than he ever had before about in-house affairs. In a tone of weary resignation, Lee counterattacked by citing the money that J. J.'s "lousy" shows had lost the firm and repeated what he had said at least privately many times before—he had long considered breaking away from J. J. This time Lee actually went as far as instructing Milton Weir to begin proceedings to dissolve the firm and split up the assets. Through Adolph Lund, J. J. invited Lee to buy him out. John, as usual, was the go-between, crossing West Forty-fourth Street to deliver messages about a mutual buyout he wasn't sure either party was serious about. "They each gave the other the chance to buy the other out, but I felt it was a test, a kind of war of nerves delivered in a way only they could truly understand."[23]

Replaying animosities that had roots in their childhood, the Shuberts challenged each other to break up the business their revered brother Sam had launched more than a half century earlier. They huffed and they puffed, but neither was able to initiate the process that would blow the house down.

Then, a week before Christmas 1953, Lee collapsed again. In his first days at Mount Sinai, he looked bright eyed as he sat up in bed to receive visitors and was as keenly interested as ever in the details of his business. But the reports by several doctors were grim: Lee had suffered serious brain damage. His upside-down vision was caused by a broken artery.

Was it time now for the brothers to heal their ancient wounds? Although Lee had not gone to see J. J. in the hospital the previous summer, J. J. considered visiting Lee nonetheless. "My father wanted to visit Lee," John said, "but he backed off when he thought about how Lee might react." If he saw J. J., Lee would surely know he was near death, and J. J. feared that when business associates learned of the visit, he would yet again be placed in a subservient role—the vassal come to seek absolution from his sovereign. In the end, J. J. did not go to Mount Sinai until after Lee had slipped into a coma and family members had gathered for a vigil.

On Christmas Day, J. J. rode to the hospital with John. "My father was white-faced and silent," John recalled. "He looked like a man in shock, and he began to weep." He was so far from his usual belligerence that he shook hands with his nephew Lawrence Shubert Lawrence, Sr., with whom he had not spoken in six or seven years. More than once, J. J. had fired Lawrence, only to have his decree countermanded by Lee. That didn't seem to matter now. J. J. and John joined Marcella, Lawrence, and Milton in an anxious vigil. At 5:24 P.M., Dr. Sidney Greenberg entered the room to inform them that Lee had died. While Marcella and the others sat in a shocked silence, J. J. began to weep uncontrollably.[24]

On Sunday, December 27, 1953, Lee's body reposed at the Universal Chapel on Lexington and Fifty-second. Funeral services were held at Temple Emanu-El at Fifth Avenue and Sixty-fifth Street on Monday, December 28, at two o'clock. There were rumors that J. J. did not attend the service and that the brothers had not talked in twenty-five years. Neither statement was accurate. "Father was all broken up at the funeral," John said. "In the small chapel before the services began, he cried out, 'What am I going to do now? I can't go on!' "[25]

Though not literally absent, J. J. had no role in organizing the funeral, and he did not participate in the service itself. Milton Shubert, Lee's second in command, took charge of all the funeral arrangements, including sending telegrams to the ninety-three honorary pallbearers, informing them to "kindly be present at the chapel at 1:30 and bring this telegram with you to expedite your admission." They constituted a veritable who's who of America's theatre, film, and television industries. George Abbott, Irving Berlin, Louis B. Mayer, Billy Rose, David Sarnoff, Spyros Skouras, Ed Sullivan, Harry Warner, and Adolph Zukor joined such long-time Shubert lieutenants as Milton Weir, William Klein, and Jack Small in paying tribute to the man who had been the single most powerful figure in the American theatre for four decades.

Rabbi Nathan A. Perilman's eulogy defined the central theme of Lee Shubert's life as "a story which we Americans dearly love to hear and tell . . . how the de-

stroyer of giants achieved the stature of a giant himself." Praising Lee for the way
he "avoided the spotlight and resisted every attempt to invade his personal and
private life," he reminded the packed congregation of

> how difficult is the role of a man who becomes a legend in his own lifetime.
> Such a one invites the blind idolatry of those who worship at the shrine of
> success, the persistent inquiry of the curious, and the immoderate flattery of
> the avid. Also such a one invites the animus of the ambitious, the resentment
> of the disappointed and the cruel barbs of those who delight in destroying
> legends. In the process of creating a legend we lose sight of the man.

As if Lee himself were reaching out to orchestrate his eulogy, Rabbi Perilman emphasized a theme Lee would surely have wanted the congregation to remember: "his devotion to the memory of his brother, Sam, was one of the most meaningful and enriching facts of his life."[26] What Rabbi Perilman pointedly omitted
was any reference whatever to Lee's other brother. In this official summation of
Lee Shubert's career, J. J. was stricken from the record.

Not for the first time, John felt bad for his father. Driving to the cemetery in
a limousine with his mother, John made the mistake of expressing his concern,
but Catherine Mary had no compassion to spare for her ex-husband. "Don't worry
about that old son of a bitch," she assured her son, with the customary scorn she
displayed whenever she talked about J. J. "He'll get his second wind."[27]

It would take a deep breath. Despite the fact that Lee could barely read or
write, he had always had the reputation as the smart Shubert; now J. J. watched as
Lee's place in theatre history quickly became elevated to the highest level. Obituaries routinely hailed Lee's death as the end of an era. "Lee Shubert played a controlling role in the destinies of more playhouses, productions and theatrical work-
ers of all types than did any other man in the known world," concluded Eugene
Burr in one of the obituaries.[28] "No critic or group of critics ever exercised Lee
Shubert's power of life and death over the drama," claimed another.[29] "He exercised more power over the drama than any one man and his death will have a
more serious effect than the passing of O'Neill," said Elliott Norton.[30] "He was the
last of the colorful showmen," *Variety* reported on January 3, 1954, placing Lee in
a line that included David Belasco, the Frohman brothers, William Brady, and
George M. Cohan. Sam was the founder and Lee the successor who did his brother
proud. Where did that leave J. J.?

Lee was remembered as the man who had saved the American theatre during
the Depression. In death, the qualities in Lee that had struck fear in the hearts of
many of his employees and partners became alchemized into virtues. Lee's greed
and his Hobbesian methods were transformed from defects into strengths. Dead,

Lee exemplified the grit and perseverance that Americans, at least in the 1950s, still liked to think were at the heart of the national character; and he was celebrated as a man who had come from nothing to build one of America's great fortunes. As Lee was canonized, J. J. saw himself reduced to a distinctly secondary role in the Shubert saga.

"Who will mind the store?" Broadway observers asked at the time of Lee's death. That the question was asked at all was yet another insult for J. J. Rumors about his being in poor health had been circulating since his hospital stay the previous summer, and Broadway gossip speculated that three administrators— Milton, Lawrence, and John—would be taking over: it would require at least three to do Lee's job. John and Milton were credible candidates, but Lawrence was not. For decades Lawrence had not strayed beyond the borders of his Philadelphia duchy; and as a severe alcoholic, he was hardly able or prepared to take on larger responsibilities.

In ARTICLE 19 of his will, dated January 27, 1949, Lee had named Milton to follow him.

> In view of the close association with me for many years of my nephew Milton Shubert in the theatrical enterprises with which I have been associated during the greater portion of my lifetime, and in view of the fact that it is my hope and expectation that said theatrical enterprises will continue for many years after my death, it is my desire that so long as the said theatrical enterprises continue, that my said nephew Milton Shubert shall be associated therewith and that he shall take my place therein and carry on said enterprises as I would have done were I alive and I request my Executors and Trustees insofar as feasible and insofar as permitted by law, that they use all of their efforts, to the end that said Milton Shubert shall carry on the said theatrical enterprises with all of the power and authority which I exercised during my lifetime, and receive such annual salary as the Shubert Enterprises agree to pay him, in excess of Twenty-five thousand ($25,000) Dollars.

Beneath the legal euphemisms, it is clear that Lee anticipated the internecine strife his act of fraternal sabotage provoked. In calling on his executors and trustees to use "all of their efforts" to support Milton, Lee was fully aware that Milton would need reinforcement to sustain his hold on the empire. In his original will, Lee had named J. J. as one of the executors and trustees assigned to shoring up Milton's sovereignty, but in the third codicil to that will, dated October 2, 1952, Lee removed J. J. from the roster, no doubt realizing that as one of the executors and trustees J. J. would be well placed for launching a civil war. Lee also had originally named J. J. (along with his sister Dora Shubert Wolf; Milton Shubert; and

William Klein) to administer his estate, but in the 1952 codicil, J. J. was replaced by Lawrence Shubert Lawrence, Sr., and (deceased) Dora was replaced by her daughter, Sylvia Wolf Golde.

Although he had been in the family shop for more than two decades (with a respite during his years in the armed services), John like Milton had not been properly trained for leadership, and too many years of being browbeaten by his father and serving as a liaison in the increasingly fevered fraternal wars had undermined his self-esteem. However, ailing at seventy-three and with decades of poor public relations to mar his track record, J. J. looked like an unpromising contender. As the producer of perennial revivals of *Blossom Time* and *The Student Prince*, he had become an industry laughingstock. Yet to anyone aware of the inner workings of the Shubert enterprises, it was inevitable that, despite his age and health and despite widespread doubts about his ability, J. J. would do what he had to do to take charge of the empire. Lee's death, then, plunged the Shubert Organization, for the first time in its history, into a crisis of leadership. "After Mr. Lee died, you didn't know where to go to get a decision," producer Alexander Cohen recalled.[31]

Lee may well have hoped that erasing J. J. from any legal role in the succession would provide some damage control, but it seems unlikely that he really believed Milton could fight off J. J.'s counterattack. "Do you dare compare yourself to me?" Lee had asked Milton in a moment that resonates with the nephew's weakness and his uncle's force. Milton was unsuited to head the Shubert outfit, as Lee had to have known, and naming Milton was simply another way for Lee to aggravate and humiliate J. J. It was Lee's last turn of the screw, from his grave—a strategy for prolonging and complicating J. J.'s rise to the position Lee had zealously occupied since Sam's death.

Playing out a charade of orderly succession, Milton moved into Lee's circular office above the Shubert Theatre. In less than a week, Milton made his first blunder. He informed Morris Jacobs, general manager for Rodgers and Hammerstein, that *The King and I*, the Rodgers and Hammerstein musical, then in its third season, would have to vacate the St. James Theatre to make way for *The Pajama Game*, a new musical, which promised heftier grosses. Without the authority or the stature to challenge Broadway royalty like Rodgers and Hammerstein, Milton warned Jacobs that, if he did not agree to close *The King and I*, the curtain would not go up that night. Relations between the Shuberts and Rodgers and Hammerstein, who were legendarily hard driving in business negotiations, had always been strained, and Milton's high-handedness opened wounds never entirely healed. Incensed, Jacobs crossed the street to complain to J. J., who had been lying in wait for Milton's first misstep. J. J. at once hammered out a truce with Rodgers and Hammerstein.

On January 1, 1954, while Milton was attending a meeting at Milton Weir's office at 1440 Broadway, J. J. made an unprecedented trip across West Forty-fourth Street to seize his kingdom. Accompanying J. J. on his errand were John; J. J.'s attorney, Adolph Lund; his longtime lieutenant Ben Mallam; and, for the occasion, the most important figure of all, a locksmith named Fisher, who had a reputation for working fast. "He broke his own record that afternoon, changing a half dozen locks in a half dozen minutes," John recalled. J. J. hurled Milton's possessions out of the office and ordered them to be taken down to the sidewalk in front of the Shubert Theatre. During J. J.'s rampage, Milton's secretary dashed to Weir's office to report what was happening. Accompanied by Weir and by his brother, Lawrence, Milton rushed to the theatre to find a cocky, bristling, buoyant J. J. seated magisterially behind Lee's desk.[32]

Winded from the hurried trip down from his office, Milton Weir challenged J. J., insisting that Milton Shubert, and Milton Shubert alone, was in rightful possession of the premises. When J. J. attempted to punch Weir in the face, Mallam (the burly ex-policeman) and Lund hustled J. J. out of the office. John remained to inform Milton, gently but firmly, that he was locked out of Lee's office for good. (Milton was to be involved in litigation over Lee's estate for many years, but he would indeed have no further role in the day-to-day operations of the business. Milton did not fight for his inheritance: J. J. had a stronger legal claim as Lee's successor, and Milton may well have realized that the job was bigger than he could handle. Milton went to Florida, where he lived in peaceful retirement until his death at age sixty-six on March 8, 1967.)

The next day, spitting fire, J. J. attended a meeting of the League of New York Theatres. He demanded Milton Weir's termination as the League's attorney. Since the Shuberts dominated the League, and since it was widely held that the League could not survive without Shubert participation, J. J. felt he was privileged to deliver on his ultimatum: "Either Weir goes, or I go."[33] J. J. would not state his reasons, but it was generally known that his long-simmering feud with Weir had ignited in the summer of 1949 over the Longacre Theatre. A radio station, WOR, had had a long-term lease on the Longacre; and when J. J. heard rumors that the station was planning to vacate when its lease expired in September, he wanted to restore the theatre so that it could be ready for a fall production. Weir rebuffed J. J., saying that WOR was in fact planning to renew its lease for another year. He was bluffing at Lee's request, as behind J. J.'s back Lee had booked in a play to open October 1 and had made arrangements to convert the theatre into the first-class house it had been before WOR took possession. Because J. J. had always been in charge of the cosmetic surgery on any Shubert theatre, Lee was finding another way to humiliate his brother; and in enlisting Weir to lie to J. J., he was drawing battle lines within the Shubert law firm.

When J. J. discovered Weir's duplicity, he threatened the lawyer verbally and physically, as he did four years later across Lee's desk. He fired Weir as his personal attorney and to replace him hired Adolph Lund, who worked in the office of Klein and Weir. From that point, Weir represented Lee's interests, while Lund represented J. J.'s.

With Lee's death, J. J. was at last in a position to avenge himself fully. J. J. was out for blood, but though he successfully forced Weir to sever his thirty-year connection with the firm of Klein and Weir, he could not force Weir out of his job at the League. Fully aware of the consequences, the League refused to capitulate. "It would be better to fold than to knuckle under to high-handed and unreasonable pressure," a League member said.[34] J. J. officially resigned from the League in April 1954. But despite Broadway insiders' opinions, the League survived without the Shuberts, who would not rejoin until 1965. The Shuberts certainly survived without the League.

J. J., though he had been stunned by Lee's death, got his second wind within a week. "The sixth floor of the Sardi Building was jumping again," John observed. Embroiled in fights with his family, former business partners, his own law firm, the League, and the United States government, J. J. was a man reborn. John, who was busy placating the general managers of every production at Shubert houses, most of whom were offended by J. J.'s tactics, watched with admiration as his father took charge of Shubert affairs. "Just let anyone try anything!" J. J. threatened, fists clenched, with a glee he made no attempt to conceal. "My father became more militant than ever," John said.[35]

J. J. did not have to wait long for his first victory. One week after Lee's death, the Shubert petition against the antitrust suit was finally answered—amazingly enough, in the Shuberts' favor. United States District Court Judge John C. Knox dismissed the suit against the Shuberts because "theatrical bookings, like organized baseball, are not subject to anti-trust laws."[36] Was Judge Knox, in this remarkable decision, suggesting that show business was no business? Herbert Bergson, handling the case for the Justice Department, immediately appealed the judgment, arguing that the motion picture industry rather than baseball would be the appropriate analogy for the Shubert operations. On April 27, 1954, the U.S. Supreme Court agreed to hear the case.

Two and one-half weeks after Lee's death, the final Messrs. Shubert production opened. Lee had acquired the play in London in May 1952, and even though it had failed there (under the title *After My Fashion*), he had decided to proceed with a New York production. A problem play, set in a British drawing room, about whether or not to expose a hero who turned out to be a scoundrel, *The Starcross Story* (as it was retitled) was the kind of material J. J. had always hated, and he was only too pleased to give it a hasty burial. With a stellar cast, including Mary Astor, Christopher Plummer, and Eva Le Gallienne, Lee's last import was a one-night flop.

With a relish he hadn't been allowed to demonstrate since the receivership period twenty years earlier, J. J. pursued every lawsuit against the firm, including a serious one from William Goldman, a former partner of Lawrence Shubert Lawrence, Sr., in the Philadelphia Erlanger Theatre, for $2.1 million; he continued the fight against the antitrust suit; and he geared up for what was to prove a long and bitter battle over Lee's will and an accounting of the estate. To represent his interests in the fight against Lee's four principal trustees—Milton Shubert, Lawrence Shubert Lawrence, Sr., William Klein, and Lee's niece Sylvia Golde—J. J. hired his own attorney, James Delehanty.

Lee's will and its numerous codicils, still unsettled by 1997, bristle with a history of familial animosity. "I give and bequeath to my nephew John Shubert the sum of Fifty Thousand ($50,000) Dollars," Lee wrote in his 1949 will. "This is in the nature of a remembrance," he added. "I feel there is no necessity of making any additional bequests or legacies to him, because his father is of sufficient means to fully and properly provide for him." "I make no provision in this will for my brother Jacob J. Shubert," Lee wrote, "for the reason that he has ample means of his own and requires no financial assistance from me." In his original will, Lee added the following: "My love and respect for him, and my utmost faith in his honesty and integrity, are evidenced by the fact that I am naming him as an Executor and Trustee of my estate, content in the knowledge that he will do all within his power to conserve and administer my estate for the benefit of my beneficiaries as herein provided." But in the 1952 codicil, written during a period John described as one of heightened tension between the brothers, only the ominous first sentence of the original will remains: "I make no provision in this will for my brother. . . . "

Clearly placing J. J. in an adversarial position, and knowing full well his brother's litigious bent, Lee seemed deliberately to have designed a will that his relatives would fight over for years. Rumors of Lee's wealth ranged from fifty million up to six hundred million; whatever his exact worth at the time of his death, Lee Shubert was a very rich man whose bequests to relatives and associates were remarkably light. Lee left his wife, Marcella, two hundred thousand dollars outright and a trust of one hundred fifty thousand from which she would receive the interest plus one-tenth percent of the principal, accruing to her annually. He left one hundred thousand dollars and a life income from one-sixth of his residuary estate to Milton, Lawrence Shubert Lawrence, Sr., and Sylvia Golde. To longtime employees, his bequests were almost mockingly small. To Joe Peters, he left ten thousand dollars in cash and one hundred dollars a week for two years from the date of his death. Jack Morris, guard at his office door for decades, received a mere five thousand dollars. For Ma Simmons, he was able to spare only one thousand dollars. The only major beneficiary, and ultimately (except for fees paid to lawyers) the only beneficiary, was the Samuel S. Shubert Foundation, established by Lee and J. J. in 1945 as a tribute to their brother. The Foundation makes annual gifts to nonprofit theatres and also owns and administers the decidedly for-profit Shubert Organization.

"Lee Shubert had three heirs," John explained.

They each receive one-third of the income of one-half of the estate. Mr. Lee prepared his will so that one-half went outright to the Foundation, and out of the remaining half, the three trust funds were set up. On Milton's death, his trust goes to Lawrence Shubert Lawrence, Jr. On Lawrence Shubert Lawrence, Sr.'s, death, his money goes to Lawrence Shubert Lawrence, Jr. So two of the trusts end at the death of Lawrence Shubert Lawrence, Jr. On Sylvia's death, her trust goes to her son, Warren.

(At this writing, Warren Golde is the only survivor.) "That would be the end of all trusts, whose principal would go back into the Foundation."[37] Lee's will ensured that the family business would outlive the family, as indeed, triumphantly, it has.

As Lee surely expected they would, J. J. and the trustees squared off for a prolonged court battle, which was to last thirteen years. In a 1956 move, (opposed by William Klein and Lawrence Shubert Lawrence, Sr.), Sylvia Golde and Milton Shubert filed suit against J. J. for an accounting of the Shubert holdings. They conservatively estimated the value at the time of Lee's death as fifty-three million; J. J. claimed fourteen and one-half million to be the accurate sum. In 1963 he revised his estimate downward to "between seven and fourteen million."[38] A court of appeals upheld the petitioners' motion for an audit, which was uncompleted at the time of J. J.'s death.

"The lawsuit within the family, between the heirs of Lee's estate and my father, was not a battle of hatred or anything like that," John maintained. "It's a battle on the interpretation of the will, which is a very complex will. That battle will continue for many years," he predicted, "unless both parties sit down and have a settlement on a common meeting ground. As long as it stays in court, there are too many dollars to interest lawyers, and things like that, to keep this thing going on for a long, long while."[39]

Lee's will seemed crafted to disprove that you can't take it with you. Not even the trustees knew the value of the estate they had been named to oversee. In league with his deceased brother, J. J. was also determined to avoid full disclosure. What the Shuberts were really worth only the Shuberts themselves knew for sure; and if J. J. was correct in his belief that Lee had cheated him over the years, then only Lee knew where all the money was. Lee wasn't telling. For ten years after Lee's death, his estate languished in confusion. On Christmas Eve, 1963, the government filed a claim against the estate in the amount of $15,705,387 in inheritance taxes, based on the assumption that the partnership had been worth fifty million dollars, a very conservative estimate according to many Broadway observers.[40]

Meanwhile the government continued to press the antitrust suit. J. J. was as prepared to fight as Lee had been—John said that "if the attorney general of the United States expected a fight from Lee, he discovered that J. J. was a knock-down-drag-out assailant."[41] But now, as ever, J. J. could not summon Lee's statesmanlike authority. At a meeting early in 1956 in the Foley Square courthouse offices of the Department of Justice, J. J. raged that he would close the UBO within one hour. The attorney general charged that J. J. would have to play by the rules and maintain business as usual until the government made its determination. The Shuberts' antitrust specialist, Alfred McCormack, realized that J. J. was a "wild card" (according to John) who might try to collapse the government's case by selling all the theatres. The lawyer, in short, had no faith in J. J.'s ability to play fair, and he urged J. J. to submit to a consent decree and thereby avoid a Supreme Court decision that he predicted might be unfavorable to the Shuberts. Under the terms of the decree, the Shuberts agreed to divest themselves of part of their empire. In effect that meant giving up twelve theatres in six cities, including four in New York, and closing the UBO and LAB Amusement Corporation. Marcus Heiman and the Shuberts were ordered to sever all business connections and were forbidden to have a financial interest in any ticket agency in any city with a Shubert house. (The UBO became an independent agency under the umbrella of the League, but it died quietly in 1986, long after it had ceased to mean anything in the theatre.) The consent decree was signed by Judge Irving Kaufman on February 17, 1956, in New York federal court, almost six years to the day after the announcement of the government's antitrust suit.[42]

Although the Shuberts were far from defeated (and, in fact, in very little time the downsizing stimulated profits), they endured the shame of being the first theatre entrepreneurs ever to be challenged and rebuked by federal authorities. In the immediate aftermath of the decree, the atmosphere on West Forty-fourth Street was dour. "It felt like a death in the family," an employee, speaking on condition of anonymity, remembered. "Many of us were worried about our jobs. No matter how brave a front they tried to put up, the Shuberts had met their Waterloo, and everyone knew it. The many people who hated their guts were secretly delighted, but others realized that, as Shubert goes, so goes the theatre. If the Shuberts were hurting, maybe that meant everyone else would suffer too."[43]

"I will live up to the decree," J. J. announced, "although I have my doubts as to whether some of its provisions will not hurt rather than benefit the American theatre." Noting that the Shuberts had never torn down or converted any theatres into supermarkets or parking lots, he warned that "many of the theatres we are forced to give up will not continue to be operated as legitimate houses." He seized, and indeed had earned the final words in the long battle.

> As the last survivor of the three Shubert brothers, who practically alone developed the present theatre districts in the large cities in the United States, I can point out what my brothers and I contributed to the development of the legitimate theatre in America. If we have been financially successful, the legitimate theatre and the public will some day benefit from the fruits of our labor through the means of the Sam S. Shubert Foundation.[44]

It took longer than the two years they had been allotted for the Shuberts to comply with the terms of the consent decree—selling legitimate theatres in an era dominated by television and films, both of which had reduced and weakened the Shubert empire long before the United States government had, wasn't easy. In two and one-half years, they managed to sell ten of the twelve theatres they had agreed to relinquish and asked for more time to find buyers for the other two; they finally sold the St. James for less money than they thought it would fetch because they were running out of time. Though operating at diminished capacity and tarnished by its defeat, Shubert enterprises remained the most powerful single force in the commercial theatre, a position it continues to occupy today.

Two years after the decree, *Variety* reported that "the Shuberts are having one of their best seasons in many years, both in New York and on the road. Not only hasn't the government's consent decree hurt, but it may even have bettered conditions for the Shuberts; they have fewer theatres to fill, and that has meant they have the pick of the strongest attractions."[45]

By the time the Shuberts had complied with the consent decree in 1958, J. J. was no longer in charge of Shubert operations on a daily basis. The son he had never trained for the job—the son he had belittled, ignored, or used as a pawn in his skirmishes with Lee—had become the man at the top. In effect, though not in title, John had become the CEO, and despite the fact that J. J.'s mental capacities began to deteriorate after 1958, John continued to feel that he was working for his father. "We've always felt we worked for some big guy, like Mr. General Motors or

something. My father used to ask me, 'Do you think I can go away to Europe?'—
like he's asking my permission. And my uncle used to say to me, 'You think I ought
to go away?' I never feel that I'm working for myself, and neither did they."

Neither his father nor his uncle ever made John feel confident about his ability to succeed them. John even interpreted his elders' establishment of the Shubert
Foundation ("something to make certain their name would live on long after they
died") as a sign that "maybe they had no hope in the second generation." As a
young man, John had been "scared of the family business," and when he took over
he still suffered from "the common illness that sons of successful fathers sometimes have": periodically, whenever he felt he couldn't measure up to being a
Shubert, he threatened to walk out. "I heard a story recently about a boy having
a nervous breakdown because his father operates six successful shopping centers,"
John said. "The son is becoming a drunkard, because he doesn't want to go into
his father's business."[46]

To cope, John developed self-protective strategies. While Lee and J. J. developed a passion for the theatre, John did not—or at least would not permit himself
to. "In the old days I said I wasn't interested in the theatre," John said.

> Well, I wasn't. It's a way of earning a living. The only reason I go to the theatre
> is to see how far off I was from judging a script from what the notices said. I
> want to see where I made my mistake in reading. I go to the theatre in a clini-
> cal way. I couldn't, and I can't, eat, sleep, and breathe it the way they did. I
> served a long apprenticeship and a hard one, and a cold one, where after you
> had an opening night, you reported to the office the next morning at ten
> o'clock, and there was no party after the show. There was no glamour to it.
> My family drilled it into me that the only way you succeed is that you make
> it the hard, cold way.

Even after he became the CEO, John worried that his father would cut him
off or at least threaten to, as he had many times in the past. "Being emotional,
quite often my father would say, 'You're fired!' And even though now [1960] I own
stock and am fairly well off financially, that thought still remains in my mind—
that any Saturday night, or even a Wednesday night, I can be thrown out of a job."
He said that, to remind himself of those difficult times when he and his mother
had to live on her small alimony or John's tuition money, he cultivated "a few ec-
centricities like riding on the subway or on the bus, or eating in a rather cheap
restaurant. I want to get the feel of what it would be like in case that difficult
moment of being cut off does occur."[47]

"John liked to be in cruddy places," said Evelyn Teichmann, the wife of writer
Howard Teichmann, a top Shubert executive in the 1960s. "He liked Ninth and

Tenth Avenues, and bars filled with drunks. He never wanted to be seated up front at Sardi's, where he could be seen and could meet and greet. John truly hated the 'magnificent' style; it made him uncomfortable."[48]

As secretary Eileen Kelly recalled, "John was a very wealthy man who acted as if he was very poor. With money, he was tight—very, very tight. He was tight with himself as well as with others. There were many times he would come in with buttons off his coat and I would sew them on."[49] "All of his suits were blue serge, from Ripley's down the block," Sandra Epstein, another of his secretaries, remembered.

> His shoes were from Thom McAn. He would go to an army-navy store when they had a sale on white shirts. He always wore the same thing—a white shirt, a blue tie, a blue serge suit, and black shoes with white socks. And a dark navy overcoat and a dark hat. It was all an eccentricity of some kind. He told me that he didn't carry any cash and that sometimes he didn't carry credit cards, and people always ended up paying for his meals. I said, "That's really ridiculous with all your money, having other people pay for you." And he said, "Well, I get away with it."[50]

Under John's watch, Shubert offices on the sixth floor of the Sardi Building became shabbier than ever. Like John's suits, the drab offices were a camouflage. "We had to badger John constantly to update the office," Eileen Kelly said.

> For years we never even had an intercom system. John thought intercoms were ridiculous: why should he have to pay money to have a whole new hookup? We would have to go back and forth, knock on his door: "David Merrick is on the phone." We used to lose weight going back and forth, knocking at the door. We had to plead for an electric typewriter. John had put up dismal partitions and installed those neon lights they use in factories.[51]

John built his own boat not to save money but because the activity gave him pleasure and a sense of accomplishment. He hoped one day to leave West Forty-fourth Street and devote himself full time to boatbuilding. "But his cheapness came out even here," according to Evelyn Teichmann. "When you went out on his yacht, you had to sit on the deck because he never bought any chairs."[52]

Yet in true Shubert style, he had a charitable streak. "He would give you a hard time if you asked for a raise and he would make you wait for it, but if there was something happening in your family and you needed money or guidance he was good," Eileen Kelly recalled. "He would never turn anyone away. He would listen, and he would give money. Out-of-work actors, musicians, usherettes—there were many he took care of, either through stipends or finding them jobs."[53]

"John was an apple without a core," Sandra Epstein observed, reflecting on her former boss. "There was a missing piece in him. He was a wasted man who never lived up to his potential, his education, and his brains. He never really had a sense of who he was. He did not want the responsibility of his inheritance—he felt it wasn't his."[54]

John may have been a mass of contradictions—a rich man who behaved like a pensioner, the head of a theatre empire who felt he was only a hired hand, someone who professed to have only "a clinical interest" in a field in which he spent his entire working life—but he did his job well. Though both his father and his uncle seem to have trained him for failure, he ultimately outwitted them. Like his elders, he kept a close watch on every aspect of the business on a day-to-day basis. He reported to work around noon and typically stayed on the job until 6:30 or 7:00. "I don't take time off in the day for anything personal of my own," he said. "I figure I've got to give them at least a few honest hours. I take home one to three hours of homework each night. Every carbon copy of everything going through the office, coming in or going out, I get. I check all statements, miscellaneous expense vouchers, and you'd be surprised how in checking those you can cut them down, if they know someone's watching the store."[55]

As in the old days, the office was flooded with people who needed to see a Shubert. "I felt like a traffic manager," Sandra Epstein recalled. "First, there were the executives who had to see him; Jack Small, the booking agent; Gertrude Ortlieb, in theatrical real estate; Howard Milley, the accountant; Howard Morrow in real estate maintenance. And then the theatre managers and theatre treasurers and the union people and the constant flow of producers and directors."[56] To act his part, John felt he had to assume his uncle's frozen mask. "Anytime I get sorry for a particular performer or director and try to help them, I know I'm making a mistake," John said. "I have a bad habit, I think most people with money have. They always get stuck on the weaklings, or they get stuck on the lost cause, the weak one in their own business. I can't make that mistake. I cannot make any mistake, and as a result I have to be able to approach it cold."[57]

John's dark, moist eyes and his foxy grin were masked by the suspicious Shubert glare he assumed whenever he was on the job. He could put on an executive air, and his brusque, gravelly staccato voice made him sound like a man in control. Finally, for all his insecurity and his resistance, he was a Shubert, and as a Shubert he knew in his bones that the only way to conduct the firm was the "hard, cold way." While Lee was truly a cold man, John playing Lee was an imposture that exacted a heavy toll. To offset the self-control his job demanded, John began to drink. During working hours and indeed up through the nightly and sacred Shubert ritual of counting the grosses, John had the discipline and the will-power to remain sober. Then, as if slipping into a different character, he would start to drink heavily. "If you get smashed, they could steal from you: that was what kept him sober," Evelyn Teichmann recalled. "But after the receipts he was free to drink, and drink he certainly did. Often he would call us at two or three in the morning, rambling and incoherent. The words wouldn't come out right."[58]

" 'Kid, you're too open with your emotions,' " John once told Sandra Epstein. "He told me that one day I would get a knife in my back because of it, and I felt that was a very revealing statement. John kept a tight rein on his emotions."[59] Nevertheless, John found ways of humanizing his job. By necessity, he usually operated according to the Shubert code; but unlike Lee or J. J., he really wanted to be liked. Conducting Shubert affairs with more of a smile than either his father or his uncle had, he was the only Shubert since Sam about whom practically everyone had a good word. "Johnny felt guilty when people talked about how cheap the Shuberts were," recalled actor-director Don Costello.

> About the time of the antitrust suit, which was when I first met him, I rented costumes from his father's warehouse for a production of *Girl Crazy* I was directing. Johnny actually wanted to pay me for using the costumes, as an appreciation for keeping J. J.'s name alive. But I insisted on paying for them. J. J. or Lee wouldn't have even thanked you for renting the costumes. When I went to the theatre for the dress rehearsal, the costumes were still at the warehouse on Sixty-first Street. When I called him, John ran up to the warehouse but forgot to bring the key. He broke the lock in order to get in, and when I told him his father would kill him, he said, "It's about time somebody broke something of the Shuberts'. Let them pay for a new lock."[60]

John was the only Shubert who talked to everyone in the family. He visited Lee's widow, Marcella; he kept up with and sent money to his mother's relatives on a monthly basis, even though Catherine Mary herself did not keep in touch with her practically poverty stricken brother in St. Louis. John talked to Lawrence Shubert Lawrence, Sr., in Philadelphia and to Milton even during the periods when J. J. was in the middle of a terrific row with one or both of the brothers. "John and Milton got along, even though there was such bad blood between Milton and J. J.," Gerald Schoenfeld recalled. "And even though Milton became an adversary in litigation involving J. J., which lasted until Milton's death in 1967, I really believe John attempted to and did maintain some relationship with Milton."[61]

As CEO, John functioned best in the guise of being a good guy. In 1959 he was instrumental in settling an actors' strike. As he sat down with both sides and listened to any union delegates who wanted to see him, he employed the skills he had spent a lifetime learning as a go-between for his warring parents and for Lee and J. J. John cultivated a pose of being flexible and reasonable and of giving petitioners what they wanted. Representatives from Actors' Equity and from the League felt comfortable talking to him. Eager to earn the respect he knew settling the strike would give him, he worked around the clock.

John himself attributed his success to "using all the tactics my family didn't use—being terribly honest, having great integrity, being conservative and making it a very sound business at the bottom instead of gambling."[62] If in his own way he tried to rectify the sins of his elders or at least wanted to create the impression that that is what he was doing, he was a Shubert nonetheless; and during his tenure, he made a few significant decisions that affirmed his blood ties to the clan. After J. J. had grown infirm, Broadway observers were betting that John would repair one of his father's most fractious acts and demonstrate his own goodwill by having the company rejoin the League. Instead, John took a hard line. "The League has asked us to come back," John said in 1958,

> and we're not going to do it. Because we are not in the League we are not identified with any group. The Shuberts will have to maintain their own independence as a stabilizing force in an industry which has always required a stabilizing force. Whether it happened to be Klaw and Erlanger in the old days, or subsequently the Shuberts, it seems a series of checks and balances are required. We feel we are the pipeline that will prevent a strike. The unions will stay with us because they knew us when.[63]

After John died, more than six hundred thousand dollars in cash was found hidden away in bank vaults. Bernard Jacobs recalled that John had

> three boxes at the Manufacturers Trust, one box at Chemical, and one box at Empire. My recollection was that there was a total of around five-hundred-and-some-odd-thousand dollars in the three boxes at Manufacturers Trust, one of which was held jointly with his mother; and about a hundred-some-odd thousand at the Chemical, and I think at the Empire there was really nothing other than some nonsense that I really don't want to talk about.[64]

Gerald Schoenfeld said that "most of the money was at Chemical," where there were "418 one-thousand-dollar bills."[65] The money represented the profits

John had raked in through ice. Ice, of course, has had a long history in the theatre; and though they were willing participants, the Shuberts did not originate the practice. Alexander Cohen said,

> John made the absurd mistake in the mid 1950s, after Lee's death, of formalizing the arrangements for ice. In the old days, and I'm going back to the forties, when I entered the theatre, if you had a great success you got ice handed to you at the end of the week by the treasurer of the theatre in which your show was playing. You got your share Saturday night or Monday night. Maybe it was about eight hundred dollars in cash, obtained from profits on, say, three-dollar tickets being sold to brokers for, say, four dollars. It was very informal, and some in the business didn't know of its existence. There were the private terms with Mr. Lee (each era had its own scams)—and when he died, there were several million dollars found in the safe in his office. If your show sold out you got a bonus, which was not written into the contract. If a producer had an "arrangement" with the Shuberts, which was never published, he could deceive his partners.
>
> After Mr. Lee died, ice exploded. By the mid fifties it had become a real factor in the business, and holier-than-thou guys like Leland Hayward took it like everyone else. Ice was split among treasurers, theatre owners, and producers, with their own managers sometimes standing between them. John set up room 504 in the Sardi Building as the "bank"—the central ticket office—which was operated by Shubert executives. Now you dealt with 504 for your ice instead of with house treasurers. You went there once a month, and you got an envelope. The practice later exploded into a public scandal.[66]

Sandra Epstein said that John set up 504 "to keep ice under wraps, to keep it under his eye, so that he would know where the money was going."[67] The arrangement continued after John's death, ending during the regime of Lawrence Shubert Lawrence, Jr.

Publicly the Shuberts had always maintained a policy of abhorring ticket agencies and scalpers. "The ticket agency is the greatest menace to show business," Lee Shubert was thundering as early as 1910. "There should be a law making it a criminal offense to sell a ticket outside the box office at an advanced price, and until such a law is enacted a manager is powerless."[68] Nevertheless, in 1912 in Chicago, the Shuberts were implicated in a scalping scandal when a prominent ticket agent, H. N. Waterfall, declared that he had paid J. J. Shubert "directly" a bonus of $250 to $1,000 every six weeks, and between November 1910 and September 1911, for the privilege of procuring control of choice seats in Shubert houses in Chicago, had paid J. J. $2,750. Waterfall's contract allowed him to return all unsold tickets; and at the end of each week, in the weekly count-up that was to become routine on Broadway after *South Pacific*, he "settled" with J. J. for tickets he had sold, "splitting the premium above the regular prices."[69]

In May 1949, Jack Pearl, the box office treasurer at the Majestic, where *South Pacific* was playing, was questioned during an official investigation into the ticket-scalping industry. (Tickets for *South Pacific* were being scalped at ten and fifteen times their five-dollar value.) Asked if he had "ever accepted tips in the selling of tickets, had ever split tips or overcharges with employers or employees and whether he was ever a party to unrecorded sales," Pearl was mute. On September 14, 1949, he was "officially" discharged. "He will not be hired at any Shubert theatre," Lee announced.[70]

In March 1951, a full-scale war erupted between the Shuberts and ticket brokers when a sizable majority of New York's ninety-odd brokers insisted that the Shuberts had financed and were in control of the recently formed Liberty Theatre Ticket Corporation. The brokers claimed that their allotments had been cut to provide the new agency with choice locations in Shubert theatres. In listing their grievances, the brokers charged the Shuberts with attempting "to control ticket brokerages [and working] for a central brokerage which would be Shubert-dominated."[71] Lee offered in defense his usual antibrokerage sentiments. Protesting the recent rise from seventy-five cents to one dollar in the brokerage fee, he proclaimed that "brokers invest nothing and have no expenses. They go and dig up tickets for hits. All they want is to sell tickets to hits at advanced prices. They're just a lot of parasites."[72]

In 1958 J. J. was still upholding the Shubert line that brokers are the "scum" of the business. "They're all gyps," he railed, "and I abhor them. I can't stop them from getting seats, and I am powerless to prevent theatre personnel from selling tickets—at a premium—to favored brokers."[73]

In addition to institutionalizing ice, John also continued another time-honored Shubert custom, whereby, to secure the most desirable Shubert theatres, producers paid under the table. "I never made a Shubert booking without paying for it," Alexander Cohen said. In John's day, petty tyrant Jack Small grew rich as the Shubert booker. "He was a great booker, and was a big factor in the Organization," Cohen said. "He'd never say no to anybody. Six different guys thought they were going into the same theatre. Small would keep everyone dangling."[74] A professional nice guy, jovial and outgoing, Jack Small asked for money right out. " 'If you want the Music Box, gimme a thousand dollars' . . . that was how he operated," said a former employee from Small's era, speaking anonymously.

Jack overbooked everything. He'd have five musicals going into the same house. He would "lose the tickets." You had a show going into the Lyceum, let's say, and somebody gave Jack a thousand or five thousand, whatever the price was to get into the theatre. Jack would have the treasurer lose the tickets, so that you would fall below the stop clause and he would get you out. The setup was Jack's baby, but John got kickbacks. "Hey, you do it, you handle it, and whatever comes my way, comes my way." That was John's attitude.[75]

"The consent decree has made my life easier," John said in 1960. "In fact, we kept selling theatres, even beyond the terms of the decree."[76] Unlike his elders, John was content to see the business shrink—he didn't have the family itch to acquire theatres and plays and property. But John did have the curse—that atavistic urge to accumulate—when it came to places to live in and women to sleep with. "I knew that John had a house in Byram [Connecticut]," Gerald Schoenfeld recalled, "and two apartments at 17 West Fifty-fourth Street. At the time of his death, he was creating an apartment for Nancy Eyerman over the then-Adelphi Theatre [in New York]. He had a room at the Hotel Astor. My recollection is he would use the Astor because he would stay late at the office and the Astor was right across the street."[77]

John needed to stay "right across the street"—even though he had two apartments only ten blocks north of the office—to continue to behave like a hot-blooded bachelor. At various times, John also had secret hideaways in the Edison Hotel and the Manhattan Hotel (now the Milford Plaza).

After hours, driven by his compulsions for sex and liquor, John was restless, edgy, and unsatisfied as he entertained a series of women in one of his secret apartments. In November 1959, he added another stopping-off place to his late-night wanderings, the Park Avenue apartment of Howard Teichmann. "The school 'Tyke' graduated from, the University of Wisconsin in Madison, asked him to get theatre people to give material to the Wisconsin Historical Society," Evelyn Teichmann recalled.

They were particularly interested in the Shuberts. Tyke, who knew John casually, asked him; John was receptive, but J. J. refused to cooperate. Almost as if to atone for his father—a role he must have played his whole life—John decided to dictate the history of the Shuberts to Tyke. When they first went out to eat, to discuss this, Tyke picked up the check, which won John over. Their first meeting was November 10, 1959, upstairs in John's office, but after that he asked if he could come here. He did, speaking into a tape recorder. In a peculiar way, as the interviews continued through 1959 and 1960, Tyke became like John's analyst. John would drop by late at night—at all hours, really—hungry to talk.[78]

John and his wife clearly had an "understanding," as Eileen Kelly recalled. "Eckie knew about all of John's girls. I believe, given the kind of relationship they had, that John discussed everything with her. She took it and she hung on—she liked being Mrs. John Shubert and she was not going to give that up."[79] But the marriage, like that of John's parents, was tempestuous. When inebriated, both had explosive tempers. "They would pick up radios and throw things at each other," said Evelyn Teichmann, a frequent guest at the Shuberts' house in Byram.

John had his own room soundproofed, to protect him against his wife's drunken rampages. At night, about 2:30, when she would be falling-down drunk, she would complain bitterly to me about what a miserable bastard he was to her, how he had forced her to have abortions. Then, in the morning, she was very regal—Lady Shubert—who had never been drunk in her life, a gracious hostess who'd ask you in a fancy accent if you'd care for muffins with your coffee.

In public, however, Mr. and Mrs. John Shubert "were like the royal family," Evelyn Teichmann added, "and like the royal family they didn't have to be together that much."[80] Eckie also had extramarital relationships, condoned by John.

When he married her in 1937, Eckie had had dainty features and porcelain skin; but over the years as she drank heavily, she gained weight, her face became bloated, and she acquired a hard, disappointed look. "There was a picture of Eckie that John kept in the office, of the time she was a dancer," Sandra Epstein recalled. "But I remember my first impression when I saw them together at an opening night. John was distinguished looking and Eckie was this dowdy woman with bags under her eyes and a double chin—completely unstylish, and not looking like someone who is stimulated by life. She was frumpy."[81]

The old-fashioned marriage of convenience of John and Eckie Shubert was seriously challenged when John met Nancy Eyerman on a cruise ship in 1958. Dark and slim and, according to Sandra Epstein, resembling "a younger female version of John—they looked like two peas in a pod"—Nancy was as zealous as Eckie for the rights and privileges of being Mrs. John Shubert. "When John started bringing her around to dinners she was introduced simply as 'Junior,' " Evelyn Teichmann said.

I didn't know who she was, or what her relationship to John was. All I knew was that one night we'd have dinner with John and Eckie, and a few nights later Eckie would be replaced by Junior, without any explanation whatsoever. She wore boots, John's fetish. She had no interest in theatre; really, she didn't seem to be interested in anything. She came from a wealthy Pennsylvania family and seemed like small-town Junior League.[82]

A complete outsider to the Broadway world (which, given John's powerfully ambivalent feelings about the business, may have been intoxicating to him), Nancy provoked in him the desire for a stable family life of the kind no Shubert male had ever enjoyed. While John had forced Eckie to have as many as a half dozen abortions, he fathered two children with Nancy. John claimed he couldn't consider having a child during his wife's childbearing years in the 1940s because his father didn't give him enough for "another mouth to feed." In 1948, when Eckie was in the early months of a pregnancy, John asked J. J. to establish a trust fund for a grandchild and a Shubert heir. "Suppose it's a daughter instead of a son?" J. J. asked, revealing in a stroke both the ingrained misogyny that runs through the Shubert saga and his tightfistedness: only a male would be worth a trust fund. When J. J. refused, John called Eckie. "The answer is no. Make an appointment with the doctor," he told her. Eckie had an abortion the next day.[83] After the showdown with his father, John gave up the idea of fathering a child "once and for all time"—until he met Nancy.

By the time he was sitting in the driver's seat at the Shubert Organization, John no longer had any illusions that he was a producer. He thought of himself as a businessman who just happened to own theatres. After having been burned, either by his father or by the critics, each time he had ventured into producing, John was content to retire from the field. But in 1960, there was a curious finale to his no-win track record, a last reckless throw of the dice in which John was accompanied, indeed led down the garden path, by some prominent names in the theatre.

"It was one of the worst shows I've ever seen," Evelyn Teichmann said of what was to be the final production actually produced by a Shubert. *Julia, Jake and Uncle Joe* was adapted by her husband, Howard Teichmann, the coauthor of the hit comedy *The Solid Gold Cadillac.*

And the terrible thing is, I'm completely responsible for that disaster. One spring day in front of the Burlington Bookstore I noticed a slim volume written by Oriana Atkinson about her visit to Russia with her husband, Brooks. It was selling for a quarter and I bought it, as a joke, I guess, probably to prove to Tyke that critics and their wives can have flops too. Not many people liked Oriana. A few nights later we had dinner with Walter Slezak, the actor, and his wife Kaasi. By dessert we had run out of real gossip—Walter loved gossip—so Tyke invented some. He told the Slezaks about my twenty-five-cent mistake, and then announced, "Oriana's book might make a good play." My God! At that point I don't think Tyke had read anything but the flyleaf on the jacket. "Oriana would be thrilled," Walter said. "She's always been so jealous of Jean Kerr's success."

Through the theatrical grapevine, Brooks Atkinson learned that Teichmann was thinking of adapting Oriana's book into a play. Atkinson called Teichmann and invited him to the *Times* offices. When Atkinson told Teichmann that Oriana was excited that he loved her book and was eagerly awaiting his call, "Tyke was dumbstruck and, facing the biggest critic in the world, cowardly," Evelyn Teichmann said. "He felt he couldn't offend the drama critic of the *New York Times*. He had to at least give it a try. When he showed his adaptation to Oriana, she cooed."

Teichmann showed the script to John Shubert, expecting a negative reaction, which he could then report to the Atkinsons. He hoped that would be the end of the matter. But the next day, John called to say that he loved the play and wanted to produce it and that he thought Claudette Colbert would be perfect as Oriana. "We're saved," Teichmann told his wife. "Claudette Colbert has good taste and she would never accept this play." Two days later, however, John called to say that Claudette loved the play and that they "had a deal." "We knew the project was lousy," Evelyn Teichmann said, "but it was rolling faster than anything we'd ever done, and we were becoming panicky." John then convinced Roger Stevens to co-produce.

"Claudette was a charming woman," Evelyn Teichmann remembered.

When I first met her, she was all her pictures rolled into one. But put her on the road in a bad show . . . She ranted and raved, and swore like a trooper. She kept calling conferences in her suite. She and Roger Stevens grew to hate each other; and one night after a particularly horrendous row, she screamed that he and John weren't producers, they were nothing but real estate men. White with rage, Stevens took Tyke and me out to an ice-cream parlor and told us, "producers are pretty helpless after a show is on, but there is one thing a producer *can* do: he can close a show. The day after the show opens, it will close." We begged him not to bring it in, but he said, "It's more humiliating to her if we go to New York."[84]

Unlike Stevens, John wanted to keep the show going. He reasoned that, with a coproducer like Roger Stevens, a star like Claudette Colbert, and the *Times* in his pocket—how could the *Times* knock a play about the Atkinsons? —he would be vindicated. But the show received unanimous pans, even from the *Times*. In the end, John deferred to his senior partner; and as Stevens had promised, *Julia, Jake and Uncle Joe* opened and closed on January 28, 1961.

"John's mind had never really been on the play," Evelyn Teichmann told me.

He was a very shy man who didn't talk a lot but screwed a lot. He was far more interested in getting laid than in producing. His own life at the time resembled a French farce and was more compelling and funnier than anything that was happening onstage. He was having an affair with our secretary, Claire Wallace, who wore boots. He had a fetish for women in boots; he liked them to walk over him. Claire was the all-American girl, with a wonderful laugh. Nothing bothered her. Once I saw her writing down, over and over again, the name she wanted: "Mrs. John Shubert." On the road his wife visited him. And he began to bring around Nancy Eyerman; we thought she was another of his girls but she turned out to be far more than that. John was more concerned with keeping the women separated from each other and with the daily calls he made to his mother than with the show. He was under a lot of stress juggling his women, and he had a vile temper: one time he took an axe to break down a locked door to get to a phone. He figured it was his theatre and he could do what he wanted. Each night he took a handful of Seconals and washed them down with Scotch. In the morning I half expected to hear that he'd died."

On the road with *Julia, Jake and Uncle Joe*, John disappeared for a few days. No one knew where he went. Only later did people learn that he had gone to Juárez, Mexico, where, on January 9, 1961, he divorced Eckie and on January 13, married Nancy.

"I think John did the show because he still wanted to prove to his family that he was a brilliant producer," Evelyn Teichmann speculated. "But at that point J. J. was far gone and I don't think he ever knew John had even produced a show."[85] Yet with the filial devotion he retained despite how ill-treated he had been, John continued to protect his father from rumors of ill health and mental incapacity. "My father isn't retired," John insisted in March 1961. "He was in the office this morning, before I arrived at noon, and he left ten minutes ahead of me, which was about a quarter to seven tonight. He generally puts in six to seven hours. His evenings, he goes to openings, but invariably, at his age of eighty-four, he likes to watch TV, have dinner in front of the set, and relax in that way, fall asleep."[86]

The reality was somewhat bleaker than John's portrait. By March 1961, J. J. had slipped into senility. Although he did make occasional visits to his sixth-floor office, taking the elevator down from his penthouse, he spent most of his time in a daze, staring blankly at the always-running television. His mouth had begun to droop; and except for intermittent flashes, his watery eyes seemed to remain uncomprehending. For companionship, he had only his wife, Muriel; John, who visited regularly; domestic servants; and John's secretaries, who were frequently summoned from the sixth floor to have lunch with J. J. or simply to provide company for an hour in the late afternoon.

An enfeebled recluse guarded by his wife, J. J. became a sympathetic, perhaps even a tragic, figure in his last few years. Far from being a theatrical dignitary to whom younger generations made respectful pilgrimage, he was mocked for having been the producer of an endless stream of girlie shows and on-the-cheap revivals of *Blossom Time* and *The Student Prince* and for having been the last and least of the three Shubert brothers, the one with the terrible temper. He continued to receive negative notices; in December 1955, he had inaugurated a one-half-million-dollar libel suit against *Variety* for a November 30, 1955, article that he maintained was intended to expose him to "public contempt, ridicule, scorn, aversion and disgrace . . . and to produce an evil opinion of him in the minds of right-thinking persons."[87] He did not collect. He still lived over the store, and nominally he remained the head of the firm, but he was a largely forgotten man, a king without a throne.

When John hired Eileen Kelly and Sandra Epstein, he told them, "If Mr. J. J. wants you up there, you go." "Not too many people visited him, and he was obviously grateful for our company," Eileen Kelly recalled.

When I would go up and see this subdued, little, white-haired old man, I wondered how he could have been as mean as people said he was. He once gave me twenty dollars for my birthday, to buy nylon stockings. He came down to the office a few times, and people shuddered when he appeared. His mind was becoming foggy—I remember once on a snowy day, he looked out the window and said that because of the snow he couldn't go to work, and of course all he had to do was go downstairs.[88]

Sandra Epstein remembered being alone in the office one day when J. J. asked her to be a witness to a new will he was writing. "It was May 27, 1958—I had started on the job in March. When he looked at my signature, he said my name aloud" in a tone Epstein recalled as wistful.

Later the same day he came down to the office again, he looked at me, shook his head, and walked out. The next day he came in and said, "Darling, how much do you make?" When I told him sixty-five dollars a week, he said, "How can you live on that?" and I said, "Mr. Shubert, one lives on what one must live on, on what one makes." And he said, "What would you like?" I was totally unprepared for this, and I said, "Well, one hundred dollars a week would be nice." And he went into his office and called Belle Jeffers, his secretary, and said, "Mrs. Jeffers, call Howard Milley [the Shubert comptroller] up here." He called me into the office and told Mr. Milley to give me a raise and that my check from that point on would have to be for one hundred dollars net. And this was just for my name being Sandra Epstein.

After having waited more than thirty years for the name that ensured financial security for her and her family, Muriel grew jealous. "She was worried J. J. would divorce her for me," Epstein said. "I thought that was the biggest kick in the whole world: I was twenty-one at the time. Can you imagine? I would have been my boss's stepmother!"

In Sandra Epstein, a pleasant young Jewish woman from Queens College majoring in elementary education, J. J. perhaps caught a glimpse of a different kind of life, one in which he hadn't grown so rich and hadn't married an Irish Catholic alcoholic whose obsession with money was as intense as his own. Epstein was often summoned upstairs to have lunch with J. J., who would do no more than pat her hand. "I never met any Jewish girls like you when I was a young man," he once told her. "And then I realized he was a man who had a history that was totally alien to what he built, and that somewhere in his 'heart of hearts' he missed that history." Sandra Epstein recalled seeing J. J. standing in John's office looking out the window at the Shubert Theatre marquee across the street and then turning to her to announce mournfully, "Darling, I created a monster."[89]

8

The Fall of the House of Shubert

On Saturday, November 17, 1962, at around half past six in the evening, the phone rang in the apartment of Gerald Schoenfeld at 541 East Twentieth Street, where he and his wife, Pat, were dressed to go out for dinner," Schoenfeld recalled.

> I was on my way out the door, as a matter of fact. Somebody on the other end identified himself as being a member of the Police Department in Clearwater, Florida, and he told me they had a DOA on the train and his name was John Shubert. I was told I was the first person called, because John had my name in his wallet.
>
> I was staggered by the news. I was just shocked. After all, the man was in his mid fifties and was in good health and . . . was going away for the weekend. I said to the policeman, "I'm not satisfied that you have John's ID. I want you to describe him to me." And he described him to me and I then realized that indeed he was telling me the truth. Although I don't have a specific recollection, but just by the sheer nature of what had happened, I'm quite sure that I must have called Bernie Jacobs immediately. I would have told him that I had just gotten news that John had died and that I was going right up to the office.

In addition to Bernard Jacobs, Schoenfeld recalls that he "notified Bernie Friedman and Howard Milley, who were then comptrollers; Jim Vaughan, who was working with me and Bernie [Jacobs] as cocounsel in matters relating to the litigation involving Lee Shubert's estate and was cocounsel to me with Bernie with respect to J. J. Shubert personally." The only Shubert relative Schoenfeld called was Lawrence Shubert Lawrence, Jr. "Lawrence was someone who had been working with John, and Lawrence was a grandnephew and someone whom I thought should be told." Schoenfeld, however, decided to exclude two other Shuberts. "J. J. could not be told," he said, and Milton, Lee's chosen successor, who might have put in a takeover bid at this point, was "really terminated, if that's the right word, by J. J. within a day or two after Lee had died. Milton was in no way connected with the business."[1] (Bernard Jacobs also adopted a carefully measured distance from Milton. "I never had a conversation with Milton Shubert," he said. "I never had anything to do with Milton Shubert other than the fact we were involved in litigation with him. As far as I know he never married. But, I wouldn't know."[2])

At an emergency meeting held at Schoenfeld's office Saturday night at nine, the men Schoenfeld had called, who were now responsible for the fate of the Shubert Organization, laid "plans to see that on Monday the business would function as it did on Friday. We wanted to make sure the ordinary conduct of the business would continue uninterruptedly, and also to give notification of his death to the banks where John may have had vaults," Schoenfeld remembered. "Of course I had no information regarding that but I wanted that information to be given out in case there were any such vaults."[3] They also decided that Jacobs was to go the next day to Florida to see Nancy and to arrange for the return of John's body to New York, and Schoenfeld was to see Eckie at her house in Byram.

To smooth the way for his meeting with Eckie, with whom he'd had only limited contact, Schoenfeld asked Howard Teichmann, who had become friendly with her, to accompany him. When the two men arrived in Byram in a downpour, Schoenfeld remembered "standing out in the rain" as Teichmann went ahead to express condolences. "I had never been to Byram before," Schoenfeld explained, "and I was concerned about whether or not I would be afforded a warm welcome in the house. I don't think she was opposed to seeing me but I perceived that she might be . . . hesitant about seeing me. But I'd rather not pursue that."[4]

Eckie invited Teichmann in but said Schoenfeld was not welcome. "You're going to have to deal with this man," Teichmann told her, and he convinced her to let Schoenfeld come in out of the rain. Eckie's lawyer, Aaron Frosch, arrived soon thereafter. "I don't remember what we discussed," Schoenfeld said. "I know that I always regarded Aaron as friendly. I know that Aaron was a personal friend of Eckie and John said that he had done some legal work for Eckie in the past, basically at John's behest."[5] ("John had arranged for Aaron Frosch to be Eckie's lawyer, because she didn't seem to trust John's lawyers," Evelyn Teichmann recalled.)

From the time that Schoenfeld entered the house in Byram on the day after

John died, he "wooed" Eckie, the presumed widow, according to Evelyn Teich-mann.

> The lawyers gave parties for her and sent limousines for her. She was worth wooing: John had left her a lot of money. When John was alive, Eckie had been in the background; now she wanted to come forward. She wanted to be on the Board of Directors, and when she was, the lawyers told her what to do. And in time they talked her into turning against Lawrence. Eckie couldn't think for herself; the only decision she made was what kind of candy to bring to opening nights.[6]

"Shock, absolute shock," Bernard Jacobs recalled of his reaction when Gerald Schoenfeld called to inform him of John's death. "I mean, John was the epitome of life. As far as I knew, he had no record of illness. It just overwhelmed me. It was a shame that he did not travel by plane and that he had traveled in a drawing room," Jacobs said. "If he had been in an airplane, where he could have gotten attention and oxygen, his life might very well have been saved. He died of a heart attack, and he was isolated in his own room when it happened." Jacobs (who took with him his wife, Betty) was selected to go to Florida as the Shubert emissary

> because, after Jack Small had died, I became sort of John's intermediary with Nancy. When Nancy needed money and John wasn't around to give it to her, he would give it to me to give to her. When Betty and I got to Clearwater, my best recollection is that we had lunch with Nancy in her simple, very plain beach bungalow, the kind you see all over in low-middle–class beach areas. There were no confrontations, no acerbity. I had a very civilized relationship with Nancy. Her father called several times during the day and spoke to me, again, in a very friendly sort of way.[7]

"I want to be buried from the Majestic Theatre if there isn't a matinee," John had written on yellow sheets of paper that Howard Teichmann found in John's desk the day John died. "He was still counting the grosses," Teichmann quipped.[8] As it happened, the week after John's death was Thanksgiving week, and *Camelot*, the Majestic's tenant, was to give a Thursday matinee. John could have his funeral on Wednesday without having to cancel the Wednesday matinee. John played to a full house. His casket rested beneath a blanket of red roses at the center of the lit stage; to the left was a lectern, to the right a single empty chair. In the front row sat the immediate family: John's mother, Catherine Mary, in deep shock at the sudden death of the son whose side she had never left; John's close cousins Milton,

Lawrence Shubert Lawrence, Jr., and Sylvia Wolf Golde; three distant cousins, Murray and Aaron Helwitz and Norman Light; and Marcella, Lee's widow. Absent were J. J., who had not been informed of his son's death, and John's stepmother, Muriel, who remained at home across the street with her ailing husband. ("I told Muriel about John's death," Gerald Schoenfeld recalled, "because J. J. could not be told."[9] In this strange, fatally divided family, so filled with rivalry and so unable to express whatever love they had for each other, there were powerful bonds that had to be respected, as so astute an employee as Schoenfeld instinctively understood. J. J. may have resented his son and feared that one day John would probably replace him, but he loved his son too; and now, infirm both mentally and physically, J. J., as those who knew him realized, had to be protected from the possibly lethal knowledge that John had died.)

At 2:15 the houselights dimmed as Roger Stevens led Eckie onto the stage, where she sat in the chair that had been placed there for her according to John's instructions. John may have loved Nancy, but it was Eckie he wanted in a conspicuous place of honor at his funeral. Roger Stevens announced that the service was "in full accord" with a letter left by John, in which he also named eleven important dates in his life, among them the year he joined the Shubert Organization, his term of military service, and his marriage to Eckie. Three men, who would be crucial figures in the transition period and beyond, read selections from the Bible: Gerald Schoenfeld recited the Twenty-third Psalm; Bernard Jacobs followed with a reading of the fourteenth chapter of the Gospel according to St. John; and—billed third—John's second cousin Lawrence Shubert Lawrence, Jr., intoned the Lord's Prayer.[10]

While Eckie sat regally onstage, John's second wife had been forbidden to attend the funeral. "That theatre was guarded very carefully so that Nancy, who wanted to come, could not get in if she showed up," Eileen Kelly said.[11] Howard Teichmann recalled that he and Sandra Epstein

> had drinks with Nancy and her father the Monday before the funeral. Bernie [Jacobs] and Gerry [Schoenfeld] had given me $750 to give to her so she could go to Florida, and she promised she would. On Tuesday they called me out of class [at Barnard College] to tell me she was still in New York. So I went back to Nancy, I think with a thousand dollars this time, and advised her to get out of town or it would be very painful for her. "The lawyers won't let you in," I told her. They had picked people who knew her by sight who were standing at the doors to the Majestic and were instructed not to let here in.[12]

The second Mrs. John Shubert did not appear at her husband's funeral.

According to John's mother, he had a second will to match his second wife.

John's original will, drawn up by Gerald Schoenfeld, who was named as coexecutor with Eckie, was dated December 8, 1960. In June 1963, seven months after her son's death, Catherine Mary discovered, in her safe-deposit box, an unwitnessed carbon copy of a will dated June 26, 1962, in which John named her sole executrix. This second will left her a half million dollars in cash and also asked her to set up a trust fund for his two children by Nancy: Sarah Catherine, three at the time, and John Jason, two. Significantly, there was no provision in this will for Eckie, Catherine Mary's longtime enemy.[13]

Ever the would-be peacemaker, John had built a cottage for Catherine Mary on the grounds of the house in Byram that he and Eckie had purchased as their country home. But Catherine Mary had only glared resentfully out her windows at John's wife; and after John's death, the two women spoke not one word to each other when they were both in residence, even though Catherine Mary's cottage was only a few feet from Eckie's patio. "I was the one John asked to take care of both Catherine Mary and Eckie, whatever they needed or wanted," Eileen Kelly recalled. "The two were so different, and they just hated each other. Catherine Mary was a big spender: she had been poor for so long, living on the alimony from J. J., that when John took over and she finally had some real money, she felt she had the right to spend all of it."[14] "Eckie was a very rich woman who acted as if she was still the poor girl from New Jersey John had married long ago," Evelyn Teichmann said. "The first time I went to their house in Byram, she showed me shoes she had just bought at a sale in Penney's. She was very proud of the purchase."[15]

Vigorously Catherine Mary insisted on the validity of the second will. "Schoenfeld and Jacobs assured my son during his lifetime that they would protect the rights of his second wife and their children in the event of death," she announced. "Instead, they attempted to enlist my support on behalf of Kerttu and they questioned the will which both they and I know my son executed during the summer of 1962."[16]

"We conducted a search for a later will, but we never found one," Gerald Schoenfeld remembered. "When Milton Weir, who was then attorney for Catherine Mary, announced that he had come into possession of a copy of what was reported to be a later will of John Shubert, we asked if we could look at it. A handwriting expert was retained, and in court, when the carbon was blown up, it was the opinion of the handwriting expert that it was not John's signature."[17] Catherine Mary angrily withdrew her suit. "We will pursue other remedies," Milton Weir stated.[18]

Schoenfeld attributed the discredited second will to Catherine Mary rather than to a collusion between Catherine Mary and Nancy. "I don't think it was Nancy," he said.[19] "We subsequently had some litigation with Catherine Mary because she managed to get access to the box which she jointly owned with John at Manufacturers Hanover after John died," Bernard Jacobs recalled. "And when the box was returned to the attendant it was much lighter than it had been before. She denied she knew anything about the box. But I would assume she was the only one who had access to that box."[20]

As early as the Monday morning after John's death, when in a hysterical state she burst into the lawyers' offices issuing demands, Catherine Mary had locked horns with Schoenfeld and Jacobs (and lost). "She was screaming, 'My son is not dead, he is alive, he is alive!' " Eileen Kelly said.[21] "Among other things," Gerald Schoenfeld recalled of Catherine Mary's visit, "she wanted to make sure where John Shubert was being buried. She was anxious that he be buried in the Shubert mausoleum, but I told her her wishes could not be agreed to because Eckie would be the one to determine where John was to be buried. John had indicated that he wished to be buried in Eckie's family plot, where he was interred."[22]

In siding with Nancy, Catherine Mary was writing her own epitaph. John may have loved Nancy, but in his will—his only verified will—it was Eckie he had provided for. He left Eckie the bulk of his estate, estimated at around six hundred thousand dollars. While Eckie would have inherited a far larger amount if J. J.'s death had preceded her husband's—a few weeks before his death, John told an associate "who did not wish to be identified that Shubert assets were worth one hundred million"[23]—John's death gave her a pivotal role in the empire and won her the support of the lawyers, who regarded Nancy as an outsider.

On May 23, 1963, six months after John's death, depositions began for an upcoming hearing, which would determine whether Eckie or Nancy had legal claim to the name Mrs. John Shubert. Given Nancy's fate at John's funeral and the sympathies of the Shubert lawyers, Eckie was the likely winner. (In the New York Post on May 3, 1974, Joseph Berger reported that Vi Fisch, a secretary, "recalled that Shubert lawyers tried to pressure her into testifying against Miss Eyerman, even threatening to cancel a contract" she had to do some typing for John. Shortly after the trial, Fisch left the Organization.) The case went to court on August 5, 1963.

"There was never any discussion of terminating our marriage," Eckie began her testimony.[24]

> In a drunken moment, John may have [said he wanted to marry Nancy] but that was the only time. All I recall is that he said he was going to Mexico to divorce me but that this so-called "divorce" wouldn't change our status whatever. I saw him off at the train station, and he said, "When you get papers, do not sign anything; it doesn't mean a thing." I was terribly hurt and distraught, but he said he had to do something to help this poor unfortunate. He said he was going to vindicate some mistake he'd made, and that he had

to do it because he was being harassed. He said he was not sure Nancy's children were his children.

Looking drawn and tense, Eckie spoke in a quiet, world-weary voice; and because of a recent fall, she was in a wheelchair.

In contrast, Nancy, though clearly just as uncomfortable, had an innate poise. She began by recalling her first meeting with the first Mrs. Shubert.

"Helene [Kerttu] wants to see you," John told me one day. "She wants to look you over—she might give you the divorce." She looked me over and sort of talked at me rather than to me. She said, "Well, I don't think she's so hot. She's kind of flat-chested and her legs aren't as good as mine." John said, "I want a divorce. Nancy and I love each other and are going to be married. Well, how about it?" And Helene said, "Well, maybe for two million dollars. At least an arm and a leg, that's all I want."

When John proposed divorcing Eckie and then marrying me in Mexico, he assured me he had been doing his own research and that our marriage would be valid. "I am a lawyer and I graduated from Harvard Law," he said [maintaining the old fiction]. "As far as that goes, I am a better lawyer than Wall Street lawyers or my own—'pardon me'—office boys. The children will be legitimate. And you will be legitimate too," he assured me. But he did not say he had talked with either Mr. Schoenfeld or Mr. Jacobs about legitimacy.

Edward Eyerman, Nancy's distinguished-looking father, recounted his first meeting, early in 1959, with the married man his daughter had fallen in love with. "John informed me that he would get a divorce because his life was unbearable, and he [mentioned] the infidelity of his wife, and her alcoholic condition, and he said her company was just obnoxious. I accepted him as a dignified gentleman and accepted his word." But when Nancy gave birth, John had still not divorced his wife. "He told me he was waiting for his wife's signature," Eyerman reported, "and he mentioned that one time when he asked her to sign papers she was drunk and tore them up."

The most damaging evidence against John was a letter, written to Eckie on the day he filed for a Mexican divorce, in which he apologized and pledged his love for her. "The divorce will be worthless, and I truly don't want it to interfere in any way with your life and mine," John wrote. Arthur N. Field, the lawyer for Nancy's children, concluded that the letter "shows a deliberate plan to obtain an invalid divorce for the purpose of tricking a girl whom he had impregnated into a sense of delusion that the subsequent marriage was going to be valid." Herbert

Polk, Edward Eyerman's attorney, stated that "the decedent was living a divided life and would appear [to have] had a dual personality."

Sitting on opposite sides of the courtroom, John's two wives—Eckie, a haggard blond at forty-seven, and Nancy, a young, lean, prosperous-looking matron—did not once glance at each other. For both women, the trial was a humiliating public spectacle to which they were willing to expose themselves for the right to be legally Mrs. John Shubert. Unlike Eckie, Nancy cared neither for the money nor for the power the Shubert name conferred; she wanted legitimacy for herself and her children. "My father knew we weren't dealing with honorable people," she said years later. "We just wanted to make sure the children were legitimate and there was no stigma. My father said, 'You don't need their money. Let's go home.' "[25]

As the hearing entered its second day, "in order to avoid testimony which might have an adverse effect" upon the two children, the two widows each got what they wanted in an out-of-court settlement. The divorce and marriage in Mexico were voided; Eckie was declared the one and only Mrs. John Shubert; but the children were legitimized and allowed to use the Shubert name. John had taken out insurance policies for Nancy and the children, and these continue to be a partial source of their income. Nancy and the children were denied property rights to John's and J. J.'s estates and at the time of the settlement, were awarded only $12,500 each.[26]

Eckie got the Shubert name and the money and acquired power in the restructured Organization. She became a member of the Board of Directors of the Shubert Foundation. A Shubert in more than name, she sued the United States Life Insurance Company for $260,574 when they refused to honor a policy John had taken out in April 1962, claiming he had "misrepresented himself" by not declaring he was "an excessive and heavy user of liquor and habit-forming drugs."[27] As Mrs. John Shubert, Eckie died, aged seventy-one, a very rich woman, on July 12, 1985.

On December 10, 1990, Evelyn Teichmann talked to Nancy, then fifty-five, who said that "some years after" the 1963 hearing, "there was a settlement so my children and I could live comfortably, the way we want to. Both children look like John. John Jason is in California; Sally likes the rural life with my mother in Pennsylvania." Nancy has never remarried, maintaining, "one man was enough for me." When asked if it ever occurred to her that the Shubert empire could have been hers if she had hired a shrewd enough lawyer, she replied, "I have no interest in the business, and neither do my children. The lawyers [Gerald Schoenfeld and Bernard Jacobs] aren't the Shuberts, they're the Organization, but they run it well."

A split decision, the out-of-court settlement agreed to by Eckie and Nancy reflected the deep ambivalence that colored John's professional, as well as his personal, history. Just as he both resented and loved his parents and felt alternately oppressed and empowered by running the business, so was he torn in his feelings about the two women he married. If Eckie was as "obnoxious" as he claimed to Nancy and her father, why did John remain with her? And if Nancy was the answer to his heart's desire, why hadn't he protected her from the embarrassment of having to go to court to sue for her rights? "I think, deep down, he really loved Eckie, and he needed her," Eileen Kelly concluded.

> He cared for her in his own way. It was a very odd relationship. He gave Eckie a twenty-fifth anniversary party at the Belasco Room at Sardi's, while he had Nancy stashed away in an apartment up at the Adelphi Theatre. It was weird. John was good to Eckie in his way, and Eckie had sweet qualities in addition to the other qualities. She was always dear to me. In her will she left me a few thousand. John loved Nancy too, but there was a deeper connection to Eckie—the other was extracurricular, and it grew into something bigger than he bargained for.[28]

Wanting to please everybody, John finally couldn't say no to either woman.

There was only slightly less confusion about who would succeed John in business. In 1953, when Lee's death had provoked rumors that the Shuberts were finished, J. J. had been eager and able to assume control, and John was the legitimate heir who would take over in the event of J. J.'s death or incapacity. Now, with John dead and J. J. grown senile, the company faced the gravest leadership crisis in its history. The problem of succession was compounded by the fact that John, according to Evelyn Teichmann, "worked in a vacuum. Once he finally had power he became jealous about keeping it. He made sure he was the only one who knew everything—everybody else knew just a little bit. He was secretive, a family trait, and he had made sure that no one else really knew how to run the show."[29]

Speaking on the Monday following John's death in 1962, producer Robert Whitehead voiced the concern of the theatre community when he declared, "John held the empire together, and in holding it together he held the theatre together. In lesser hands it would have torn apart. There are now two alternatives: either get a board of directors and make it a public company, or disband it." Another producer, Emmett Rogers, predicted that, if "the empire should dissolve, you could kiss goodbye to the commercial theatre."[30]

Right after John's death, the lawyers turned to Howard Teichmann for help. In addition to accompanying Gerald Schoenfeld in his state visit to Eckie, Teichmann had also selected a casket ("a very simple, inexpensive one, which is what John would have wanted") and had directed the funeral at the Majestic Theatre so successfully that Campbell's (a Madison Avenue mortuary) offered him a job. "The lawyers were in charge, and yet they weren't sure what to do," Evelyn Teichmann recalled. "My husband told them that Lawrence [Shubert Lawrence, Jr.] had to be head—there was no one else. Lawrence was the only Shubert; his father was still alive but ill and quite unable to take over."[31] To provide the illusion of continuity, Lawrence was immediately appointed as John's successor.

"I was next in line, nobody questioned that," Lawrence said in 1988. "I had worked for the Shuberts for thirty-six years, integrated into the business since the time I was a youngster. Employees like Schoenfeld and Jacobs sat outside John's office and mine and waited their turn. I sat in with John on all meetings behind closed doors—and the lawyers came in only when John asked them to."[32]

Lawrence was born in Philadelphia on February 18, 1916. "The Shuberts were a strange family, not at all like normal people," he reminisced.

> Their life was their business. My father wouldn't make that same commitment, and Lee and J. J. always treated him like an outsider. The only time I can ever remember anything resembling a family get-together was when I was a little boy, when Lee and J. J. had houses in Darien [Connecticut] and on weekends they'd sit down to dinner together. They sold their houses in Darien and went to Mamaroneck [on Long Island Sound], where they also bought houses across the street from each other. They had grown farther apart by then. J. J. used to be so awful to Lee at family dinners; yet, even so, there they were with houses facing each other, just the way their offices did. Deep down, I think they cared for each other, in the peculiar way the Shuberts had, but they cared most for their business.[33]

In the Shubert mold, Lawrence's immediate family was also divided. When his parents separated when he was young, Lawrence, like John an only child, remained with his mother, Frances Von Summerfield, a thin, aristocratic-looking woman with the air of a society hostess. He described his father as "odd" and was never close to him. "He was a practical joker who had an electric chair he used to sit unsuspecting guests in, for instance, and he was a real character, a hail-fellow-well-met kind of guy on the surface but a loner underneath."[34] "Lawrence's father hated him," said Shubert in-law and good friend Marjorie Light.[35] Lawrence resented Milton Shubert, his uncle. "My father and Milton couldn't stand each other, just like Lee and J. J.," Lawrence said. "It was a family curse for brothers to be at war, I guess. Milton had delusions of grandeur, and he was almost as unpopular as J. J. Milton was always buzzing around Lee—he was overbearing."[36]

At nine, Lawrence was sent to military schools, where he was "in trouble all the time." In June 1934, he graduated from the Lawrenceville School and in 1938 earned his B.A. from the University of Pennsylvania, from which John, who was six years older than Lawrence, had also graduated. "I wasn't trained in business," Lawrence recalled. "John was, though. I don't regret not having the business background: you learn by osmosis, anyway, on the job, as both John and I did. But I wish now I had been a lawyer, so I could have protected myself against Schoenfeld and Jacobs."

After graduating from college, Lawrence became the manager of the Locust Street Theatre in Philadelphia. In 1939, soon after he got married (it was to be the first of three marriages, followed by an equal number of divorces), he went to New York to become the manager of the big new hit at the Winter Garden, *Hellzapoppin'*, "a wild show which I enjoyed seeing again and again, because Olsen and Johnson kept changing it." He was then company manager for another Olsen and Johnson free-for-all, *Sons o' Fun*, after which, during the run of *Porgy and Bess*, he became the manager of the 44th Street Theatre. In 1944, when *Winged Victory* was at his theatre, he enlisted in the navy, where he remained until 1946. Returning to New York, he became the manager of the Cort and then took the same post at the National.

> The Shuberts were taskmasters, especially to their relatives. They'd give us jobs, but they made us work harder than others. I wanted to get out of the Shubert Organization, because I didn't think I was getting anywhere. After *Call Me Mister* had played at the National [1946] for over a year, I asked the show's producer, Herman Lewin, to go on the road as the company manager of the national company. I wanted to be out of New York, away from my uncles.

Lawrence returned to New York in 1948 to become the manager of the Majestic, a key Shubert house, where he was in residence throughout the runs of a number of smash hits, including *South Pacific* and *The Music Man*, and up until the time of John's death, when he was suddenly promoted.

"If Abe Lincoln had been born in Philadelphia, he would have looked tall, lean and honest like Larry Lawrence," wrote Broadway columnist Earl Wilson.[37] But Lawrence was Lincolnesque in height only: in all the ways that counted, he was unequal to the Hobbesian world into which he had been tossed. Eileen Kelly, who became Lawrence's secretary and stayed on the job until 1969, recalled that Lawrence "never wanted the job—until it was taken from him. He really didn't want to have to make huge decisions. He was never a catalyst, the way John was, and he was never as involved or concerned as John. He never wanted to be more than the manager of the Majestic. John trained him—and Larry certainly needed help—but John thought Larry had absolutely no brains at all."[38]

As the overseer of what was still the world's largest theatrical empire, Lawrence Shubert Lawrence, Jr., lacked the relish for power and for making money that even John had revealed once he was in charge. "I always regarded the business as purely mercantile," Lawrence said, revealing an attitude that was ultimately to cost him his job.[39] Lawrence didn't have John's sense of family—"I had to remind him that he was a Shubert, and that he mustn't forget that," Howard Teichmann said[40]—or John's need to prove himself to a demanding, disapproving, competitive father. Lawrence seemed to have inherited his own father's lack of drive; and, fatally, Lawrence acquired another of his father's traits—he drank. Eileen Kelly remembered, that "Lawrence said he drove John to the station the day John died. I don't think he ever took John anyplace . . . to the cleaners maybe. Lawrence couldn't drive half the time; he wouldn't have been in any condition to take John."[41]

"Lawrence was a decent guy, but he was less interested in show business than in hanging around at the bar on the second floor of Sardi's," producer Alexander Cohen recalled.

> He had his own phone extension there. I saw him at the bar for eight hours straight. He was built—people remarked on his military bearing—and he could certainly hold his liquor. When I took him to London, he spent his time at the Savoy Bar, asking the bartender about shows. "How's *Stop the World?*" he asked. "It stinks!" the bartender answered. He never saw one show. The lawyers had to stay with him at the hotel, because he didn't want to be alone. He never studied a contract, but signed where he saw his initials. Lawrence reduced himself to being a titular head.[42]

Like John, and like the elder Shuberts too, Lawrence was a womanizer. But unlike John, he was not secretive. During his tenure as Shubert grand marshal, he was publicly involved with a number of women. There was a blond from Washington, D.C.; "they wouldn't let her into the Beverly Hills Hotel with him because they thought she was a hooker," Howard Teichmann recalled (she had an abortion when she was pregnant by Lawrence). Another blond, named Dolores, came in and out of his life until she committed suicide. Regularly, Evelyn Teichmann said, Lawrence saw a bevy of "high-priced fancy ladies he'd spend a lot of money for and then in the morning couldn't remember if he'd slept with them or not." But "number one" was award-winning choreographer Onna White. "They were going to get married, but didn't," Howard Teichmann said. "She left, I guess because she couldn't take it anymore. The smartest thing she ever did was not to marry him."[43] In retirement in Boca Raton, Lawrence's companion was an attractive, pleasant blond named Gloria Anderson.

"Right after John died, the lawyers called every day with a new crisis," said Evelyn Teichmann.

> John had been so secretive, and Tyke was the only one who knew some of the secrets. They were grateful to Tyke for keeping Nancy's name out of the paper when John died. We were at Sardi's, after the opening night of *Little Me*, when Val, the headwaiter, approached with a concerned expression. "Mr. Teichmann, the *Times* is calling, they told me that a Mr. Shubert died on a train in Florida." He paused, then lowered his voice. "That can't be *our* Mr. Shubert, can it? They want us to verify that the widow's name is Nancy somebody." Tyke got up and went to the pay phone, about five feet away from me. "No, no, I don't care what he told you," Tyke told the *Times*. "They're good friends of mine; his wife's name isn't Nancy, it's Helene, Helene Kerttu, but everyone calls her 'Eckie.'"
>
> The lawyers were grateful that Eckie was saved the humiliation of having another woman named as John Shubert's widow on the obituary page of the *New York Times*. And it's my opinion that that's how my husband happened to spend the next ten years as a Shubert executive. The lawyers realized Tyke could be useful to them: they knew the legal end, but they didn't know much about the theatre, while Tyke did. Once at Sardi's they asked Tyke who Ruth Gordon was; they asked if she was married to [producer] Max Gordon.[44]

A playwright and for many years the teacher of a famous course in creative writing at Barnard College, Howard Teichmann had a strong background in theatre. When he arrived in New York in 1939, he worked for Orson Welles and John Houseman. Later he studied lighting with Jean Rosenthal. "Because my husband loved the theatre, he took the ten-thousand-dollar-a-year job that Schoenfeld offered him. It was really the lawyers who hired Tyke, but they allowed Lawrence to think he did."[45]

Witty, urbane, well liked by the staff, and sounding like Henry Fonda, Teichmann "was totally different from Mr. Lawrence," said Lori Inman, a secretary. "Mr. Teichmann was a writer—that's where his heart was—rather than an administrator. There will always be misunderstandings between artists and businessmen. Mr. Lawrence was very concerned about box office receipts because Broadway was kind of dying."[46]

Teichmann wrote Lawrence's speeches, Shubert press releases, and the articles that appeared under Lawrence's byline in *Variety*. Valerie Mitchell, Teichmann's secretary from 1963–1969, said that he was "the cultural attaché for Mr. Lawrence, who was not an erudite, cultivated man."[47] Teichmann was placed in charge of administering Shubert Foundation awards in playwriting to college students.

He was also hired to be Lawrence's companion—to attend opening nights with him, to accompany him to auditions of shows seeking a Shubert house, and to go drinking with him whenever asked. Drinking on the job became an occupational hazard for Teichmann until he decided to quit drinking in the summer of 1968. He still had to pretend to drink whenever he went out with Lawrence, however; and as Evelyn Teichmann explained, "Tyke made arrangements with the bartenders at their regular places. He'd order a gin and tonic and the bartenders would bring him a club soda with a slice of lime."

"My husband had no interest in business, and so he never represented a threat to the lawyers," Evelyn Teichmann said. "But perhaps for those reasons too, he was always an outsider. They paid everybody a little cash in addition to a check; Tyke said right at the first that he wanted to be paid on the books. After that, though he lasted ten years, he was on borrowed time, because if you're not going to play by the lawyers' rules, ultimately you're out."[48]

In February 1963, for their second major appointment following John's death, the lawyers (and Lawrence) selected Alvin Cooperman, a former television executive and producer. As the chief booker, Cooperman took on Jack Small's position, becoming the number two man to the man in charge. "If for nothing else but a single line his name will remain in the modern American theatre," Howard Teichmann recalled about his former colleague. "Saying 'one David Merrick musical is just like another David Merrick musical,' he chose *110° in the Shade* for the Broadhurst and permitted *Hello, Dolly!* to go to an opposition house."[49]

With the Shubert empire in transition all around him, J. J. was both unaware and largely forgotten. Never having known that his son was gone, J. J., aged eighty-six, died on December 26, 1963, almost a decade to the day after Lee. Muriel was right beside him, as she had been for nearly forty years. J. J.'s passing did not command the same attention or genuflections as Lee's had. Rabbi Nathan A. Perilman, Lee's eulogist, spoke more briefly this time and with greater restraint. "Like persons of great dimension, J. J. had contradictory personal characteristics and qualities," the rabbi began, immediately opening a space in which the congregants could read between the lines. "When he was disappointed or felt betrayed, he withdrew and could be adamantine." As he had for Lee, Rabbi Perilman underlined the ways in which J. J. differed from the conventional image of a Broadway showman. "He was almost painfully shy of personal attention. There was nothing of the flamboyant in this retiring, almost self-effacing man. He was as reticent in his public benefactions as he was in his private life." And as one would expect, the rabbi sounded the great theme of the Shuberts' self-constructed mythology, citing J. J.'s dedication "to the memory of his brother, Sam," as "one of the most meaningful and enriching factors of his life." About J. J.'s show-business achievements Rabbi Perilman had virtually nothing to say.[50]

Newspaper obituaries were also reserved but on the whole less grudging than Rabbi Perilman. The most generous, and the most accurate assessment of J. J.'s legacy was John Molleson's on December 28 in the *New York Herald-Tribune.* "He was known as a man who produced a thousand shows," Molleson opened, conferring on J. J. a moniker he would have appreciated. "The actual number, many of which he both co-produced and directed, was 520, a record which seems likely to endure." He saluted J. J. both as an astute talent scout, listing Al Jolson, Eddie Cantor, Marilyn Miller, Ed Wynn, Fanny Brice, Ray Bolger, Bert Lahr, and the Dolly Sisters as among the performers J. J. provided with their first important jobs; and as a pioneer who led Broadway's move northward from Herald Square to Times Square. In correctly citing the twenties as J. J.'s and the Shuberts' high period, Molleson evoked the might and extent of the empire at its zenith—"a domain that extended from coast to coast and that included not only theatres but extensive other real estate holdings, a music publishing company, scenery and costume warehouses." In the twenties, the Shuberts "furnished attractions for one thousand theatres, employed seven thousand persons, and had an income estimated at more than one million dollars a week. Often there were as many as twenty Shubert companies touring the country at one time; and in a single season, *The Student Prince* had eight companies on the road." And yet, as Molleson noted, concurring in this one single regard with Rabbi Perilman, J. J. maintained an amazingly modest profile. "Few men had done so much for the theatre and been so little known. J. J. seldom gave interviews, except to announce new shows. He didn't address luncheons and attended night clubs only to view new talent. He neither drank nor smoked."

In his will, J. J., like Lee, left the bulk of his estate to the Shubert Foundation. Ironically, his largest specific bequest was to John; the revenue—three hundred thousand dollars outright, plus the income from a two-million-dollar trust—was turned over to the Foundation. For surviving a thirty-one-year engagement and the care of a senile husband, Muriel was rewarded with three hundred thousand, plus a life income from an eight-hundred-thousand-dollar trust fund, as well as "whatever she chooses from the art collection and the furniture" in J. J.'s baronial penthouse.[51] (After J. J.'s death, Muriel moved to the Rockefeller Apartments at 17 West Fifty-fourth Street, where John and Eckie had had two apartments. When Muriel died, on March 26, 1970, leaving an estate estimated to be no more than one million dollars, she asked that her ashes be scattered over Shubert Alley.[52])

Surprisingly, Catherine Mary, J. J.'s dreaded first wife, was left ten thousand dollars annually. The Lawrence Shubert Lawrences, father and son, with both of whom J. J. had often quarreled, were left fifty thousand and twenty-five thousand dollars, respectively; and John's first wife, Eckie, of whom J. J. had never approved, was left twenty-five thousand. To his longtime secretary Belle Jeffers, he bequeathed twenty-five thousand dollars. Approximately fifty other employees and friends received modest sums. Pointedly, J. J. left nothing to Milton Shubert, Sylvia Golde, and Marcella Shubert, Lee's chief beneficiaries.

It took thirteen years for J. J.'s estate to be settled—speedy when compared with the disposition of Lee's still-unsettled estate. In death, as in life, the brothers continued to fight each other. Round one of the complicated legal tug-of-war between J. J.'s side and Lee's side concluded on January 31, 1966, when New York State Supreme Court Justice John L. Flynn decreed that the estate of Lee Shubert was entitled to receive about twenty-eight million dollars from J. J.'s estate.[53] In May 1968, the Internal Revenue Service (IRS) slapped J. J.'s estate with a bill for $624,407.82 in taxes, which the government claimed the deceased tycoon had tried to avoid paying.[54] In April 1977, J. J.'s wealth was finally given a specific figure, appraised for a sum that exceeded the expectations of the executors of both brothers' estates: over ninety-seven million dollars.[55] In 1977 J. J.'s executors were the Morgan Guaranty Trust and Eckie, but virtually the sole heir was the Shubert Foundation.

J. J.'s death only emphasized the relative youth of the new triumvirate heading the Shubert Organization. Lawrence Shubert Lawrence, Jr., and his "cultural consultant," Howard Teichmann, were both forty-seven; "executive director" Alvin Cooperman was thirty-nine. Trying to remake the Shuberts' moldy image, the new team was depicted in press releases as bringing a much-needed youthful progressivism and vitality to the Organization, which was as old as the century. "The public image of the Shubert empire, which for many years has been compounded of decaying theatres, bedraggled revivals of Blossom Time or The Student Prince, and an aura of penny-pinching, is undergoing a complete revamping under Lawrence Shubert Lawrence," claimed an article in Theatre Arts, timed to coincide with the fiftieth anniversary of Shubert Alley in September 1963. "The theatres are being cleaned up and redecorated."

For years there had been reports about scandalous conditions backstage at Shubert houses. In August 1959, Actors' Equity had threatened to pull out the entire cast of The Music Man before a performance, citing "deplorable" maintenance. On John's orders, the indictable conditions were quickly corrected.[56] "I could never get Mr. Lee to refurbish," Lawrence recalled. "I went to all the opposition houses, then reported what they had done. 'Oh, this is good,' he'd say, but he never did a thing." On Lawrence's watch, however, theatres that hadn't been touched since they were built were given a new polish and made to gleam and shimmer once again. In the first three years of Lawrence's administration, more than two million dollars were spent to transform the Broadhurst, Shubert, Booth, Royale and Golden Theatres.[57]

Reflecting on his accomplishments as head of the family business, Lawrence was particularly proud of having "brought most of Shubert's outdated playhouses up to today's theatrical standards." He also cited having built the Shubert in the Century City section of Los Angeles in 1972 (the first Shubert-built theatre since 1928; the company applied for and was granted release from the 1956 consent decree) and his efforts to attract younger audiences. "I instituted the policy of free distribution of tickets to high school students and the Police Athletic League, of giving cut-rate tickets to American Airlines–ID cardholders, and of selling theatre tickets at Macy's at box office prices."[58] ("It was the lawyers who had the idea to build the Shubert in Los Angeles," Evelyn Teichmann said, "and it was my husband who instituted the other programs Lawrence took credit for.")[59]

While Lawrence was superintending the cleaning of the Shubert theatres, the company was forced to clean up its operation in another way as well. On January 5, 1965, Murray Helwitz, described as the manager of the central ticket office of Shubert theatres, pleaded guilty to "forcing" nine ticket brokers to pay more than seventy thousand dollars above the box office prices for tickets to shows in Shubert houses in 1963. Helwitz "forced" the brokers to pay twenty-five to fifty cents above box office prices for all tickets to all shows, regardless of the show or the seat location. The guilty plea covered all ninety-one counts of a case filed by a grand jury in May 1964. In sentencing Helwitz, the criminal court judge said, "I suspect somebody above you got some of the money."[60]

One of a number of Shubert relatives hired in subsidiary jobs, Helwitz is related to the Helwitz family with whom David and Catherine Shubart and their children lived when they first arrived in America. His admission of guilt and his subsequent jail sentence put the cap on the long history of Shuberts and ice. Living in retirement in Santa Monica, California, Helwitz wouldn't talk about his case, except to say that "the company has treated him well."[61] After he was convicted and sentenced to prison, however, the Shubert Organization publicly shunned him. "He was not treated well after he went to prison," Sandra Epstein remembered.[62] When Helwitz was in prison, Evelyn Teichmann called Mrs. Helwitz to offer her condolences. "I was the only person from Shubert to call, and I was reprimanded by Gerald Schoenfeld," she said. "He told me I was not to do that ever again."[63]

While Lawrence launched a theatre restoration program, he left the sixth floor of the Sardi Building in the same woebegone condition it had been in for decades. "There was linoleum on the floor of the elevator, and rust, and when you got off at the sixth floor the office was incredibly grungy," according to Valerie Mitchell.

> The walls were a horrible false wood, which was turd brown. Across the street the lawyers, (who came over to the sixth floor frequently) had offices that were palatial—absolutely glorious. Mr. Lee's shower, next to Mr. Schoenfeld's office, had five jets. Mr. Teichmann and I redid Mr. Lawrence's office; we bought tasteful furniture, to replace the old stuff that looked like rejects from stage sets from the Stone Age.[64]

In addition to the down-at-the-heels surroundings and the poor pay ("they were stingy beyond belief; there was never a Christmas bonus, and when Mr. Lawrence announced he was raising my salary from $95 to $105 he expected me to do a song and dance"), Valerie Mitchell had to endure Lawrence's flareups. "I never saw Mr. Lawrence fall down or not be in control, and his speech was never slurred, but he had a fierce temper, and usually he would scream behind closed doors. Eileen Kelly, his secretary, would often emerge from his office in tears. At one Christmas party Mr. Lawrence got drunk and insulted [Mayor] John Lindsay, who turned heel and left." She also had to put up with the behavior of Lawrence's alcoholic cousin Norman Light, the manager of managers whose office was down the hall. "Opening night of *Golden Boy*, a Sammy Davis, Jr., musical, Norman Light staggered up to me and asked, 'What are all those niggers doing on the stage?' "

In the end, Lawrence's demeaning chauvinism was unbearable. When Eileen Kelly left, Lawrence told Teichmann, "I'm taking your girl." (At a party, when Walter Pidgeon asked him for house seats, Lawrence said, "Talk to the girl here.") When Mitchell wouldn't leave Teichmann, Lawrence's attitude toward her darkened. Lawrence instead "took" Jean Rosen, "who had survived Alvin Cooperman, who was difficult," Mitchell said. Mitchell was in charge of Lawrence's house seats, "the best pair in the house every night. In some theatres he had sixteen seats." The lawyers had four house seats per theatre per night, and if they needed house seats they also went to her. "There were certain house seats I couldn't use. Hickey [Irving Katz, named for the character in *The Iceman Cometh*] picked up those house seats for his ticket agency and sold them with Murray Helwitz's help. Some of that ice came back to Mr. Lawrence," Mitchell said.

On one especially busy day, when Jean Rosen went to Mitchell's office after lunch to ask for Lawrence's house seats, Mitchell said she would get back to her at four. After Rosen told Lawrence he would have to wait for his own house seats, he stormed into Mitchell's office, screaming, "Valerie, if you can't take orders there's the door!" Mitchell thought about it and said, "And maybe I'd better use it." After Lawrence stalked back to his office,

> All the anger I felt toward this vulgar man all those years welled up and I burst into his office, grabbed him, and said, "How dare you treat me like that?" I looked at him and Jean and said, "You two deserve each other." Mr. Teichmann and Mr. Schoenfeld said they would fix it, but it wouldn't have worked. Mr. Teichmann helped me get a job with David Susskind. Mr. Lawrence refused to give me unemployment insurance, but Mr. Teichmann got me some.[65]

To give Lawrence the illusion of stature, the lawyers arranged for him to receive awards. "When I won a gold medal for encouraging young writers, my associates, including Schoenfeld and Jacobs, gave me a luncheon at Sardi's," Lawrence said. In 1968 Lawrence was honored with the Man of the Year Award from the City of Hope, a hospital. Irving Goldman, the lawyers' close associate and soon to become an infamous figure in Shubert history, arranged the award, which was presented by Surrogate Court Judge Samuel DiFalco, who would become another blot on the Shubert ledgers. "Both Schoenfeld and Jacobs signed the City of Hope plaque presented to me," Lawrence recalled bitterly in 1990.[66]

"We asked Earl Wilson to write nice things about Lawrence in his column," Evelyn Teichmann said. "Wilson was a friend of ours; like us, he was from the Midwest."[67] Wilson complied, and in "The Fifth Reigning Shubert," a typical pro-Lawrence column (which appeared in the *New York Post* on October 15, 1966), he gushed that "Lawrence must be doing something right because the Shuberts are making more money than ever. His office has large photographs of his uncles and of Johnny. It's reported that when he rings for the elevator he looks at his four predecessors and asks softly, 'How am I doing?' It's also reported that the four Shubert photos shout, 'Bravo!' "

"People laughed behind Mr. Lawrence's back, and even though he only spoke Mr. Teichmann's words, Mr. Lawrence had some real power too," Valerie Mitchell said.[68] But ultimately, as Evelyn Teichmann observed, "Lawrence was the lawyers' stooge. They pretended Lawrence was the head, but he was only playing a role: he was a figurehead CEO, and all he really did was to take the bows and the cash."[69]

9

The Lawyers

After John Shubert's funeral, Gerald Schoenfeld, Bernard Jacobs, and their wives got into "the second car" in the cortege. "I think that Lawrence was with us, Lawrence and his mother," Bernard Jacobs recalled. "Now I don't remember whether it was Lawrence and his mother or Lawrence and Onna [White]. But I do remember that Lawrence was in the car with us. But, you know, I could be confused about that, though I am almost sure that Lawrence was in the car with us."[1] Lawrence, Gerald Schoenfeld said coolly, "was someone I thought should be told" of John's death. "Lawrence was someone who had been working with John. He used to sit in John's office in some sort of . . . in some sort of learning capacity, to see and I guess absorb what was going on during the course of the business days. He was there to oversee what John was participating in. But his primary responsibility was as manager of the Majestic Theatre."[2] Is it possible to infer that Jacobs and Schoenfeld did not have a high opinion of the man who was the most likely candidate to take John Shubert's place?

While Lawrence assumed his position as head of the firm, in the belief that it was his "birthright," he was in fact an employee who served at the discretion of the Board of Directors of the Shubert Foundation. When, in his grief and anxiety ("John was more like a brother than a cousin," Lawrence maintained[3]), he became CEO of the Shubert Organization, Inc., he was not aware that his days were numbered. "The lawyers made remarks about how they planned to take over in ten years," Evelyn Teichmann said. "We thought they were kidding. In 1962 they were not the same men they are today. They were terribly insecure, and when they'd say they were going to take over it seemed at the time like a joke."[4]

During Lawrence's tenure, Schoenfeld and Jacobs orchestrated Shubert affairs from behind the scenes with increasing skill and confidence. Their gradual takeover campaign began with terminating Lawrence's right-hand man, Howard Teichmann. "To isolate Lawrence, they kicked Tyke out of the office he had occupied right next to Lawrence's and put him in the back near the secretarial pool," as Evelyn Teichmann recalled.

> They really wanted him to quit, but he wouldn't. Norman Light became seriously ill and was put into Lenox Hill Hospital, across from where we live; his wife, Marjorie, stayed with us. When the lawyers found out, they were angry: they loathed Norman even more than they did Lawrence. Norman was very close to Lawrence, as Tyke was, and by the late sixties the lawyers wanted Lawrence to be alone so they could depose him.[5]

"The lawyers were out to get rid of Norman," agreed his widow, Marjorie Light. "And they were working on Eckie, pitting her against Larry. After Norman died in 1970, Larry didn't stand a snowball's chance in hell."[6] "Norman did stand up for Lawrence, but he wasn't the Maginot Line," according to Teichmann's daughter, Judith Teichmann Steckler. "This was bowling, and Lawrence would have been knocked down anyway."[7]

On June 30, 1972, at a meeting of the Board of Directors of the Shubert Foundation, Lawrence Shubert Lawrence, Jr., was voted out as chief executive officer. Named chairman of the board, he had no role in the day-to-day operations of the company; and for the first time since its founding in 1900, the largest and most durable theatrical empire in the history of the American theatre was managed by people who were not members of the Shubert family. "I didn't see it coming," Lawrence reflected sixteen years after he had been removed. "I had no prior notice but I couldn't have done anything had I known: when men of bad faith and little integrity conspire to gain power there's very little that can be done. I worked right beside John, who was training me to take over. It was my inheritance, everyone knows that. I call what the lawyers did the hundred-million-dollar train robbery."[8]

Prominently displayed on a coffee table in his airy, pastel-colored living room in Boca Raton, where Larry Lawrence lived in quiet retirement until his death from cancer at age seventy-six on July 18, 1992, was a book with the blunt title *The Terrible Truth about Lawyers*. "In 1972 I wished I had been a lawyer, so I could have dealt with these treasonable guys. The lawyers get a million apiece a year, which

Lee and J. J. never got; I get a stipend from them, a pension of $ 2,100 a year—that's it," he said. "At the time I felt I let my ancestors down." But once he was out of the line of fire, he was "strangely relieved. I'd have been dead long ago if I had stayed up there," he said in 1990.

> I don't like New York anymore. Here in Boca Raton I've gotten used to a nice quiet life. I play golf, I swim, I read, I have friends, I go to local theatres.
>
> All the Shuberts are gone now, except for me and my progeny—five children and six grandchildren—and my cousin, Warren Golde. I once called up Bernie Jacobs to taunt him. "Are you a Shubert? Are you a relative of mine?" I asked, but he wouldn't talk to me. Neither Warren nor any of my kids went into the theatre, and thank God for that. It was a blessing they didn't.[9]

"I knew something was up when Schoenfeld and Jacobs sat in front of us at the closing night of *Fiddler on the Roof* and didn't speak," Evelyn Teichmann said. And though she and her husband were in Los Angeles at the time, promoting Howard's biography of George Kaufman, the Teichmanns were not invited to the opening of the Shubert Theatre in Century City. Stopping for messages at their hotel one day, they found a curt letter of dismissal (dated July 27, 1972) from Gerald Schoenfeld.[10] With Teichmann gone, the key players from Lawrence's regime were no longer a part of the Shubert Organization.

In a December 12, 1972, memorandum written at the request of Robert M. Morgenthau, a lawyer who was to become Manhattan district attorney in 1975 (a post he continues to hold at this writing), Howard Teichmann compiled a history of how the lawyers had seized control.[11] He noted that "upon John's death Schoenfeld and Jacobs began to wield an amount of influence that was far out of line with their positions as house counsel." Circumstances, however, were certainly on their side. First, Lawrence was a distracted, gullible, easily led CEO; and understandably enough, the lawyers worked Lawrence's manifold deficiencies to their advantage. Second, as coexecutor of John Shubert's will, Schoenfeld, according to Teichmann, "took unto himself and his partner an authority over everything in the Shubert Organization." Third, Schoenfeld and Jacobs were cocounsel to the estate of J. J. Shubert, advising on assets evaluated by Surrogate Court Judge Samuel DiFalco in 1972 as worth sixty million dollars. On June 30, 1973, one year to the day after Lawrence was deposed, the Morgan Guaranty Trust, which had chaperoned J. J.'s estate, turned over its administration to the trustees of the Shubert Foundation, of which Schoenfeld and Jacobs were by then the chief officers.

A fourth factor in the lawyers' favor was their successful courtship of John's widow, Eckie, who had been hostile to them at the time of John's death and in the weeks following had refused to meet either of the lawyers unless her own lawyer, Aaron Frosch, was present. Like Lawrence, Eckie was an alcoholic. She was also notoriously thrifty and, according to Teichmann, Schoenfeld and Jacobs won points with her by "doing her legal work free of charge while the firm of Weissberger & Frosch sent bills." Her increasing dependence on Schoenfeld and Jacobs had a decisive impact. In 1971, pressure from Attorney General Louis Lefkowitz forced Lawrence and Eckie, the sole surviving family members, to expand the Board of Directors of the Shubert Foundation. By this point, a schism had developed between the last two Shuberts. "I didn't care for Eckie," Lawrence recalled, "and I helped Nancy, who also got a raw deal from the lawyers."[12] Schoenfeld and Jacobs did not want relations between the feuding Shuberts to be repaired. "When I attempted to patch the rift between Mrs. Shubert and Mr. Lawrence, [the lawyers] became downright hostile," Teichmann wrote.

Lawrence and Eckie each appointed two new members to the board. Eckie named Gerald Schoenfeld and Bernard Jacobs. Lawrence named Irving "Rocky" Wall, his own lawyer, and Irving Goldman, a paint salesman with powerful political connections who seemed to materialize out of the air during Lawrence's tenure and who had skillfully managed to convince Lawrence that he was his best friend. Once the new members, all of whom professed public support of Lawrence, had been chosen, Lawrence in fact was doomed. On June 30, 1972, when he was voted up and out, even his own appointees voted against him.

"A three-man executive committee has taken over in an atmosphere of almost Elizabethan conspiracy," the New York Times reported on July 11, 1972. The self-appointed new troika—Schoenfeld, Jacobs, and their cohort, the mysterious Irving Goldman—took charge of the cluster of twenty-three corporations that comprised the Shubert empire. Schoenfeld was to be responsible for all nontheatrical real estate, labor relations, and pensions. Jacobs assumed control of theatrical operations. And Goldman was to be in charge of theatre maintenance, vendors, and concessions.

"For their first appointment the lawyers chose a crook," a former employee said. "My God, can you believe it? A paint salesman in a position of such power!"[13] "Irving Goldman was the Jewish version of the godfather," according to Evelyn Teichmann.

> Suddenly he was there, as a shadow behind Gerald Schoenfeld. Tyke and I didn't know who he was, or what his function was. I first met him at a luau at his house, which had the thickest rugs I've ever walked on. The lawyers were at the party, and Lawrence, who got drunker by the minute. Irving Goldman kept saying to Lawrence, like a litany, "I'm your best friend; I'm your best friend." Lawrence believed Goldman, and it helped to ruin him.[14]

If the rise of Irving Goldman was to be bad news for both Lawrence Shubert Lawrence, Jr., and Howard Teichmann, it was to be even worse news for the lawyers who promoted him. Their devotion to Goldman was nearly to cost them their newly won empire.

Irving Goldman's background was similar to that of the elder Shuberts. Born into poverty in the Brownsville section of Brooklyn, Goldman was three when his father died and at fourteen was forced to quit school to support his mother. He claimed what few have ever claimed, a long and warm relationship with J. J., which he said began when he was a seventeen-year-old messenger boy for a paint company who in the course of his errands made frequent deliveries to the Shubert offices. With his native brashness, which could be brushed up to resemble charm, and his determination to become a millionaire, the young errand boy attracted J. J.'s attention. "You won't be an errand boy long," J. J. predicted.[15] Goldman said that J. J. gave him five thousand dollars to start his own theatrical paint company. "Take it and return it whenever you can," J. J. told him, adding, "I don't want your note; if you're not good your note is no good."[16] Goldman started Gothic Color with the seed money from J. J. By 1960 Goldman's company serviced about 95 percent of Broadway shows. "I repaid J. J.'s loan in full in six months," Goldman boasted. "My friendship with both J. J. and John, wonderful men, has been one of the greatest things in my life."[17]

In a later version of the tale of his friendship with J. J., Goldman embellished on the details. "J. J. called me 'son,' " he recalled. "Maybe it was because I once fronted for him in buying valuable sets and costumes from a movie outfit that had folded. If they'd heard his name they'd have jacked up the price: I saved him $10,000."[18]

"J. J. never saw or heard of Irving Goldman," claimed Walter J. Keyser, the man who handled Shubert insurance for over forty years and who knew J. J. well enough to make five trips to Europe with him. "J. J. wasn't generous, and he wouldn't have given five thousand dollars to anyone," Keyser told Howard Teichmann in 1972.[19] Apocryphal or not, Goldman had been claiming J. J.'s friendship for many years, at least since 1942, more than twenty years before he began to work for the Shubert Organization. There is no evidence that J. J. or John ever publicly denied or substantiated Goldman's boast. What is beyond dispute, however, is that Goldman made a lot of money selling theatrical paint and that he had a gift for courting people in high places. In 1963 he was honored at a dinner for three thousand as Man of the Year by the City of Hope—the same year he began to appear on West Forty-fourth Street. "There he was, just like that," Howard Teichmann recalled.[20]

One of Teichmann's duties was to co-sign, with Lawrence, all funds disbursed by the Shubert Foundation. "It was in this latter category—charitable bequests—

that I began encountering and having difficulties with Irving Goldman," Teichmann wrote.

> He was a fund raiser, Schoenfeld and Jacobs told me at the beginning. The charity for which Goldman raised more and more money was a California hospital called the City of Hope. It was an eminently qualified institution but for reasons I didn't understand it was receiving money completely out of proportion to hospitals in New York. In point of fact, it was completely out of proportion to anything the Foundation was giving to the next twenty charities combined. Schoenfeld and Jacobs constantly badgered Lawrence on behalf of Goldman to give more and more money to this California-based charity. My continued opposition deepened the animosity between Goldman and me. I began to believe, contrary to the expressions of Schoenfeld and Jacobs, that Goldman was much more than a fund raiser.

Teichmann had what he described as his first "run-in" with Irving Goldman two days before the fiftieth anniversary celebration of Shubert Alley on September 13, 1963.

> Two days before, a furious Alvin Cooperman handed me a long list of names given to him by Irving Goldman, who was then seated behind Schoenfeld's desk, using Schoenfeld's telephone—names which meant nothing to me— whom we were to place on the bleachers set up in the Alley. When I asked Goldman who these men were, he told me they were judges. "The Dago judges run this town and I run the Dago judges," he boasted. When I protested to Schoenfeld and Jacobs, I was told he was a fund raiser and to pay no attention to him. Nevertheless, two days later, there were all those judges, and I had a hell of a time finding a place for Helen Hayes to sit.

Goldman's dual roles, as fund-raiser and as the man with political contacts, escalated in importance throughout Lawrence's regime. "Goldman began to expand his requests for charities," Teichmann wrote. "He would claim that this was 'Judge So-and-so's favorite charity' or the pet project of 'Judge So-and-so's wife.'" By 1967 Goldman began receiving a regular allotment of house seats. "In this, as in so much else, his entire attitude was that he had to look after his friends. And he certainly had a great many friends who needed looking after."

Among Goldman's many boasts was that he had influenced decisions handed down by Judge Samuel DiFalco in the Nancy Eyerman case and in probating the estates of John and J. J. "All were in favor of the Shuberts," as Howard Teichmann noted. "In each instance the decision might very well have been proper, but Goldman took credit for them and Schoenfeld and Jacobs never allowed Lawrence to forget this for a moment."

Goldman began to receive a number of favors. "Word was passed to the maintenance department that the firm employed in painting the theatres should be changed to Campbell's, a company Irving Goldman controlled," Teichmann observed. "Further, all paint was to be purchased from Gothic Color, another Irving Goldman company. The exterminating business was to go to the brother-in-law of [Samuel] DiFalco; the carpeting was to be bought from a friend of [Samuel] DiFalco."

After Lawrence, prodded by the lawyers, made the mistake of appointing Goldman to the Board of Directors in 1971, the man became increasingly autocratic in his demands. At the first meeting of the now board, a lawyer from a firm hired by Lawrence—under pressure from Goldman, Schoenfeld, and Jacobs—as legal counsel to the Foundation attacked Teichmann's handling of Foundation gifts. The lawyer suggested that larger sums of money should be given to fewer institutions so that, according to Teichmann, "members of the Board of Directors of the Shubert Foundation could become members of the boards of directors of great hospitals and universities." Only Eckie and Lawrence came to Teichmann's defense. Teichmann was instructed to prepare a paper justifying the expenditure of fellowships in playwriting.

When he made his presentation a few meetings later, Goldman made comments about each of the schools on Teichmann's list. " 'Catholic University—out! That son of a bitch, Father Hartke, hasn't bought a quart of paint from me in twenty-five years. Not a dime for Catholic University.' 'He's a good boy up at Brown'—Brown University bought paint from Gothic—give him $10,000.' " Teichmann was "horrified." "The meeting ended in a shambles," he wrote.

Goldman, Schoenfeld, and Jacobs kept clamoring that they had to take care of their friends. I protested. Mrs. Shubert wasn't even present. "Rocky" Wall appeared uninterested. By the next week, my secretary had resigned. Her replacement did not know enough to say anything whenever a record of the Foundation was moved from my files. The inevitable handwriting was on the usual wall. It didn't take long. The Playwriting Fellowship program was dropped almost immediately. More money went to the City of Hope. Curious gifts began to be sent out to the School of Minerals and Mining at the University of Colorado, and to Purdue University, another engineering school. Were they friends of Irving Goldman's? Did they buy paint from Gothic Color? The money that had been made by the Shuberts in theatre—was it going back to aid the theatre? Or was it going back to aid somebody else? Or somebody else's friends?

Goldman is a man who sells paint and political influence. Schoenfeld and Jacobs, like their partner Goldman, know nothing about the theatre as an art form, a profession, or even a craft. [Goldman's primary connection to the theatre was as a fan bedazzled by its glamour; in the tradition of Harry Kaufman, he claimed to have seen every Broadway show since 1930.] I believe that what Schoenfeld, Jacobs, and Goldman are running is not the Shubert theatres but a partnership in which each man shares in everything from house seats to concessions to real estate ventures to maintenance contracts and who knows what else. It is my opinion that they have been milking the theatres with the same brashness they have used as trustees of the Foundation. These so-called executive directors are using their power for their own personal gain. Salaries, services, contracts, legal fees should all be exposed for the public to see, for the Foundation which controls the Shubert Organization is a public trust and I must assume there are laws dealing with persons who misuse that trust."[21]

Evelyn Teichmann recalled that, after her husband wrote the memorandum that Morgenthau, "who was a personal friend of ours, had asked Tyke to write," and after he "sent in his letter, we decided not to pursue it. How are you going to fight lawyers? Frankly, we didn't have the heart or the resources to go any further than the letter to Morgenthau."[22]

Another disgruntled former employee, however, was out for blood. On January 5, 1973, in a blistering seventy-seven-page document the New York Times called "a virtual declaration of war," Lawrence Shubert Lawrence, Jr., accused his deposers of conflicts of interest (the lawyers, he asserted, were both management and counsel to the management), of "excessive largesse" in distributing funds to their favorite charities, and of "acting invalidly" in having removed him from office. (The complaints were filed in New York State Supreme Court by Lawrence's lawyer, William Klein II, who like his client bore a name that resounded with Shubert history.) While Schoenfeld and Jacobs received the brunt of Lawrence's outrages Irving Goldman, described as their "cohort," was also blasted, particularly for his close association with Samuel DiFalco—"they made no secret of their long friendship"—and for claiming a friendship with J. J. that Lawrence maintained had never existed. Lawrence asked that the June 30 election be invalidated and that the new Board of Directors be ousted.

"Free this great business from the Schoenfeld and Jacobs vise," Lawrence's suit concluded ringingly, "through which they have perpetuated themselves as directors and principal officers of the subsidiaries, as attorneys for the subsidiaries, as member-directors and officers of the Foundation and thereby ensconced themselves and their cohort Goldman as dictators of each and every charitable bequest which the multimillion-dollar Foundation makes in their lifetime."[23] (Under the new regime, there was no separation of powers as in the past—the officers of the necessarily not-for-profit Foundation and of the decidedly for-profit Organization were the same.[24])

Lawrence's suit indicted the new triumvirate as men of unsurpassed rapacity, but it also, perhaps unwittingly, revealed why he lost his kingdom. He presented himself as "powerless" during his ten-year term to cope with the "manipulations" of his enemies and as generally unaware of what they were doing. Lawrence emerged from his own testimony as a weak-willed, remarkably unobservant CEO. "I didn't act because I didn't know and couldn't have done anything had I known," he stated, claiming he had no prior notice of "what was coming" the previous June 30. Unlike his ancestors, in other words, he did not properly mind the store.

On April 10, 1973, Justice Thomas C. Chimera rejected Lawrence's requests on both a technicality—Lawrence's lawyer had not filed in time and thereby missed the six-month statute of limitations on challenges to the validity of corporate elections—and on legal imprecision. Unconvinced by Lawrence's charges, which he characterized as "seasoned with unqualified conclusory statements such as 'pay-offs,' 'undue influence,' 'self-aggrandizement,' " Justice Chimera refused to remove the new officers and concluded that, however enflamed, Lawrence's document lacked "sufficient particularity" and did not "elicit intelligent pleading in response."[25] As to the technicality of William Klein II missing a deadline, a former Shubert employee asked incredulously, "How could a lawyer miss a deadline? And he missed by a mere five days. That's what you pay a lawyer to know. It has always smelled funny to me, and to a lot of others as well."[26]

New York Attorney General Louis Lefkowitz, however, had a different opinion from Justice Chimera and decided to conduct his own investigation. On March 28, 1974, he released a sixty-six-point recital of allegations in which, ironically, Lawrence was hoist with his own petard. The burden of Lefkowitz's indictment was that the chief officers of the firm, including Lawrence Shubert Lawrence, Jr., had squandered assets of the charitable Foundation and used some of the Foundation's funds for their personal benefit. Lefkowitz also noted that, over the prior nine years, J. J. Shubert's estate had lost millions through "excessively" paid legal advisers and that legal fees of $4,249,300 shared by the firm of Schoenfeld and Jacobs and $173,000 paid to them individually represented a conflict of interest and must be returned, with interest. Among numerous other abuses, Lefkowitz accused the lawyers of getting rent-free space in a Shubert building, "replenishing" their law library, and receiving "lucrative" insurance and pension benefits at the estate's expense. "Through unexplained and excessive payments Lawrence Shubert Lawrence, Jr., received more than one million dollars in salary and reimbursements for European trips, entertaining friends at swank restaurants, chauffeur-driven limousines and for flowers"—in short, for living high on the hog at company expense. The report also noted that the Campbell Paint Company, in which Irving Goldman had a substantial interest, received "unjustified and excessive" payments of $1,030,538 "for painting Shubert properties."[27]

On April 27, 1974, one month after he had released his indictment, Lefkowitz asked that the entire Board of Directors of the Shubert Foundation step down during his investigation. "No way," the normally reticent Rocky Wall responded. "They'll have to get a court of law to remove me."[28]

On May 3, a group of producers, union leaders, and theatre owners assembled in Lefkowitz's office to support the beleaguered lawyers. The convocation was organized by producer Alexander Cohen, who for many years had an office in the Shubert Theatre Building and who was to develop a close relationship with Schoenfeld and Jacobs; for a time, before a falling-out in the mid eighties, Cohen was popularly known along Broadway as "the third Shubert." "I was in Cannes when I got a call telling me that the board had been asked to step down," Cohen said.

> I returned to Now York that night, and next day hired seven limousines to take all the important theatre people down to Lefkowitz's office in the World Trade Center. We gave character references; and our request that the board be allowed to continue their duties during the probe warned Lefkowitz that in going after Schoenfeld and Jacobs he would, in effect, be taking on the entire theatre. It was at that point that Lefkowitz began to back off.

At the meeting, Cohen, as he recalled, led off by voicing his belief that this "is the best possible management of the Shuberts." In the nearly two decades since Lee's death, Cohen had witnessed what he felt was a steady decline in Shubert operations; he felt that Schoenfeld and Jacobs had the experience and the skill to lead the firm into a much-needed renaissance. "Most of the support was for the lawyers," Cohen noted. "Irving Goldman was still an unfamiliar figure to most of the theatre community."[29]

Although the comments made to Lefkowitz seem like the merest window dressing, what counted was the fact that so many prominent theatre people had chosen to affirm the new "Shuberts." Lefkowitz was impressed.

Emboldened by the vote of confidence they had received at the meeting, on May 10 the Board of Directors refused to step down. But the Lefkowitz probe continued, and the lawyers' problems were far from over. After Lefkowitz's indictment had been published, Joe Berger, then a reporter for the *New York Post*, began a series of hard-hitting accounts of alleged misconduct by the lawyers and by

Irving Goldman, whom he pursued with particular vigor. "Retaining Schoenfeld and Jacobs as counsel helped some producers [Berger cited Alexander Cohen and Stuart Ostrow] get their plays into select Shubert theatres," Berger wrote on April 2, 1974. "In some cases, retaining the two lawyers was a prerequisite," he continued. "They are also lawyers for Mohawk Maintenance Company, which supervises the cleaning operations at the fifteen Shubert theatres."

The civil suit against the Organization, filed by Lefkowitz in March 1974, lasted until April 1977, when Lefkowitz withdrew sixty-four of his original sixty-six accusations. "There were rumors that Lefkowitz had been paid off," a former employee said, "but nothing was ever proven."[30] Officially, then, Schoenfeld and Jacobs were completely exonerated of the charges Lefkowitz had brought against them. "The [remaining two] charges were dropped because Lefkowitz, finally, had nothing to go on," said veteran *Variety* reporter Hobe Morrison, who covered the case.

> I believe the Lefkowitz crusade against the "Shuberts" was inspired by Governor [Nelson] Rockefeller and the Rockefeller interests, who wanted to replace Schoenfeld and Jacobs with their own people. Rockefeller interests wanted to control all that real estate, I believe. And Lefkowitz's charges of favoritism were absurd: so what if Gerald Schoenfeld's mother-in-law handled mail orders? She was damn good at the job. Historically speaking, *Variety* had never hesitated to smack the Shuberts, who had in turn held a longtime grudge against *Variety*. When they started, Bernie and Gerry were leery of *Variety* and I couldn't blame them. But when I came out strongly in their favor they were grateful to me. But I was only doing my job. They asked what they could do for me after I came out on their side, but I don't want to be beholden. When I go to lunch with them I split the check.[31]

The lawyers survived the Lefkowitz indictments and the aura of "Elizabethan conspiracy" under which their takeover was launched and outlasted and outmaneuvered virtually all of their adversaries. However, their partner, Irving Goldman—the man they selected to help them seize Shubert from a Shubert—had a notably short tenure. In 1972 Goldman was a seemingly equal partner; by May 1975, he was out of a job.

On March 6, 1974, Goldman, a leading fund-raiser in his good friend Abe Beame's campaign for New York City mayor, was appointed New York's first full-time commissioner of cultural affairs, a dollar-a-year post with hefty influence. The swearing-in ceremony was Goldman's greatest—and last—hurrah. One year later, on March 13, 1975, Goldman was indicted by Special New York State Prosecutor Maurice H. Nadjari on fifteen counts of bribery, grand larceny, perjury,

and conspiracy involving "an alleged scheme to pay off Transit Authority offi-
cials to protect his subway vending machines," as Joe Berger reported in the *New
York Post*. Less than three weeks later, on April 1, 1975, Goldman was indicted on
forty-four counts of federal tax evasion and of conspiring to defraud the Transit Authority, a vending-machine company, and the United States government by
violating federal tax laws.[32]

When the first charges were announced, on March 13, Goldman resigned as
commissioner of cultural affairs; on March 19, he took a leave of absence from
the Shubert Foundation and resigned as officer and director of two Shubert holding corporations, the Select Theaters Corporation and the Shubert Organization,
though he continued working in the office on personnel and maintenance and
continued to receive his salary. Nonetheless, at the Shubert Organization Goldman began to live on borrowed time. On May 27, 1975, Goldman and Lawrence
Shubert Lawrence, Jr., were unanimously voted off the Board of Directors of the
Shubert Foundation. Goldman, then on leave as president and director, did not
attend; Lawrence, who was present, abstained. The board, which had voted to reduce its membership from nine to seven, Berger reported, added three new members in addition to Schoenfeld, Jacobs, Eckie, and Wall: socialite Helen Hollerith;
New York University accounting Professor Lee Seidler; and Metromedia President
John W. Kluge, reputedly the richest man in America.[33]

Schoenfeld and Jacobs reacted quickly to an October 7 indictment against
Goldman, which charged in part that he gave one million dollars' worth of contracts to a company for painting Shubert theatres that then returned half its
profits to him as kickbacks and that he bribed a potential witness to keep that
witness from testifying about allegedly receiving kickbacks from a Shubert paint
contract. For Schoenfeld and Jacobs, who themselves continued to be tainted by
the ongoing Lefkowitz probe, this was too close to home. Irving Goldman's ability
to win the friendship of judges may have been attractive to ambitious lawyers
planning a corporate takeover, but it proved an attraction with nearly fatal consequences. If Schoenfeld and Jacobs were to have any chance (in 1975, when they
themselves were under government scrutiny) of retaining their fragile purchase
on their newly won positions, Goldman had to go—and fast.

On October 8, after Goldman had refused the board's request that he provide
a detailed affidavit denying the charges against him, he was suspended from the
Shubert Organization by unanimous vote. Joshua Sokolow, a Shubert comptroller
and Goldman's personal accountant, was dismissed at the same time. Stripped
of his $65,000-a-year salary and barred from his office in Shubert Alley, Gold-
man, as suddenly as he had appeared on the scene as a Shubert power broker, was
just as quickly terminated. No longer useful as either fund-raiser or political go-
between, he had become a decided liability. The board's suspension did not rep-

resent "prejudgment," announced Milton S. Gould, counsel for the Shubert Foundation, but had been done "to protect the welfare" of the Foundation.[34] After the dismissal, Goldman wrote a stinging letter to his erstwhile colleagues, branding their action "an injustice." "I will be vindicated elsewhere," he promised.[35]

Whether by sheer luck or by manipulation, Goldman proved as resourceful in eluding conviction as he had been in cultivating powerful associates. "There was overwhelming evidence against Goldman," said Joseph A. Phillips, Nadjari's chief assistant. "We thought this was the strongest case we had against a public official."[36] Nonetheless, Nadjari's indictment was dismissed on a technicality. On September 5, 1977, Judge Kevin Thomas Duffy declared a mistrial in the Transit Authority bribery case, with the disclosure that the prosecution's chief witness had not told the truth about money he had received from Goldman. Although the judge's decision did not prohibit the government from seeking a new indictment based on untainted testimony, the case was not renewed in deference to the defendant's age (sixty-eight) and poor health (in March 1976, Goldman had undergone open-heart surgery).[37] The October 7, 1975, indictment concerning kickbacks in the Shubert paint contract was dropped for the same reason.

Retiring in 1975 from the kind of public life he had always craved, Goldman continued to run his paint company until his death at seventy-three on May 30, 1983. In 1980 he had one final brush with the Shubert lawyers. *Variety* reported on June 4 that Goldman had begun a series of talks with the rival Nederlander Organization, Inc. Goldman, it was rumored, was advising Nederlander in its fight to block the Shubert application to take over the management of Washington's National Theatre. While Goldman reputedly boasted to acquaintances that he was to become an executive with Nederlander, the firm denied it. Goldman never did join the opposition, at least not in any official capacity. The lawyers were outraged, but James Nederlander noted blandly that "Goldman *does* have experience in the theatre."[38]

After they had succeeded in removing Lawrence Shubert Lawrence, Jr., Schoenfeld and Jacobs faced enormous challenges. Not only did they have to overcome doubts about how they came to power, they also had to prove equal to the power they had won. Not only did they have to endure Lawrence's accusations and the prolonged government probe that followed, they also had to restructure a theatre empire that had become seriously frayed. "Something had to be done . . . to halt the deterioration which had occurred under Mr. Lawrence's sole managerial direction," Irving Goldman explained during the initial transition phase. "The Organization had sustained a loss of hundreds of thousands of dollars."[39] Goldman, in effect, became the spokesman for the transition team, at least as far as public criticisms of Lawrence. The lawyers did not retaliate against Lawrence's denunciations, prudently deciding not to honor the biblical injunction of an eye for an eye. "The man's abilities and shortcomings are well known in the business, and I don't think it would be appropriate for me to make any comment about him," said Gerald Schoenfeld, in a typically restrained statement.[40]

In 1971–1972, Lawrence's last season in power, the Shubert empire lost more than two million dollars in its theatrical operations, though it made about $1.5 million in nontheatrical real estate. "The ability of our theatres to operate depends in large measure upon the success of our non-theatrical real estate," Schoenfeld said at the time.[41] The *New York Times* called Lawrence's final season "the worst Shubert season since the Depression."[42]

Along Broadway there was concern that the lawyers had seized control of the empire only to dismantle it; some insiders felt that they were venture capitalists more interested in real estate than in preserving the cultural heritage represented by the collection of historic Shubert theatres. They also had to confront widespread suspicion that they were outsiders who knew nothing about either the creative or the practical aspects of putting on a show. "These two guys are not really theatre people," Garson Kanin said, still branding them mere lawyers two decades after their rise to power. "The theatre community looks upon them as real interlopers and newcomers and feels no bond with them. It's like a Jew who has a bond with other Jews while a Gentile never understands them—Bernie and Gerry remain 'Gentiles' in the eyes of the theatre community."[43]

However, Schoenfeld and Jacobs were hardly newcomers or outsiders in the house of Shubert or in the practice of theatrical law. Although when Schoenfeld joined the firm of Klein and Weir in 1949 Klein himself was no longer active, Schoenfeld could legitimately claim a Shubert tie that could be traced back to the Organization's origins. He could also claim a baptism by fire, having cut his teeth representing Shubert in the antitrust suit, one of the toughest cases in Shubert history.

He received extensive on-the-job training from J. J. When Adolph Lund (who became the principal Shubert lawyer after J. J. fired Milton Weir in 1953) died suddenly on New Year's Day 1957, J. J. approached Schoenfeld. "On that very day J. J. Shubert asked me if . . . ah, the way he put it was, 'I would like to know if you would handle our affairs,' " Schoenfeld recalled.

> I said that I would and he said, "Good, because I want you to know that I don't want old men handling our affairs because old men have old ideas." Now, J. J. Shubert was no youngster at that particular time but it was interesting to me that somebody who was as advanced as he would have that attitude towards younger people. I was then thirty-two years old. After ten weeks, he said to me, "I think you need help." And indeed I did. So he said,

"Go out and get somebody to help you." And that's how Bernie came here. Bernie came to work here on March 17, 1957, St. Patrick's Day.[44]

"When I was married in October 1950, I don't think I had met either Lee or J. J.," Schoenfeld remembered, although he had been working for the Shuberts' law firm for over a year. "In fact, I met Lee only once before he died," Schoenfeld said. But after Lee's death, J. J. became a major presence in Schoenfeld's professional life. "We were told by J. J., 'Ours is a twenty-four-hour day, seven days a week, and I expect my lawyers to be on the grounds at all times.' When you were called you'd wait on a bench outside J. J.'s office, maybe three or four hours."[45] Once they were in the office, the two lawyers would be seated on opposite sides of J. J.'s desk, with their backs to the front door and their faces toward the boss. "J. J. liked it that way," Jacobs recalled.[46]

When Schoenfeld became Shubert counsel in 1957, J. J. was heading into a decline, but he continued to exhibit his famous temper. He would typically explode at least once during the morning, invite both men up to his apartment for a sumptuous lunch, and then have another "tantrum" in the afternoon (according to Schoenfeld). After Schoenfeld had asked Jacobs to come to work with him, J. J. sent Schoenfeld a memo: "Anything Mr. Jacobs does wrong, you will be held accountable for."[47] Jacobs recalled that J. J. once summoned him into the office and told him to fire his partner.[48]

Learning to be "Shubert" from one of the founding brothers, and acting as principal participants in long and complicated litigation in the estates of Lee, J. J., and John, Schoenfeld and Jacobs could claim intimate knowledge of the Organization. And therefore, when a weak Shubert was nominally in charge, Schoenfeld and Jacobs were uniquely prepared to apply lessons gleaned from their many years of service. "Somebody had to run the business while Lawrence was titular head," Alexander Cohen said. "It got to the point where you talked to Bernie or Gerry to get a studied, rational answer. They represented new thinking in the business, and it was apparent to insiders that Schoenfeld and Jacobs were running the outfit even before Lawrence was out."[49]

"These are two smart guys who came along when the Shubert Organization was wobbling," said longtime Broadway insider and director Harold Prince.

What followed after Lee died jeopardized Shubert history. In the days of John, you could be promised a theatre and good luck as to whether or not you'd get the theatre he said you would. Lawrence was sweet but drank; Eckie was sweet but drank. And then there was the ice scandal, when Murray Helwitz was sent to jail; what had been going on in the box office was dangerous. The present-day 'Shuberts' are honest—you can trust what they tell you.[50]

Once they became the new Shuberts, another hurdle the lawyers had to confront was one the historical Shuberts never quite mastered: developing good public relations. They first had to position themselves with respect to the company's founders. Both Schoenfeld and Jacobs admitted that the historical Shuberts were the strictest of taskmasters who nonetheless, according to Schoenfeld, "evoked the loyalest kind of employees, even though they treated them like slaves."[51] Indeed, it has become an article of faith in the post-Shubert phase of Shubert history that the founders were true theatrical heroes. "It was Lee and J. J. who sustained the theatre during the Depression while others fell, and without their tenacity and their love of the theatre, today's business would not be what it is," Schoenfeld said.[52] "They preserved a heritage for this country that you would never have without these buildings," Jacobs said. "These buildings are a national treasure. The Shuberts also had the foresight and good sense and love for the theatre which compelled them to leave these buildings to a foundation so they could continue as part of that tradition. They loved this business and they persevered in this business in very difficult times and they worked their asses off and they died on the job and they never gave up, either one of them."[53]

At the same time, Schoenfeld and Jacobs tried to distance themselves from the Shubert family and from past practices. "John was very devoted to his father, but at the same time I think he was aware that both his father and his uncle were very stern, difficult men of another era and that, as the next generation, he wanted to project a different image," Schoenfeld observed.[54] The lawyers adopted the same stance, solicitous on the one hand and eager to "project a different image" on the other. And rather than conducting themselves as colorful showmen, they were corporate functionaries who operated in a bland, modern mode.

Ten days into his reign, on July 10, 1972, the *New York Times* described Gerald Schoenfeld, at fifty, as a "genial and cherubic envoy at large on everything from improving the Times Square area to encouraging Off-Broadway endeavor." "Quiet and solemn" was the muted evocation of Bernard Jacobs.

"They are really *very* different," Hal Prince said about the two most powerful men in the American theatre of the prior two decades.[55] Schoenfeld, the seemingly friendlier, more approachable partner, "has a hail-fellow-well-met facade," a former employee said. Smiling frequently ("he used to smile a lot more, before he became so powerful," the same former employee noted) and cultivating the impression of a desire to be liked,[56] his appearance of bonhomie clearly set him apart from Jacobs, who made no ingratiating gestures whatsoever. "He always walks in looking like he's just been told the human race has twenty-four hours to live," producer Harry Rigby memorably quipped.[57] Dyspeptic, sallow, and saturnine, Jacobs, was, according to a former employee, "an absolutely frightening-looking man."[58] As a public speaker, he had all the verve and charm of Bartleby the Scrivener. When he stepped to the podium of the Grand Ballroom of the Waldorf-Astoria Hotel on June 15, 1992, to accept an award as Man of the Year from the Actors' Fund, he launched into a dryasdust recitation of the fund's financial status.

But appearances, after all, can be deceiving. "Bernie appears dour, but is actually a beloved figure," said Executive Secretary Alan Eisenberg of Actors' Equity. "He can be outrageous, but his remarks are often tempered with a twinkle. You don't know if he means it."[59] "Mr. Jacobs has a sneaky, wicked sense of humor, and a marvelous deadpan delivery," said Grafton Nunes, coordinator of the Theatre Administration Program at Columbia University, where the two lawyers were adjunct professors.[60] "Everyone who doesn't know him thinks Bernie is awful," said playwright Joe Masteroff. "Just looking at him, people are afraid of him. But the word is that he's nice once you get to know him."[61]

"Schoenfeld is a West Side guy who has cultivated this pretentious accent, and his stylish wife, Pat, is interested in society," an associate said, speaking anonymously. "He doesn't realize how he's playing, whether or not he's getting over. This opinion is widely held." But Jacobs spoke in deep New Yorkese. "You couldn't mistake him for coming from anywhere else," the same associate commented. "He's really without pretense and so is his wife, Betty, who is liked by everyone."[62]

Schoenfeld's "cool" gray office, filled with crystal, which insiders dubbed "the ice palace," contrasted markedly with the classically dour Jacobs's "hot" red office, likened to an Oriental bordello. Unlike the historical Shuberts, the lawyers seemed quite comfortable both with each other and in their private lives. "They're nicely married men," Hal Prince observed.[63] Their titles—Gerald Schoenfeld as chairman, Bernard Jacobs as president—carried no real differences. They divided the responsibilities amicably and shared great power in an outwardly peaceable fashion for more than twenty years. In his speech at the Actors' Fund tribute, Jacobs acknowledged that his award "must be shared with my partner, Gerald Schoenfeld, and our wives, who saw us through some rough periods. Neither of us would be here tonight but for the loyalty of our wives."[64]

Jacobs did most of the contract negotiations; Schoenfeld is in charge of real estate and represents the Shubert Organization in matters of urban concern. After the formal ceremonies at the Actors' Fund salute, Schoenfeld began to work the room, shaking hands, dancing briefly with a variety of partners, and smiling all the while, as Jacobs held court dourly at a side table. For a moment the two men passed close to each other and exchanged whispered confidences. In that fleeting exchange could be glimpsed the history of their seemingly unshakable personal and professional bond: like Lee and J. J., the lawyers clearly spoke the same language, a kind of code or shorthand they elaborated over the course of their long partnership.

J. J., and later John, referred to them, behind their backs, as "Itsik and Pit-sik"; others had called them "Bernie and Bernie." But whatever they were called, whether "the Shuberts" or "Schoenfeld and Jacobs" or simply "the lawyers," for more than two official decades and, in truth, for many years before the palace revolt of June 1972, they had been the American theatre's preeminent power brokers.

Although one of the complaints against the lawyers made by Lawrence Shubert Lawrence, Jr., had been their refusal to let him invest significant amounts of money in any single production, Schoenfeld and Jacobs were merely conforming to guidelines laid down in J. J.'s will, which specified twenty-five thousand dollars as the upper limit the Organization could contribute to any one show. (J. J. may have wished to ensure that no future Shubert head would achieve the recognition as a producer he always felt had been withheld from him.) One of the first signs that Schoenfeld and Jacobs were guiding the Organization into a more expansive era than the one Lawrence presided over was when they began to exceed the stipulations in J. J.'s will.

The new Shuberts "got their feet wet" as coproducers, as Schoenfeld recalled to William Glover, on *Pippin*, a musical that opened at the Shubert-owned Imperial Theatre on October 23, 1972, at the start of the new team's first theatre season.[65] Over the summer, the show's producer, Stuart Ostrow, had approached them to put up the remaining $225,000 his show needed to open at the Imperial. The lawyers offered to contribute $50,000 and then brought in Roger Stevens, who put in $100,000, while Ostrow himself obtained the remaining $75,000. Before *Pippin* opened, however, the new Shuberts decided to adhere to the letter of J. J.'s instructions and sold half their investment. But by the end of their second season in power, Jacobs boasted that "there's hardly a show running today that we have not given financial aid to in some way—and that is not limited to what is in our theatres."[66] "We do not demand billing unless it's actually our production," Schoenfeld said, "but in nine out of ten cases where we're involved our name does not appear in the program."[67]

Setting themselves up as coproducers rather than as investors with minimal participation, Schoenfeld and Jacobs contradicted J. J.'s will for a reason J. J. would surely have understood: they began to invest in other producers' shows to be able to keep Shubert theatres lit. Providing end money to financially strapped producers (like Stuart Ostrow) ensured tenants for Shubert houses that otherwise might remain empty. "The important thing is the development of a constant, dynamic flow of productions," Schoenfeld said.[68] For the new Shuberts, as for the first Shubert, Sam, who faced the monopolistic practices of the fledgling Syndicate, producing became a necessary form of self-protection.

By the time the new Shuberts came to power, not only had the flow of product begun to dry up but so had the pool of active producers. Escalating costs made many theatrical producers shy away from Broadway, and the ones who remained had begun to depend on corporate investors and theatre owners to secure the hefty capitalization that any show on Broadway now requires. Indeed, the Shubert Organization itself has sought the kind of corporate connection that, alas, it now requires to mount most Broadway shows. In 1980 Shubert attracted the interest of Capital Cities/ABC, which began investing in shows for Shubert theatres. In March 1989, they signed a five-year agreement with Suntory, a Japanese multinational corporation best known for its whiskey and beer. (On August 15, 1992, as Jeremy Gerard reported in *Variety*, "with little more than red ink to show after four disappointing years, Suntory International Corporation has nixed an extension of its ground-breaking partnership with the Shubert Organization.")

"Broadway was in the cemetery and the road was already in the crematorium" is the way Bernard Jacobs described the state of the theatre at the time he and Schoenfeld took over.[69]

There was a severe dearth of product and urban centers were in a state of decay, due largely to the unrestricted growth of crime and pornography. It was clear that unless remedial measures were undertaken, there would be no Broadway theatre left to survive. Under Gerald Schoenfeld we instituted a comprehensive clean-up campaign [to improve general conditions in the theatre district]. To deal with the critical problem of productivity we have pursued a calculated course of stimulating play production. From June 1972 to November 1976 we have invested in excess of four million dollars in shows.[70]

As coproducers Schoenfeld and Jacobs demonstrated consistent good taste. *Amadeus* (1980), *Dreamgirls* (1981), *Nicholas Nickleby* (1981), *Sunday in the Park with George* (1984), *Jerome Robbins' Broadway* (1989), *The Grapes of Wrath* (1989), and *The Heidi Chronicles* (1990) are a few of the productions that Shubert investment helped stage. But as producers, the Broadway community, for the most part, faulted Schoenfeld and Jacobs on at least two counts: their failure to be creative and to develop new plays and musicals. The new Shuberts were the men with the money rather than the ideas. They provided completion funds for a number of worthy shows that might not have opened otherwise, but they originated no shows, helped encourage and nurture no new talent. "They should put people in offices in a Shubert building, give them an annual salary and seed money to develop plays and musicals," Hal Prince argued. "They should have created their own equivalent of the Arthur Freed unit at MGM. But they haven't wanted to share that responsibility with young people."[71] "The old Shuberts were crooks and monstrous, but during the Depression they saved the theatre," playwright Joe Masteroff said. "In another Depression—the one we're in now—the new Shuberts haven't done anything, and they have all that money. They used to give twenty-five thousand dollars a year to New Dramatists [a support group for selected play-wrights], and they have millions. They have done nothing to develop talent; they provide end money but not seed money, which is just as important."[72] "New, smart young people are the future," Prince said, "and neither the Shuberts nor the League [which the Shubert Organization dominates] understands that. They and the League have an old club mentality that's not good for the future of the theatre."[73]

Bowing at last to repeated criticism, in August 1993 Schoenfeld and Jacobs provided an office and a salary for writer-director James Lapine, best known for his collaborations with Stephen Sondheim and William Finn on inventive musical theatre projects, such as *Sunday in the Park with George* and *Falsettos*. "The affilia-tion is a tacit acknowledgment by Jacobs and Schoenfeld of their need, after thirty years at the top of Broadway's dominant theatre-owning concern, to bring new blood into Shubert," Jeremy Gerard wrote in the August 30, 1993, *Variety*. "Asked when Shubert last had a creative force such as Lapine on staff, Schoenfeld paused briefly and replied, 'Sigmund Romberg and Dorothy Donnelly.' "

Like the historical Shuberts, Schoenfeld and Jacobs negotiated with unions on behalf of the industry. Often they adopted a strong antiunion stance. "There has to be some willingness by all the unions to give back a little of what they've gotten or the theatre will be in worse trouble than it is," Jacobs said in 1985, ex-pressing the official house line. "Lots of people get paid for not working, and that has to come to an end," he continued. "I think theatre owners and producers have been squeezed as far as they can go."[74] On the street, however, there was and is a widely held belief that too often the Shuberts have been entirely too accommo-dating toward union demands. "They make deals with unions only they could af-ford to pay," Joe Masteroff said, "and in meetings Bernie says he will not partici-pate in union busting."[75] "They agreed to contracts most independent producers could never have countenanced," a former theatrical lawyer said. "They agreed to union demands in order to keep their theatres open, and the concessions helped to raise the price of tickets."[76] "Through the years the Shuberts negotiated expen-sive contracts with the fourteen unions represented on Broadway that only theatre owners with deep pockets could afford," a prominent independent producer said.[77]

"People have said that Bernie has been too kind to actors, but there's no such thing," noted Alan Eisenberg of Actors' Equity.

Actors are beleaguered people. When I came in in 1981 the minimum salary was five hundred dollars; now [1991] it is nine hundred. When Bernie started, the minimum was two hundred dollars. So actors and Equity have done well. Bernie, who is chief negotiator for the League in drawing up the Equity–League contracts, is tough and fair. You have to play up to his vanity and ego, but you can press his moral button. He has been sympathetic to medical needs. He's obsessive, sometimes to his detriment. He is a bulldog, and he'll call three, four, five times a day—he can wear you down. Our positions are inevitably oppositional, but I really want him to like me. To keep his goodwill, I will do him a favor.[78]

In June 1996, for the first time since 1961, Jacobs did not represent Broadway producers in contract negotiations with Actors' Equity. "This spells out a victory of sorts for Broadway's increasingly powerful independent producers, who have been determined for some time to separate the theatre owners from labor negotiations—or at least to reduce their influence," Jeremy Gerard noted in *Variety*.[79]

If Jacobs maintained a fragile peace with Actors' Equity and with the musicians and stagehands' unions, his and Schoenfeld's relations with the Dramatists Guild were contentious. "They want to wreck the playwrights," Garson Kanin said in 1991. "They don't have any appreciation of playwrights, though when they give interviews they say they do. There's not a breath of truth to it. The Dramatists Guild lives with them in a truce, though things got sticky in the last contract negotiations."[80] (Ironically, for thirty-five years, until a move in October 1996, the Dramatists Guild was located in the penthouse of the Shubert-owned Sardi Building, in what was formerly J. J.'s apartment; the Shubert Foundation now occupies the space.)

"Authors don't bother to learn about the totality of the business," Schoenfeld chastised, in a May 23, 1988, meeting of the Dramatists Guild.

There are two parts to the business . . . producing and theatre ownership. In union negotiations nobody figures the cost to the theatre owners of carrying theatres that don't pay their way. When you have to carry weak sisters, theatres that don't get booked, theatres *you* and your agents won't play in, that affects terms. It's a burden. We carry twenty-three theatres and nobody is there with a parachute to help us land safely.[81]

"You have an inherent resistance to us as representing real estates," Schoenfeld stated candidly at that meeting. And as the men with the real estate, the Shuberts became embroiled in a prolonged contretemps with the New York City Landmarks Commission. The battle began in earnest in 1982, when the Morosco, Bijou, and Helen Hayes Theatres were razed to permit the construction of the Marriott Marquis Hotel. The new Shuberts, leaders of the theatre owners' fight with the Landmarks Commission, were cast as yahoos fulminating against the guardians of historical and cultural preservation. "One-third of the older houses are economically obsolete," Schoenfeld said, adding that "they represent the last vestige of a nonsubsidized, tax-paying performing arts discipline in America. Broadway's physical plants—its theatres—have had a financial burden imposed on them as have no other business or art form in America: the enactment of a legislative mandate by the New York City Board of Estimate in May 1982 prohibiting the demolition of theatres regardless of the attendant financial consequences."[82]

Many preservationists, on the other hand, viewed the theatre owners' stance as an eruption of Shubert greed. "Jacobs and Schoenfeld would like to see every brick of the beautiful Belasco Theatre crumble to the ground, so they could build an office complex on the site that would make them a thousand times richer than they already are," a commission employee said. "They are real estate men who love money far more than they love the theatre. If they had their way they'd tear down all the marginal theatres and Midtown would have new hotels and office towers it doesn't need. But we've been here all along to see that that doesn't happen, and with the Supreme Court decision, we won." In May 1992, the United States Supreme Court refused to hear an appeal by Shubert, Nederlander, and Jujamcyn to overturn the 1988 landmark designation of twenty-two Broadway theatres. "The Shuberts will have to be content with a few hundred million dollars less."[83]

Although the Shuberts suffered a rare court defeat on the landmark issue, even foes have admitted that Schoenfeld and Jacobs were conscientious custodians of Shubert theatres. "They respect their theatres, which are in better shape than those of the opposition," Hal Prince said.[84] Nonetheless, as is so often the case, even praise for the Shuberts carries a sting. "They can fix up their theatres because of the weird way the Foundation is woven into the commercial affairs of the Organization," said a former employee. "They can get tax benefits that Jujamcyn and Nederlander, who function without a Foundation to help them, cannot."[85]

Where Lee and J. J. were rough-and-tumble tycoons who operated with a Broadway-style version of frontier justice, the lawyers worked to upgrade and "correct" the Shubert image through good-works programs. They taught at Yale, New York University, and Columbia, where beginning in 1972, they conducted a weekly course in theatre management, a course Schoenfeld continues to teach. They also expanded contributions to nonprofit theatres in an awards program administered by the Shubert Foundation.

"The rebirth of the theatre program at Columbia in 1972 is directly connected to the interest of the Shubert Organization," said Grafton Nunes, director of the Theatre Administration Program. (Former Columbia University President Michael Sovern serves on the Board of Directors of the Shubert Foundation.) "Schoenfeld and Jacobs wanted commercial theatre to be considered in academic courses," Nunes said,

> and they wanted the chance to correct the widespread assumptions in academe that commercial theatre is "bad," and nonprofit theatre is "good." They had felt that at Yale, where they had been treated like the enemy. They wanted a program where commercial theatre would have a chance to explain itself. During the semester they teach a course every Friday afternoon—students go down to their offices in the Shubert Theatre Building—where they speak extemporaneously for two hours. Students go in skeptical, assuming they are the dragons of Broadway, and come out charmed.[86]

The Samuel S. Shubert Foundation, which was formed in 1945 but not announced until October 1947, operated in secrecy for many years. When Howard Teichmann was in charge of Foundation awards during the sixties, the lawyers put stringent restrictions on the amounts he was able to give. In the post-Goldman years, however, Jacobs and Schoenfeld turned the Foundation into a major source of funding for not-for-profit theatre groups throughout the United States. Ironically, through the Foundation they established to honor their brother, Lee and J. J. have become America's chief donors to the kind of theatre they did not understand or enjoy and would have been unlikely to produce. In a typical year—1989—the Foundation presented a total of $2,758,200 in awards. Among the grateful recipients were the American Conservatory Theatre of San Francisco; the American Repertory Theatre at Harvard; the Arena Stage in Washington, D.C.; the Vivian Beaumont Theatre at Lincoln Center; the New York Shakespeare Festival; Columbia University; the Metropolitan Opera Association; the Theatre Collection of the Museum of the City of New York; the Harlem School for the Arts; and the American Jewish Theatre.

"The Shubert Foundation has given me money from time to time," Agnes de Mille, no Shubert fan, said.

> A friend of mine, Mrs. Charles [Helen] Hollerith, whose husband was executive director of my dance foundation and who herself served on the Shubert board for a time, got me some money: three thousand dollars, though that was nothing to the Shuberts. When the Foundation gave me an award recently, I gave the present fellows a nod, saying the present generation was not like the old Shuberts. My late husband, Walter Prude, liked Gerald Schoen-

feld, and so I said nice things for the sake of my husband. I hoped I believed what I was saying.[87]

In the old days, when the theatre was a thriving industry, the Shuberts fought their way to preeminence among a group of avaricious wheeler-dealers. The latter-day Shuberts reigned over both an empire and and industry drastically reduced from the time when Lee Shubert commanded the American commercial theatre from his circular office atop the Shubert Theatre. Nonetheless, Schoenfeld and Jacobs presided very much in the spirit of the house of Shubert. As contract negotiators, as landlords who owned more theatres than their rivals, as the dominant voice in the League, as coproducers, and as de facto spokesmen for the industry, they ruled what was left of Broadway and the road as mightily as the Shubert Organization they represented had ever done. Show people, now as before, are by and large awed by the aura of authority and retribution the Shubert name conjures. "They are very powerful and can get rid of anybody they want," a prominent Broadway producer said.[88] Even people who liked the lawyers proceeded warily. "I sense the potential for revenge," Alan Eisenberg said, adding, "Many people are afraid of them."[89] Even Lawrence Shubert Lawrence, Jr., in exile in Boca Raton, said, "I have to be very careful what I say about those guys up there: they're very shrewd."[90]

Although the atmosphere of conspiracy and manipulation through which they came to power had never entirely been forgotten, Schoenfeld and Jacobs proved to be better caretakers of the Shubert fortunes than any blood relative. "Gerald Schoenfeld and Bernard Jacobs saved the Shubert Organization," claimed Alexander Cohen, a generous tribute from a former intimate. "The lawyers decided to turn Shubert into a business: they saw what was there," Cohen said. "They determined they were going to get rid of ice—when Lee died, several million dollars were found in the safe in the office; the lawyers would have been shocked the most. They were determined to upgrade the theatres, to change the booking system, to revamp the road."[91]

Cohen's opinion was shared by many in the industry who genuinely respected the team of Schoenfeld and Jacobs and readily acknowledged that, by virtue of their experience and ability, they were entirely justified in wresting control of a family business from a family that had become unable to control it. But, as with all the dramatis personae in the Shubert story, the lawyers too elicited strongly divided reviews—they were admired for their astute business practices, on the one hand, and excoriated for playing hardball, on the other. "I have never heard anyone say a good word about the Shuberts of today," Garson Kanin maintained.[92] "It's true they don't participate in ice, but then why should they? When you live in Fort Knox you don't have to steal from the neighborhood," Judith Teichmann

Steckler said.[93] Playwright Ruth Goetz claimed that "only their press agents would say good things about them."[94] The latter-day Shuberts, in short, were respected, feared, and reviled in about the same proportions as their predecessors. And, like the historical Shuberts, who were satisfied to be the theatre's most powerful figures *behind* the scenes, Schoenfeld and Jacobs did not relish being written about.

The inevitable question of who's up next at Shubert was first raised in May 1986, when Bernard Jacobs had an attack of transient global amnesia—"I woke up one morning and didn't know where I was"—and the Broadway community was reminded that the new Shuberts too were mortal.[95] In 1991, Alan Eisenberg said, "He's never quite recovered, and Gerald Schoenfeld has been encroaching on Bernie's territory a little ever since."[96] Rumors of Jacobs being in ill health continued to circulate—mixed with speculation that the longtime partners were not as friendly as they used to be.

After having kept a noticeably lower profile for many months, Bernard B. Jacobs died, aged eighty, on August 27, 1996, from complications following heart surgery. Obituaries routinely cited him as one of the most powerful men in the American theatre; indeed, no Shubert captain since Lee had received such an outpouring of public praise, fealty, and awe. In death, Jacobs's gruff, curt style was remembered fondly, and he was all but canonized not only as a savior of the commercial American theatre but, owing to the munificent sums distributed by the Shubert Foundation under his watch, of the nonprofit theatre as well.

Speculation about Schoenfeld's ability to continue in power without his longtime business associate and lifelong friend swept through the theatre community. Like the historical Shuberts, the lawyers had never talked about succession; but Schoenfeld acted quickly and, on September 17, 1996, appointed two presidents to oversee Jacobs's former responsibilities: Michael Sovern, sixty-four, Shubert board member and former president of Columbia University, became president of the Shubert Foundation; and longtime Shubert employee and Jacobs's chief assistant, Philip J. Smith, sixty-five, was advanced to president of the Shubert Organization, Inc. Schoenfeld retained his title as chairman of both the Foundation and the Organization, thereby confirming his continued dominance over the business he has known intimately for nearly fifty years.

"They had no formal education of any kind," Gerald Schoenfeld said about the founders of the empire he still runs. "They had nothing but native intelligence, yet they built a dynasty. We brought a lot of different talents than those they had. So when people ask what will happen in the next generation, I don't know that you can say that there are any criteria out there." Maintaining that the Organization was structured to continue without him or Jacobs, Schoenfeld said that "Shubert is sui generis, one of a kind."[97] In other words, there's no business like Shubert business.

Notes
Bibliography
Index

Notes

Prologue: The Last Shubert

1. John Shubert to Howard Teichmann, November 10, 1959. All quotations from John Shubert are from a series of exclusive interviews given to Howard Teichmann from November 10, 1959, to September 23, 1960. In 1985 Teichmann began research for a biography of John Shubert to be called "The Man in the Blue Serge Suit." Teichmann died in July 1987. When I took over the project, deciding to expand the book into a history of the Shubert empire, from its beginnings up to the present, Evelyn Teichmann presented me with the five hundred pages of interview material John and others had given her husband. All further quotations from this material are designated as, for example, "John Shubert to Howard Teichmann," followed by the date of the interview.

2. Sandra Epstein to Howard Teichmann, November 17, 1985.

3. Lawrence Shubert Lawrence, Jr., interview with the author, January 5, 1988.

4. Eileen Kelly to Howard Teichmann, August 30, 1985.

5. Garson Kanin, interview with the author, February 26, 1991.

6. Lawrence Shubert Lawrence, Jr., interview with the author, January 5, 1988.

7. Lawrence Shubert Lawrence, Jr., telephone interview with the author, June 20, 1990.

8. Lawrence Shubert Lawrence, Jr., interview with the author, January 5, 1988.

9. Agnes de Mille, interview with the author, December 10, 1990.

10. Gerson Werner, telephone interview with the author, June 12, 1991.

11. "Anonymous," interview with the author, December 15, 1990.

12. Lawrence Shubert Lawrence, Jr., interview with the author, January 5, 1988.

1. The Boys in Syracuse

1. Lee Shubert, *Passing Show*, 8.

2. John Shubert to Howard Teichmann, November 10, 1959.

3. The Syracuse census is on file at the Onondaga Historical Society, Syracuse, New York.

4. "There's a big cloud, a tremendous cloud, over Grandfather David's side of the family," John said. "Nobody can quite figure out where they go or where they're from, but David apparently had two sisters. One of them married a fellow by the name of Grossman

in Syracuse." (To this day there is a Shubert-related Grossman family living in Syracuse.) "We're not sure about the identity of the other sister. She was either a Cohen and the mother of Lord Henry Cohen, Lord Birkenhead, the king of England's physician, or she married a Mendelsohn, a diamond dealer in Brussels and Amsterdam." John Shubert to Howard Teichmann, November 10, 1959.

5. Ibid.

6. For Syracuse in the 1880s and 1890s, see contemporary newspapers at the Onondaga Historical Society and Rudolph, *From a Minyan to a Community*.

7. For an account of peddling in upstate New York, see Provol, *Pack Peddler*.

8. John Shubert to Howard Teichmann, November 10, 1959.

9. John Shubert to Howard Teichmann, November 17, 1959.

10. Ibid.

11. John Shubert to Howard Teichmann, December 15, 1959.

12. John Shubert to Howard Teichmann, November 10, 1959.

13. John Shubert to Howard Teichmann, November 17, 1959.

14. In a September 12, 1990, letter to the author, D. Sloane Hurwitz, the son of one of Mrs. Shubart's boarders, recalled the story of his father's life in Syracuse.

My father, Louis Lee Hurwitz, came to Syracuse about 1886 from Russia, when he was sixteen years old. He came in steerage with about fifty cents in his pocket. People came out of Russia in the late eighties to escape service in the army. When my father was leaving Russia he passed a friend's house; his friend was shoveling dirt in his front yard. He said, "Louis, where are you going?" My father said, "America." His friend threw his shovel down and said, "Wait, I'll go with you," and he did. About twenty-five years after he arrived in Syracuse my father had every good scrap iron account in town.

Louis Hurwitz, who was unlike David Shubart in every way, was a joiner who started many Jewish organizations and who handed down a thriving business to his son, who in turn passed it on to his son.

15. Provol, *Pack Peddler*, 27.

16. John Shubert to Howard Teichmann, November 17, 1959.

17. John Kenley, interview with the author, October 11, 1990.

18. John Shubert to Howard Teichmann, November 17, 1959.

19. My account of Lee Shubert's early years in Syracuse is based on material in the interviews John Shubert gave to Howard Teichmann, November 10, November 17, and December 15, 1959.

20. John Shubert to Howard Teichmann, November 17, 1959.

21. Ibid.

22. John Shubert to Howard Teichmann, December 15, 1959.

23. Lee Shubert, *Passing Show*, 9.

24. Ibid.

25. Provol, *Pack Peddler*, 28.

26. John Shubert to Howard Teichmann, November 17, 1959.

27. Lee Shubert, *Passing Show*, 10.

28. Ibid.

29. George Abbott, interview with the author, January 4, 1991.

30. Hunt, "Charles Hoyt," 15.

31. Provol, *Pack Peddler*, 29.

32. It was at Wallack's Theatre, a stock house in New York City, that Augustin Daly learned his trade in the 1850s. A typical bill at Wallack's might consist of a five-act tragedy followed by entr'actes, such as a solo dance or a comic song, which in turn might be followed by a farce or extravaganza. By the time Daly established a theatre of his own, he conformed to the evolving custom by simplifying his program to one play a night. For his 1869–1870 season at the Fifth Avenue Theatre, Daly presented his company in twenty-one plays in six months. Daly's dedication to stock company repertory was absolute, but even he caught the star fever that swept through American theatre in the decades after the Civil War. He began to hire actors, including Maurice Barrymore and John Drew, who developed into stars with loyal followings. Both performers would eventually leave to pursue independent careers and larger salaries than Daly could afford. Nor did Daly disdain commercial success—hits were extended, failures quickly retired from the repertoire. As the combination system began to take hold, Daly's offerings became increasingly commercial, and to survive he was forced to present lightweight fare with such titles as *Frou-Frou* and *Fernande*, which resembled touring star vehicles. For a full account of the career of Augustin Daly, see Daly, *Life of Augustin Daly*; and Felheim, *Theatre of Augustin Daly*.

33. Clipping from the *Syracuse Standard*, December 1897. On file at the Onondaga Historical Society, Syracuse, New York.

34. J. J. Shubert gave his unfinished memoirs to his son, John, who in turn read them to Howard Teichmann, February 24, 1960.

35. Ibid.

36. Ibid.

37. Charles Frohman was a popular figure, the only Syndicate founder who was respected professionally and personally. Even J. J. admitted in his unfinished memoir that "very little can be said against him. I doubt very much if he approved of Erlanger's methods. He usually kept to himself, and never made a companion of either Klaw or Erlanger— I know that personally he detested Erlanger. 'C. F.' never would go deliberately out of his way to do you an injustice. He was very much liked by his star actors and the associates he came in contact with." (Read by John Shubert to Howard Teichmann, February 24, 1960.) Frohman had a cherubic countenance, setting him apart from his confreres. A man who kept his word—with his actors he had verbal agreements only, and unlike the Shuberts was

rarely sued—and personally both modest and affable, he truly loved the theatre in a way none of his Syndicate partners did. He was nonetheless a practical man of the theatre, a commercial producer who built up a stable of stars, took no chances on unknown writers, and favored British over American playwrights. J. J. called him "artistic," but he was so only in comparison to the other Syndicate members. The lives of the Frohman brothers— Charles, Gustave, and Daniel—in many ways paralleled those of the Shuberts. All were sons of peddlers; all were born or raised away from New York (the Frohmans in Sandusky, Ohio); and all eventually entered the theatre barely out of childhood. When Henry Froh- man took his family to New York and opened a cigar shop, his three sons began to go to the theatre on passes given to Henry for displaying show posters in his store windows. After Gustave, the eldest, started hawking souvenir books at the old Academy of Music on Irving Place, he pulled his brothers into the theatre business. As Gustave's career progressed, so did his brothers'. He got Charles a job in the box office at Hooley's Theatre in Brooklyn, then he sent Charles to St. Paul, Minnesota, to break him in as advance man for a touring company. Step by step, C. F. made his way back to New York, where he became the most successful producer-manager of his era, the maestro of his own sparkling Empire Theatre, and a familiar and significant figure in London's West End. When Charles, at fifty-five, went down on the *Lusitania* in 1915, he left an estate after debts of $452. For a full account of Frohman's life and career, see Marcosson and Frohman, *Charles Frohman*.

38. Bernheim, *Business of Theatre*, 47.

39. Lee Shubert, *Passing Show*, 16.

40. Timberlake, *Bishop of Broadway*, 241.

41. John Shubert to Howard Teichmann, November 17, 1959.

42. Ibid.

43. Ibid.

44. J. J. Shubert, unfinished memoir, read by John Shubert to Howard Teichmann, February 24, 1960.

45. John Shubert to Howard Teichmann, November 17, 1959.

46. Ibid.

47. Programs cited are on file at the Onondaga Historical Society, Syracuse, New York.

48. In his early career, Sam worked at the three leading theatres in Syracuse, the Grand, the Wieting, and the Bastable; their histories are emblematic of the changing place of the- atrical entertainment in the cultural life of nineteenth-century America. The first Wieting Theatre (there were three in all) dated from 1851. The Grand opened in 1869. The Bastable, a newcomer, opened in 1893. The Wieting was built by the colorful Dr. John Wieting, a local schoolteacher and civil engineer interested in medicine who traveled widely to deliver popular lectures on public health. The first Wieting, in fact, was not a theatre but a lecture hall where Syracusans heard, in addition to Wieting, Charles Dickens, Ralph Waldo Emerson, Buffalo Bill, Henry Ward Beecher, and others. In 1851 "theatre" carried racy connotations,

especially in the provinces where there were lingering traces of the Puritan disapproval of theatrical mimesis and of the Puritan conviction that theatres were glorified bawdy houses. (And, in fact, theatres before the 1850s tended to be rowdy: in the pit, seated on rude wooden benches or standing, groups of single working-class men noisily interrupted performances, demanded encores, or hissed a scene or performer. Upstairs, prostitutes and johns congregated in the crowded gallery. Some theatres offered a bar. The gentry who ventured into a theatre felt safe only in the boxes that bordered the pit in horseshoe style. The assertiveness of audiences reached a peak in the 1849 Astor Place Riot, after which managers claimed a steadily growing power in shaping the tastes and behavior of theatre-goers.) Dr. Wieting wanted his auditorium to be a place of edification rather than entertainment. When his lecture hall burned down in the 1860s, he had it rebuilt and reopened it in 1870 as the Wieting Opera House, with a seating capacity of 1,017. There was no opera at this opera house (at least not until 1886, when the American Opera Company made a brief appearance), nor was opera intended to be the theatre's staple. At the time, towns throughout the country had opera houses where operas were seldom or never performed. The "opera house" designation simply provided a respectable cover for places that presented a variety of popular entertainments. (The other common euphemism was "museum," in imitation of P. T. Barnum's hugely successful museum in New York, where on the ground floor patrons could see sideshow-style freaks and curiosities and then walk to the upstairs auditorium to hear a lecture or, heavens, actually to see a show.) In 1897, when Dr. Wieting's widow built the third theatre, it was no longer necessary to be coy about calling it a theatre. The third Wieting was a resplendent edifice with ornate chandeliers, a floor of Italian mosaic tile, marble walls, a rich gold and rose color scheme, draperies of silk and velvet, and bronze doors—in short, a theatre rather than a lecture hall, "museum," or "opera house." Like the Wieting, the Grand first opened as a hall. In 1869, a cigar maker named Barton built the Barton Block, which on the third floor contained a hall called Barton's Opera House for lectures and occasional musical entertainment. Seven years later, the theatre was rechristened the Park Opera House; and then it was rebuilt in 1879 as the Grand. When the Grand burned in 1886, it was immediately rebuilt and, like others throughout the country, featured popular fare, alternating between musical comedy and sensation melodrama. In 1884, foreshadowing the Shuberts' methods, Dr. Wieting, who had by now overcome his moral objections to theatrical entertainment, moved in on the Grand, taking a three-year lease because in bidding against each other for popular New York shows neither the Wieting nor the Grand had been able to make a profit. By 1893 the Wieting and the Grand were making so much money that one Frederick Bastable felt there was room enough for an opposition house, though his theatre did not become profitable until Sam took over the lease in 1897. Housed in a commercial building called the Bastable, the new theatre abandoned the horseshoe-style configuration that had been traditional in the 1800s. The Bastable had two balconies and three profusely decorated boxes on each side of the proscenium. Though it was to have rough times over the next five years, the Bastable hit the jackpot with its opening attraction, Richard Mansfield in *Beau Brummel* then in *A Parisian Romance.* The policies of the three Syracuse theatres shifted over the years, but in time each established its own specialty. The Wieting became the house of stars in touring combinations; the Grand evolved into a vaudeville house; the Bastable featured stock companies and melodramas and was called the "house of 10–20–30¢ shows": gallery, ten cents; balcony, twenty cents; orchestra, thirty cents. A fourth theatre, the Dunfee, built around 1895 and a born loser, was the only Syracuse house with which the Shuberts had no connection. With daily matinees, the Dunfee pursued a lower-class audience with wrestling bouts, motorcycle races, and the "hottest burlesque show that ever came down the pike," as the desperate management advertised in 1898. (In their fight against the Syndicate, the Shuberts were never too proud to present vaudeville or stock, but they drew the line at burlesque, at least the brand offered at the Dunfee, which bore little resemblance to the genre as it was first performed in 1868, when Lydia Thompson and her troupe of British Blondes appeared at Niblo's Garden, New York's leading theatre. Parodying *Axion*, an ancient Greek drama about mighty warriors, Thompson's company was dressed in formfitting male military gear and spoke in rhymed couplets as they sent up—burlesqued—masculine behavior. While it would be disingenuous to dismiss the purely visual appeal of tall, chesty blonds in tight clothes, Thompsonian burlesque was sly, essentially chaste, and decidedly feminist. As the form rapidly evolved, however, the female performers were reduced to mobile but silent objects displayed for male pleasure and made the butt of jokes that the imported male comics shared with the male audience. By the time the Shuberts began to produce, the form had already embarked on its long slide into permanent disrepute. Burlesque in its original form as parody and topical satire was kept alive briefly, from 1896 to 1904, at Weber and Fields's famed Music Hall.) For a detailed history of the theatres of Syracuse in the nineteenth century, see Nesbitt, "Early Concert Life at the Wieting"; and Rabe, "History of the Wieting."

49. John Shubert to Howard Teichmann, November 30, 1959.

50. Ibid.

51. Ibid.

52. Ibid.

53. The incident is described by William Klein in an autobiographical fragment; see Klein, *Passing Show,* 3.

54. John Shubert to Howard Teichmann, November 30, 1959.

55. Klein, *Passing Show,* 5.

56. John Shubert to Howard Teichmann, November 30, 1959.

57. John Kenley, interview with the author, October 11, 1990.

58. John Shubert to Howard Teichmann, November 30, 1959.

59. Lawrence Shubert Lawrence, Jr., interview with the author, January 5, 1988.

2. Sam Shubert Goes to Town

1. *New York Sun*, May 14, 1905.
2. *New York Herald-Tribune*, May 14, 1905.
3. Pollock, *Harvest of My Years*, 107.
4. Leavitt, *Fifty Years in Theatrical Management*, 286.
5. Grau, *Business Man in the Amusement World*, 195.
6. John Kenley, interview with the author, October 11, 1990. At this point, it is not possible to establish Sam's sexual orientation with any certainty.
7. For detailed accounts of the lobster-palace phenomenon, see Churchill, *Great White Way*; Erenberg, *Steppin' Out*.
8. Quoted in the *Chicago Sunday Herald*, June 5, 1900.
9. Peter Davis, "Syndicate/Shubert War," 154.
10. Ibid.
11. Lee Shubert, *Passing Show*, 12.
12. Wilstach, *Richard Mansfield*, 289.
13. Lee Shubert, *Passing Show*, 12.
14. Wilstach, *Richard Mansfield*, 290.
15. Lee Shubert, *Passing Show*, 13.
16. Ibid.
17. Klein, *Passing Show*, 3.
18. *New York Herald-Tribune*, May 27, 1902.
19. Lee Shubert, *Passing Show*, 13.
20. Quoted in Sheean, *Oscar Hammerstein I*, 83.
21. Sam's Lyric Theatre opened first, but Klaw and Erlanger's New Amsterdam won the architectural honors. The Lyric, designed by V. Hugo Koebler in a chastened style of classical revival, had a broad, shallow auditorium, a new shape at the time, which created an illusion of intimacy. The seats were wider and the rows farther apart than in most theatres; and with double exits, the fifteen-hundred-seat house could be emptied quickly. With its sinuous shapes and its stylized floral and aviary motifs, Henry B. Herts and Hugh Tallant's New Amsterdam was a dazzling example of a new style, art nouveau; and as the home of *Ziegfeld Follies* from 1909 to 1927, the theatre was to enjoy a renown the Shuberts never achieved at the Lyric. The trio of historic theatres—the Belasco, the Lyric, and the New Amsterdam—would become the foundation of the new Forty-second Street. At this writing, the Belasco, which has been renamed the New Victory, has been restored to its original splendor and is being operated as a theatre for children's shows; the Disney organization has refurbished the New Amsterdam; and the Lyric has been combined with the adjacent Apollo Theatre into the Ford Center for the Performing Arts, a musical theatre venue for Garth Drabinsky's Canadian-based Livent Productions. After nearly seven decades as an increasingly disreputable movie house, the Lyric had been architecturally de-

nuded. Inside, there were no vestiges whatever of an auditorium hailed by the *New York Times* on its opening in October 1903 as exuding a "dainty, salad-like effect." Only its arresting beaux-arts facade on Forty-third Street, a riot of cupids, masks, false balconies, and bas-reliefs, serves notice of the theatre's former grandeur.

22. J. J. Shubert, unfinished memoir, read by John Shubert to Howard Teichmann, February 24, 1960.

23. Lee Shubert, *Passing Show*, 19.

24. *New York Times*, December 25, 1904.

25. Quoted in Swartz, "Waldorf Venture," 30.

26. Quoted in *Billboard*, March 11, 1922.

27. John Shubert to Howard Teichmann, November 17, 1959.

28. Quoted in the *Syracuse Journal*, May 12, 1905.

29. *New York Times*, May 13, 1905.

30. John Shubert to Howard Teichmann, November 17, 1959.

31. J. J. Shubert, unfinished memoir, read by John Shubert to Howard Teichmann, February 24, 1960.

32. *Syracuse Journal*, May 14, 1905.

33. John Shubert presented Howard Teichmann with a copy of Sam Shubert's will on November 30, 1959.

34. Quoted by Swartz, "Waldorf Venture," 28.

35. In the fall of 1903, after Sam and Lee had established a foothold in New York, Sam summoned his mother and sisters from Syracuse and confined them behind closed doors at the home of actress Fay Templeton, then under contract to Sam. Templeton instructed the ungainly, foreign-seeming Shubert women in how to walk and dress and dine in the style of a prosperous American matron. "Fay Templeton, a very, very elegant lady of the theatre, took in Catherine and three rather unattractive girls from Syracuse, and wouldn't let them out in public for about six months," John told Howard Teichmann on November 10, 1959. "It took about that long to get them into shape to assume a position of importance in the theatre." In hiring Templeton, famed for her expert imitations of celebrities of the day, to "improve" his mother and sisters, Sam was trying to erase the Old World traces he and his brothers felt shamed by. Conferring an illusion of respectability on his uncultivated family was another attempt to eradicate his father's legacy. Even after they had been carefully coached by Templeton, however, the women were not allowed to "assume a position of importance in the theatre," nor is there any indication that any of them ever wanted to. They were given choice box seats on opening nights, but as John said, "a lot of people who watched them in the theatre for years never even knew who they were. They were always shy, they never pushed themselves forward. My three aunts always entertained very nicely in their own homes—friends of their own, but usually nobody from show business." Catherine and her daughters—Fanny, Sarah, and Dora—remained shadowy figures in Shubert history. A June 12, 1934, obituary of Sarah in the *New York Times* rumbles with a

subtext of female suppression: "She was a steady first night playgoer and keenly interested in every venture of her brothers, but she avoided all publicity; unassuming also was her charitable activity."

    36. Lawrence Shubert Lawrence, Jr., telephone interview with the author, June 20, 1990.

3. Lee and J. J., Front and Center

    1. John Shubert to Howard Teichmann, November 30, 1959.

    2. Ibid.

    3. J. J. Shubert, unfinished memoir, read by John Shubert to Howard Teichmann, February 24, 1960.

    4. Quoted in Hapgood, *Stage in America*, 118.

    5. Eaton, *At the New Theatre and Others*, 3.

    6. Winter, *Life and Art of Richard Mansfield*, 220.

    7. Quoted in Binns, *Mrs. Fiske and the American Theatre*, 79.

    8. Ibid., 81.

    9. Wilson, *Francis Wilson's Life of Himself*, 151.

    10. Ibid., 161.

    11. J. J. Shubert, unfinished memoir, read by John Shubert to Howard Teichmann, February 24, 1960.

    12. Quoted in Timberlake, *Bishop of Broadway*, 274.

    13. Pollock, *Harvest of My Years*, 124.

    14. John Shubert to Howard Teichmann, February 24, 1960.

    15. Bernheim, *Business of Theatre*, 65.

    16. For details about the Hippodrome, see Clarke, *Mighty Hippodrome*; and Register, "New York's Gigantic Toy."

    17. Quoted in Clarke, *Mighty Hippodrome*, 101.

    18. As reported in the *Morning Telegraph*, November 2, 1907.

    19. Clarke, *Mighty Hippodrome*, 54.

    20. Quoted in *Variety*, April 3, 1907.

    21. Leavitt, *Fifty Years in Theatrical Management*, 190.

    22. Robert Taylor, *Fred Allen*, 55.

    23. Obituary of B. F. Keith in the *New York Review*, March 28, 1914.

    24. Robert Taylor, *Fred Allen*, 55.

    25. "Scarcely anyone mentions E. F. Albee without intense bitterness," Marian Spitzer writes in *The Palace*, 86:

With his relentless air of holiness, Mr. Albee was totally without humor and grim of visage as he wielded his destructive power. Mr. Albee's office on the sixth floor of the Palace Theatre was not only a throne room, it was a command post. The fate of thousands hung on his decisions. Anyone who incurred his displeasure was summarily banished, whether performer, office employee, or agent. And he rarely gave reasons for his dismissals beyond the brief comment that this one or that one had been what he considered "disloyal."

At the end of his career in the late twenties, Albee was to be outsmarted by a business lord even more brutal than he: Joseph P. Kennedy.

26. *New York Review*, March 28, 1914.

27. Quoted in the *New York Review*, September 12, 1909.

28. Quoted in Swartz, "Waldorf Venture," 35.

29. Ibid., 32.

30. *New York Review*, August 29, 1909.

31. Bernheim, *Business of Theatre*, 69.

32. Quoted in the *Morning Telegraph*, May 1, 1909.

33. John Shubert to Howard Teichmann, March 11, 1960.

34. Ibid.

35. Quoted in the *New York Review*, June 5, 1909.

36. Quoted in the *Saturday Evening Post*, August 14, 1909.

37. Quoted in the *Theatre*, January 1911.

38. John Shubert to Howard Teichmann, March 11, 1960.

39. *Green Book*, January 1910.

40. *Cleveland Plain Dealer*, May 2, 1910.

41. *Morning Telegraph*, June 1, 1908.

42. *New York Review*, November 12, 1909.

43. Eaton, *At the New Theatre and Others*, 15.

44. *Theatre*, May 1910.

45. *New York Evening Post*, April 19, 1910.

46. Quoted in the *New York Times*, September 16, 1913.

47. Quoted in the *New York Review*, September 21, 1913.

48. *Variety*, July 27, 1919.

49. Details about Worm's misdeeds are recounted in *Variety*, July 27, 1919.

50. Details about J. J.'s meeting with Catherine Mary Dealey are based on material in John Shubert's March 5, 1960, interview with Howard Teichmann.

51. John Shubert to Howard Teichmann, March 5, 1960.

52. J. J.'s account of the founding of the Winter Garden Theatre is based on details drawn from John Shubert's April 6, 1960, interview with Howard Teichmann.

53. Fields and Fields, *From the Bowery to Broadway*; the history of Lew Fields's involvement in the planning of the Winter Garden is based on material on pp. 280–283. Also L. Marc Fields, interview with the author, November 21, 1993.

54. *New York Times*, March 21, 1911.

55. Irving Caesar, interview with the author, June 14, 1992.

56. John Shubert to Howard Teichmann, May 17, 1960.

57. John Shubert to Howard Teichmann, April 5, 1960.

58. A copy of the opening night program of the Winter Garden Theatre is at the Billy Rose Theatre Collection, the New York Public Library for the Performing Arts at Lincoln Center.

59. Quoted in Sieben, *Immortal Jolson*, 68–69.

60. Irving Caesar, interview with the author, December 2, 1990.

61. John Shubert to Howard Teichmann, April 5, 1960.

62. John Kenley, interview with the author, October 11, 1990.

63. John Shubert to Howard Teichmann, April 5, 1960.

64. Janet Cantor Gari, interview with the author, December 8, 1990.

65. Irving Caesar, interview with the author, December 2, 1990.

66. Janet Cantor Gari, interview with the author, December 8, 1990.

67. Irving Caesar, interview with the author, December 2, 1990.

68. John Shubert to Howard Teichmann, April 5, 1960.

69. Minstrel shows were divided into three parts. In the first section, the minstrels (in blackface) sat in a semicircle as an interlocutor joked with the low-comedy end men—tambo and bones, so-called because of the instruments (tambourine and bones, respectively) they played. The jokes were interspersed with musical numbers performed by the onstage musicians. In the second part, which was called an olio, a series of performers came on one at a time to sing or dance or tell jokes (this section became the model for vaudeville). The third part of the minstrel show was a farcical sketch, usually in blackface, about some aspect of plantation life. If the ethnic comedy that was a staple of early variety and vaudeville was a way of addressing and including the urban immigrants who comprised the bulk of the audience, the humor in minstrelsy—the only theatrical form native to America—was exclusionary, a way of dispossessing African Americans, who were prevented from participating in making fun of themselves. Variety, minstrelsy, vaudeville, revue, and burlesque shared a mosaiclike format in which one number, or "turn," followed another. The various forms were distinguished by how much cohesion existed among the acts. Variety and its upwardly mobile cousin, vaudeville, had no thematic continuity; variety became revue when performers or visual and thematic motifs reappeared throughout a show; and if the musical numbers were enfolded within a more or less stable story line, with characters who held the audience's attention for the length of the show, variety became musical comedy. Burlesque, in its original form, and minstrelsy were more tightly woven than vaudeville, whose main appeal lay precisely in its serendipity, its apparent structural looseness. Minstrelsy faded because it was locked into a specific formula that became repetitive.

70. John Shubert to Howard Teichmann, April 5, 1960.

71. Ibid.

72. Irving Caesar, interview with the author, June 14, 1992.

73. Janet Cantor Gari, interview with the author, December 8, 1990.

74. John Shubert to Howard Teichmann, April 5, 1960.

75. Quoted in Gardiner, *Gaby Deslys*, 108.

76. *Variety*, September 23, 1914.

77. A copy of *The Passing Show* program is at the Billy Rose Theatre Collection, the New York Public Library for the Performing Arts at Lincoln Center.

78. Bernheim, *Business of Theatre*, 70.

79. Ibid., 65.

4. Power Plays

1. Lawrence Shubert Lawrence, Jr., interview with the author, January 5, 1988.

2. John Shubert to Howard Teichmann, March 15, 1960.

3. Viola Seff Goldberg, interview with the author, October 12, 1991.

4. Agnes de Mille, interview with the author, December 10, 1990.

5. Alvin Klipstein, interview with the author, December 15, 1990.

6. Garson Kanin, interview with the author, February 26, 1991.

7. Ruth Goetz, interview with the author, September 29, 1990.

8. Barbara Barondess, interview with the author, April 14, 1991.

9. Ezra Stone, interview with the author, December 22, 1990.

10. Alexander Cohen, interview with the author, December 5, 1990.

11. John Kenley, interview with the author, October 11, 1990.

12. Garson Kanin, interview with the author, February 26, 1991.

13. Alvin Klipstein, interview with the author, December 15, 1990.

14. Irving Caesar, interview with the author, June 14, 1992.

15. Sol Jacobson, interview with the author, October 8, 1990.

16. Agnes de Mille, interview with the author, December 10, 1990.

17. John Shubert to Howard Teichmann, March 11, 1960.

18. John Shubert to Howard Teichmann, March 5, 1960.

19. As reported by John Shubert to Howard Teichmann, March 11, 1960.

20. Ibid.

21. Ibid.

22. Ibid. Details about John's parents' divorce are based on material in this interview.

23. John Shubert to Howard Teichmann, April 5, 1960.

24. Programs for *Robinson Crusoe, Jr.*, for both the original Winter Garden edition and the road tour, are on file at the Billy Rose Theatre Collection, the New York Public Library for the Performing Arts at Lincoln Center.

25. Irving Caesar, interview with the author, June 14, 1992.

26. John Shubert to Howard Teichmann, April 23, 1960.

27. In addition to the original Syracuse investors, Lee had acquired the backing of a far-wealthier group from Cincinnati, including George B. Cox, Max Anderson, and Con-

gressman Joseph Rhinock, as well as a New York group consisting of Samuel Untermyer, a New York attorney well connected with bankers and investors; Andrew Freedman, the owner of the New York Giants, who also had extensive New York property; and several New York banks. John Shubert to Howard Teichmann, April 23, 1960.

28. Another Shubert strategy was to buy land under various names and corporations. "The Shubert Theatrical Company didn't own everything," John explained. "Lee and J. J. leased things they owned personally to the Shubert theatres. Their personal companies leased the theatres to a company they called Select Theatres—I'd say Select owns only one out of the twelve theatres they operate, or two out of twelve. That was the success formula which illustrates that they were real estate operators." John Shubert to Howard Teichmann, April 23, 1960.

29. Architectural details are based on notes by Eugenie Hoffmeyer and Anthony W. Robins for the Landmarks Preservation Commission and made available to me by Mr. Robins, June 1991.

30. Quoted in descriptions of theatres in reports filed by the Landmarks Preservation Commission.

31. As reported in the *New York Times*, March 31, 1915.

32. John Shubert to Howard Teichmann, May 5, 1960.

33. As reported in *Variety*, April 15, 1911.

34. John Shubert to Howard Teichmann, May 5, 1960.

35. Max Gendel, letter to the author, November 16, 1990.

36. Harding, *Revolt of the Actors*, 85.

37. *Variety*, December 15, 1917.

38. Blue laws against Sunday performances were a persistent thorn in the Shuberts' side. The concerts were lucrative, especially since in pre-Equity days the Shuberts required actors under contract to perform for no extra pay. The *New York Review* heatedly claimed (November 25, 1916) that the prohibition against Sunday performances represented "a heritage of narrow-minded Puritanism which has no place on the statute book in this generation. New and more liberal Sunday laws in this State are imperative. It is unfair to permit motion picture and vaudeville theatres to remain open while drama and opera are prohibited. Why deny intellectual recreation to the public on the day of rest?"

39. Quoted in *Variety*, March 15, 1913.

40. As reported in *Variety*, June 11, 1914.

41. Bernheim, *Business of Theatre*, 132.

42. Wilson, *Francis Wilson's Life of Himself*, 252.

43. Quoted in the *New York Times*, September 3, 1919.

44. Bernheim, *Business of Theatre*, 134.

45. Harding, *Revolt of the Actors*, 231.

46. Ibid., 311.

47. Kevin Lewis, interview with the author, July 10, 1991.

48. "Klaw and Erlanger and Daniel Frohman were the forerunners, the first theatre producers to invest in motion pictures," Kevin Lewis told me on July 10, 1991. Their films, straightforward adaptations of plays, were commercial and artistic failures, but other Broadway managers were eager to make movies too. Ignoring his brother Charles's derision, Daniel Frohman entered into partnership with Adolph Zukor for a series called "Famous Players in Famous Plays"; the first, Sarah Bernhardt in *Queen Elizabeth* (1912), was given a prestigious road-show presentation at Frohman's own Lyceum Theatre. Films like *Queen Elizabeth*, however, and such later Zukor–Frohman offerings as James O'Neill in *The Count of Monte Cristo* (1913) and James K. Hackett in *The Prisoner of Zenda* (1913) indicated that the theatre moguls seriously misunderstood the new medium. Promoting *Queen Elizabeth* in an interview in the November 2, 1912, issue of the *New York Review*, Zukor expressed his intention "to embalm the art of all our greatest players for future generations," which is exactly what his filmed plays accomplished. In a medium that demands a more naturalistic, intimate style than the one she was accustomed to, for instance, Bernhardt in *Queen Elizabeth* looks denatured—a foolish old woman with a merely superficial gift for picturesque posturing.

49. Kevin Lewis, interview with the author, July 10, 1991.

50. Ibid.

51. Lewis, "Shuberts and the Movies," 49–50.

52. Lewis, "Include Me Out," 138.

53. Quoted in Lewis, "Include Me Out," 150.

54. Ibid., 152.

55. John Shubert to Howard Teichmann, June 5, 1960.

56. John Shubert to Howard Teichmann, May 17, 1960.

57. Ibid.

58. *New York Times*, December 7, 1916.

59. Irving Caesar, interview with the author, June 14, 1992.

60. Bernheim, *Business of Theatre*, 71.

61. Details about the dissolution of the Klaw and Erlanger partnership were reported in *Variety*, March 11, 1930.

62. John Shubert to Howard Teichmann, May 17, 1960.

5. The Long-Distance Runners

1. Garson Kanin, interview with the author, February 26, 1991.

2. Agnes de Mille, interview with the author, December 10, 1990.

3. Dorothy Terolow Reissman, interview with the author, September 30, 1990.

4. John Shubert to Howard Teichmann, June 15, 1960.

5. "Anonymous," interview with the author, September 16, 1991.

6. John Shubert to Howard Teichmann, June 15, 1960.

7. Ibid.

8. Miriam Krengel Pulvers, letter to the author, April 15, 1990.

9. Dorothy Derman, telephone interview with the author, October 9, 1990.

10. Miriam Krengel Pulvers, letter to the author, May 7, 1990.

11. John Shubert to Howard Teichmann, June 22, 1960.

12. Sol Jacobson, interview with the author, October 8, 1990.

13. Henry Senker, telephone interview with the author, October 25, 1990.

14. John Shubert to Howard Teichmann, June 22, 1960.

15. Sol Jacobson, interview with the author, October 8, 1990.

16. Alvin Klipstein, interview with the author, April 14, 1991.

17. Examples of Shubert malapropisms told by John Shubert to Howard Teichmann, January 12, 1960.

18. Max Wilk, interview with the author, June 15, 1991.

19. Alvin Klipstein, interview with the author, April 14, 1991.

20. Viola Seff Goldberg, interview with the author, October 12, 1991.

21. Quoted in the *Syracuse Post-Standard*, March 22, 1942.

22. John Shubert to Howard Teichmann, June 5, 1960.

23. Ibid.

24. To the Shuberts, warlords of the legitimate stage, vaudeville like motion pictures was second-rate. Their *New York Review* maintained a superior attitude toward vaudeville. "Stars in musical comedy and drama at last are beginning to realize that engagements in vaudeville are detrimental to their subsequent prestige and drawing power," trumpeted an editorial in the January 7, 1914, edition. "A tour in the two-a-day, where they can be seen from orchestra seats for fifty cents, takes away that glamor of personality which makes people willing to pay two dollars. Their individuality has become cheapened, and they do not attract at the higher price." As if priming the pump for their own return to vaudeville, throughout the teens the Shuberts planted items in the *New York Review* that downgraded Keith–Albee vaudeville, that exposed the abuses of Keith and Albee's United Booking Office, and that sided, oddly enough, with the vaudevillians' union, the White Rats, in their attempts to demand fair play from Albee. "Salaries raised to those who follow UBO demands," a *New York Review* headline on September 25, 1915, announced. "Vaudeville actors are disgusted by unfair salary reductions, cut-weeks and lay-offs, and feel the White Rats must stand up vigorously to secure a square deal from the booking offices," an editorial stated on October 2, 1915. But when the White Rats rose up in 1916 and 1917 to the UBO and fought the Vaudeville Managers' Protective Association, threatening to strike, the *New York Review* took management's side. To the Shuberts, strikes were anathema—even if it was the opposition who was facing a strike. On January 6, 1917, the *New York Review* supported the conservative faction within the White Rats and attacked the militant group within the union as "labor agitators" attempting to "plunge the profession into a disastrous strike."

25. Quoted in the *New York Times*, March 12, 1923.

26. Quoted in Harding, *Revolt of the Actors*, 443.

27. Quoted in Middleton, *Dramatists Guild*, 5.

28. Owen Davis, *I'd Like to Do It Again*, 36–37.

29. George Abbott, interview with the author, January 5, 1991.

30. John Shubert to Howard Teichmann, May 17, 1960.

31. Ibid.

32. Ibid.

33. Peters, *House of Barrymore*, 330.

34. John Shubert to Howard Teichmann, March 11, 1960.

35. *New York Review*, June 5, 1915.

36. Ibid.

37. Quoted in the *New York Review*, April 13, 1918.

38. Ibid.

39. Ibid.

40. Quoted in the *New York Review*, June 5, 1915.

41. Ibid.

42. Agnes de Mille, interview with the author, December 10, 1990.

43. Quoted in Gilmartin, "Joseph Urban," 276.

44. Quoted in the *New York Times*, March 25, 1934.

45. Quoted in the *New York Times*, October 25, 1936.

46. Agnes de Mille, interview with the author, December 10, 1990.

47. Ethel Lynne, interview with the author, January 5, 1991.

48. Agnes de Mille, interview with the author, December 10, 1990.

49. John Kenley, interview with the author, October 11, 1990.

50. Ibid.

51. *New York Review*, April 23, 1918.

52. John Shubert to Howard Teichmann, March 11, 1960.

53. *Variety*, January 8, 1964.

54. John Shubert to Howard Teichmann, April 11, 1960.

55. *New York Journal American*, September 7, 1943.

56. *Boston Transcript*, October 12, 1943.

57. *New York Times*, January 30, 1931.

58. *New York Daily News*, October 7, 1921.

59. Details about *Bombo* are drawn from contemporary newspaper reviews on file at the Billy Rose Theatre Collection, the New York Public Library for the Performing Arts at Lincoln Center.

60. *Globe*, October 7, 1921.

61. *New York Times*, October 7, 1921.

62. John Kenley, interview with the author, October 11, 1990.

63. Quoted in Sieben, *Immortal Jolson*, 71–72. Details about Jolson's contractual disputes are in Sieben as well.

64. John Shubert to Howard Teichmann, May 17, 1960.

65. Janet Cantor Gari, interview with the author, December 8, 1990.

66. Cantor, *My Life Is in Your Hands*, 312.

67. Janet Cantor Gari, interview with the author, December 8, 1990.

68. Irving Caesar, interview with the author, June 14, 1992.

69. John Shubert to Howard Teichmann, May 17, 1960.

70. Details about the contretemps between Price and the Shuberts are based on Stagg, *Brothers Shubert*, 180–194.

71. Closer to musical comedy than extravaganza, *Big Boy* was a more realistic show than its Winter Garden predecessors. But despite its "modern" touches, it could never have worked on film, though Warner Brothers tried in 1930. The aboriginal musical theatre stitching was cruelly exposed on-screen without the spark of Jolson in the flesh to play against it. Forced to stick to the script, Jolson was lackluster; and appearing throughout the film in blackface, it seemed (according to *Variety*'s review on November 12) "as if the Messrs. Warner had hired a ghost actor for their star."

72. Quoted in Goldman, *Jolson*, 141.

73. Quoted in Leiter, *Encyclopedia of the New York Stage*, vol. 1, 85.

74. Details about the battle over *The Student Prince* are drawn from John Shubert's account to Howard Teichmann, April 5, 1960.

75. *Theatre*, January 1925.

76. John Shubert to Howard Teichmann, May 17, 1960.

77. Ruth Goetz, interview with the author, September 29, 1990.

78. Garson Kanin, interview with the author, February 26, 1991.

79. John Shubert to Howard Teichmann, May 17, 1960.

80. *New York Times*, September 1, 1921.

81. *New York American*, August 21, 1923.

82. Irving Caesar, interview with the author, June 14, 1992.

83. Alvin Klipstein, interview with the author, April 14, 1991.

84. Dorothy Seegar, telephone interview with the author, June 12, 1991.

85. Ethel Lynne, interview with the author, January 5, 1991.

86. Barbara Barondess, interview with the author, April 10, 1991.

87. Dorothy Terolow Reissman, interview with the author, September 30, 1990.

88. *New York Mirror*, November 3, 1925.

89. Ibid.

90. When Jeffery John Archer Amherst, later Lord Amherst, reviewed *My Maryland* for the *New York World*, he rated it "a run-of-the-mill production with a score by Sigmund Romberg but by no means one of his best." The Messrs. Shubert "blew their tops," Lord

Amherst writes, demanding that Amherst's boss, Herbert Bayard Swope, fire him. Shrewdly, Swope told Lee that "he had always regarded the Shuberts as efficient theatre managers and he hoped they would regard him as an efficient editor, the right of dismissal being his prerogative and his alone." Lee barred Amherst from Shubert openings and threatened to withdraw advertising—the standard Shubert ploy—but was told that if he did he "need not ever try to get it back again at the same advantageous rates." After the furor subsided, Amherst went again to Shubert openings and indeed became well acquainted with Lee. One day, asking Amherst if he knew French, Lee said he had a French script he would like to have translated. Lee pulled out a checkbook as he said, "Look, you newspaper boys are always hard up. Take this as an advance." Amherst said he would rather see the script first. "He never sent it. I doubt if there ever was one. But it might have suited his purpose to have my endorsement on the back of one of his checks if only to claim to Swope that I was bribable." Amherst, *Wandering Abroad*, 90–91.

91. The Romberg operettas were not, of course, the only ones J. J. produced, but they were the pacesetters for his operetta factory. The Romberg shows, often enough, were imitations of earlier hits; and, in turn, the other Shubert operettas tended to be imitations of Romberg's imitations. *The Love Song* (1925) copied the *Blossom Time* formula, with a fictionalized Jacques Offenbach replacing Franz Schubert; the libretto concocted an imagined romance between the composer and the woman who was to become the Empress Eugénie and who thereby gives up love for power. For *A Wonderful Night* (1929), J. J. tried to duplicate *Die Fledermaus*, borrowing the story and the music of Johann Strauss, as well as stealing the staging of Max Reinhardt's successful contemporary production in Berlin, the high point of which was a revolving stage. When the show opened on Broadway, J. J. advertised the revolving stage as the only one in America. (*Fledermaus* had been used for two earlier Shubert operettas, *Night Birds* and *The Merry Countess*.) The leading man of *A Wonderful Night* was Archie Leach (to become Cary Grant after he was released by the Shuberts), who couldn't sing. J. J. had him mouth the words while a member of the chorus sang. *Countess Maritza* (1926), with music by Emmerich Kalman and a story (about a countess who falls for her overseer, who turns out to be an impoverished count in disguise) that had seen service in many earlier operettas, was a big hit. Brooks Atkinson in the September 19, 1926, *New York Times* hailed the sumptuous show as "a pleasing operetta of the old school." "The chorus calls up memories of the rare old singing corps of the Oscar Hammerstein [I] nights at the Manhattan Opera House. With the highly colored paper-petalled scenery more familiar fifteen years ago than today, the show is a throwback." The next season, J. J. was ready with another adaptation of a Viennese original, with a score by Kalman: *The Circus Princess* was about another royal romance in which one of the partners is temporarily disguised as a commoner. There were genuine circus acts in the show; and perhaps because of its setting, J. J. booked the operetta into his extravaganza house, the Winter Garden.

92. John Shubert to Howard Teichmann, April 15, 1960.

93. Ibid.

94. The Shuberts had harsh feelings about Victor Herbert. "Both Lee and my father thought he was a mean, vicious German," John reported. "Even though he was supposed to be Irish, he had this German training. He was a vulgar man, a four-letter-word type of man who, God knows, wrote good stuff, but they didn't respect him." John Shubert to Howard Teichmann, April 15, 1960.

95. Ethel Lynne, interview with the author, January 5, 1991.

6. All in the Family

1. John Shubert to Howard Teichmann, March 16, 1960.

2. As reported in *Variety*, October 25, 1931.

3. As reported in the *New York Times*, December 4, 1931.

4. David Feinstone's daughter, Emily Hewlett, remembered that her father "had a great deal of respect for Mr. Lee and spoke sadly and lovingly of Sam, whom he knew from his early years in Syracuse. When I would ask about adverse newspaper articles about the Shuberts, my father was kind and understanding, the same way he was with everyone he knew. He never tolerated adverse criticism of anyone. I visited with Mr. Lee at his office shortly after Dad's death and will always remember him, that day, as very kind. That was the last time I saw him." Emily Hewlett, interview with the author, March 14, 1991. Ezra Stone had a less idealized version of his relative's association with the Shuberts. "As long-time general manager of Shubert theatres David Feinstone had to do all the Shubert dirty work. He was a lovely, sweet man, and quite unlike the Shuberts he was beloved. But the job ate him out: it hastened his demise from a heart attack at age fifty-five." Ezra Stone, interview with the author, December 22, 1990.

5. Quoted in an interview with Ward Morehouse, *New York Sun*, July 25, 1932.

6. As reported in *Variety*, December 12, 1931.

7. As reported in the *New York Times*, April 9, 1933.

8. Quoted in the *New York Times*, June 5, 1933.

9. Quoted in the *New York Times*, August 12, 1933. On October 8, 1958, *Variety* reported that, for the first time in the firm's history, the Shubert-controlled Select Theatres Corporation paid a dividend on its common stock. The payment totaled $120,000 at sixty cents per share on two hundred thousand shares. "The bulk of the coin paid went out to members of the Shubert family, who own approximately 90% of the stock. Another $22,000 dividend was paid on 38,000 shares of preferred stock, entirely owned by the Shuberts."

10. Garson Kanin, interview with the author, February 26, 1991.

11. John Shubert to Howard Teichmann, March 16, 1960.

12. *New York Times*, January 31, 1933.

13. Bordman, *American Musical Revue*, 103.

14. John Shubert to Howard Teichmann, March 31, 1960.

15. John Shubert to Howard Teichmann, April 5, 1960. The details about John Shubert's upbringing, education, and residences, are based on material in this interview.

16. John Shubert to Howard Teichmann, April 11, 1960.

17. Ibid.

18. As reported in *Variety*, November 12, 1933.

19. *Variety*, January 7, 1934.

20. Quoted in the *New York Times*, September 19, 1943. Details about Harry Kaufman's background are drawn from this same source.

21. Ibid.

22. John Shubert to Howard Teichmann, April 11, 1960.

23. John Shubert to Howard Teichmann, March 11, 1960.

24. Ibid.

25. *New York Times*, August 28, 1934.

26. *New York Evening Post*, August 28, 1934.

27. John Shubert to Howard Teichmann, March 11, 1960.

28. *New York Times*, September 20, 1935.

29. *Variety*, September 22, 1935.

30. Bordman, *American Musical Revue*, 88.

31. *New York Times*, December 26, 1936.

32. John Shubert to Howard Teichmann, March 11, 1960.

33. Imogene Coca, interview with the author, October 18, 1990.

34. John Shubert to Howard Teichmann, March 11, 1960.

35. Arden, *Three Phases of Eve*, 30.

36. Agnes de Mille, interview with the author, December 10, 1990.

37. Ibid.

38. *New York Evening Post*, September 19, 1937.

39. Ethel Lynne, interview with the author, January 5, 1991.

40. Miriam Krengel Pulvers, letter to the author, April 15, 1990.

41. William Packer, telephone interview with the author, December 6, 1990.

42. Annette Packer, telephone interview with the author, December 1, 1990.

43. John Kenley, interview with the author, October 11, 1990.

44. Ruth Goetz, interview with the author, September 29, 1990.

45. John Shubert to Howard Teichmann, February 24, 1960.

46. Quoted in *Variety*, January 7, 1970.

47. As reported in the *New York Times*, May 18, 1983.

48. John Shubert to Howard Teichmann, March 11, 1960.

49. *New York Times*, December 30, 1934.

50. *New York Evening Post*, December 30, 1934. Oddly enough, in the thirties, when the operettas J. J. favored were no longer popular on Broadway, they served as the basis of a series of commercially successful films starring Jeanette MacDonald and Nelson Eddy.

The films, however, treated their sources cavalierly, often replacing most of the original scores with more contemporary-sounding numbers by MGM house composers or else "apologizing" for the original music by placing it within a self-conscious performance framework, as if the only place for genuine operetta songs was onstage.

51. John Shubert to Howard Teichmann, March 11, 1960.

52. Alvin Klipstein, interview with the author, April 14, 1991.

53. John Shubert to Howard Teichmann, April 11, 1960.

54. Ibid. Details about the Shuberts' involvement in coproducing *Hellzapoppin'* are drawn from this interview.

55. Quoted in the *Daily Mirror*, December 7, 1938.

56. Quoted in Gil-Montero, *Brazilian Bombshell*, 86. Details about the Shuberts' promotional campaign for Miranda are drawn from this same source.

57. Imogene Coca, interview with the author, October 18, 1990.

58. Alvin Klipstein, interview with the author, April 14, 1991.

59. For Miranda's breakup with the Shuberts, see Gil-Montero, *Brazilian Bombshell*, 140–141. Carmen performed in only one other show for Lee, *Sons o' Fun*, which opened in Boston on October 31, 1940. As in her short-lived but dynamic Hollywood career, Carmen was already tagged as a glittering guest star who comes on for a specialty number or two but is not asked to carry a show. In *Sons o' Fun*, although she was playing second fiddle to props, audience-participation gags, guns, firecrackers, and the improvised shenanigans of Olsen and Johnson, Carmen was the audience favorite nonetheless.

60. John Shubert to Howard Teichmann, April 11, 1960.

61. Ibid.

62. *New York Evening Post*, September 12, 1940.

63. Quoted in *Variety*, January 1, 1970.

64. Miriam Krengel Pulvers, letter to the author, April 15, 1990.

65. Dorothy Terolow Reissman, interview with the author, September 30, 1990.

66. Miriam Krengel Pulvers, letter to the author, May 7, 1990.

67. Dorothy Derman, telephone interview with the author, October 24, 1990. For all his brusqueness at the office, J. J. had a kindly side too. "He was plumper than Mr. Lee, and I wasn't so afraid of him," Alvin Klipstein told me, smiling at the image he had conjured up of his boss from long ago. "He was a family man, after all—he had a son who made him almost human." Klipstein remembered going in to see J. J. during the run of *The Streets of Paris* to present an unusual publicity idea.

When I went to Shubert theatres at night trying to pick up column items I talked to Jackie Gately, one of the showgirls in the revue. She was an Arkansas native who had won a hog-calling contest. One of the columnists told me he had a great stunt: "Take the girl into Central Park at night and have her give a hog call. When you get arrested, tell them she had a nostalgic urge." I went in to tell Mr. J. J., and when I explained the stunt to him, he started to smile. He told me to go see a Mr. [Ben] Mallam, who was the Shuberts' general troubleshooter, an ex-policeman in control of opening nights. We went to Central Park; she gave a hog call—and nothing happened. But I was impressed that Mr. J. J. had gone for the idea, and I still remember his smile. I saw his famous temper too, of course. When A. J. Liebling was doing an article on the Shuberts for the *New Yorker*, he came to the office of my boss, Claude Greneker. I walked over to the Winter Garden with Mr. Liebling and Mr. Greneker, to watch a rehearsal. It was raining, and I took Mr. Liebling's raincoat and placed it over a chair. When Mr. J. J. came in, he happened to put his hand on the wet raincoat and blew his top. I ran out of the theatre. Mr. Liebling reported in his article that Mr. J. J. was outraged about the damage to his theatre, but that wasn't it. He was concerned for the opening night audience with their fancy clothes.

Alvin Klipstein, interview with the author, April 14, 1991. "J. J. was accessible in his office," Alexander Cohen recalled. "I didn't find him at all unkind. Once when I was in the office, in the early forties, I admired a book of sketches from shows he had produced. On the spot he made me a present of two volumes of revue sketches; there were seven hundred pages in volume one alone." Alexander Cohen, interview with the author, December 5, 1990.

68. *Variety*, May 5, 1975.

69. Dorothy Terolow Reissman, interview with the author, September 30, 1990.

70. Iva Withers, interview with the author, September 28, 1990.

71. Details about John Shubert's secret marriage are drawn from his interview with Howard Teichmann, January 21, 1960.

72. Details about John Shubert's career in the army are drawn from his interview with Howard Teichmann, January 25, 1960.

73. The family meeting in the Edison Hotel Green Room was described by John Shubert to Howard Teichmann, February 24, 1960.

74. John Shubert's comments about Milton Shubert and Lawrence Shubert Lawrence, Sr., are drawn from his interview with Howard Teichmann, February 28, 1960.

75. *New York Times*, April 11, 1947.

76. Ezra Stone, interview with the author, December 22, 1990.

77. Abraham Grossman, letter to the author, August 11, 1990.

78. Ethel Lynne, interview with the author, January 5, 1991.

79. Dorothy Seegar, telephone interview with the author, June 12, 1991.

80. Lawrence Shubert Lawrence, Jr., interview with the author, January 5, 1988.

81. Ezra Stone, interview with the author, December 22, 1990.

82. Ibid.

83. Joan Lavender, telephone interviews with the author, March 15, 1991, and June 12, 1992.

84. John Shubert to Howard Teichmann, February 28, 1960.

85. Lucille Lawrence, letter to the author, January 22, 1991.

86. Marjorie Light, telephone interview with the author, January 3, 1991.

87. *New York Times*, January 11, 1945.

88. Anne Jeffreys, telephone interview with the author, December 1, 1993.

89. Ibid.

90. John Shubert to Howard Teichmann, April 11, 1960.

91. Anne Jeffreys, telephone interview with the author, December 1, 1993.

92. John Shubert to Howard Teichmann, April 11, 1960.

93. Quoted in the *New York Times*, September 6, 1948.

94. Details about William Klein's dismissal are drawn from John Shubert's interview with Howard Teichmann, April 11, 1960.

95. Alvin Klipstein, interview with the author, April 14, 1991.

96. Garson Kanin, interview with the author, February 26, 1991.

97. William Packer, telephone interview with the author, December 6, 1990.

98. Annette Packer, telephone interview with the author, December 1, 1990.

99. William Packer, telephone interview with the author, December 6, 1990.

100. *Variety*, September 15, 1973.

101. A few years earlier, also at an advanced age, William Klein had married. Sometime in the mid 1940s, after she had left Klein's office and had settled with her husband in Miami Beach, Miriam Krengel Pulvers met Lee and William Klein at the Roney Plaza Hotel.

> Mr. Klein and Lee were sitting in the lobby playing gin rummy; their girlfriends, Peggy Gallimore and Marcella Swanson, were sitting on the beach with two young lifeguards. I was shocked when I later learned that Mr. Lee was already married to Marcella, and that Mr. Klein later married Peggy Gallimore—Mr. Klein believed he was a confirmed bachelor. Peggy was a tiny, small-featured, reddish-brown-haired girl, pert and pretty, with a dancer's figure. She was a "pony" in Shubert musicals. Her boyfriend was a dancer, but she went out with William Klein, who was much older than she. Peggy's mother wanted her to marry William Klein, but she was reluctant, as she loved the young man.

"Mr. Klein and someone from his office came to the Winter Garden every night to pick up their girls," Alvin Klipstein said. "Though everyone knew he was seeing Peggy Gallimore more than anyone else, he said his mother would object if he married an Irish girl. When his mother passed away, he married Peggy." Klipstein, interview with the author, April 14, 1991. Marrying for money rather than for love, Peggy Gallimore ended up in an institution for alcoholism. "Although Mr. Klein was a very wealthy man, I don't know how much Miss Gallimore benefited from it in the long run," Mrs. Pulvers wrote. Miriam Krengel Pulvers, letter to the author, April 15, 1990.

102. John Shubert to Howard Teichmann, April 11, 1960.

103. Anne Jeffreys, telephone interview with the author, December 1, 1993.

104. Dorothy Terolow Reissman, September 30, 1990.

105. Iva Withers, interview with the author, September 28, 1990.

106. Eileen Kelly to Howard Teichmann, August 30, 1985.

107. John Shubert to Howard Teichmann, April 11, 1960.

108. Ibid.

109. John Shubert to Howard Teichmann, April 15, 1960.

110. Details about Joe Peters are from John Shubert's interview with Howard Teichmann, April 15, 1960.

111. Garson Kanin, interview with the author, February 26, 1991.

112. John Shubert to Howard Teichmann, September 17, 1960.

7. The Man in the Blue Serge Suit

1. Quoted in the New York Times, February 26, 1950.

2. Quoted in the New York Times, March 15, 1950.

3. Eileen Kelly to Howard Teichmann, August 30, 1985.

4. John Shubert to Howard Teichmann, June 1, 1960.

5. New York Times, February 26, 1950.

6. Quoted in the New York Times, February 22, 1950.

7. Ibid.

8. Quoted in the New York Times, March 8, 1950.

9. New York Journal American, March 20, 1950.

10. Variety, February 15, 1941.

11. John Shubert to Howard Teichmann, June 1, 1960.

12. Quoted in the New York Times, February 10, 1950.

13. Ibid.

14. John Shubert to Howard Teichmann, June 1, 1960.

15. Quoted in the New York Times, February 15, 1950.

16. Quoted in Variety, March 7, 1950.

17. Quoted in the New York Daily News, March 22, 1950.

18. New York Journal American, March 20, 1950.

19. Gerald Schoenfeld to Howard Teichmann, September 19, 1985.

20. Variety, August 12, 1953.

21. Ibid.

22. Details about the 1953 illnesses of Lee and J. J. are drawn from John Shubert's interview with Howard Teichmann, June 5, 1960.

23. Ibid.

24. Details about Lee's death are drawn from John Shubert's interview with Howard Teichmann, June 8, 1960.

25. Ibid.

26. Quoted in the *New York Times* on December 29, 1953.

27. John Shubert to Howard Teichmann, June 8, 1960.

28. *Playbill,* February 1954.

29. *New York Daily News,* December 27, 1953.

30. *Boston Post,* January 3, 1954.

31. Alexander Cohen, interview with the author, December 5, 1990.

32. Details about J. J.'s takeover are drawn from John Shubert's interview with Howard Teichmann, June 8, 1960; and from *Variety,* January 3, 1954.

33. Quoted in *Variety,* January 3, 1954

34. Ibid.

35. John Shubert to Howard Teichmann, June 8, 1960.

36. Quoted in the *New York Times,* January 2, 1954.

37. John Shubert to Howard Teichmann, June 8, 1960.

38. Quoted in the *New York Times,* April 12, 1963.

39. John Shubert to Howard Teichmann, June 8, 1960.

40. *New York Times,* December 24, 1963.

41. John Shubert to Howard Teichmann, June 8, 1960.

42. Details about the consent decree are based on accounts in the *New York Times,* February 18, 1956; and *Variety,* February 20, 1956.

43. "Anonymous," interview with the author, February 3, 1991.

44. Quoted in the *New York Times,* March 1, 1956.

45. *Variety,* January 22, 1958.

46. John Shubert to Howard Teichmann, September 15, 1960.

47. Ibid.

48. Evelyn Teichmann, interview with the author, October 13, 1990.

49. Eileen Kelly to Howard Teichmann, August 30, 1985.

50. Sandra Epstein to Howard Teichmann, November 17, 1985.

51. Eileen Kelly to Howard Teichmann, August 30, 1985.

52. Evelyn Teichmann, interview with the author, October 13, 1990.

53. Eileen Kelly to Howard Teichmann, August 30, 1985.

54. Sandra Epstein to Howard Teichmann, November 17, 1985.

55. John Shubert to Howard Teichmann, September 15, 1960.

56. Sandra Epstein to Howard Teichmann, November 17, 1985.

57. John Shubert to Howard Teichmann, September 15, 1960.

58. Evelyn Teichmann, interview with the author, October 16, 1990.

59. Sandra Epstein to Howard Teichmann, November 17, 1985.

60. Don Costello, interview with the author, October 17, 1990.

61. Gerald Schoenfeld to Howard Teichmann, September 19, 1985.

62. John Shubert to Howard Teichmann, September 15, 1960.

63. Quoted in the *New York Times,* March 23, 1958.

64. Bernard Jacobs to Howard Teichmann, September 17, 1985.

65. Gerald Schoenfeld to Howard Teichmann, September 19, 1985.

66. Alexander Cohen, interview with the author, December 5, 1990.

67. Sandra Epstein to Howard Teichmann, November 17, 1985.

68. Quoted in the *New York Review*, February 16, 1910.

69. *Morning Telegraph*, November 5, 1912.

70. Quoted in the *New York Herald-Tribune*, September 15, 1949.

71. Quoted in the *New York Times*, March 6, 1951.

72. Ibid.

73. Quoted in *Variety*, January 29, 1958.

74. Alexander Cohen, interview with the author, December 5, 1990.

75. "Anonymous," interview with the author, March 15, 1991.

76. John Shubert to Howard Teichmann, September 15, 1960.

77. Gerald Schoenfeld to Howard Teichmann, September 19, 1985.

78. Evelyn Teichmann, interview with the author, October 19, 1990.

79. Eileen Kelly to Howard Teichmann, August 30, 1985.

80. Evelyn Teichmann, interview with the author, January 2, 1991.

81. Sandra Epstein to Howard Teichmann, November 17, 1985.

82. Evelyn Teichmann, interview with the author, January 2, 1991.

83. John Shubert to Howard Teichmann, August 1, 1960.

84. Evelyn Teichmann, interview with the author, November 5, 1990.

85. Ibid.

86. Quoted in the *New York Times*, March 12, 1961.

87. As reported in *Variety*, December 12, 1955.

88. Eileen Kelly to Howard Teichmann, August 30, 1985.

89. Sandra Epstein to Howard Teichmann, November 17, 1985.

8. The Fall of the House of Shubert

1. Gerald Schoenfeld to Howard Teichmann, September 19, 1985.

2. Bernard Jacobs to Howard Teichmann, September 17, 1985.

3. Gerald Schoenfeld to Howard Teichmann, September 19, 1985.

4. Ibid.

5. Ibid.

6. Evelyn Teichmann, interview with the author, October 5, 1990.

7. Bernard Jacobs to Howard Teichmann, September 17, 1985.

8. As recounted by Evelyn Teichmann to the author, October 5, 1990.

9. Gerald Schoenfeld to Howard Teichmann, September 19, 1990.

10. As recounted by Evelyn Teichmann to the author, October 5, 1990.

11. Eileen Kelly, telephone interview with the author, April 16, 1991.

12. As recounted by Evelyn Teichmann to the author, October 5, 1990.

13. Details of John's second will are as reported in *Variety*, June 23, 1963.

14. Eileen Kelly, telephone interview with the author, April 16, 1991.

15. Evelyn Teichmann, interview with the author, October 15, 1960.

16. Quoted in the *New York Times*, June 20, 1963.

17. Gerald Schoenfeld to Howard Teichmann, September 19, 1985.

18. Quoted in the *New York Times*, July 11, 1963.

19. Gerald Schoenfeld to Howard Teichmann, September 19, 1985.

20. Bernard Jacobs to Howard Teichmann, September 17, 1985.

21. Eileen Kelly, telephone interview with the author, April 16, 1991.

22. Gerald Schoenfeld to Howard Teichmann, September 19, 1985.

23. Quoted in *Variety*, January 29, 1964.

24. All quotations are from the court transcriptions of the hearing.

25. Quoted in the *New York Post*, May 3, 1974.

26. As reported in the *New York Times*, August 7, 1963.

27. *New York Times*, October 5, 1963.

28. Eileen Kelly, telephone interview with the author, April 16, 1991.

29. Evelyn Teichmann, interview with the author, November 6, 1990.

30. Both men quoted in the *New York Times*, November 20, 1962.

31. Evelyn Teichmann, interview with the author, November 6, 1990.

32. Lawrence Shubert Lawrence, Jr., interview with the author, January 5, 1988.

33. Ibid.

34. Ibid.

35. Marjorie Light, interview with the author, January 5, 1991.

36. Lawrence Shubert Lawrence, Jr., interview with the author, January 5, 1988. Details about his life are based on material in this interview.

37. *New York Post*, August 27, 1970.

38. Eileen Kelly, telephone interview with the author, April 16, 1991.

39. Lawrence Shubert Lawrence, Jr., interview with the author, January 5, 1988.

40. As recounted by Evelyn Teichmann to the author, November 6, 1990.

41. Eileen Kelly to Howard Teichmann, August 30, 1985.

42. Alexander Cohen, interview with the author, December 5, 1990.

43. Howard Teichmann, in conversation with Eileen Kelly, August 30, 1985. Details about Lawrence Shubert Lawrence, Jr.'s relationships are based on comments made by Howard Teichmann during this interview; and Evelyn Teichmann, interview with the author, October 15, 1990.

44. Evelyn Teichmann, interview with the author, October 15, 1990. Ruth Gordon was, of course, married to Garson Kanin.

45. Ibid.

46. Lori Inman, telephone interview with the author, July 22, 1992.

47. Valerie Mitchell, interview with the author, November 13, 1990.

48. Evelyn Teichmann, interview with the author, October 15, 1990.

49. Memorandum from Howard Teichmann to Robert Morgenthau, December 12, 1972.

50. As reported in *Variety*, December 30, 1963.

51. Details about J. J.'s will as reported in the *New York Times*, January 15, 1964.

52. *New York Times*, March 27, 1970.

53. *New York Times*, January 31, 1966.

54. *New York Times*, May 12, 1968.

55. *New York Times*, April 5, 1977.

56. *New York Times*, August 11, 1959.

57. Lawrence Shubert Lawrence, Jr., interview with the author, January 5, 1988.

58. Ibid.

59. Evelyn Teichmann, interview with the author, November 6, 1990.

60. Quoted in the *New York Herald-Tribune*, January 6, 1965.

61. Murray Helwitz, letter to the author, May 2, 1990.

62. Sandra Epstein to Howard Teichmann, November 17, 1985.

63. Evelyn Teichmann, interview with the author, November 6, 1990.

64. Valerie Mitchell, interview with the author, November 13, 1990.

65. Ibid.

66. Lawrence Shubert Lawrence, Jr., telephone interview with the author, June 20, 1990.

67. Evelyn Teichmann, interview with the author, November 6, 1990.

68. Valerie Mitchell, interview with the author, November 13, 1990.

69. Evelyn Teichmann, interview with the author, November 6, 1990.

9. The Lawyers

1. Bernard Jacobs to Howard Teichmann, September 17, 1985.

2. Gerald Schoenfeld to Howard Teichmann, September 19, 1985.

3. Lawrence Shubert Lawrence, Jr., interview with the author, January 5, 1988.

4. Evelyn Teichmann, interview with the author, October 20, 1990.

5. Ibid.

6. Marjorie Light, interview with the author, January 6, 1991.

7. Judith Teichmann Steckler, interview with the author, October 22, 1990.

8. Lawrence Shubert Lawrence, Jr., interview with the author, January 5, 1988.
Evelyn Teichmann said that Lawrence Shubert Lawrence, Jr., had bitter feelings about
Howard Teichmann, as well as the lawyers. "Lawrence felt that Tyke should have advised
and protected him, and instead he felt he had been deserted. There were hundreds of harsh
words exchanged, and by the fall of 1973 there was no more contact. Tyke did phone Lawrence
after he heard that Dolores had killed herself. But when he heard Tyke starting to offer

sympathy, Lawrence slammed the receiver in Tyke's ear. They never spoke again." Evelyn Teichmann, interview with the author, October 20, 1990.

9. Lawrence Shubert Lawrence, Jr., telephone interview with the author, June 20, 1990.

10. "At a meeting of the Board of Directors held on July 26, 1972, certain reorganizational changes were discussed in the context of a restructuring of various departments," begins Howard Teichmann's dismissal notice.

As a consequence of this discussion it was determined by the Board to eliminate your department. Since the Board felt that your services were peculiarly related to your department it was agreed that your services would no longer be required subsequent to the conclusion of your vacation period. I wish to express on behalf of the Board its appreciation for the past services rendered by you. Sincerely, Gerald Schoenfeld, Trebuhs Realty Company, Inc.

"They had become powerful enough to get rid of anyone they didn't want," said Evelyn Teichmann, "and when they're through with you, they're through with you. There was no severance pay either. I was shattered: these were people I'd grown to think of as family. For at least seven years we saw Pat and Gerry, and Betty and Bernie socially three or four times a week." Evelyn Teichmann, interview with the author, November 8, 1990.

11. Memorandum from Howard Teichmann to Robert Morgenthau, December 12, 1972.

12. Lawrence Shubert Lawrence, Jr., interview with the author, January 5, 1988.

13. "Anonymous," interview with the author, March 15, 1991.

14. Evelyn Teichmann, interview with the author, November 18, 1990.

15. Quoted in an interview with Stan Bair, *New York Journal American*, November 8, 1964.

16. Quoted in the *Morning Telegraph*, November 22, 1942.

17. Quoted in the *Theatre*, June 1960.

18. Quoted in the *New York Journal American*, November 8, 1964.

19. Quoted in memorandum from Howard Teichmann to Robert Morgenthau, December 12, 1972.

20. Ibid. Details about Goldman's role are from this memorandum.

21. Joe Berger, a reporter for the *New York Post*, kept a close watch on Irving Goldman at the time when Goldman was under investigation for alleged financial misconduct. Berger's conclusions support Howard Teichmann's. On May 3, 1974, Berger wrote that

Goldman's influence with Surrogate Court Judge Samuel DiFalco to arrange a controversial 1963 settlement favorable to 'Eckie' resulted in Goldman [being] given control over lucrative painting jobs at seventeen Shubert theatres. DiFalco's former law partner, Arthur N. Field, was appointed guardian for the children's interests and paid $15,000. Nancy Eyerman says she knew of Goldman's influence on the case.

In another column in the *New York Post*, on April 17, 1975, Berger wrote that Goldman

> channeled an increasing share of the Foundation's grants into charities that appear to reap political and personal benefits for him. A 1968 City of Hope dinner was one of several pivotal events in Goldman's climb to the top of the Shubert empire. That year the Shubert Foundation gave the City of Hope $113,000, one-eighth of its total contributions. Lawrence Shubert Lawrence, Jr., said that Goldman persuaded him to make the donations and Gerald Schoenfeld and Bernard Jacobs urged him to agree. "The last straw was when Goldman asked for $150,000 for the City of Hope in June 1972," Lawrence said.

22. Evelyn Teichmann, interview with the author, November 18, 1990.

23. Quoted in the *New York Times*, January 5, 1973.

24. After J. J.'s deaths the ties between the Foundation and the Organization became murky to the point of opacity, but the officers of the Foundation did control the Shubert Organization and sometimes had official positions on the profit-making side of the business. "It is highly unlikely that today the Shubert set-up between its non-profit and commercial branches would be allowed to pass," *New York Times* reporter N. R. Kleinfield told me in an interview, November 20, 1993. In its application for tax-exempt status, the Foundation explained that its investment in the Organization

> is solely to carry out the cultural, educational purposes for which it is exempt. The investment is used directly in carrying out the Foundation's exempt purposes. . . . Over the years profits and losses of the theatre business have been erratic and, in total, accumulated profits are modest for the amount of capital invested. Nevertheless, Foundation is invested in the Organization to help maintain and preserve the theatre. . . . The investments were made to carry out the Foundation's educational and charitable purposes . . . and were not made for the production of income or the appreciation of property.

In other words, the legal justification under which the Foundation invests in the Organization is that the business of the Organization is uncertain, and therefore the Foundation contributes to the Organization for primarily cultural reasons, as a means of preserving an endangered species, the (shakily commercial) commercial theatre. In 1979, in an extremely unusual decision (and one that ensured the future of both the Shubert empire and its two heads of state), the Foundation was granted an exemption to federal tax laws that normally do not allow a private charity to own a controlling share in a profit-making business. If the ruling had gone against the Shuberts, the Foundation would have been forced to sell the theatres and Schoenfeld and Jacobs might have been unemployed. As a result of the ruling in their favor, the lawyers were able to continue as chief executive officers of both the Foundation and the Organization. Under the terms of the ruling, the profits of the Organization are taxed at the standard corporate rate, and the remainder of the profits can then be invested to produce tax-exempt income for the Foundation. During the Schoenfeld–Jacobs regime, the Foundation significantly increased its support of nonprofit theatre and dance companies; and in an era in which government support has diminished, the Foundation is a principal mainstay of the arts in America. At the time of Jacobs's death on August 27, 1996, the Foundation's assets were cited in the *New York Times* as "more than $149 million." The Foundation is the sole shareholder in the Organization and owns the Shubert theatres. For a thorough account of the intricate connections between the two branches of the Shubert enterprises, see N. R. Kleinfield's two-part article in the *New York Times*, July 10 and 11, 1994.

25. Quoted in the *New York Times*, April 10, 1973.

26. "Anonymous," interview with the author, April 12, 1991.

27. Quoted in the *New York Times*, March 28, 1974.

28. Quoted in the *New York Times*, April 29, 1974.

29. Alexander Cohen, interview with the author, December 5, 1990.

30. "Anonymous," interview with the author, March 23, 1991.

31. Hobe Morrison, interview with the authors, September 24, 1990.

32. *New York Post*, April 1, 1975.

33. *New York Post*, May 27, 1975.

34. Quoted in *Variety*, October 15, 1975.

35. Ibid.

36. Quoted in the *New York Post*, March 23, 1977.

37. *New York Times*, December 6, 1978.

38. Quoted in the *New York Times*, September 14, 1980.

39. Quoted in *Variety*, January 10, 1973.

40. Quoted in McMorrow, "New Shuberts."

41. Quoted in the *New York Times*, December 12, 1972.

42. Ibid.

43. Garson Kanin, interview with the author, February 26, 1991.

44. Gerald Schoenfeld to Howard Teichmann, September 19, 1985.

45. Ibid.

46. Bernard Jacobs to Howard Teichmann, September 17, 1985.

47. Gerald Schoenfeld to Howard Teichmann, September 19, 1985.

48. Bernard Jacobs to Howard Teichmann, September 17, 1985.

49. Alexander Cohen, interview with the author, December 5, 1990.

50. Harold Prince, interview with the author, May 20, 1990.

51. Quoted in Nadel, "When the Shuberts Fit."

52. Gerald Schoenfeld, speaking at the American Theatre Wing seminar, October 16, 1981.

53. Quoted in Nadel, "When the Shuberts Fit."

54. Gerald Schoenfeld to Howard Teichmann, September 19, 1985.

55. Harold Prince, interview with the author, May 20, 1990.

56. "Anonymous," interview with the author, March 25, 1991.

57. Quoted in McMorrow, "New Shubert."

58. "Anonymous," interview with the author, June 28, 1991.

59. Alan Eisenberg, interview with the author, July 12, 1991.

60. Grafton Nunes, interview with the author, October 1, 1990.

61. Joe Masteroff, interview with the author, May 22, 1991.

62. "Anonymous," interview with the author, July 16, 1991.

63. Harold Prince, interview with the author, May 20, 1990.

64. Notes taken by the author, Actors' Fund tribute to Bernard B. Jacobs, June 15, 1992.

65. Quoted in the *New York Times*, June 12, 1974.

66. Ibid.

67. Quoted in McMorrow, "New Shubert."

68. Quoted in the *New York Times*, June 12, 1974.

69. Quoted in *Variety*, July 5, 1977.

70. Quoted in *Show Business*, March 10, 1977.

71. Harold Prince, interview with the author, May 20, 1990.

72. Joe Masteroff, interview with the author, May 22, 1991.

73. Harold Prince, interview with the author, May 20, 1990.

74. Quoted in *Variety*, November 3, 1985.

75. Joe Masteroff, interview with the author, May 22, 1991.

76. "Anonymous," interview with the author, May 4, 1991.

77. "Anonymous," interview with the author, December 7, 1990.

78. Alan Eisenberg, interview with the author, July 12, 1991.

79. *Variety*, April 22, 1996.

80. Garson Kanin, interview with the author, February 28, 1991.

81. Notes taken by the author, the Dramatists Guild, May 23, 1988.

82. Quoted in the *New York Times*, November 16, 1986.

83. "Anonymous," interview with the author, June 18, 1991.

84. Harold Prince, interview with the author, May 20, 1990.

85. "Anonymous," interview with the author, May 1, 1991.

86. Grafton Nunes, interview with the author, October 1, 1990.

87. Agnes de Mille, interview with the author, December 10, 1990.

88. "Anonymous," interview with the author, March 13, 1991.

89. Alan Eisenberg, interview with the author, July 12, 1991.

90. Lawrence Shubert Lawrence, Jr., telephone interview with the author, June 20, 1990.

91. Alexander Cohen, interview with the author, December 5, 1990.

92. Garson Kanin, interview with the author, February 28, 1991.

93. Judith Teichmann Steckler, interview with the author, October 22, 1990.

94. Ruth Goetz, interview with the author, September 29, 1990.

95. Bernard Jacobs quoted in the *New York Times*, May 24, 1986.

96. Alan Eisenberg, interview with the author, July 12, 1991.

97. Quoted in the *New York Times*, March 14, 1982.

Bibliography

Abbott, George. *Mister Abbott*. New York: Random House, 1963.

Adams, Samuel Hopkins. *Alexander Woollcott. His Life and His World*. New York: Reynal and Hitchcock, 1945.

Allen, Fred. *Much Ado about Me*. Boston: Little, Brown and Company, 1956.

Allen, Robert C. *Horrible Prettiness. Burlesque and American Culture*. Chapel Hill: University of North Carolina Press, 1991.

Amherst, Jeffery John Archer (Lord Amherst). *Wandering Abroad*. Secker and Warburg, Ltd., 1976.

Arden, Eve. *Three Phases of Eve*. New York: St. Martin's Press, 1985.

Arnold, Elliott. *Deep in My Heart. A Story Based on the Life of Sigmund Romberg*. New York: Duell, Sloan and Pearce, 1949.

Balaban, A. J. *Continuous Performance. The Story of A. J. Balaban as Told to His Wife, Carrie Balaban*. New York: G. P. Putnam's Sons, 1942.

Baral, Robert. *Revue. A Nostalgic Reprise of the Great Broadway Period*. New York: Fleet Publishing Corporation, 1962.

Barker, Barbara M. *Bolossy Kiralfy. Creator of Great Musical Spectacles*. Ann Arbor: UMI Research Press, 1988.

Batterbury, Michael, and Ariane Batterbury. *On the Town in New York: A History of Eating, Drinking and Entertainments from 1776 to the Present*. New York: Charles Scribner's Sons, 1973.

Beer, Thomas. *The Mauve Decade. American Life at the End of the Nineteenth Century*. New York: Alfred A. Knopf, 1926.

Berg, A. Scott. *Goldwyn*. New York: Knopf, 1989.

Bergreen, Laurence. *As Thousands Cheer. The Life of Irving Berlin*. New York: Viking Press, 1990.

Berliner, Louise. *Texas Guinan: Queen of the Nightclubs*. Austin: University of Texas Press, 1993.

Bernheim, Alfred L. *The Business of Theatre*. New York: Actors' Equity Association, 1932.

Binns, Archie. *Mrs. Fiske and the American Theatre*. New York: Crown, 1955.

Bordman, Gerald. *American Musical Comedy. From Adonis to Dreamgirls*. New York: Oxford University Press, 1982.

——. *American Musical Revue. From The Passing Show to Sugar Babies.* New York: Oxford University Press, 1985.

——. *American Musical Theatre.* New York: Oxford University Press, 1978.

——. *American Operetta.* New York: Oxford University Press, 1981.

Brown, Henry Collins. *In the Golden Nineties.* Hastings-on-Hudson: Valentine's Manual, 1928.

Burke, Billie, with Cameron Shipp. *With a Feather on My Nose.* New York: Appleton-Century-Crofts, 1949.

Cantor, Eddie, as told to David Freedman. *My Life Is in Your Hands.* New York: Harper and Brothers, 1928.

Carter, Randolph. *Ziegfeld. The Time of His Life.* London: Bernard Press, 1988.

Churchill, Allen. *The Great White Way. A Re-creation of Broadway's Golden Era of Theatrical Entertainment.* New York: E. P. Dutton and Company, 1962.

Clarke, Norman. *The Mighty Hippodrome.* Cranbury, New Jersey: A. S. Barnes and Company, 1968.

Cone, John F. *Oscar Hammerstein's Manhattan Opera Company.* Norman, Oklahoma: University of Oklahoma Press, 1964.

Courtney, Marguerite. *Laurette.* New York: Atheneum, 1968.

Daly, Joseph Francis. *The Life of Augustin Daly.* New York: Macmillan, 1917.

Davis, Owen. *I'd Like to Do It Again.* New York: Farrar and Rinehart, 1931.

Davis, Peter. "The Syndicate/Shubert War." In *Inventing Times Square. Commerce and Culture at the Crossroads of the World.* Edited by W. R. Taylor. New York: Russell Sage Foundation, 1991.

De Angelis, Jefferson, and Alvin F. Harlow. *A Vagabond Trouper.* New York: Harcourt, Brace and Company, 1931.

De Cordova, Fred. *Johnny Came Lately.* New York: Simon and Schuster, 1988.

de Mille, Agnes. *Portrait Gallery. Artists, Impresarios, Intimates.* Boston: Houghton Mifflin, 1990.

Dietz, Howard. *Dancing in the Dark.* New York: Quadrangle, 1974.

Eaton, Walter Prichard. *At the New Theatre and Others. The American Stage: Its Problems and Performances 1908–1910.* Boston: Small, Maynard and Company, 1910.

——. *Plays and Players. Leaves from a Critic's Notebook.* Cincinnati: Stewart and Kidd Company, 1916.

Erenberg, Lewis A. *Steppin' Out. New York Nightlife and the Transformation of American Culture, 1890–1930.* Westport, Connecticut: Greenwood Press, 1981.

Felheim, Marvin. *The Theater of Augustin Daly. An Account of the Late Nineteenth Century American Stage.* Cambridge: Harvard University Press, 1956.

Fields, Armond, and Marc L. Fields. *From the Bowery to Broadway. Lew Fields and the Roots of American Popular Theatre.* New York: Oxford University Press, 1993.

Fisher, Judith L., and Stephen Watt, editors. *When They Weren't Doing Shakespeare. Essays on Nineteenth-Century British and American Theatre.* Athens, Georgia: University of Georgia Press, 1989.

Foy, Eddie, and Alvin F. Harlow. *Clowning Through Life.* New York: E. P. Dutton and Company, 1928.

Freedland, Michael. *Jolson.* New York: Stein and Day, 1972.

Frick, John W., and Carlton Ward, editors. *Dictionary of Historic American Theatres.* Westport, Connecticut: Greenwood Press, 1987.

———. *New York's First Theatrical Center. The Rialto at Union Square.* Ann Arbor: UMI Research Press, 1985.

Frohman, Daniel. *Daniel Frohman Presents.* New York: Claude Kendall and Willoughby Sharp, 1935.

Gardiner, James. *Gaby Deslys. A Fatal Attraction.* London: Sidgwick and Jackson, 1986.

Gilbert, Douglas. *American Vaudeville, Its Life and Times.* New York: Dover, 1963.

Gilmartin, Gregory F. "Joseph Urban." In *Inventing Times Square. Commerce and Culture at the Crossroads of the World.* Edited by W. R. Taylor. New York: Russell Sage Foundation, 1991.

Gil-Montero, Martha. *Brazilian Bombshell. The Biography of Carmen Miranda.* New York: Donald I. Fine, 1989.

Goldman, Herbert G. *Jolson. The Legend Comes to Life.* New York: Oxford University Press, 1988.

Gordon, Ruth. *Myself among Others.* New York: Atheneum, 1971.

Gottlieb, Polly Rose. *The Nine Lives of Billy Rose.* New York: Crown, 1968.

Grau, Robert. *The Business Man in the Amusement World. A Volume of Progress in the Field of the Theatre.* 1910. Reprint, New York: Jerome S. Ozer, 1971.

Green, Abel, and Joe Laurie, Jr. *Show Biz from Vaude to Video.* New York: Henry Holt and Company, 1951.

Green, Stanley. *The Great Clowns of Broadway.* New York: Oxford University Press, 1984.

Grimsted, David. *Melodrama Unveiled. American Theatre and Culture 1800–1850.* Chicago: University of Chicago Press, 1968.

Hapgood, Norman. *The Stage in America, 1897–1900.* New York: Macmillan, 1901.

Harding, Alfred. *The Revolt of the Actors.* New York: William Morrow and Company, 1929.

Harris, Warren G. *The Other Marilyn. A Biography of Marilyn Miller.* New York: Arbor House, 1985.

Hayes, Helen, with Katherine Harch. *My Life in Three Acts.* San Diego: Harcourt Brace Jovanovich, 1990.

———. *On Reflection.* New York: M. Evans and Company, 1968.

Henderson, Mary C. *Broadway Ballyhoo.* New York: Abrams, 1989.

———. *The City and the Theatre. New York Playhouses from Bowling Green to Times Square.* Clifton, New Jersey: James T. White and Company, 1973.

———. *Theatre in America.* New York: Abrams, 1988.

Henneke, Ben Graf. *Laura Keene. Actress, Innovator and Impresario.* Tulsa, Oklahoma: Council Oaks Books, 1990.

Hirschfeld, Al. *Show Business Is No Business.* New York: Simon and Schuster, 1951.

Hoyt, Charles, *Five Plays.* Princeton, New Jersey: Princeton University Press, 1941.

Hoyt, Harlowe R. *Town Hall Tonight. Intimate Memories of the Grassroots Days of the American Theatre.* New York: Bramhall House, 1955.

Hunt, Douglas L. "Charles Hoyt." *Theatre Annual* (1942).

Isman, Felix. *Weber and Fields. Their Tribulations, Triumphs and Their Associates.* New York: Boni and Liveright, 1924.

Johnson, Stephen Burge. *The Roof Gardens of Broadway Theatres, 1883–1942.* Ann Arbor: UMI Research Press, 1985.

Kahn, E. J. *The Merry Partners: The Age and Stage of Harrigan and Hart.* New York: Random House, 1955.

Kelly, Kevin. *One Singular Sensation. The Michael Bennett Story.* New York: Doubleday, 1990.

Klein, William. "William Klein's Early Years with the Shuberts," edited by Maryann Chach. *Passing Show* 13/14, no. 1/2 (fall 1990/spring 1991): 2–7.

Langley, Stephen. *Theatre Management in America. Principle and Practice.* New York: Drama Book Specialists, 1980.

Leavitt, M. B. *Fifty Years in Theatrical Management.* New York: Broadway Publishing, 1912.

Leiter, Samuel L., editor. *The Encyclopedia of the New York Stage, 1920–1930.* 2 vols. Westport, Connecticut: Greenwood Press, 1985.

Lewis, Kevin. "Include Me Out. Samuel Goldwyn and Joe Godsol." *Film History* 2, no. 1 (1988): 135–154.

———. "A World Across from Broadway: The Shuberts and the Movies." *Film History* 1, no. 1 (1987): 47–62.

———. "A World Across from Broadway (II): Filmography of the World Film Corporation, 1913–1922." *Film History* 1, no. 2 (1987): 2–10.

Liebling, A. J. "The Boys from Syracuse." *New Yorker*, November 18, 26–30; November 25, 23–27; December 2, 1939, 33–37.

Marbury, Elisabeth. *My Crystal Ball.* New York: Boni and Liveright, 1923.

Marcosson, Isaac F., and Daniel Frohman. *Charles Frohman: Manager and Man.* New York: Harper and Brothers, 1916.

Marker, Lise-Lone. *David Belasco. Naturalism in the American Theatre.* Princeton, New Jersey: Princeton University Press, 1975.

Marston, William Moulton, and John Henry Feller. *F. F. Proctor, Vaudeville Pioneer.* New York: Richard R. Smith, 1943.

McArthur, Benjamin. *Actors and American Culture, 1880–1920.* Philadelphia: Temple University Press, 1984.

McLean, Albert F., Jr. *American Vaudeville as Ritual*. Knoxville, Kentucky: University of Kentucky Press, 1965.

McMorrow, Tom. "The New Shuberts." *New York Theatre Review* (Spring/Summer 1977).

McNamara, Brooks. *The Shuberts of Broadway*. New York: Oxford University Press, 1990.

Middleton, George. *The Dramatists Guild: What It Is and Does. How It Happened and Why*. Fifth edition. New York: Dramatists Guild, 1966.

Morell, Parker. *Lillian Russell. The Era of Plush*. New York: Random House, 1940.

Morris, Lloyd. *Curtain Time. The Story of the American Theatre from 1820 to the Present*. New York: Random House, 1953.

Nadel, Norman. "When the Shuberts Fit." *Horizon* (October 1981).

Nesbitt, Robert D. "Early Concert Life at the Wieting Opera House in Syracuse, New York." Master's thesis, Syracuse University, 1947.

Oberfirst, Robert. *Al Jolson: You Ain't Heard Nothin' Yet!* San Diego: A. S. Barnes, 1980.

Peiss, Kathy. *Cheap Amusements. Working Women and Leisure in Turn-of-the-Century New York*. Philadelphia: Temple University Press, 1986.

Peters, Margot. *The House of Barrymore*. New York: Knopf, 1990.

Pollock, Channing. *Harvest of My Years*. Indianapolis: Bobbs-Merrill Company, 1943.

Postlewait, Thomas, and Bruce A. McConachie, editors. *Interpreting the Theatrical Past. Essays in the Historiography of Performance*. Iowa City: University of Iowa Press, 1989.

Provol, W. Lee. *The Pack Peddler*. Syracuse: Syracuse University Press, 1937.

Rabe, Mary M. "A History of the Wieting." Term paper, Syracuse University, n.d. On file at the Onondaga Historical Society, Syracuse, New York.

Register, William Wood, Jr. "New York's Gigantic Toy." In *Inventing Times Square. Commerce and Culture at the Crossroads of the World*. Edited by W. R. Taylor. New York: Russell Sage Foundation, 1991.

Rose, Phyllis. *Jazz Cleopatra. Josephine Baker in Her Time*. New York: Doubleday, 1989.

Rourke, Constance. *Troupers of the Gold Coast, or the Rise of Lotta Crabtree*. New York: Harcourt, Brace and Company, 1928.

Rudolph, B. G. *From a Minyan to a Community. A History of the Jews of Syracuse*. Syracuse: Syracuse University Press, 1970.

Russell, Charles Edward. *Julia Marlowe. Her Life and Art*. New York: D. Appleton and Company, 1926.

Saxon, A. H. *P. T. Barnum. The Legend and the Man*. New York: Columbia University Press, 1989.

Senelick, Laurence. *The Age and Stage of George L. Fox 1825–1877*. Hanover, New Hampshire: University Press of New England, 1988.

Sheean, Vincent. *Oscar Hammerstein I. The Life and Exploits of an Impresario*. New York: Simon and Schuster, 1956.

Shubert, Lee. "Lee Shubert's Reminiscences," edited by Maryann Chach.

Sieben, Pearl. *The Immortal Jolson. His Life and Times*. New York: Frederick Fell, 1962.

Skinner, Cornelia Otis. *Madame Sarah*. Boston: Houghton Mifflin, 1966.

Slezak, Walter. *What Time's the Next Swan?* New York: Doubleday and Company, 1962.

Smith, Sol. *Theatrical Management in the West and South for Thirty Years*. 1868. Reprint, New York: Benjamin Blom, 1968.

Smith, Wendy. *Real Life Drama. The Group Theatre and America, 1931–40*. New York: Knopf, 1990.

Snyder, Robert W. *The Voice of the City. Vaudeville and Popular Culture in New York*. New York: Oxford University Press, 1989.

Spitzer, Marian. *The Palace*. New York: Atheneum, 1969.

Stagg, Jerry. *The Brothers Shubert*. New York: Random House, 1968.

Stein, Charles W. *American Vaudeville. As Seen by Its Contemporaries*. New York: Alfred A. Knopf, 1984.

Sullivan, Mark. *The Turn of the Century*. Vol. 1 of *Our Times. The United States 1900–1925*. New York: Charles Scribner's Sons, 1928.

Swartz, Mark. "The Waldorf Venture." *Passing Show* 13/14, no. 1/2 (fall 1990/spring 1991): 28–34.

Taylor, Robert. *Fred Allen. His Life and Wit*. Boston: Little, Brown and Company, 1989.

Taylor, William Ried, editor. *Inventing Times Square. Commerce and Culture at the Crossroads of the World*. New York: Russell Sage Foundation, 1991.

Teichmann, Howard. *Smart Aleck. The Wit, World and Life of Alexander Woollcott*. New York: William Morrow and Company, 1976.

Timberlake, Craig. *The Bishop of Broadway. The Life and Work of David Belasco*. New York: Library Publishers, 1954.

Toll, Robert C. *Blacking Up. The Minstrel Show in Nineteenth-Century America*. New York: Oxford University Press, 1974.

———. *On with the Show. The First Century of Show Business in America*. New York: Oxford University Press, 1976.

Trauber, Richard. *Operetta. A Theatrical History*. New York: Doubleday and Company, 1983.

Vardac, A. Nicholas. *Stage to Screen. Theatrical Origins of Early Film: David Garrick to D. W. Griffith*. Cambridge: Harvard University Press, 1949.

Wilson, Francis. *Francis Wilson's Life of Himself*. Boston: Houghton Mifflin, 1924.

Wilstach, Paul. *Richard Mansfield. The Man and the Actor*. New York: Charles Scribner's Sons, 1908.

Winter, William. *The Life and Art of Richard Mansfield*. 2 vols. New York: Moffat, Yard, 1910.

———. *The Life of David Belasco*. 2 vols. New York: Moffat, Yard, 1918.

———. *Vagrant Memories*. New York: George H. Doran Company, 1915.

Wodehouse, P. G., and Guy Bolton. *Bring on the Girls! The Improbable Story of Our Life in Musical Comedy.* New York: Simon and Schuster, 1953.

Wynn, Keenan, as told to James Brough. *Ed Wynn's Son.* Garden City: Doubleday and Company, 1959.

Young, William, editor. *Famous American Playhouses, 1716–1971.* 2 vols. Chicago: American Library Association, 1973.

Zierold, Norman. *The Moguls.* New York: Coward-McCann, 1969.

Ziff, Larzer. *The American 1890s. Life and Times of a Lost Generation.* New York: Viking Press, 1966.

Index

Foster Hirsch is a professor of film at Brooklyn College of the City University of New York. He has published fifteen books on film and theatre, including *A Method to Their Madness: The History of the Actors Studio*; *Harold Prince and the American Musical Theatre*; *Acting Hollywood Style*; *The Dark Side of the Screen: Film Noir*; *Love, Sex, Death, and the Meaning of Life: The Films of Woody Allen*; and *A Portrait of the Artist: The Plays of Tennessee Williams*.

CONVERSATIONS WITH BRANDO
Lawrence Grobel
Updated Edition
238 pp., 17 b/w photos
0-8154-1014-X
$15.95 U.S.

HOLY TERROR
Andy Warhol Close Up
Bob Colacello
560 pp., 74 b/w photos
0-8154-1008-5
$17.95 U.S.

CLARA BOW
Runnin' Wild
David Stenn
with a new filmography
368 pp., 27 b/w photos
0-8154-1025-5
$21.95 U.S.

THE HUSTONS
The Life and Times of a Hollywood Dynasty
Lawrence Grobel
Updated Edition
872 pp., 61 b/w photos
0-8154-1026-3
$29.95 U.S.

FRANÇOIS TRUFFAUT
Correspondence, 1945-1984
Edited by Gilles Jacob and Claude de Givray
Foreword by Jean-Luc Godard
608 pp., 81 b/w photos
0-8154-1024-7
$24.95 U.S.

BLUE ANGEL
The Life of Marlene Dietrich
Donald Spoto
376 pp., 57 b/w photos
0-8154-1061-1
$16.95 U.S.

MY LIFE IS IN YOUR HANDS & TAKE MY LIFE
The Autobiographies of Eddie Cantor
Eddie Cantor
with David Freedman / Jane Kesner Ardmore
Foreword by Will Rogers
New introduction by Leonard Maltin
650 pp., 63 b/w photos
0-8154-1057-3
$22.95 U.S.

MY STORY
Marilyn Monroe
Co-authored with Ben Hecht
New introduction by Andrea Dworkin
152 pp., 16 b/w photos, 8 color photos
0-8154-1102-2
$22.95 U.S.

REBEL
The Life and Legend of James Dean
Donald Spoto
352 pp., 41 b/w illustrations
0-8154-1001-8
$18.95 U.S.

REMINISCING WITH NOBLE SISSLE AND EUBIE BLAKE
Robert Kimball and William Bolcom
256 pp., 244 b/w photos
0-8154-1045-X
$24.95 U.S.

A SILENT SIREN SONG
The Aitken Brothers' Hollywood Odyssey, 1905-1926
Al P. Nelson and Mel R. Jones
288 pp., 47 b/w photos
0-8154-1069-7
$25.95 U.S.

STEPS IN TIME
Fred Astaire
Foreword by Ginger Rogers
New introduction by Jennifer Dunning
376 pp., 46 b/w photos
0-8154-1058-1
$19.95 U.S.

Available at bookstores; or call 1-800-462-6420

 Cooper Square Press

150 Fifth Avenue
Suite 911
New York, NY 10011